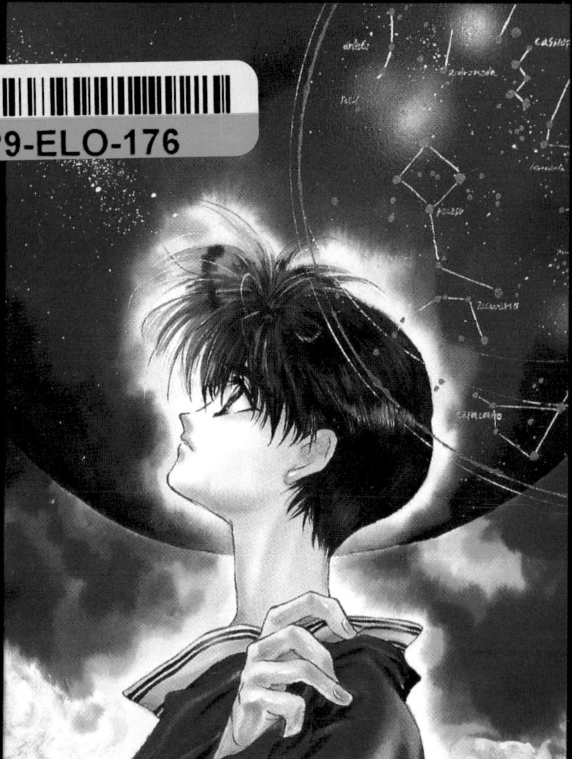

E'S

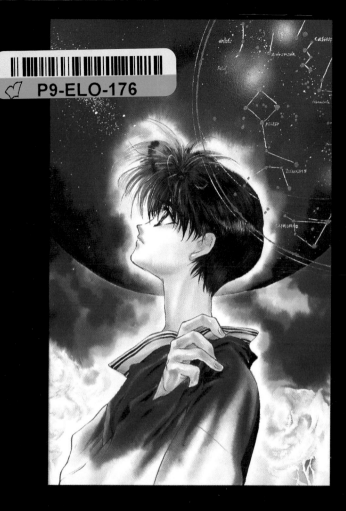

02 B – BERTH

PRESENTED BY SATOL YUIGA

02

SATOL YUIGA

™ brought to you by
BROCCOLI BOOKS
A DIVISION OF BROCCOLI INTERNATIONAL USA

E'S Volume 2

English Adaptation Staff
Translation: Satsuki Yamashita
English Adaptation: Elizabeth Hanel
Cover, Touch-Up & Lettering: Keiran O'Leary
Graphic Supervision: Christopher McDougall
Graphic Assistant: Krystal Sae Eua

Editor: Dietrich Seto
Associate Editor: Satsuki Yamashita
Sales Manager: Ardith D. Santiago
Managing Editor: Shizuki Yamashita
Publisher: Kaname Tezuka

Email: editor@broccolibooks.com
Website: www.bro-usa.com

A BROCCOLI BOOKS Manga
Broccoli Books is a division of Broccoli International USA, Inc.
1728 S. La Cienega Blvd., Los Angeles, CA 90035

ISBN-13: 978-1-5974-1120-2
ISBN-10: 1-59741-120-5

Published by Broccoli International USA, Inc.
First printing, February 2007
All illustrations by Satol Yuiga.

Distributed by Publishers Group West

ANIME GAMERS

BROCCOLI INTERNATIONAL USA
www.bro-usa.com

10 9 8 7 6 5 4 3 2 1
Printed in Canada

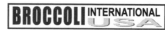

Other titles available from Broccoli Books

CONTENTS

02 B – BERTH
PRESENTED BY SATOL YUIGA

EIJI SAGIMIYA
Age 27

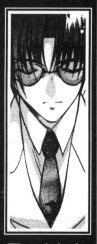

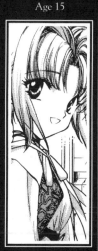

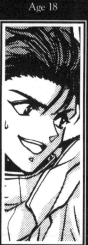

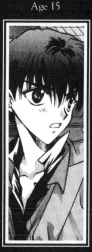

Eiji is the head of the Ashurum psychic research facility. He has a mysterious interest in both Kai and his sister Hikaru. He may have some hidden agendas of his own.

ASUKA TOKUGAWA
Age 15

Asuka is Yuuki's adopted sister. She is cheerful and innocent, and likes to take in stray animals. She cannot cook to save her life. She takes in Kai when he is lost and wounded in Gald.

YUUKI TOKUGAWA
Age 18

Yuuki is a mercenary gun-for-hire who will take most any job. He has been hired by Erimiya to find the Sacrament of Calvarias.

KAI KUDOU
Age 15

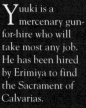

Kai is a psychic member of Ashurum. He wants to put his powers to good use. He has a little sister named Hikaru in the Ashurum hospital. He hates sweets; even the smell gives him a headache.

SHEN-LONG BELVEDERE
Age 15

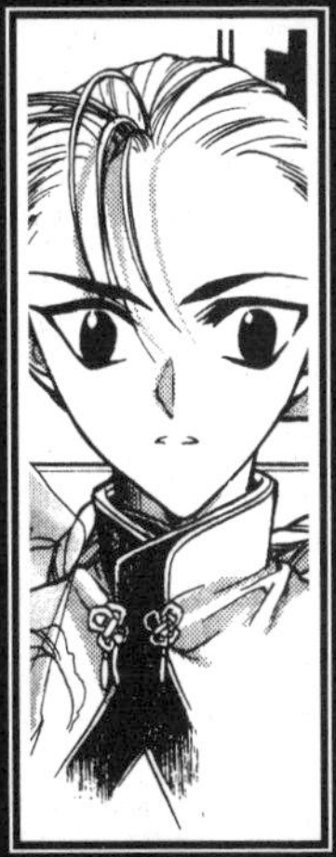

Shen-long is a psychic member of Ashurum and twin of Shin-lu. Shen-long believes in the superiority of psychics and hates normal humans with a murderous passion. He is very attached to his sister.

SHIN-LU BELVEDERE
Age 15

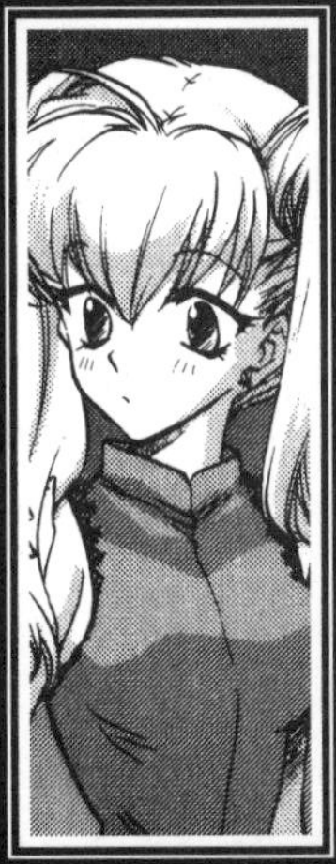

Shin-lu is a psychic member of Ashurum and twin of Shen-long. She is a friend of Kai who tries to look out for him and keep the peace between Kai and her brother.

MARIA
Age 17

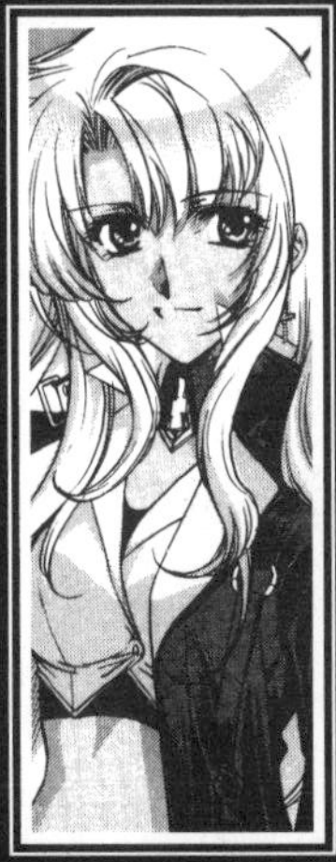

Maria is the adopted granddaughter of Erimiya, and a member of the Gald guerillas. She admires her grandfather and hopes to find the Sacrament of Calvarias for him. She is also a psychic.

DR. ASAKURA
Age ??

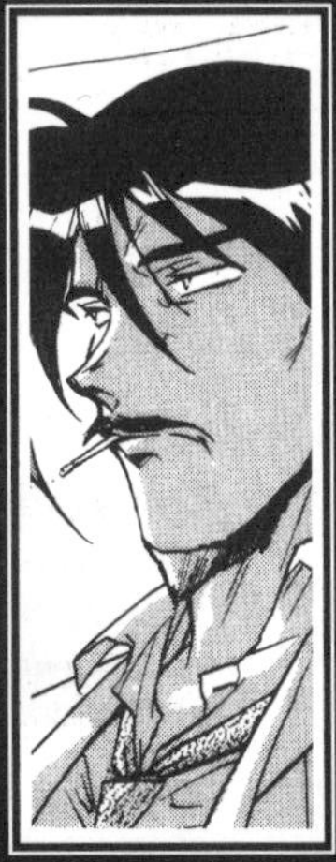

Shugo Asakura is a doctor who has a medical clinic in Gald. He is very knowledgeable about psychics.

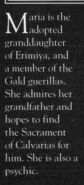

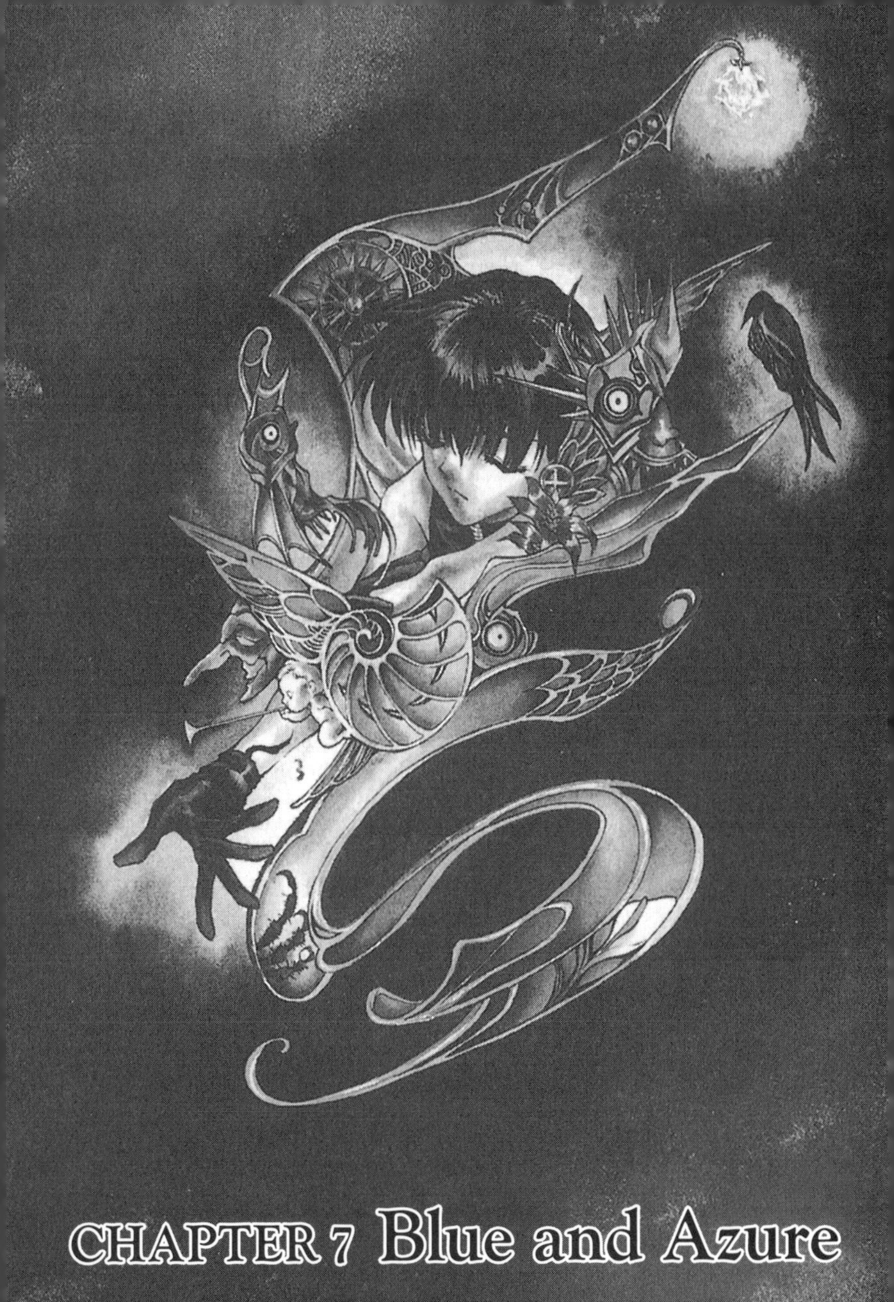

CHAPTER 7 Blue and Azure

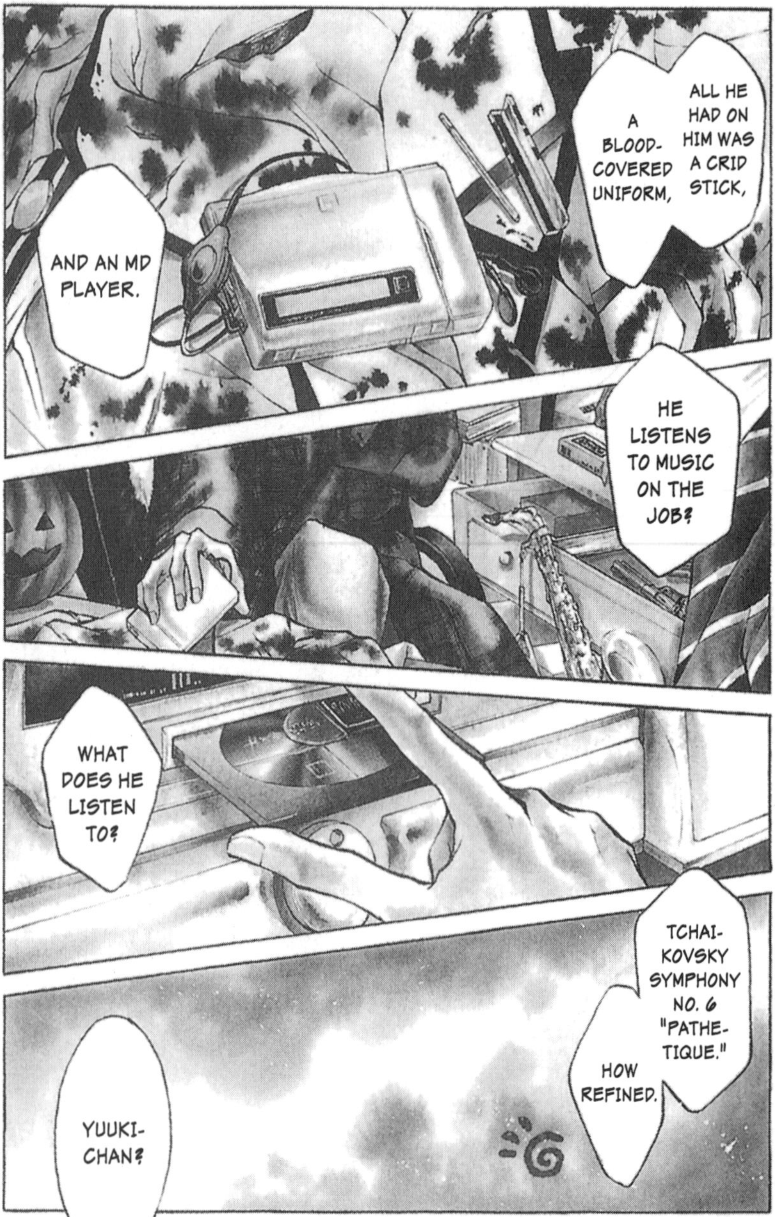
ALL HE HAD ON HIM WAS A CRID STICK,
A BLOOD-COVERED UNIFORM,
AND AN MD PLAYER.
HE LISTENS TO MUSIC ON THE JOB?
WHAT DOES HE LISTEN TO?
TCHAIKOVSKY SYMPHONY NO. 6 "PATHETIQUE."
HOW REFINED.
YUUKI-CHAN?

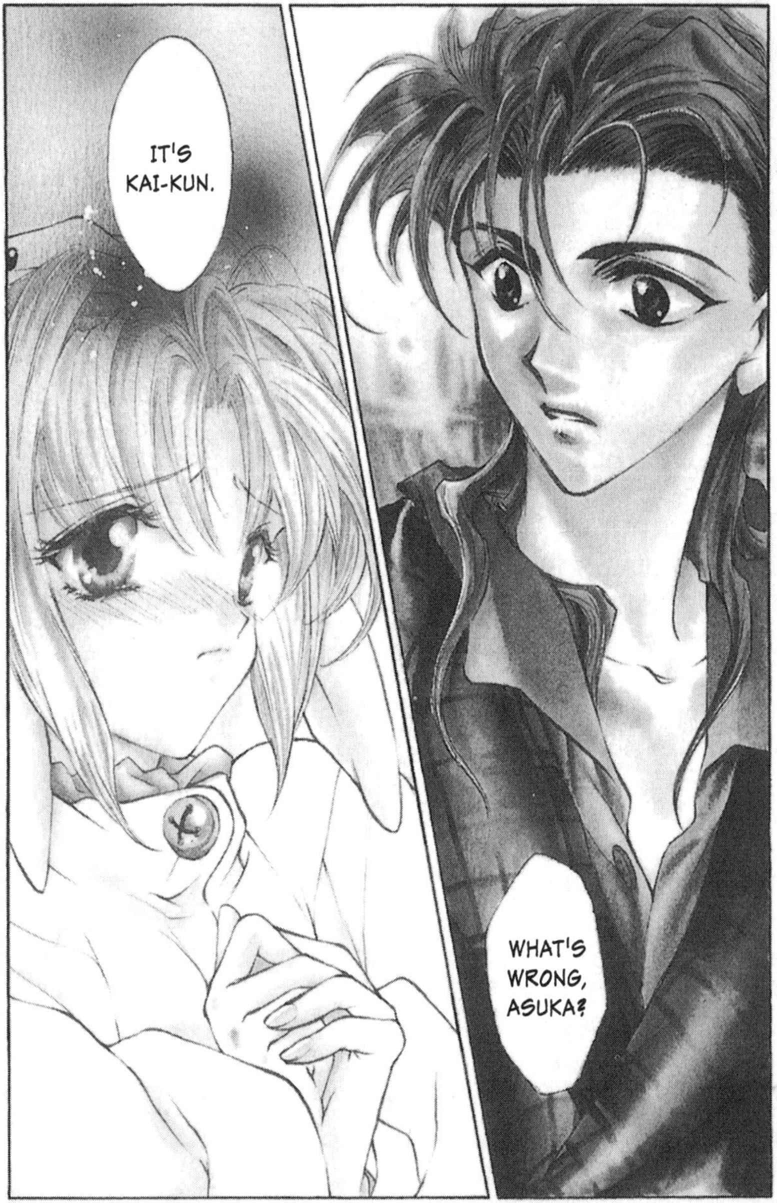
WHAT'S WRONG, ASUKA?
IT'S KAI-KUN.

E'S CHARACTER PROFILE FILE: 2

Asuka Tokugawa (age 15)

Birthday: June 25 (Cancer)

Blood Type: O

Favorite Food: Pumpkin.

Least Favorite Food: Anything that doesn't taste good.

Hobbies: Collecting hats and chokers.

Playing with animals.

Special Abilities: Taking care of plants in the green house.

Favorite Color: Orange.

Family: Guardian and adopted brother (Yuuki).

Other: Likes pumpkin as a pudding or pie or cooked as a side dish; also likes pumpkin-shaped objects like Jack O' Lanterns.

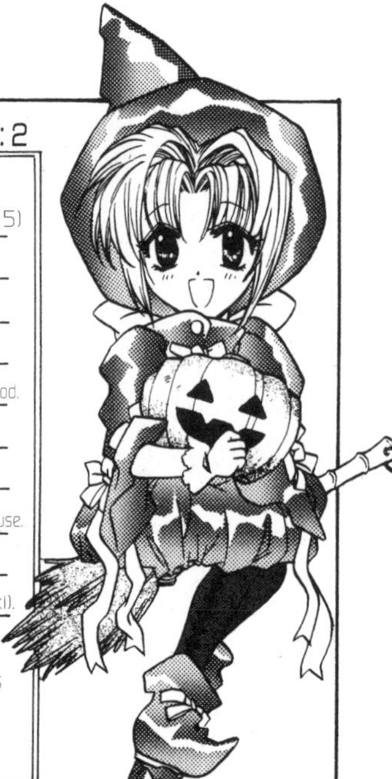

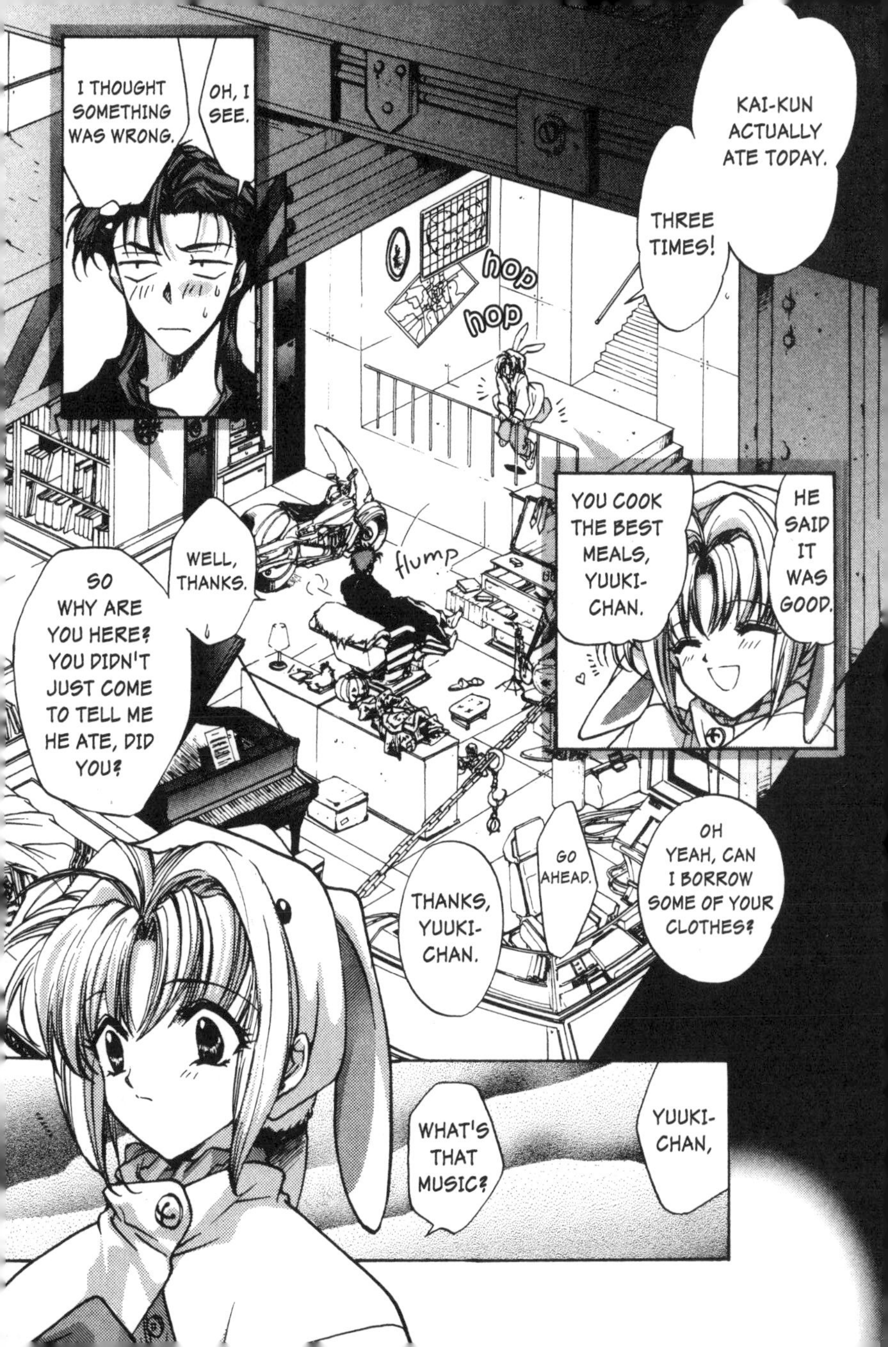
KAI-KUN ACTUALLY ATE TODAY.
THREE TIMES!
hop
hop
OH, I SEE.
I THOUGHT SOMETHING WAS WRONG.
HE SAID IT WAS GOOD.
YOU COOK THE BEST MEALS, YUUKI-CHAN.
WELL, THANKS.
flump
SO WHY ARE YOU HERE? YOU DIDN'T JUST COME TO TELL ME HE ATE, DID YOU?
OH YEAH, CAN I BORROW SOME OF YOUR CLOTHES?
GO AHEAD.
THANKS, YUUKI-CHAN.
YUUKI-CHAN,
WHAT'S THAT MUSIC?

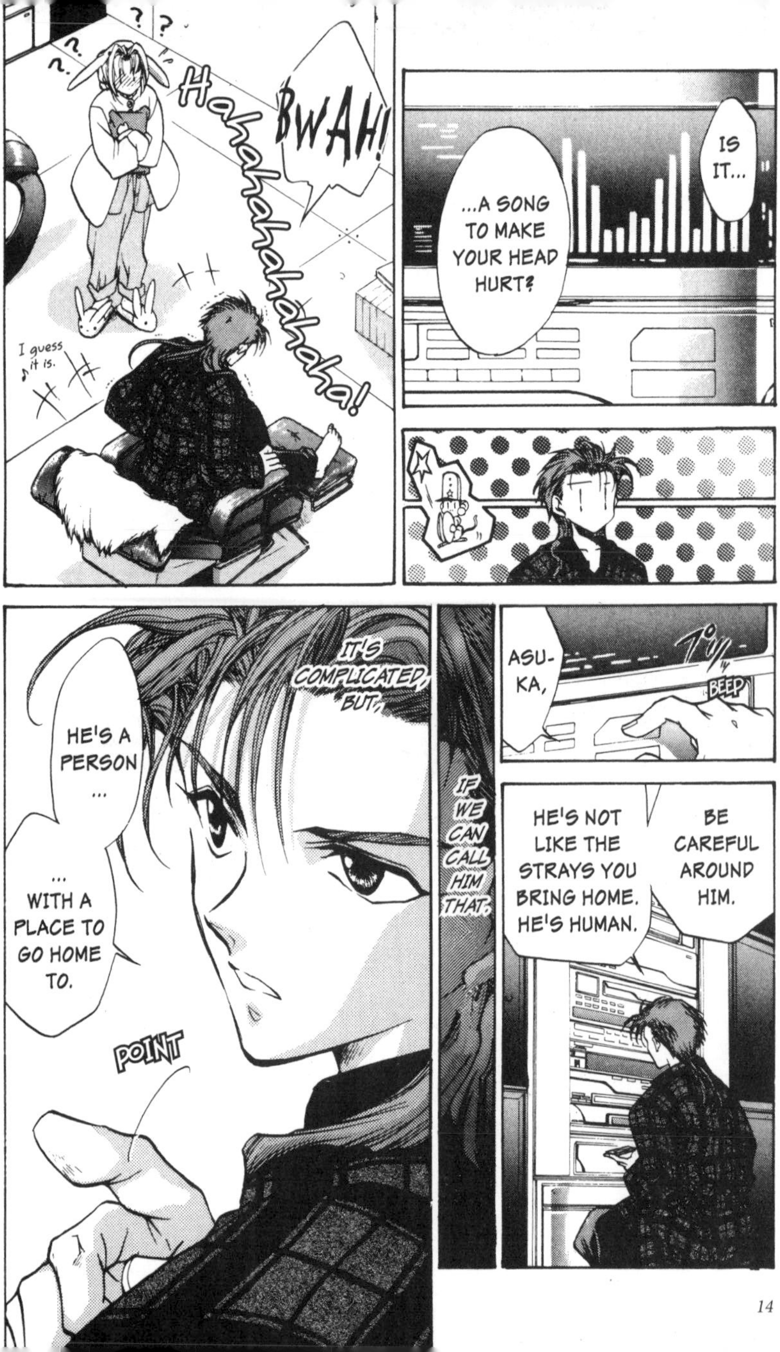
IS IT...
...A SONG TO MAKE YOUR HEAD HURT?
BWAH!
Hahahahahaha!
I guess it is.
ASU-KA,
BEEP
BE CAREFUL AROUND HIM.
HE'S NOT LIKE THE STRAYS YOU BRING HOME. HE'S HUMAN.
IF WE CAN CALL HIM THAT.
IT'S COMPLICATED, BUT,
HE'S A PERSON ...
... WITH A PLACE TO GO HOME TO.
POINT

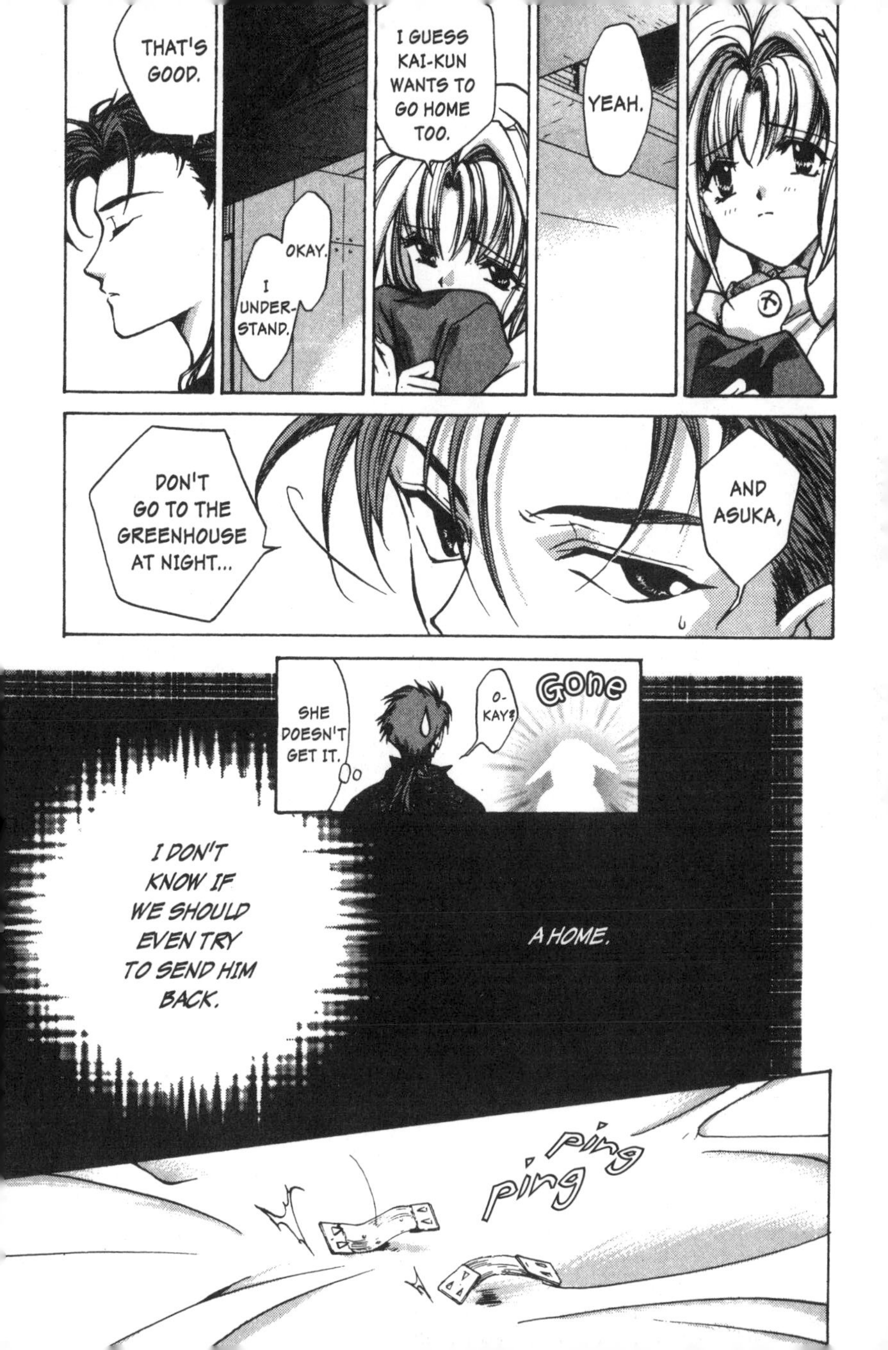
YEAH.
I GUESS KAI-KUN WANTS TO GO HOME TOO.
OKAY.
I UNDERSTAND.
THAT'S GOOD.
AND ASUKA,
DON'T GO TO THE GREENHOUSE AT NIGHT...
Gone
O-KAY?!
SHE DOESN'T GET IT.
A HOME.
I DON'T KNOW IF WE SHOULD EVEN TRY TO SEND HIM BACK.
ping
ping

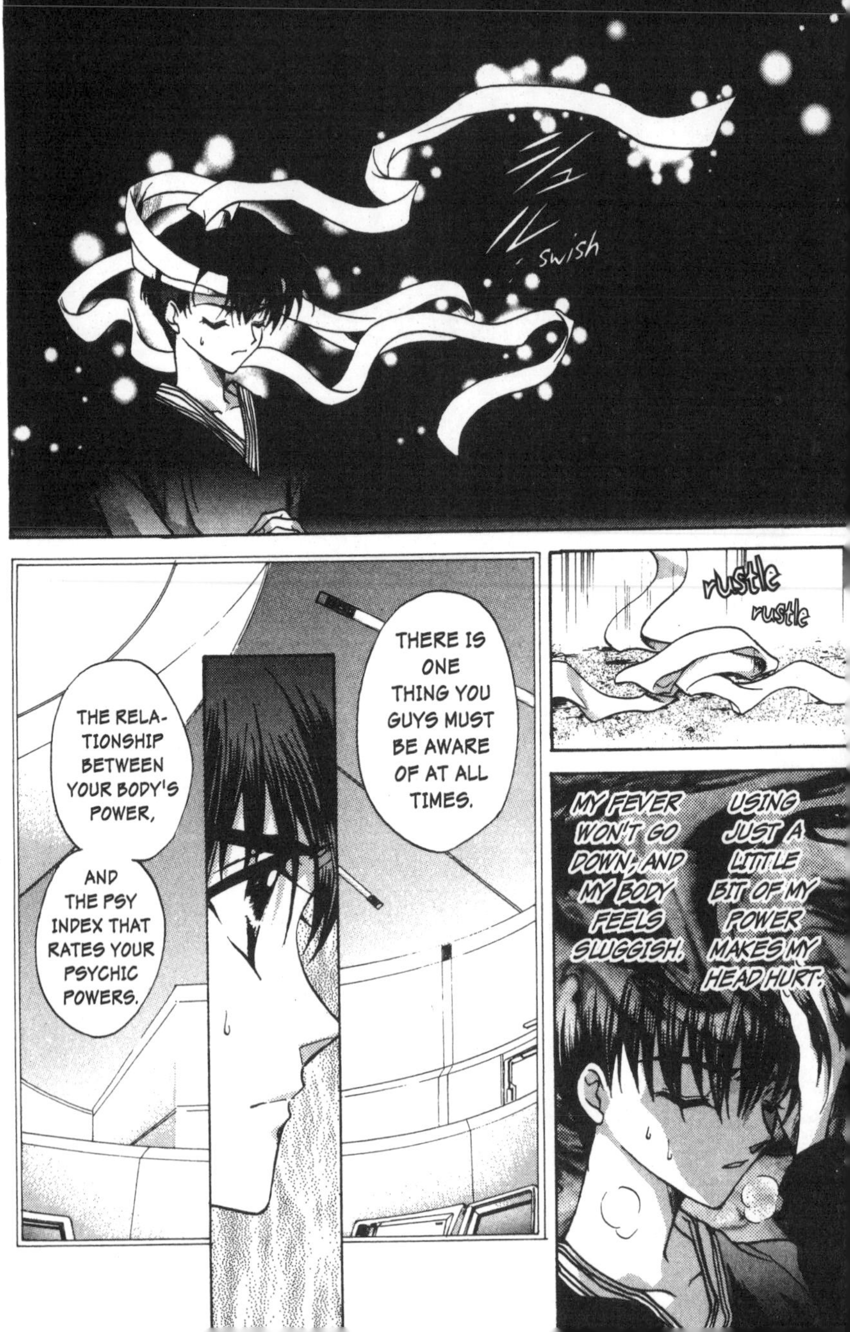
swish
rustle
rustle
USING JUST A LITTLE BIT OF MY POWER MAKES MY HEAD HURT.
MY FEVER WON'T GO DOWN, AND MY BODY FEELS SLUGGISH.
THERE IS ONE THING YOU GUYS MUST BE AWARE OF AT ALL TIMES.
THE RELA- TIONSHIP BETWEEN YOUR BODY'S POWER,
AND THE PSY INDEX THAT RATES YOUR PSYCHIC POWERS.

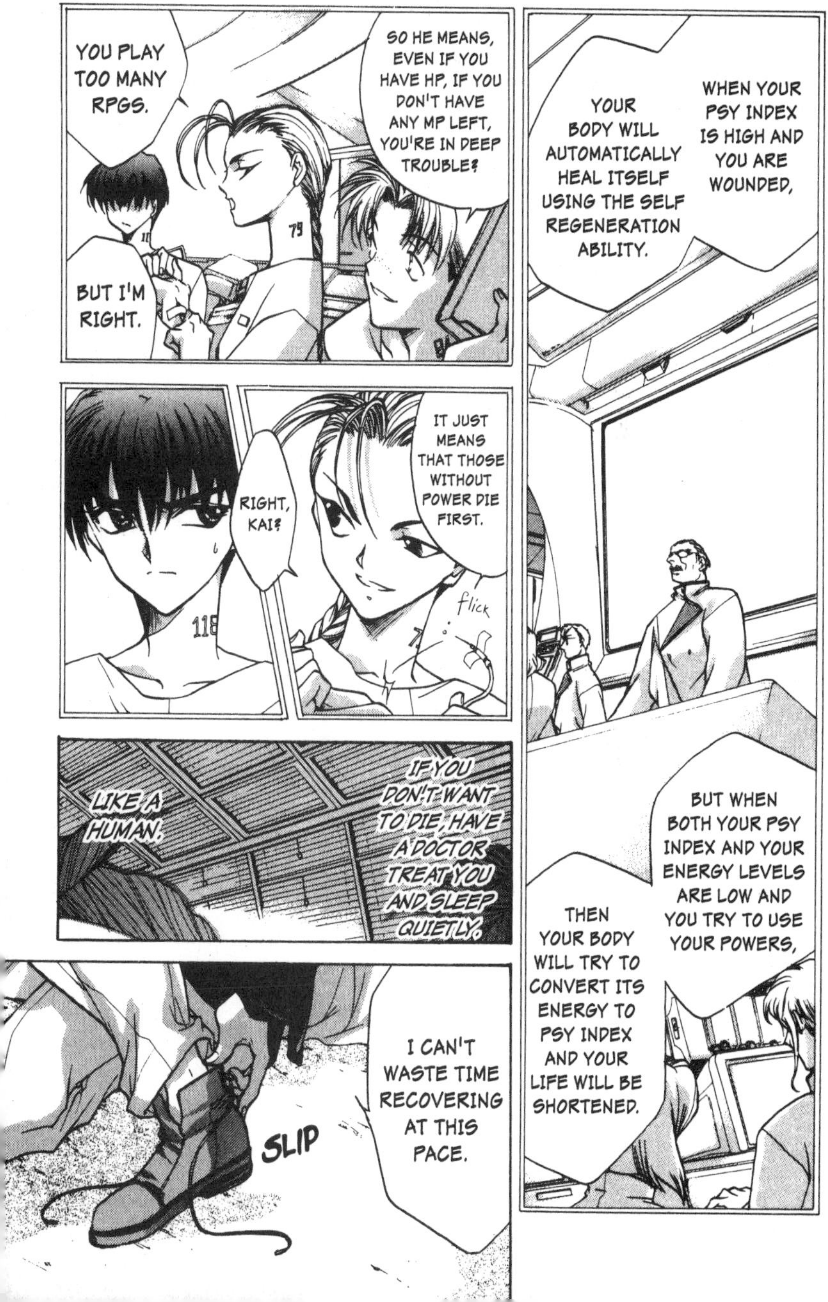
WHEN YOUR PSY INDEX IS HIGH AND YOU ARE WOUNDED,
YOUR BODY WILL AUTOMATICALLY HEAL ITSELF USING THE SELF REGENERATION ABILITY.
BUT WHEN BOTH YOUR PSY INDEX AND YOUR ENERGY LEVELS ARE LOW AND YOU TRY TO USE YOUR POWERS,
THEN YOUR BODY WILL TRY TO CONVERT ITS ENERGY TO PSY INDEX AND YOUR LIFE WILL BE SHORTENED.
SO HE MEANS, EVEN IF YOU HAVE HP, IF YOU DON'T HAVE ANY MP LEFT, YOU'RE IN DEEP TROUBLE?
YOU PLAY TOO MANY RPGS.
BUT I'M RIGHT.
IT JUST MEANS THAT THOSE WITHOUT POWER DIE FIRST.
RIGHT, KAI?
flick
IF YOU DON'T WANT TO DIE, HAVE A DOCTOR TREAT YOU AND SLEEP QUIETLY.
LIKE A HUMAN.
I CAN'T WASTE TIME RECOVERING AT THIS PACE.
SLIP

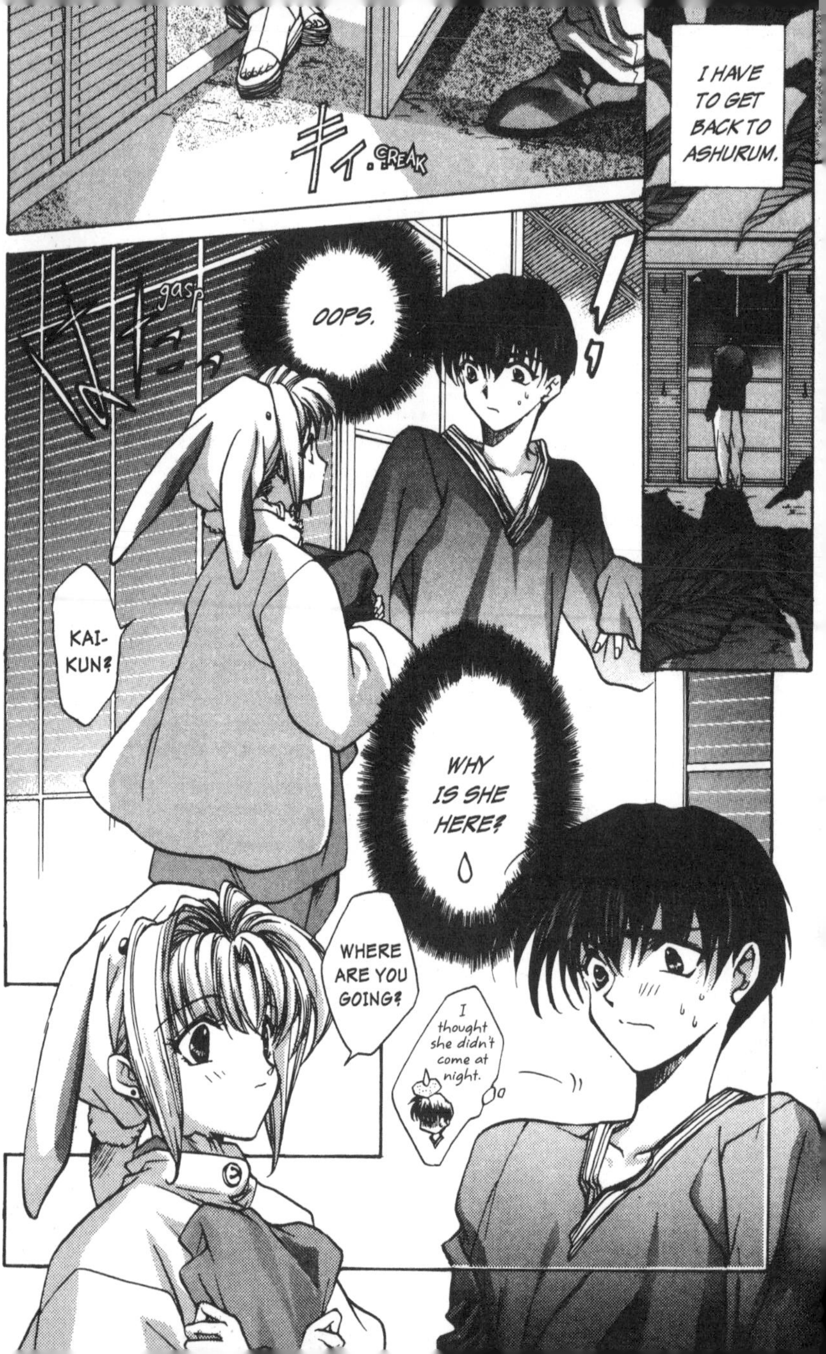
I HAVE TO GET BACK TO ASHURUM.
CREAK
OOPS.
gasp
KAI-KUN?
WHY IS SHE HERE?
I thought she didn't come at night.
WHERE ARE YOU GOING?

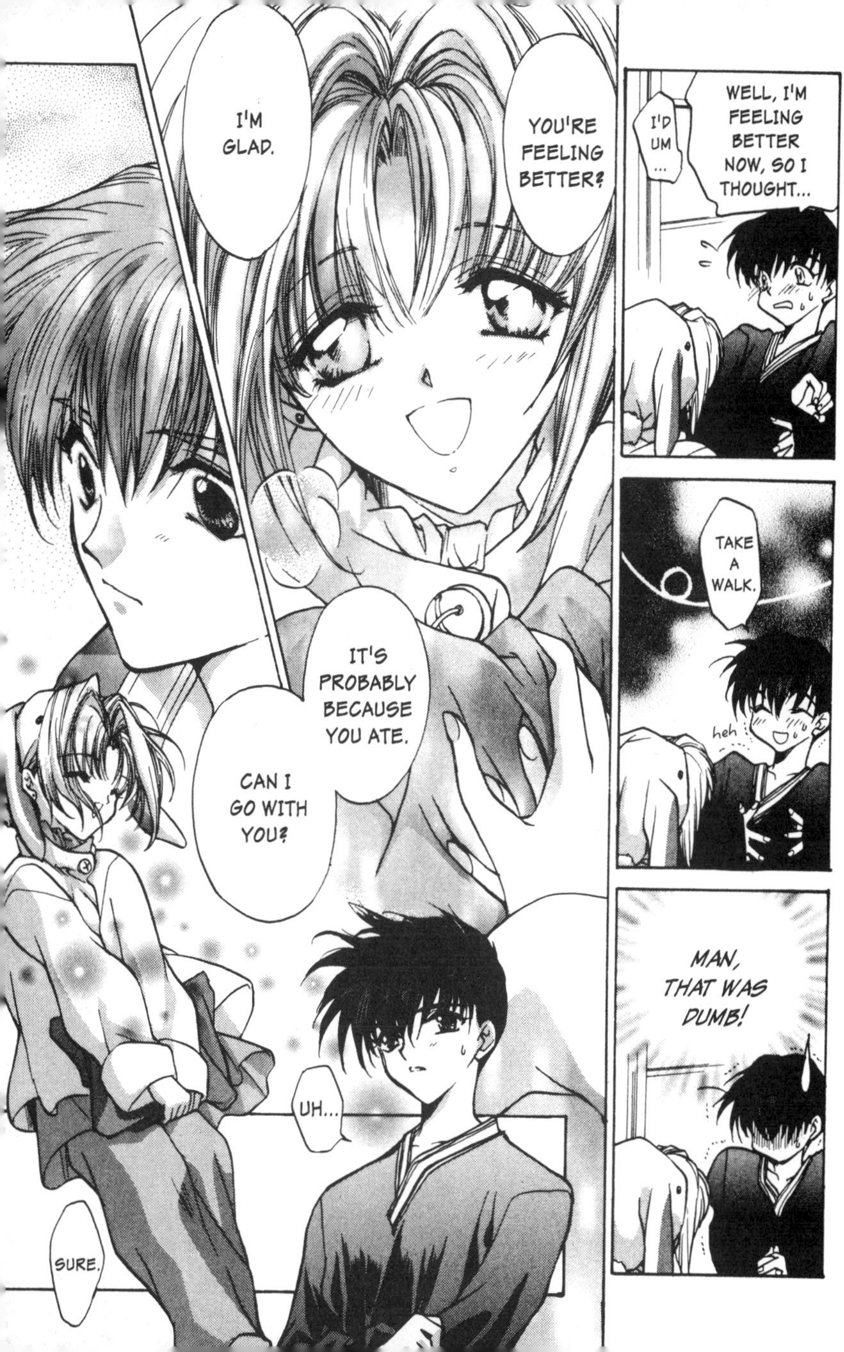
WELL, I'M FEELING BETTER NOW, SO I THOUGHT...
I'D UM ...
TAKE A WALK.
heh
MAN, THAT WAS DUMB!
YOU'RE FEELING BETTER?
I'M GLAD.
IT'S PROBABLY BECAUSE YOU ATE.
CAN I GO WITH YOU?
UH...
SURE.

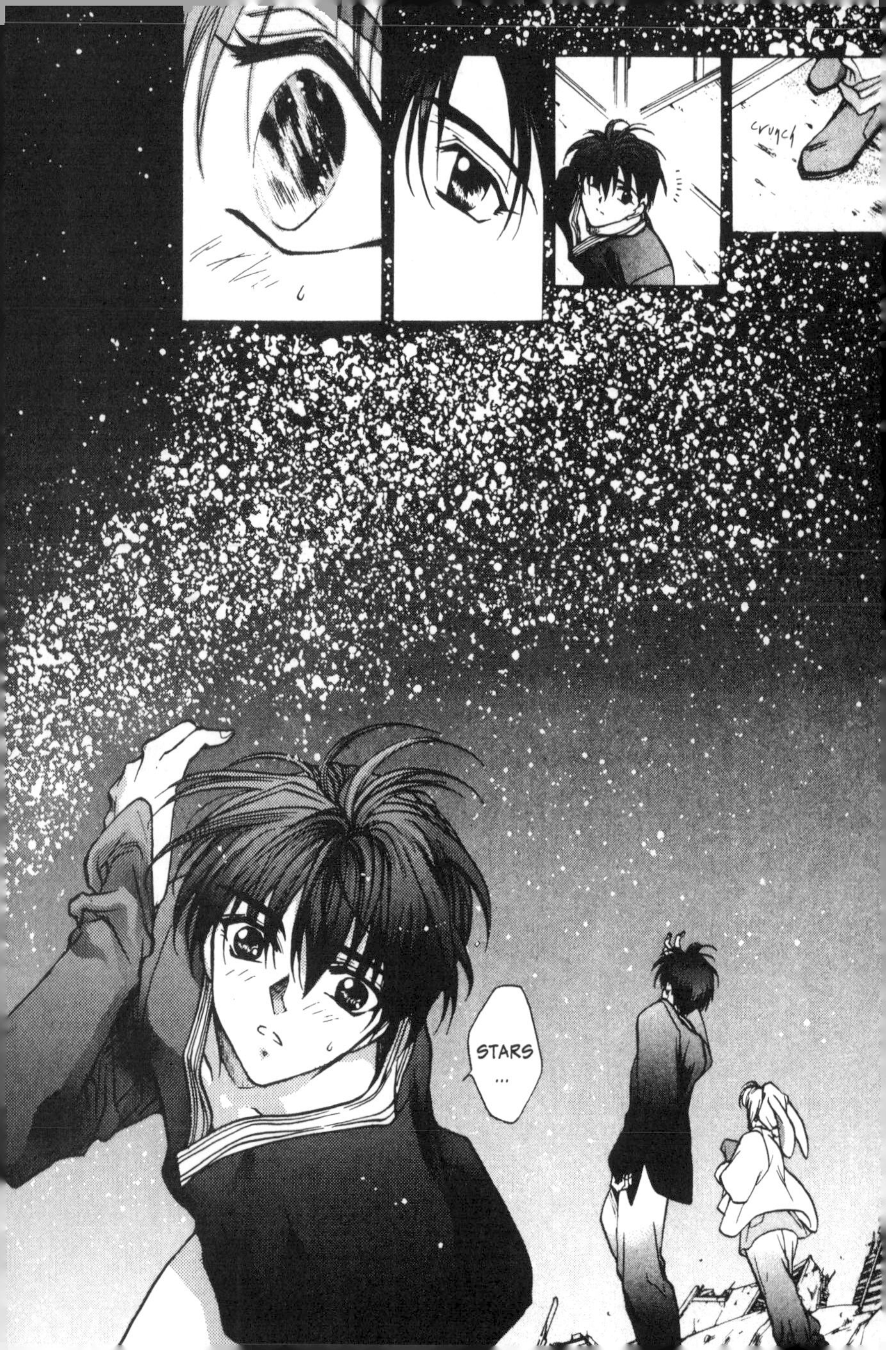
crunch
STARS ...

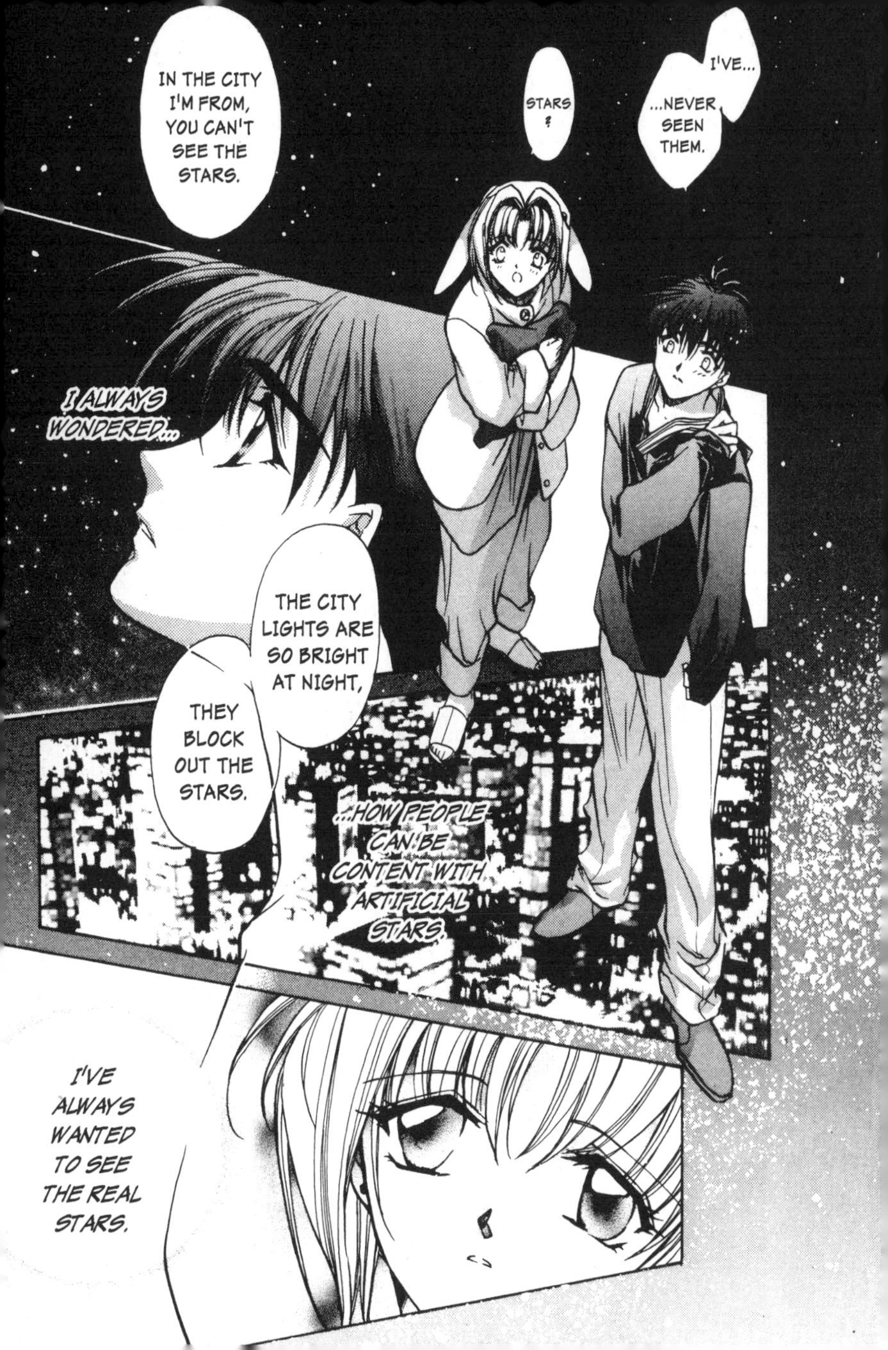
I'VE...
...NEVER SEEN THEM.
STARS?
IN THE CITY I'M FROM, YOU CAN'T SEE THE STARS.
THE CITY LIGHTS ARE SO BRIGHT AT NIGHT,
THEY BLOCK OUT THE STARS.
I ALWAYS WONDERED...
...HOW PEOPLE CAN BE CONTENT WITH ARTIFICIAL STARS.
I'VE ALWAYS WANTED TO SEE THE REAL STARS.

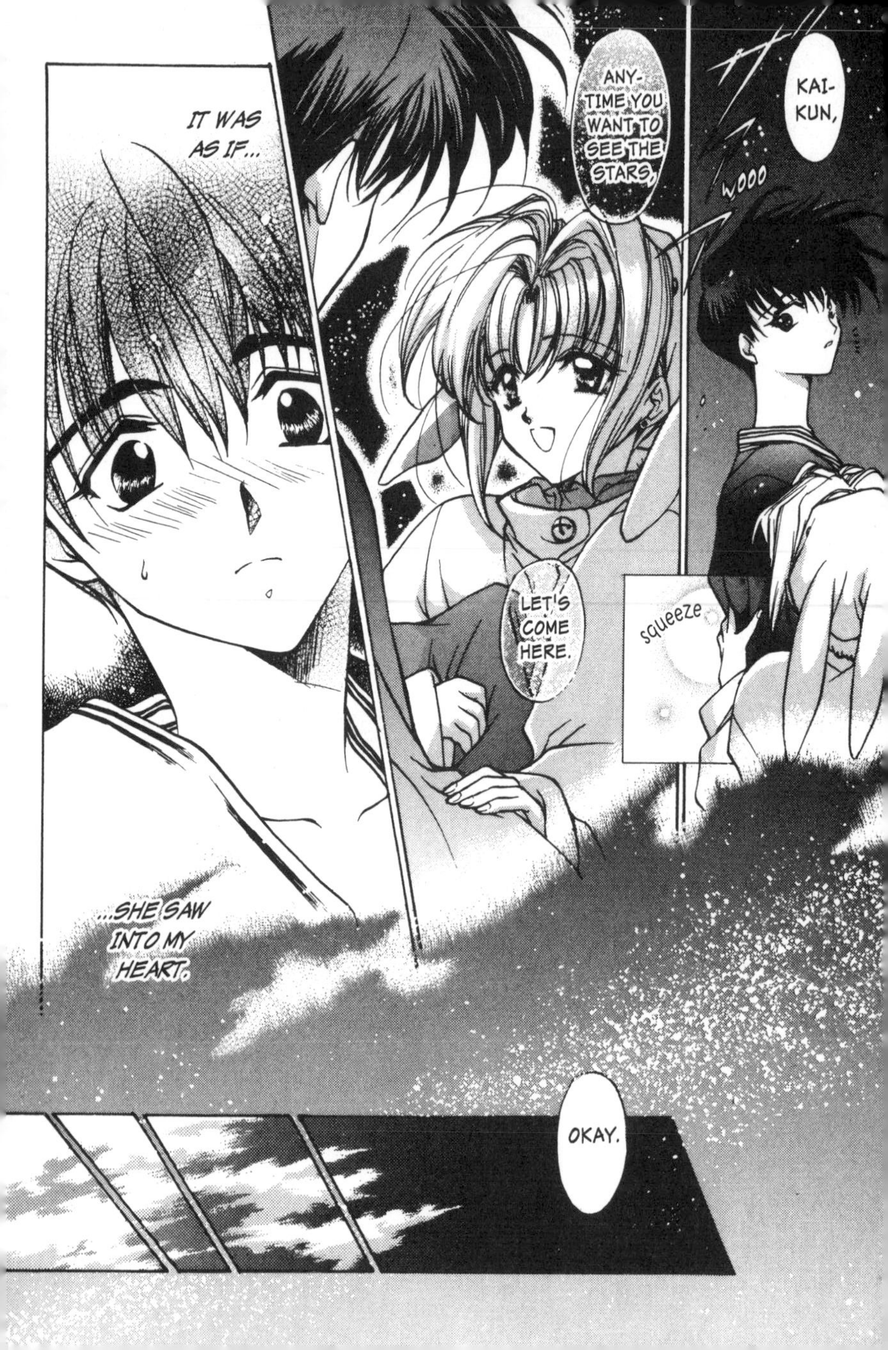
KAI-KUN,
WOOO
ANY-TIME YOU WANT TO SEE THE STARS,
LET'S COME HERE.
squeeze
IT WAS AS IF...
...SHE SAW INTO MY HEART.
OKAY.

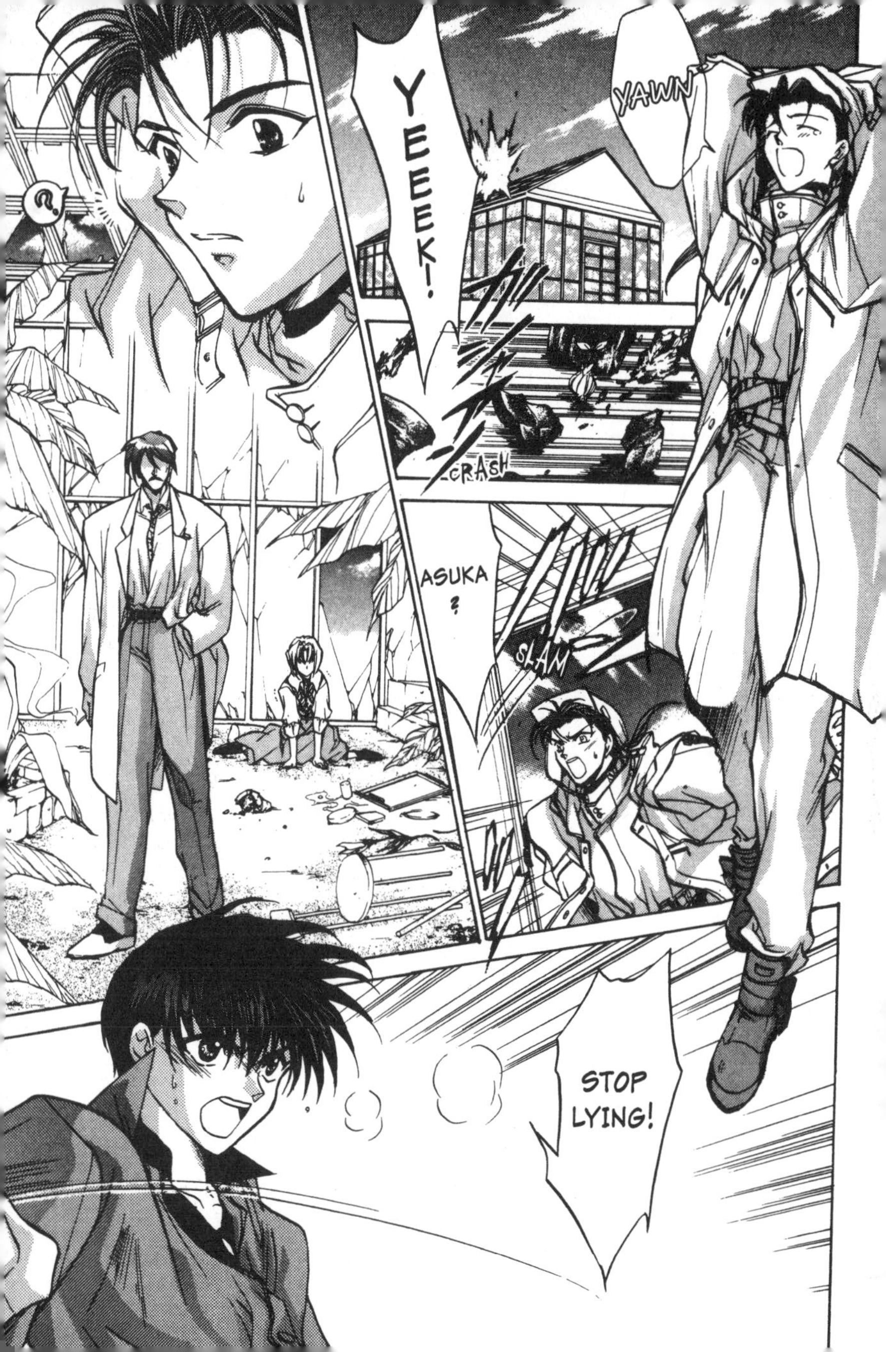
YAWN
YEEEEK!
CRASH
ASUKA?
SLAM
STOP LYING!

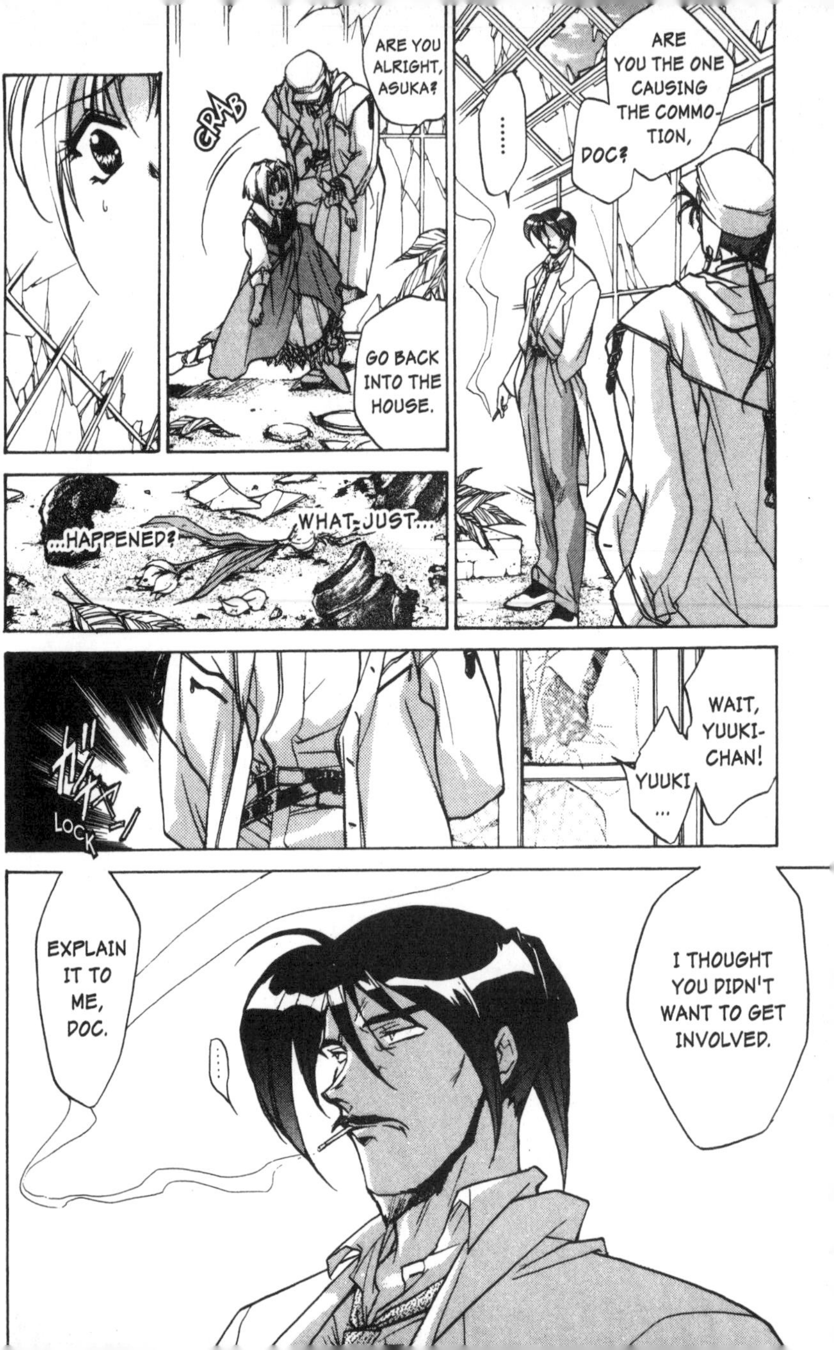
ARE YOU THE ONE CAUSING THE COMMOTION, DOC?
......
ARE YOU ALRIGHT, ASUKA?
GRAB
GO BACK INTO THE HOUSE.
WHAT JUST...
...HAPPENED?
WAIT, YUUKI-CHAN!
YUUKI ...
LOCK
I THOUGHT YOU DIDN'T WANT TO GET INVOLVED.
....
EXPLAIN IT TO ME, DOC.

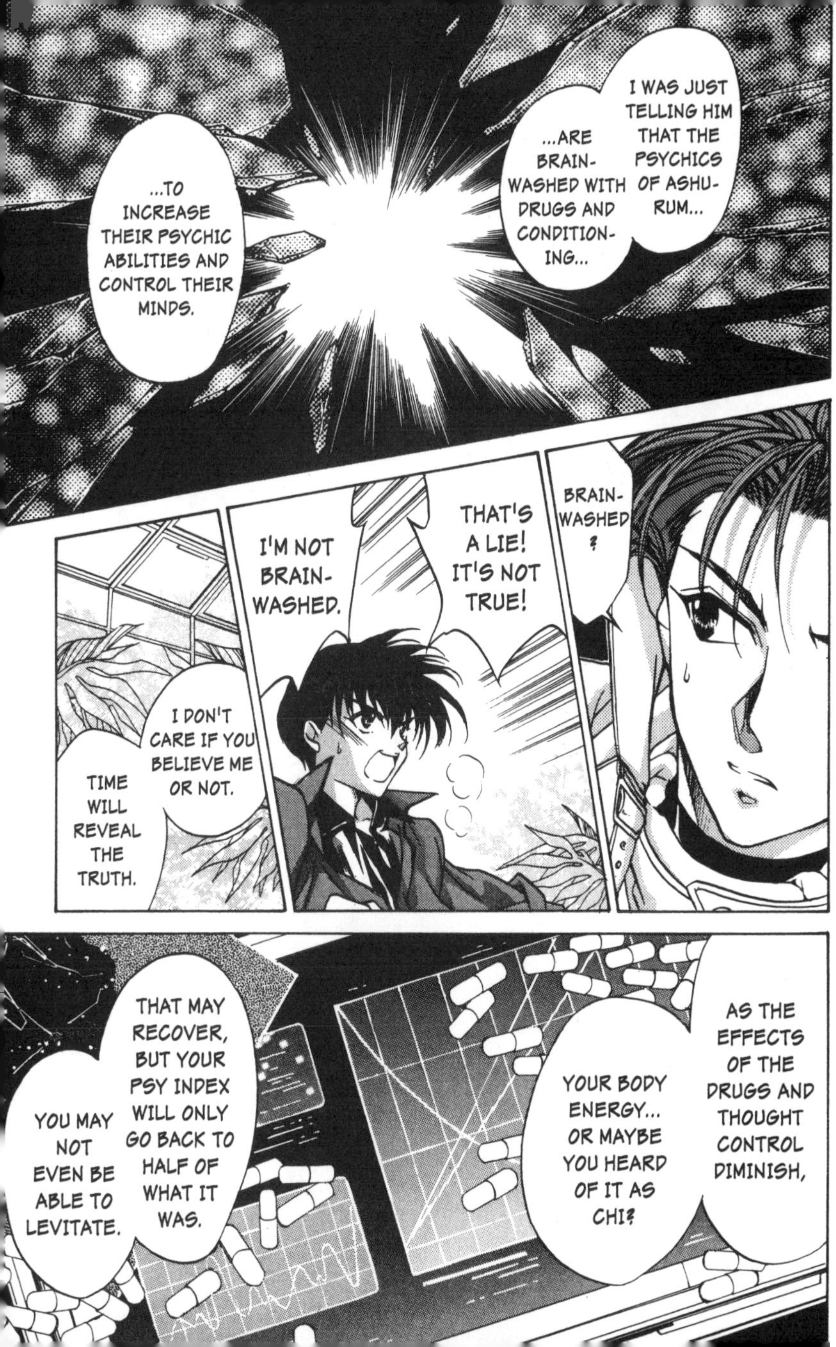
I WAS JUST TELLING HIM THAT THE PSYCHICS OF ASHURUM...
...ARE BRAIN-WASHED WITH DRUGS AND CONDITIONING...
...TO INCREASE THEIR PSYCHIC ABILITIES AND CONTROL THEIR MINDS.
BRAIN-WASHED?
THAT'S A LIE! IT'S NOT TRUE!
I'M NOT BRAIN-WASHED.
I DON'T CARE IF YOU BELIEVE ME OR NOT.
TIME WILL REVEAL THE TRUTH.
AS THE EFFECTS OF THE DRUGS AND THOUGHT CONTROL DIMINISH,
YOUR BODY ENERGY... OR MAYBE YOU HEARD OF IT AS CHI?
THAT MAY RECOVER, BUT YOUR PSY INDEX WILL ONLY GO BACK TO HALF OF WHAT IT WAS.
YOU MAY NOT EVEN BE ABLE TO LEVITATE.

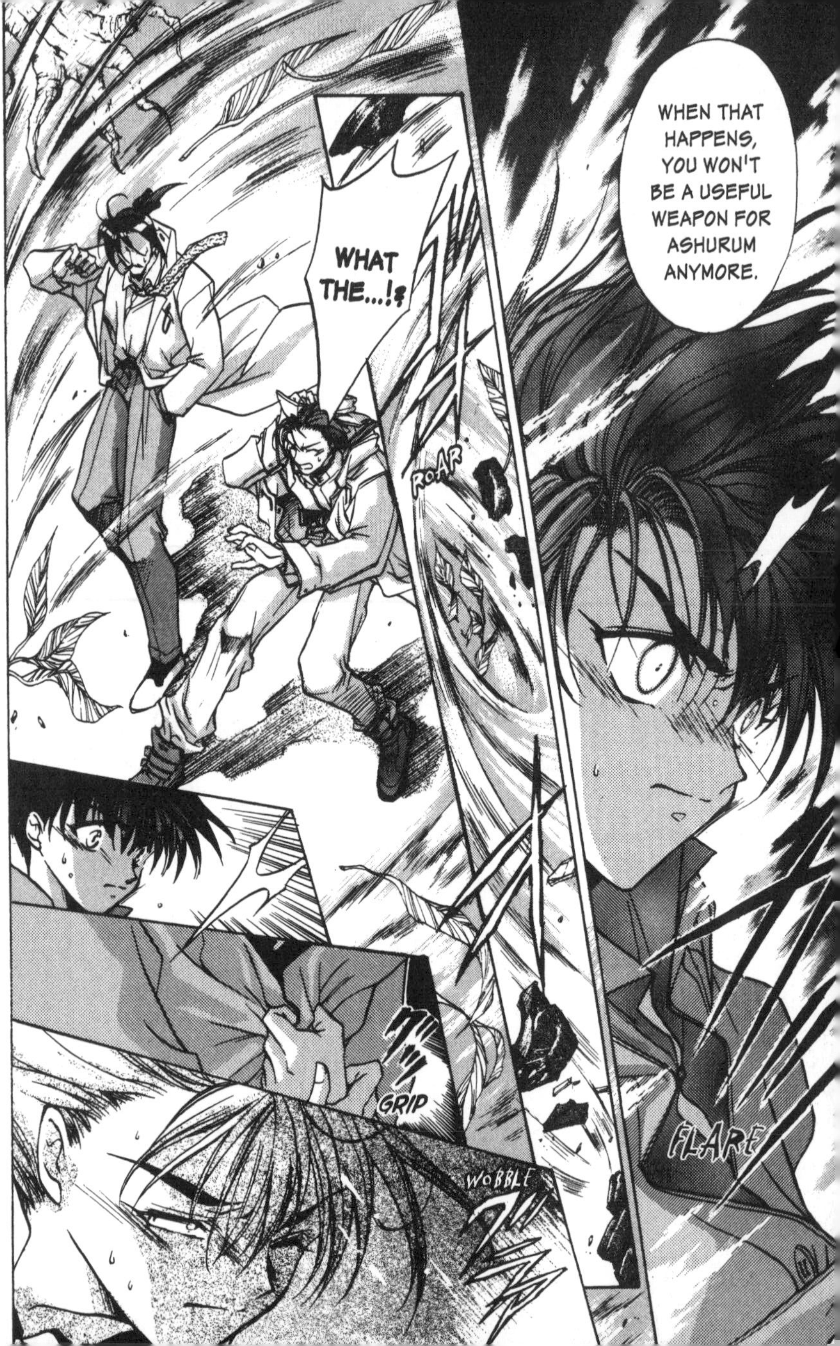
WHEN THAT HAPPENS, YOU WON'T BE A USEFUL WEAPON FOR ASHURUM ANYMORE.
FLARE
WHAT THE...!?
ROAR
GRIP
WOBBLE

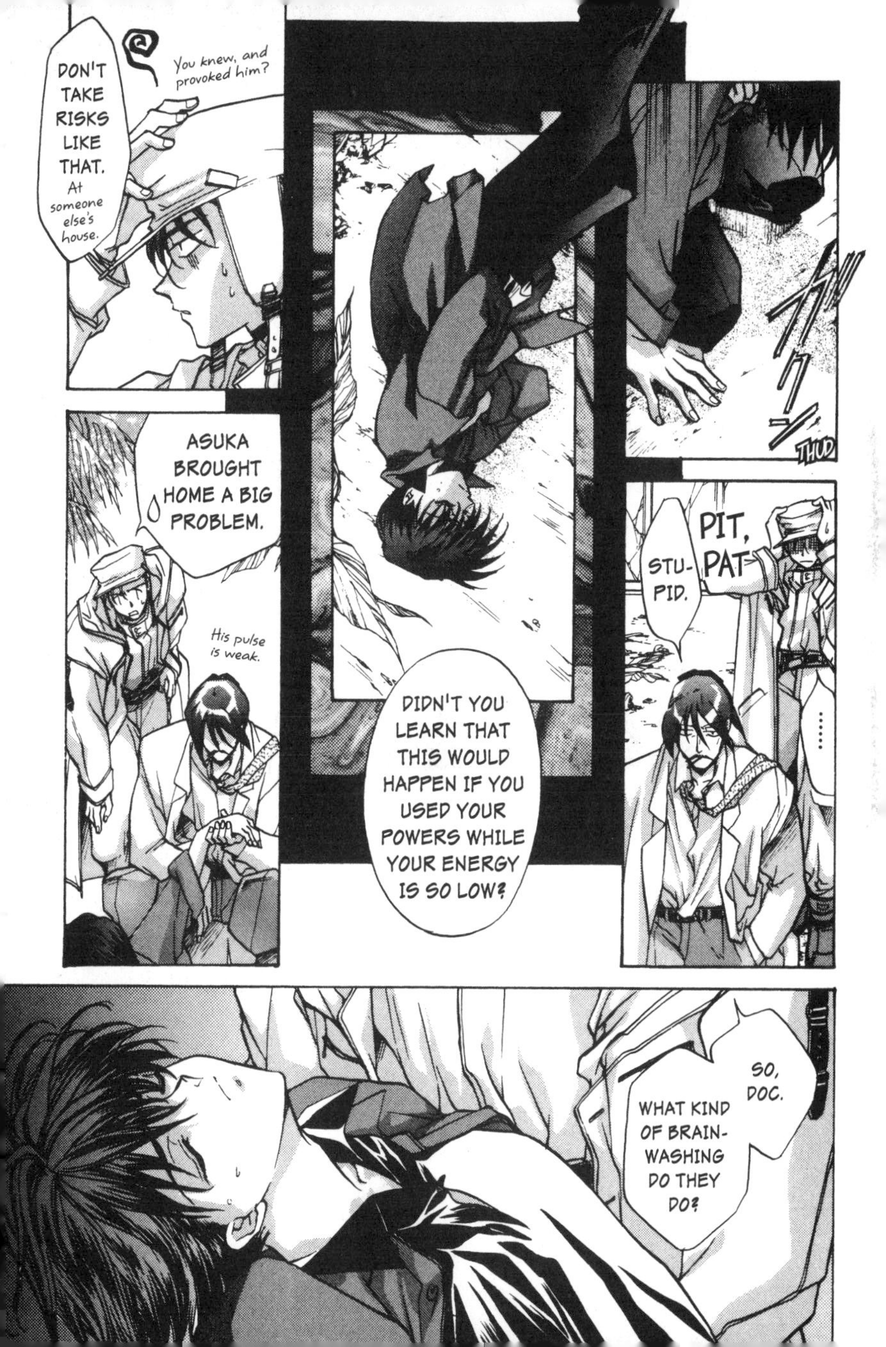
THUD
STU-PID.
PIT, PAT
......
DIDN'T YOU LEARN THAT THIS WOULD HAPPEN IF YOU USED YOUR POWERS WHILE YOUR ENERGY IS SO LOW?
DON'T TAKE RISKS LIKE THAT. At someone else's house.
You knew, and provoked him?
ASUKA BROUGHT HOME A BIG PROBLEM.
His pulse is weak.
SO, DOC.
WHAT KIND OF BRAIN-WASHING DO THEY DO?

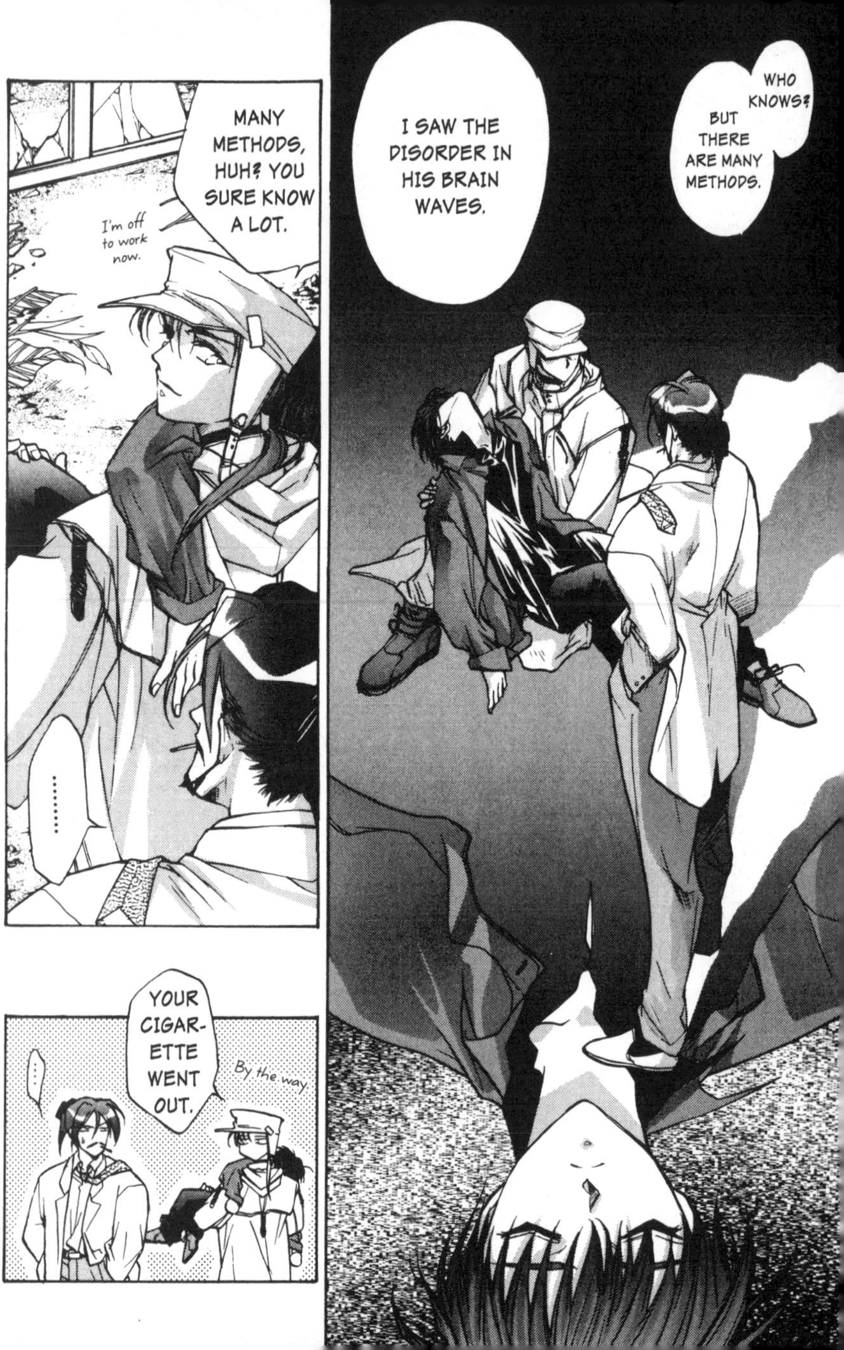
WHO KNOWS? BUT THERE ARE MANY METHODS.
I SAW THE DISORDER IN HIS BRAIN WAVES.
MANY METHODS, HUH? YOU SURE KNOW A LOT.
I'm off to work now.
....
By the way,
YOUR CIGAR-ETTE WENT OUT.
...

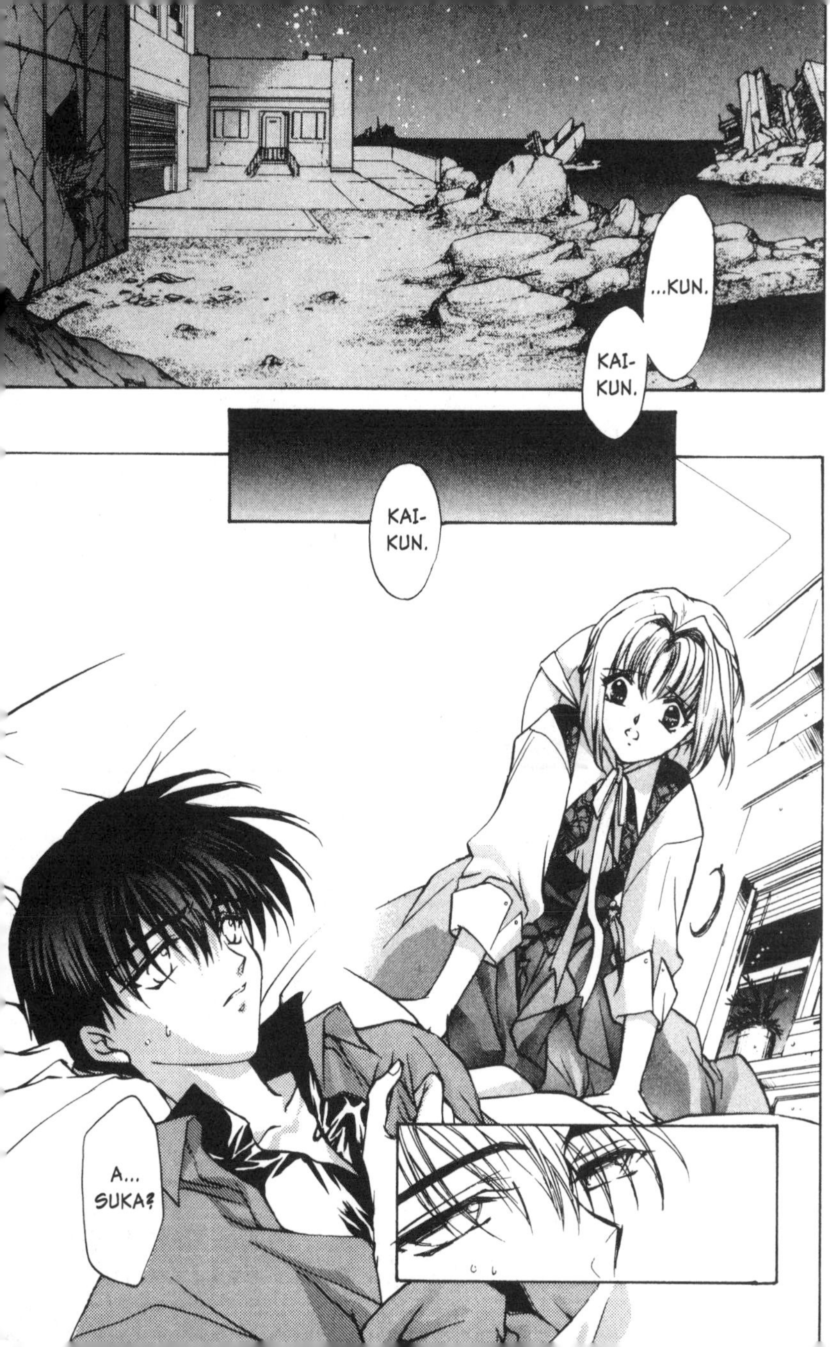
...KUN.
KAI-KUN.
KAI-KUN.
A... SUKA?

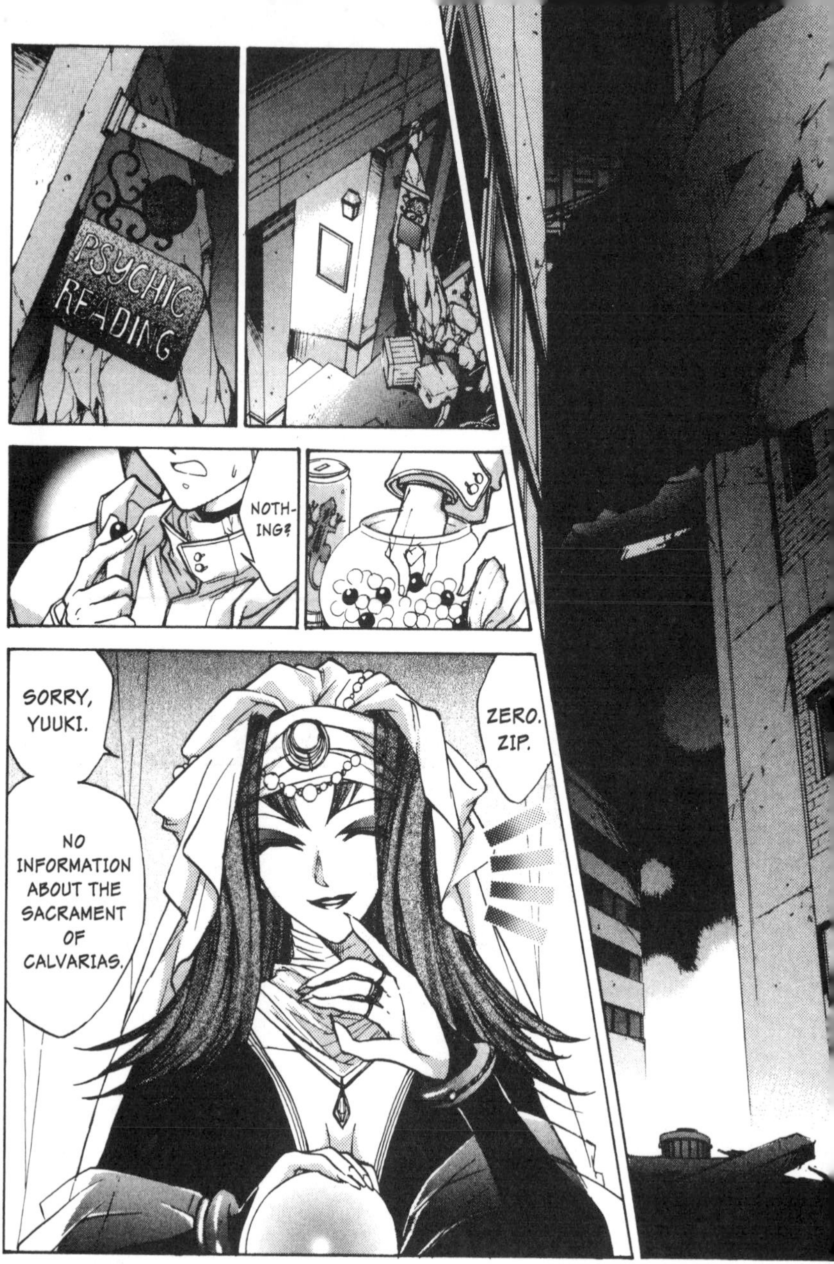
PSYCHIC READING
NOTH-ING?
ZERO. ZIP.
SORRY, YUUKI.
NO INFORMATION ABOUT THE SACRAMENT OF CALVARIAS.

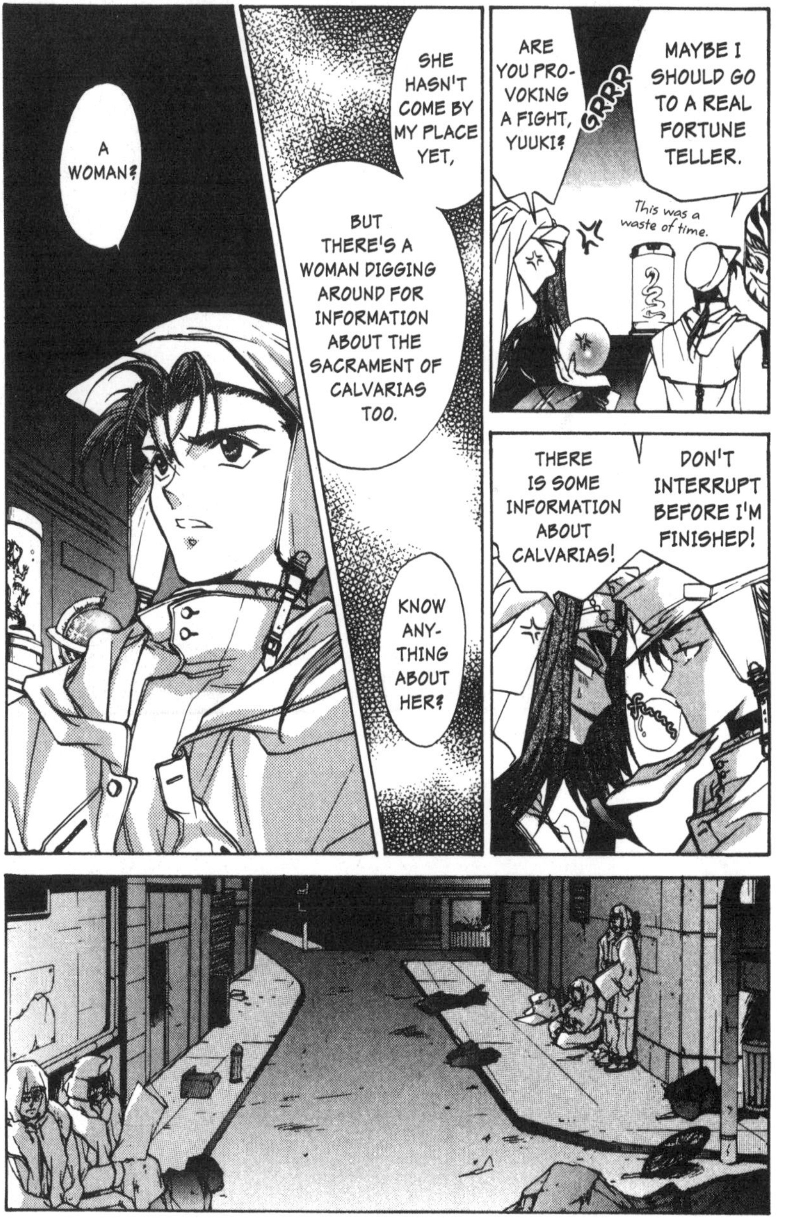
MAYBE I SHOULD GO TO A REAL FORTUNE TELLER.
GRRR
ARE YOU PRO-VOKING A FIGHT, YUUKI?
This was a waste of time.
DON'T INTERRUPT BEFORE I'M FINISHED!
THERE IS SOME INFORMATION ABOUT CALVARIAS!
SHE HASN'T COME BY MY PLACE YET,
BUT THERE'S A WOMAN DIGGING AROUND FOR INFORMATION ABOUT THE SACRAMENT OF CALVARIAS TOO.
KNOW ANY-THING ABOUT HER?
A WOMAN?

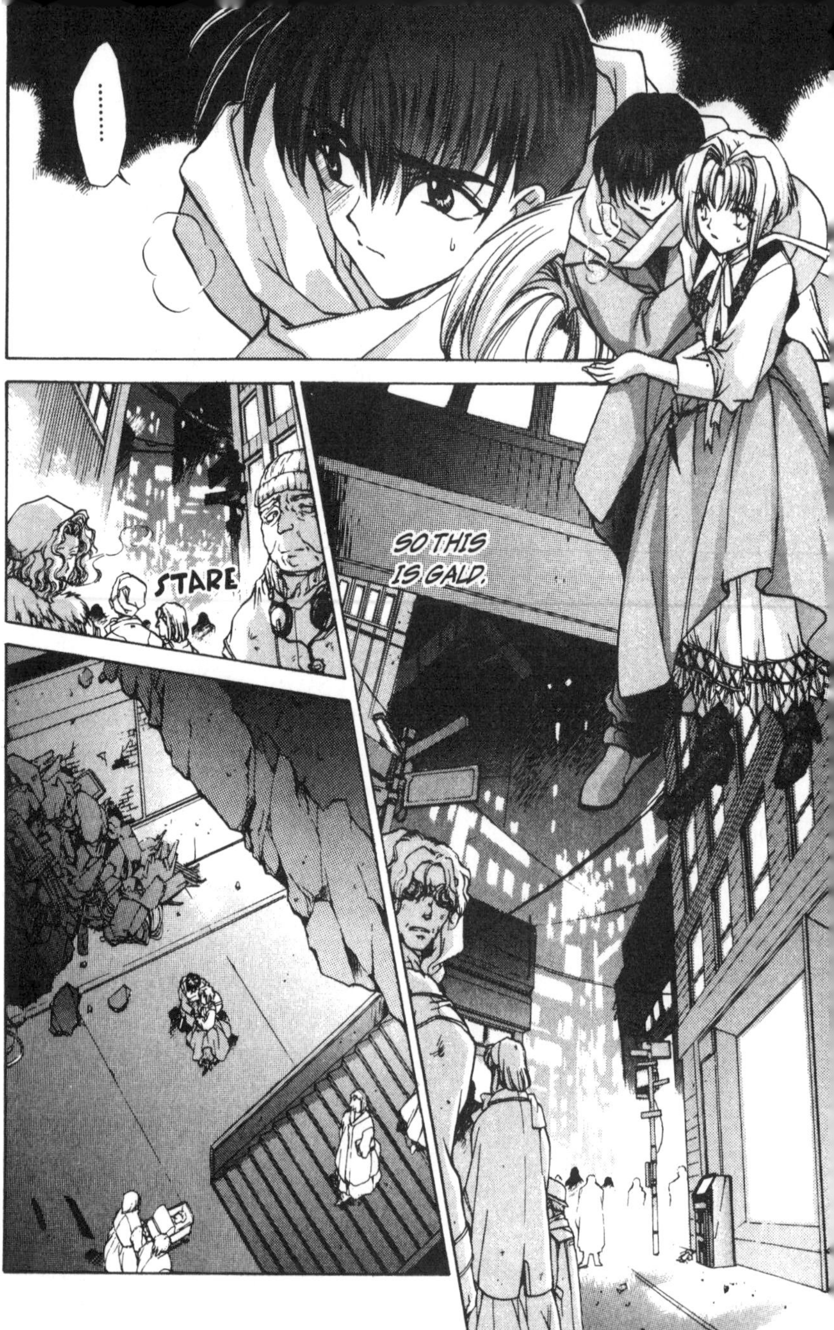
……
SO THIS IS GALD.
STARE

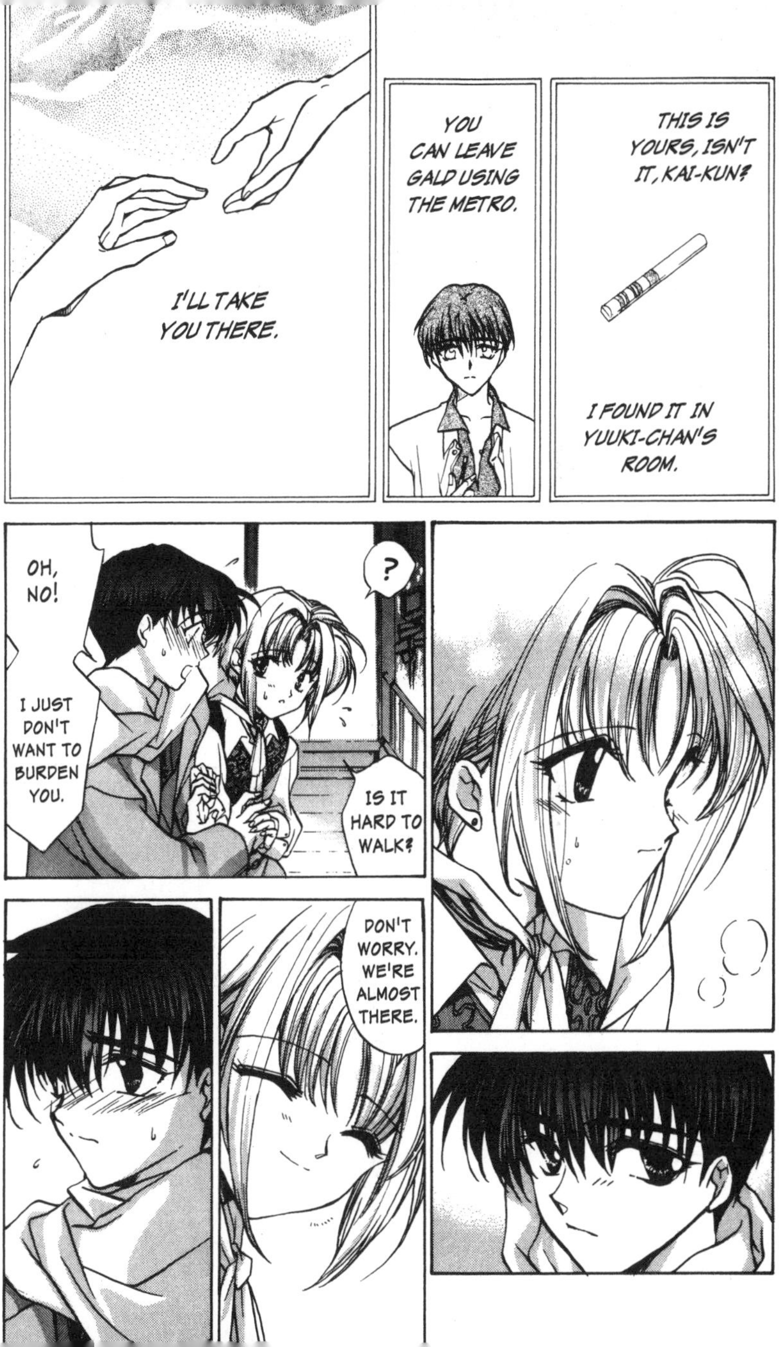
THIS IS YOURS, ISN'T IT, KAI-KUN?
I FOUND IT IN YUUKI-CHAN'S ROOM.
YOU CAN LEAVE GALD USING THE METRO.
I'LL TAKE YOU THERE.
?
IS IT HARD TO WALK?
OH, NO!
I JUST DON'T WANT TO BURDEN YOU.
DON'T WORRY. WE'RE ALMOST THERE.

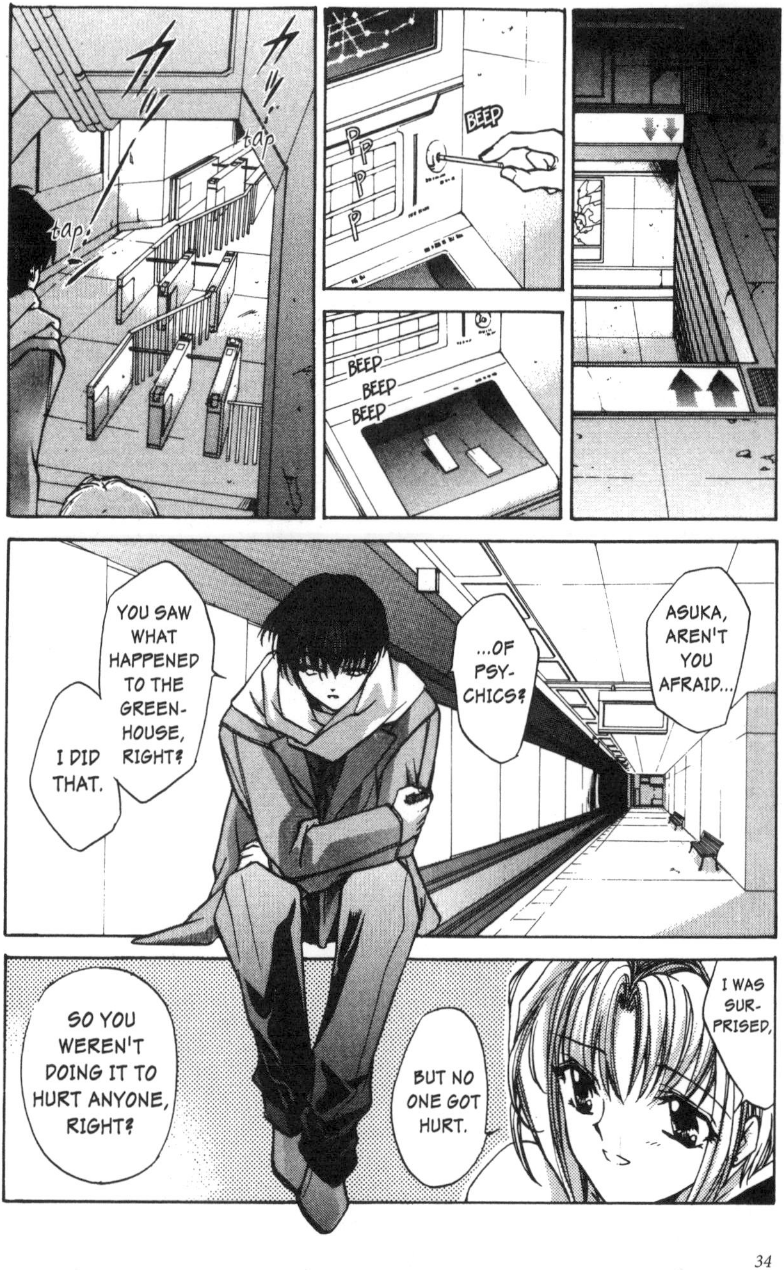
BEEP
P P P P
BEEP BEEP BEEP
tap
tap!
ASUKA, AREN'T YOU AFRAID...
...OF PSYCHICS?
YOU SAW WHAT HAPPENED TO THE GREENHOUSE, RIGHT?
I DID THAT.
I WAS SURPRISED,
BUT NO ONE GOT HURT.
SO YOU WEREN'T DOING IT TO HURT ANYONE, RIGHT?

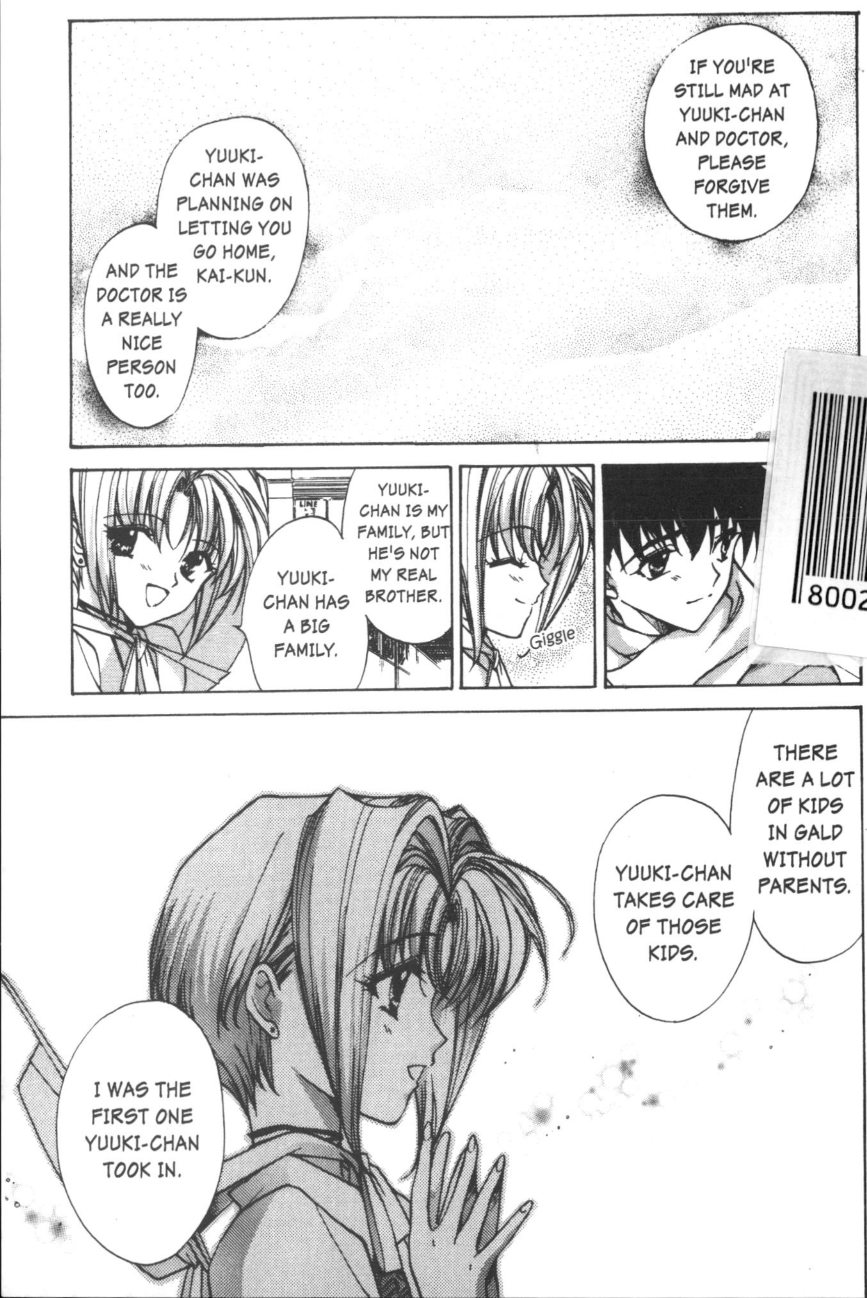
IF YOU'RE STILL MAD AT YUUKI-CHAN AND DOCTOR, PLEASE FORGIVE THEM.
YUUKI-CHAN WAS PLANNING ON LETTING YOU GO HOME, KAI-KUN.
AND THE DOCTOR IS A REALLY NICE PERSON TOO.
Giggle
YUUKI-CHAN IS MY FAMILY, BUT HE'S NOT MY REAL BROTHER.
YUUKI-CHAN HAS A BIG FAMILY.
THERE ARE A LOT OF KIDS IN GALD WITHOUT PARENTS.
YUUKI-CHAN TAKES CARE OF THOSE KIDS.
I WAS THE FIRST ONE YUUKI-CHAN TOOK IN.

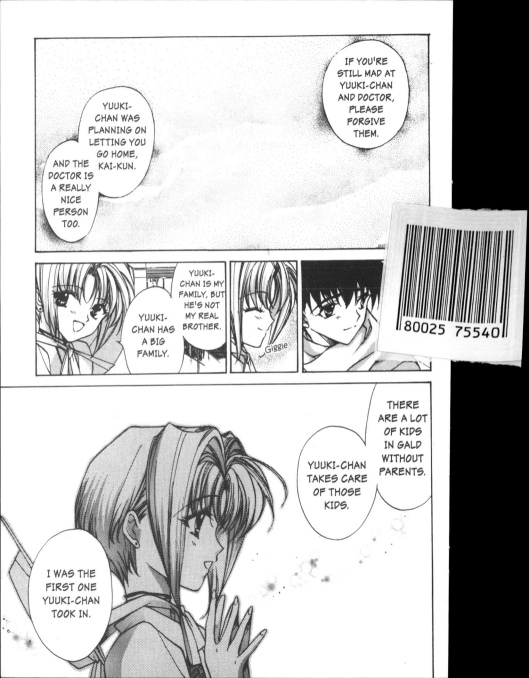

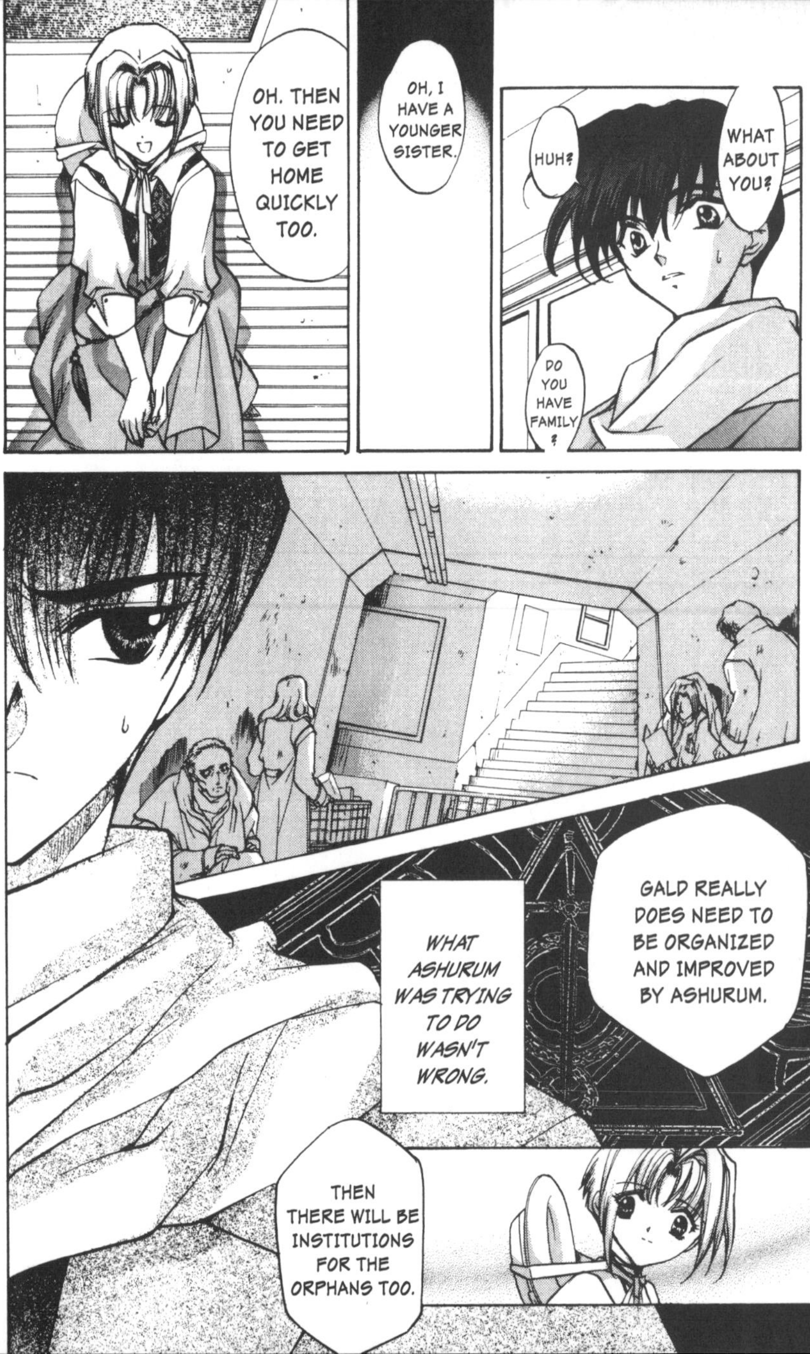
WHAT ABOUT YOU?
HUH?
DO YOU HAVE FAMILY?
OH, I HAVE A YOUNGER SISTER.
OH. THEN YOU NEED TO GET HOME QUICKLY TOO.
GALD REALLY DOES NEED TO BE ORGANIZED AND IMPROVED BY ASHURUM.
WHAT ASHURUM WAS TRYING TO DO WASN'T WRONG.
THEN THERE WILL BE INSTITUTIONS FOR THE ORPHANS TOO.

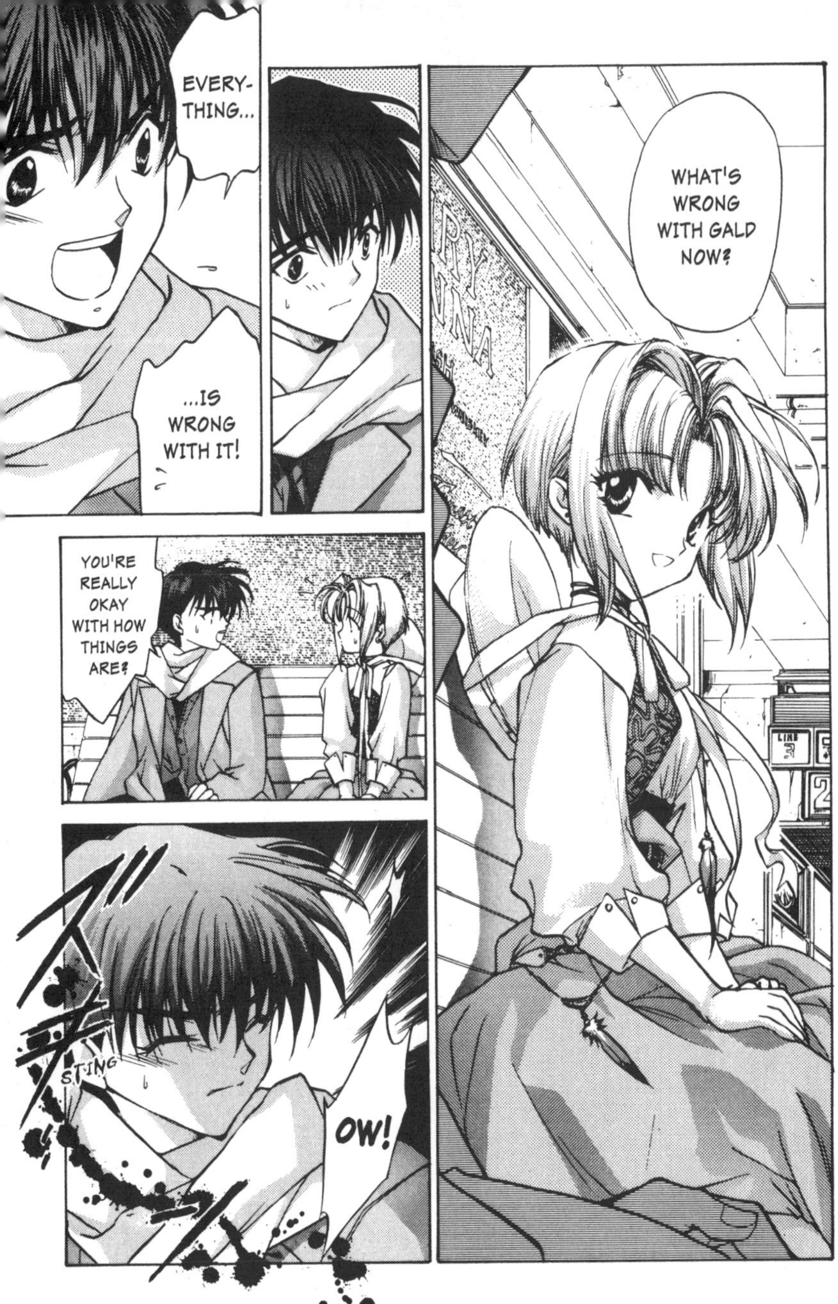
WHAT'S WRONG WITH GALD NOW?
EVERY-THING...
...IS WRONG WITH IT!
YOU'RE REALLY OKAY WITH HOW THINGS ARE?
STING
OW!

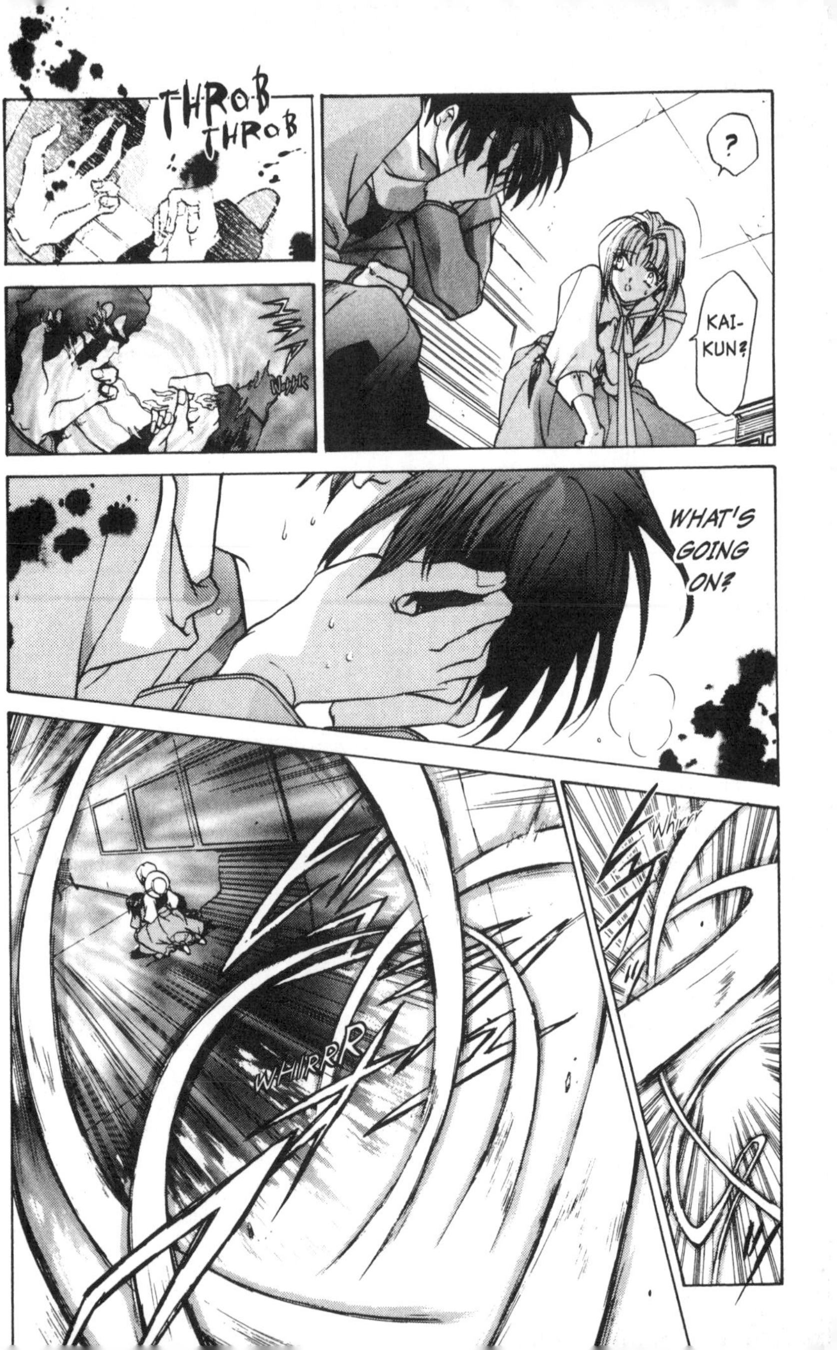
?
KAI-KUN?
THROB THROB
Wobble
WHAT'S GOING ON?
Whirrr
WHIRRR

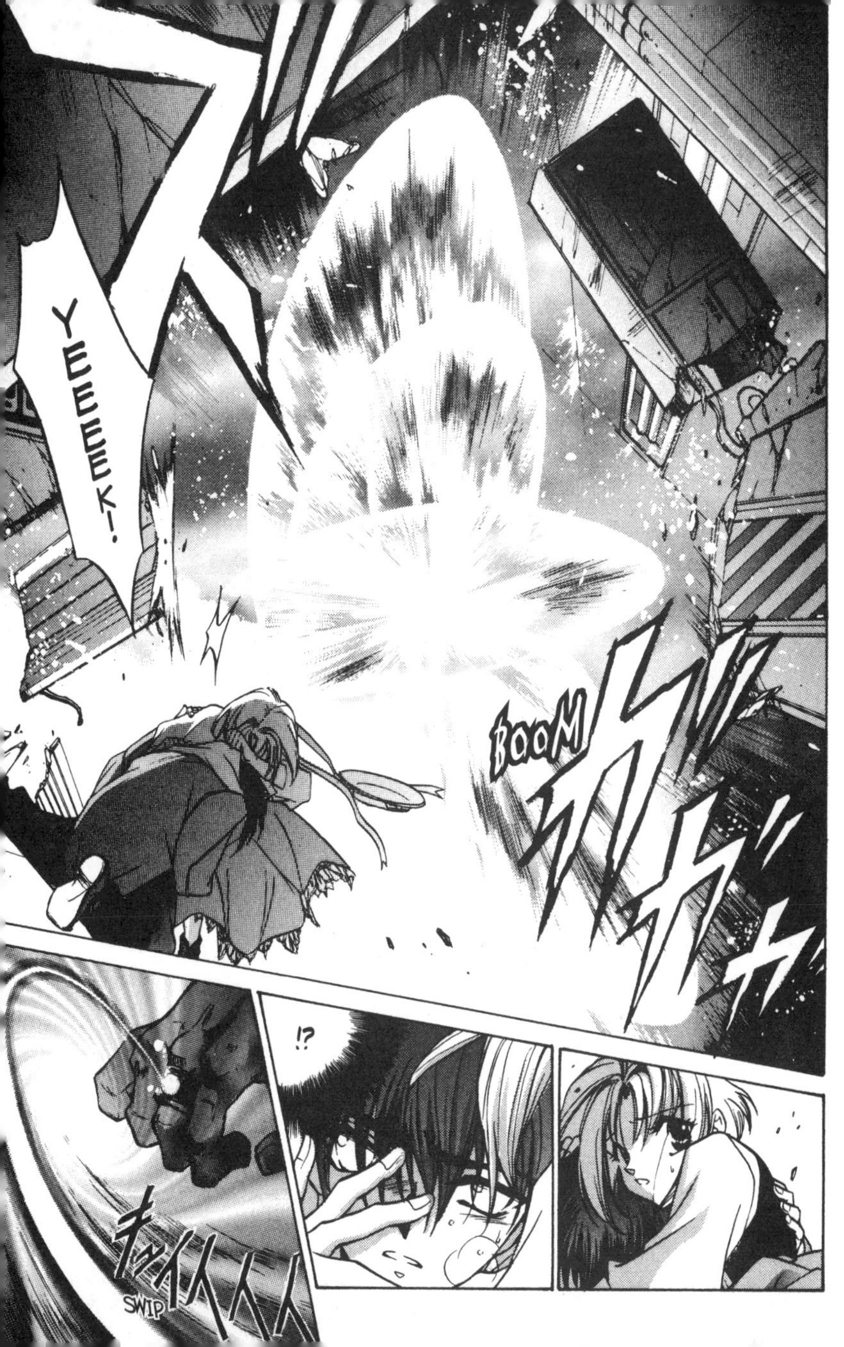
YEEEEEK!
BOOM
!?
SWIP

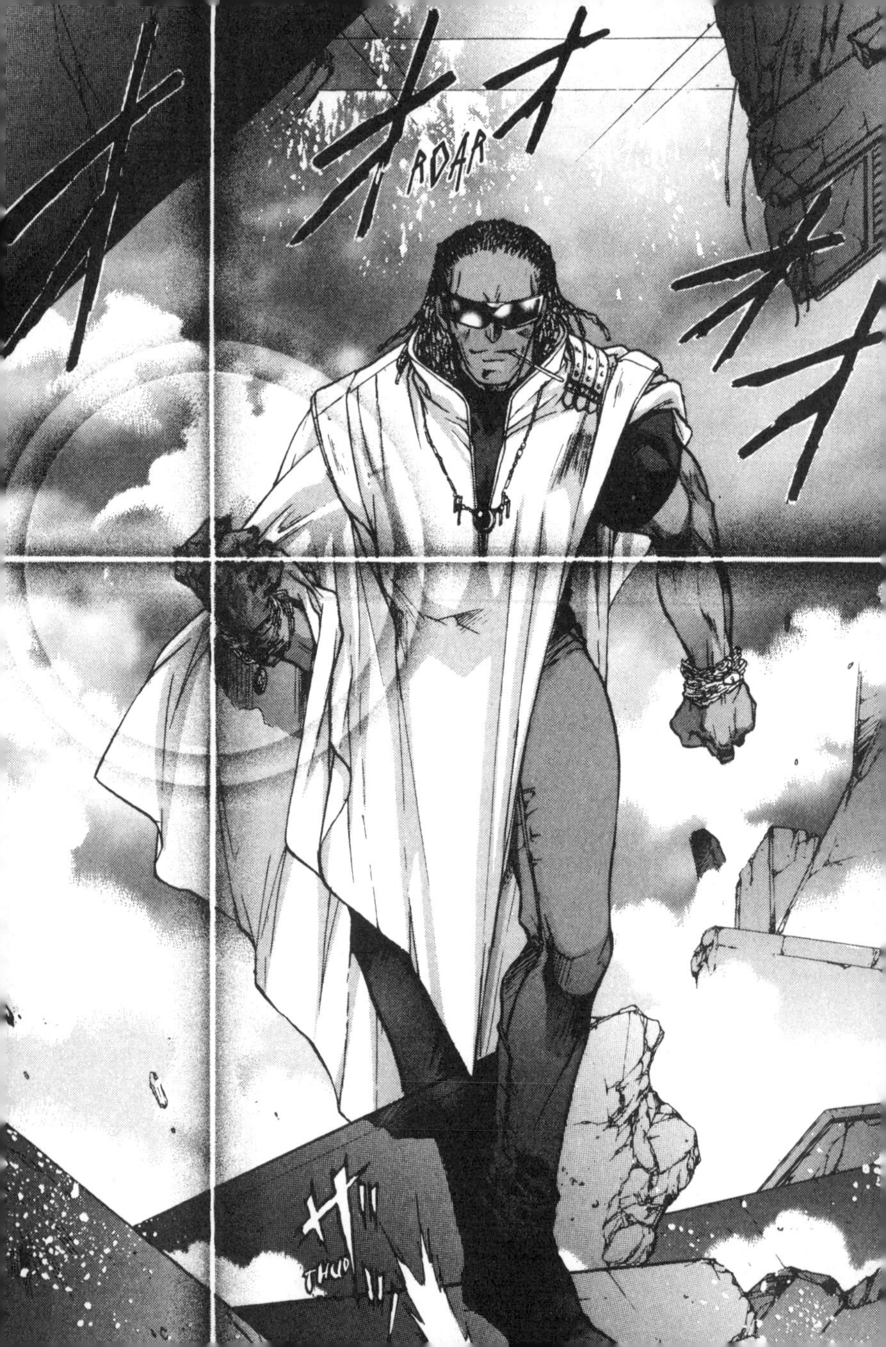
ROAR
THUD

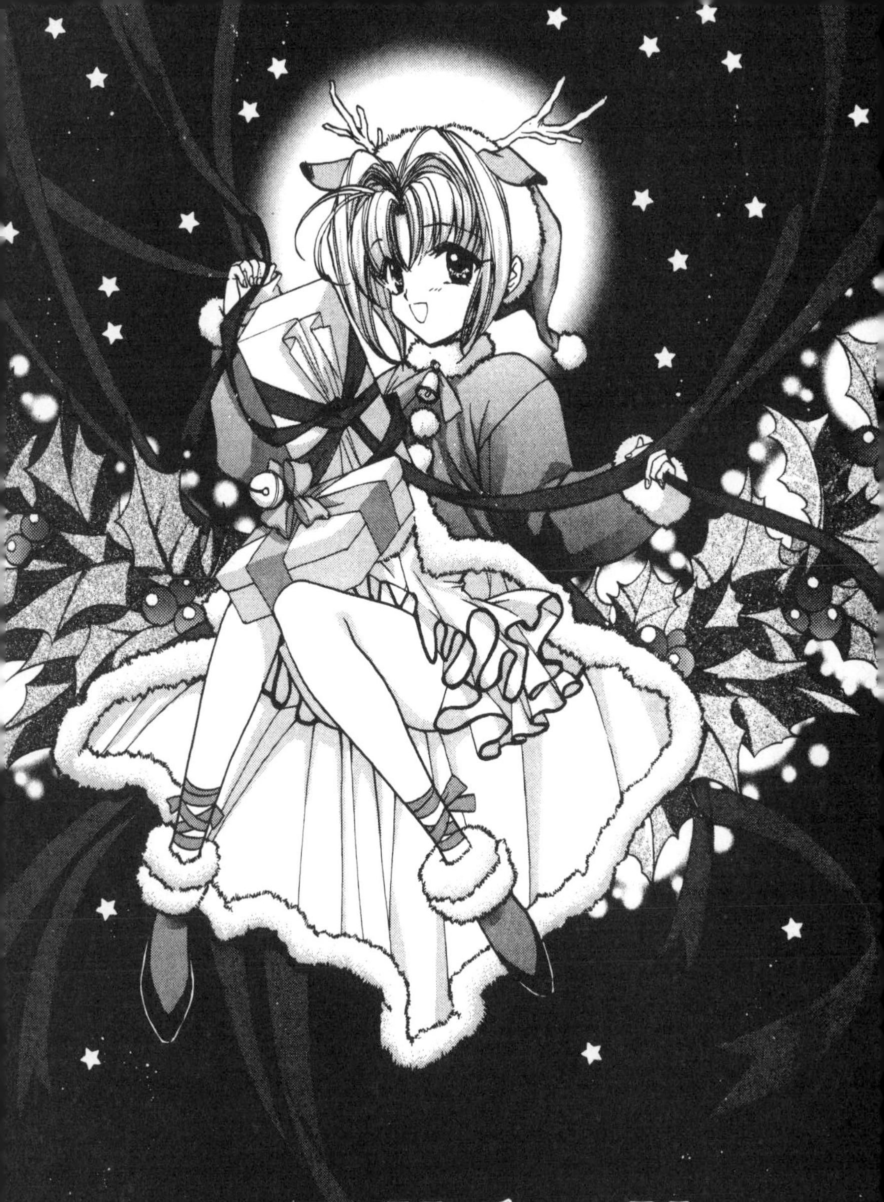

CHAPTER 8 Violent Urges

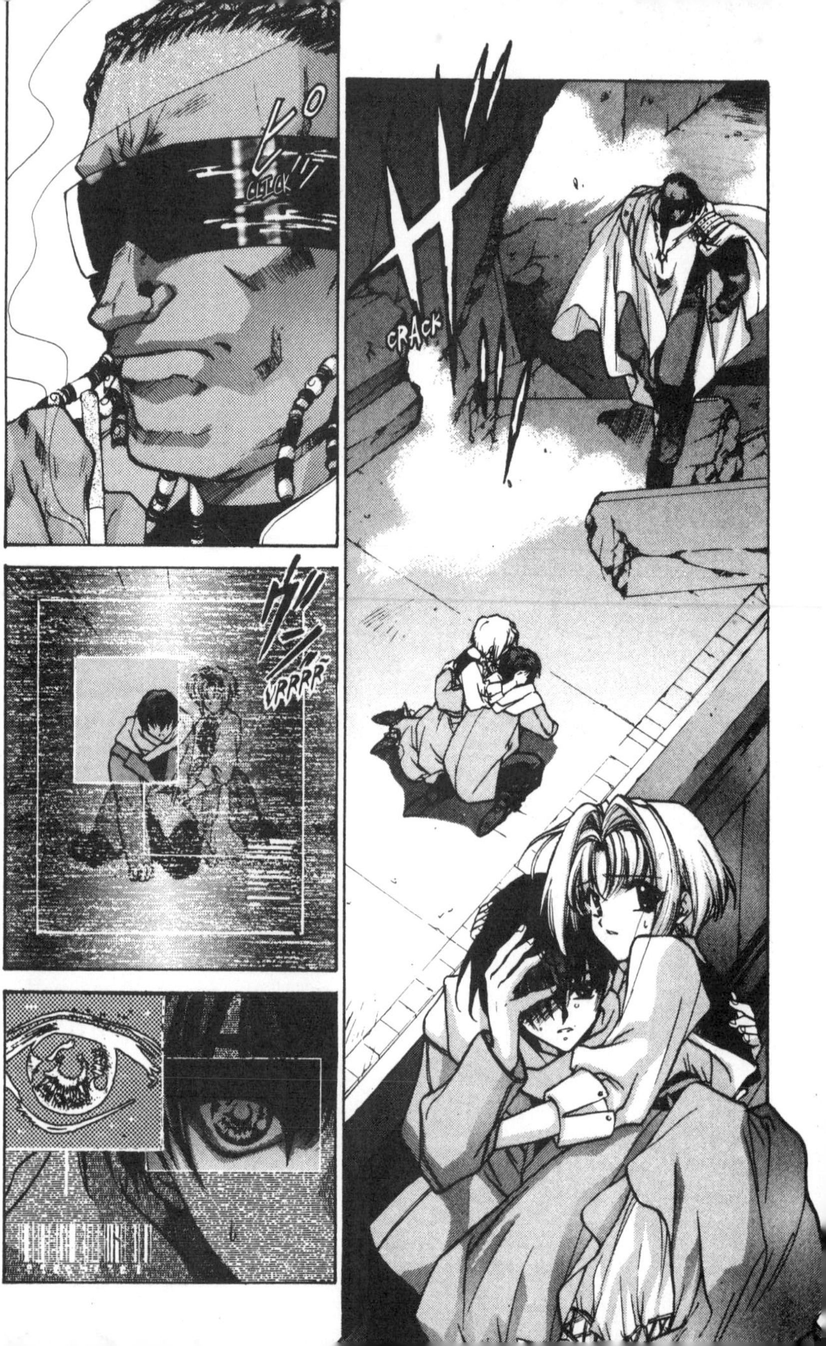
CRACK
CLICK
VRRRR

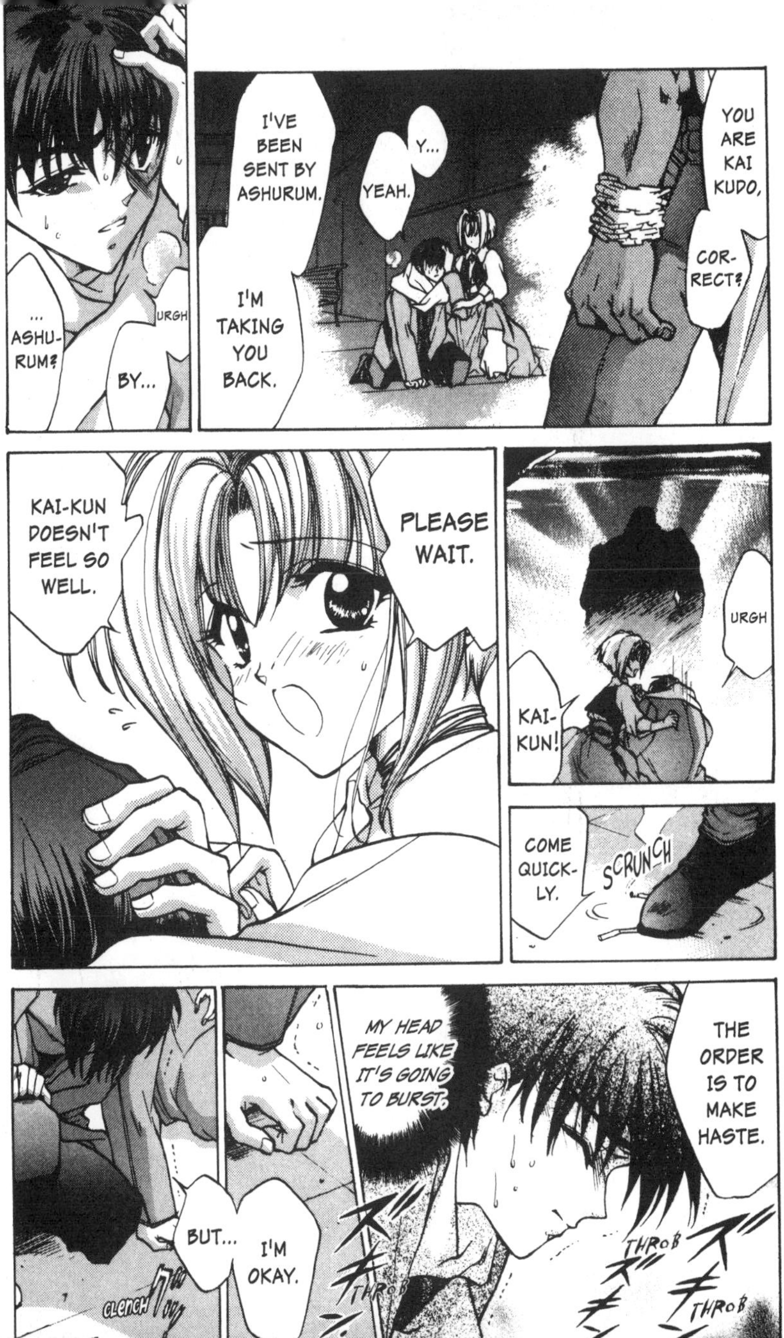

YOU ARE KAI KUDO,
CORRECT?
Y...
YEAH.
I'VE BEEN SENT BY ASHURUM.
I'M TAKING YOU BACK.
URGH
BY...
... ASHURUM?
URGH
KAI-KUN!
SCRUNCH
COME QUICKLY.
PLEASE WAIT.
KAI-KUN DOESN'T FEEL SO WELL.
THE ORDER IS TO MAKE HASTE.
MY HEAD FEELS LIKE IT'S GOING TO BURST.
THROB
THROB
THROB
BUT...
I'M OKAY.
CLENCH

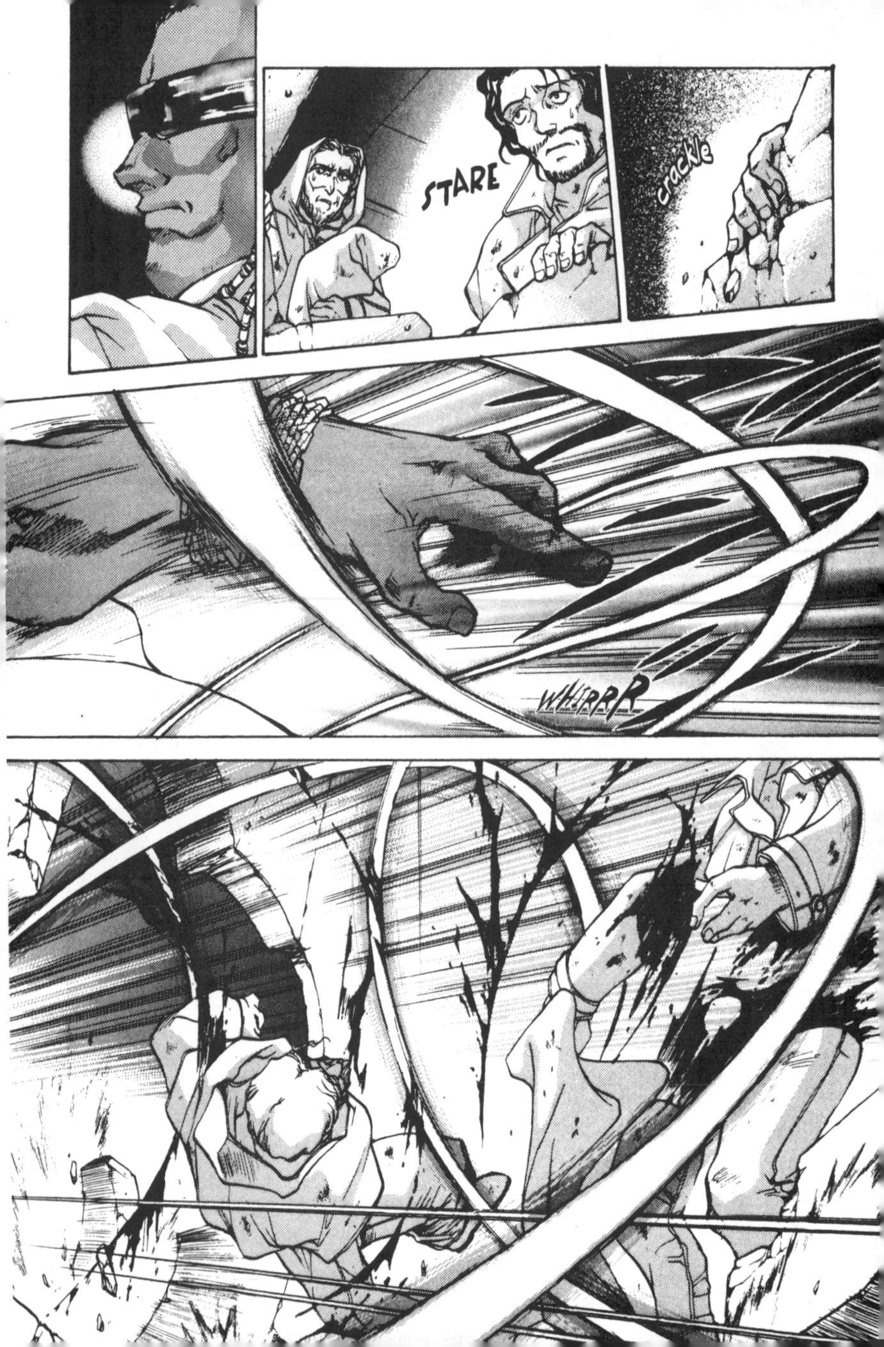
crackle
STARE
WHIRRR

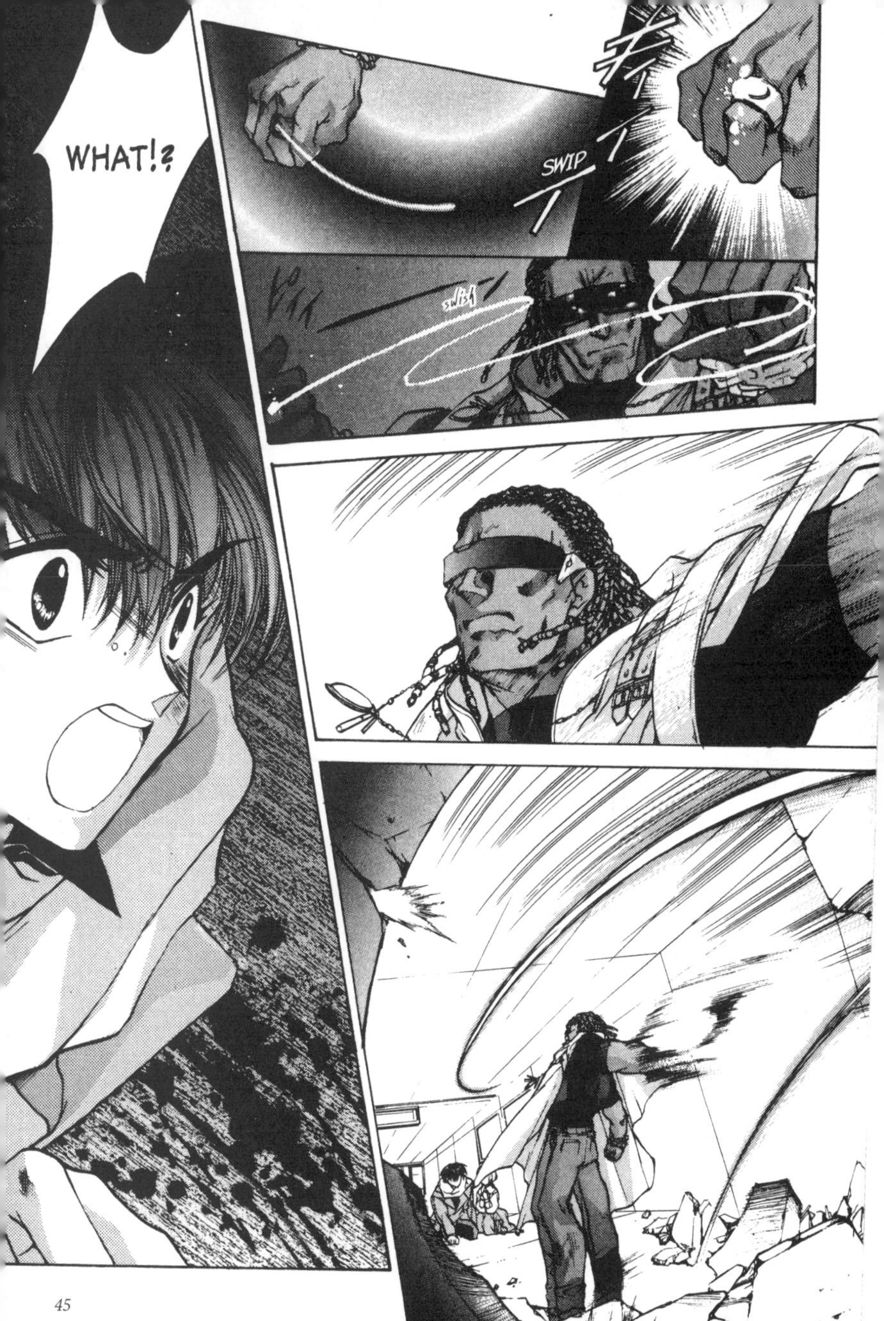
SWIP
swish
WHAT!?

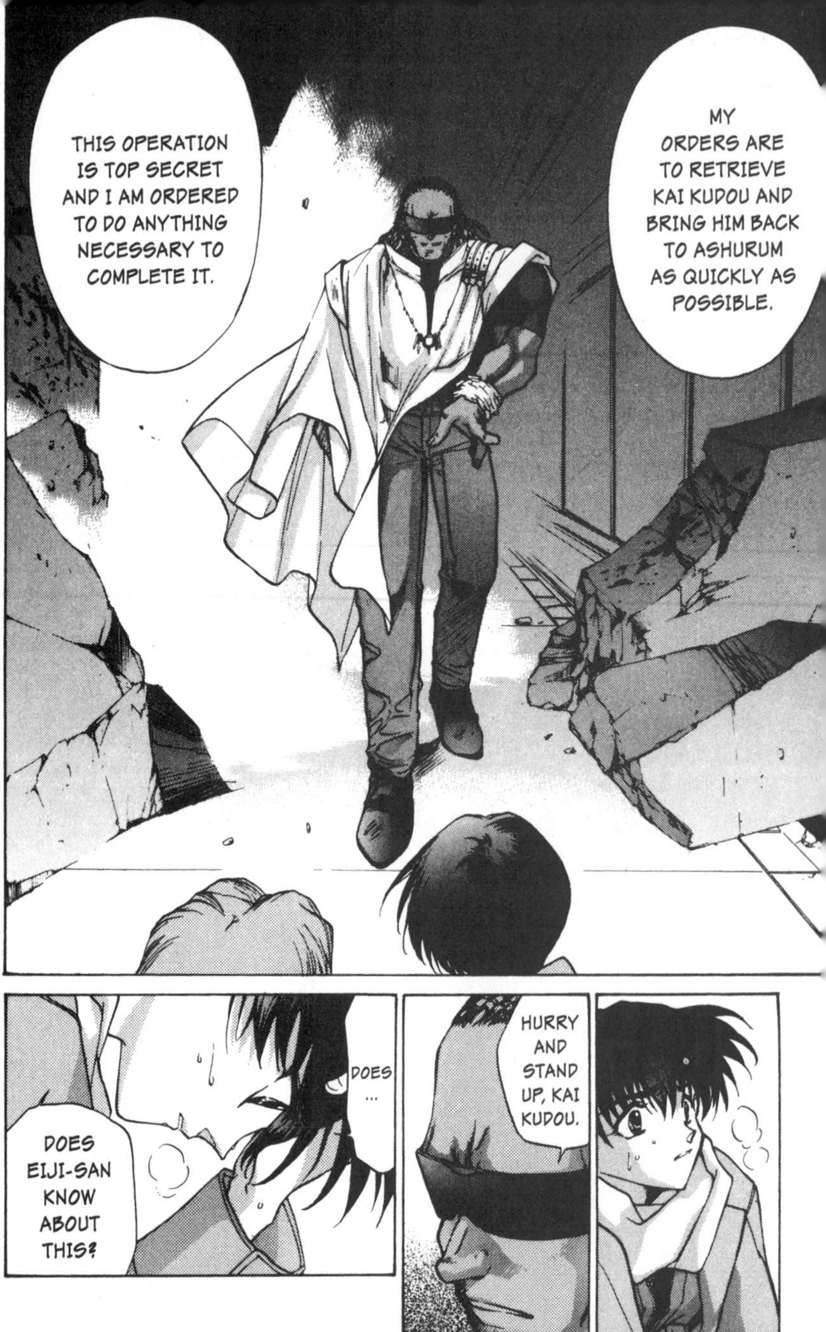
MY ORDERS ARE TO RETRIEVE KAI KUDOU AND BRING HIM BACK TO ASHURUM AS QUICKLY AS POSSIBLE.
THIS OPERATION IS TOP SECRET AND I AM ORDERED TO DO ANYTHING NECESSARY TO COMPLETE IT.
HURRY AND STAND UP, KAI KUDOU.
DOES ...
DOES EIJI-SAN KNOW ABOUT THIS?

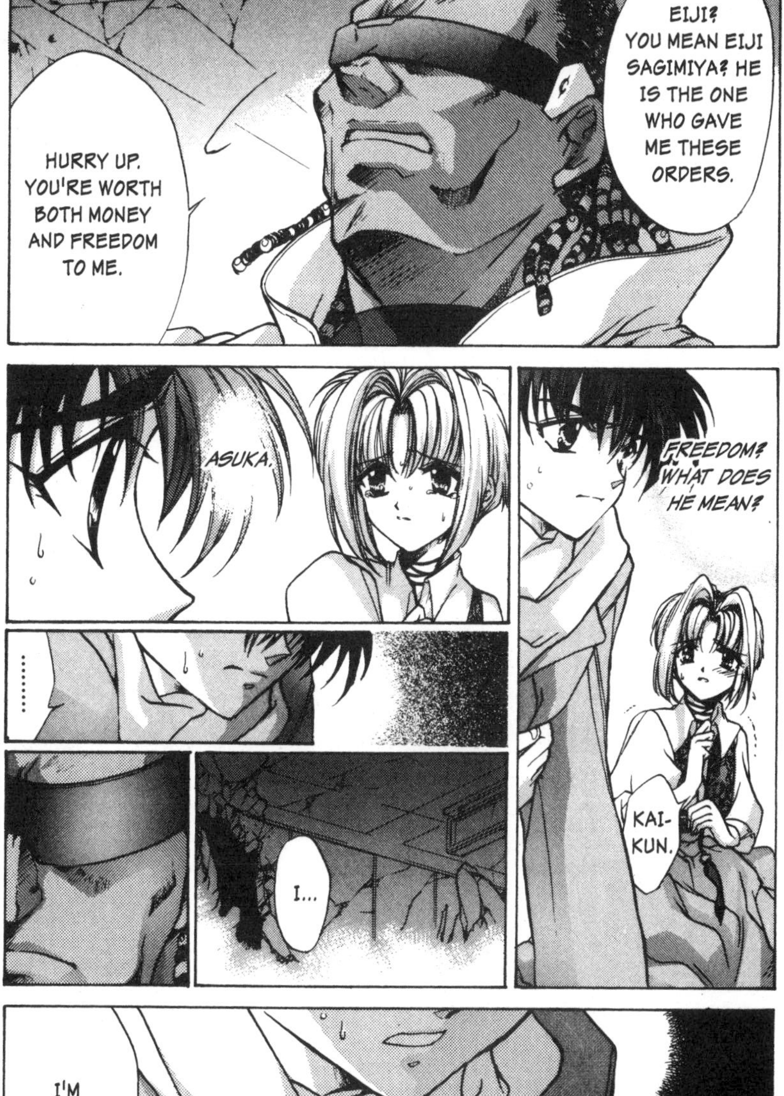
EIJI? YOU MEAN EIJI SAGIMIYA? HE IS THE ONE WHO GAVE ME THESE ORDERS.
HURRY UP. YOU'RE WORTH BOTH MONEY AND FREEDOM TO ME.
FREEDOM? WHAT DOES HE MEAN?
KAI-KUN.
ASUKA.
....
I...
I'M THIRSTY.

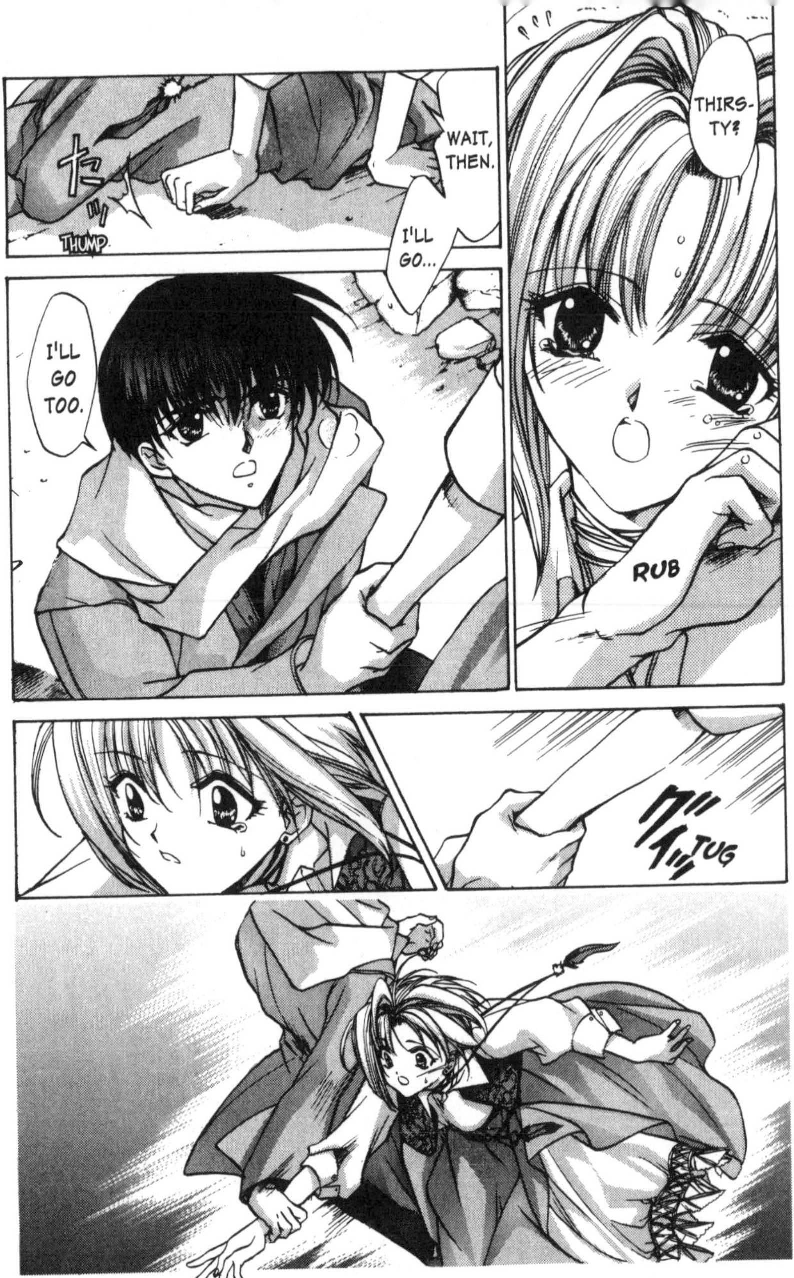

THIRS-TY?
RUB
WAIT, THEN.
I'LL GO...
THUMP
I'LL GO TOO.
TUG

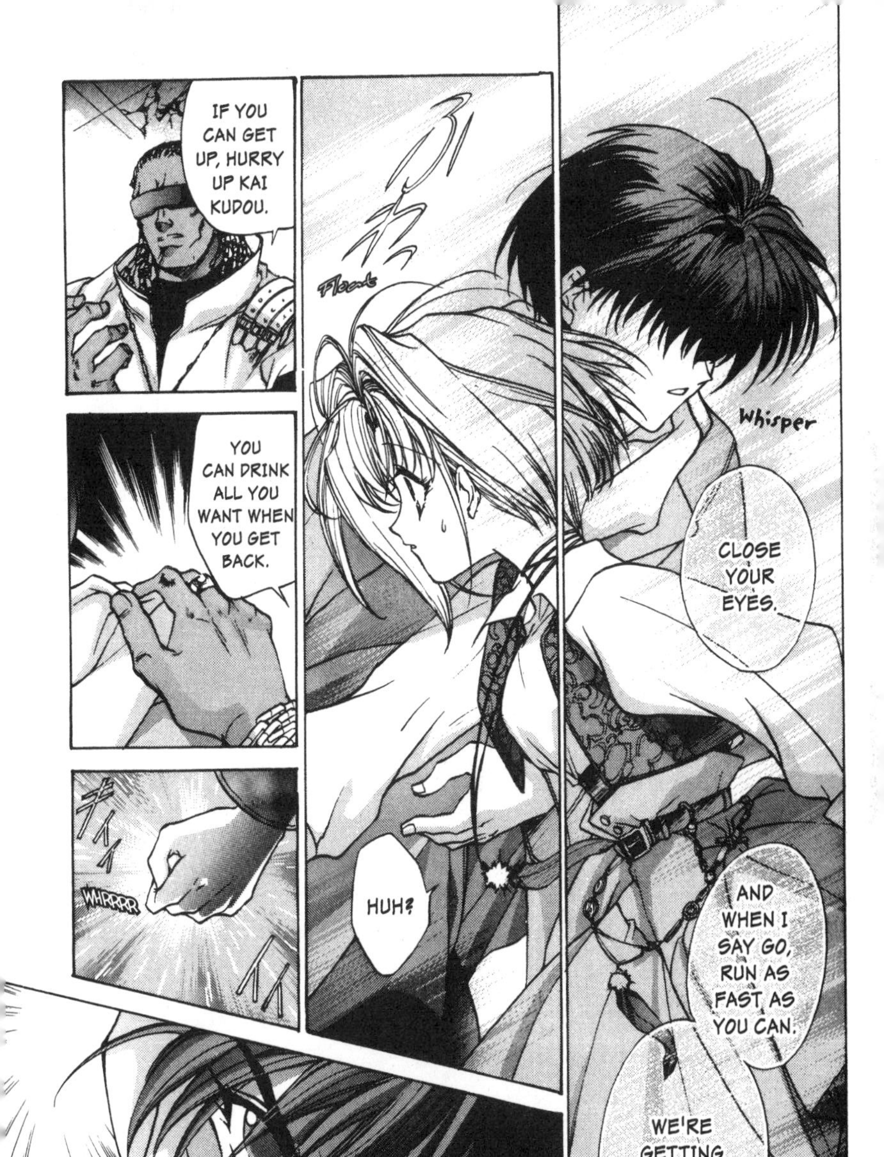

Whisper
CLOSE YOUR EYES.
AND WHEN I SAY GO, RUN AS FAST AS YOU CAN.
WE'RE GETTING OUT OF HERE!
Float
HUH?
IF YOU CAN GET UP, HURRY UP KAI KUDOU.
YOU CAN DRINK ALL YOU WANT WHEN YOU GET BACK.
WHRRRR

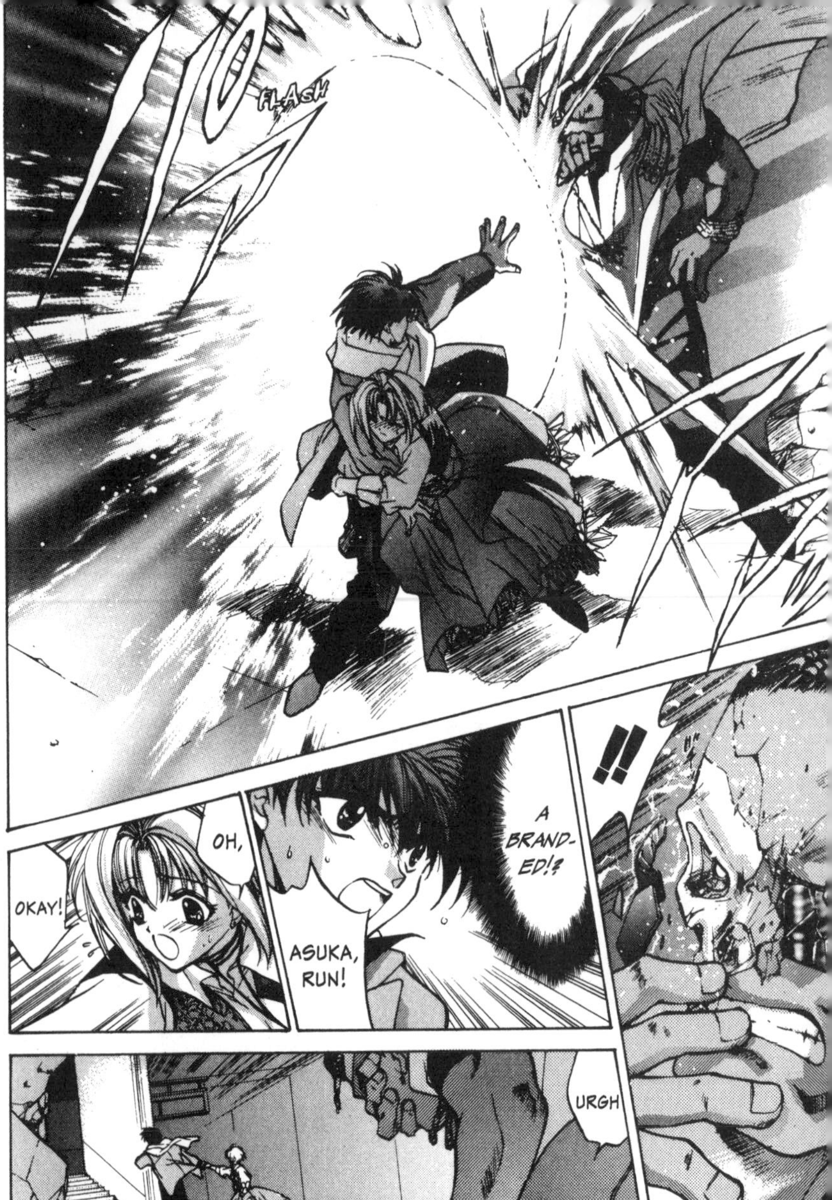
FLASH
!!
URGH
A BRAND-ED!?
ASUKA, RUN!
OH,
OKAY!

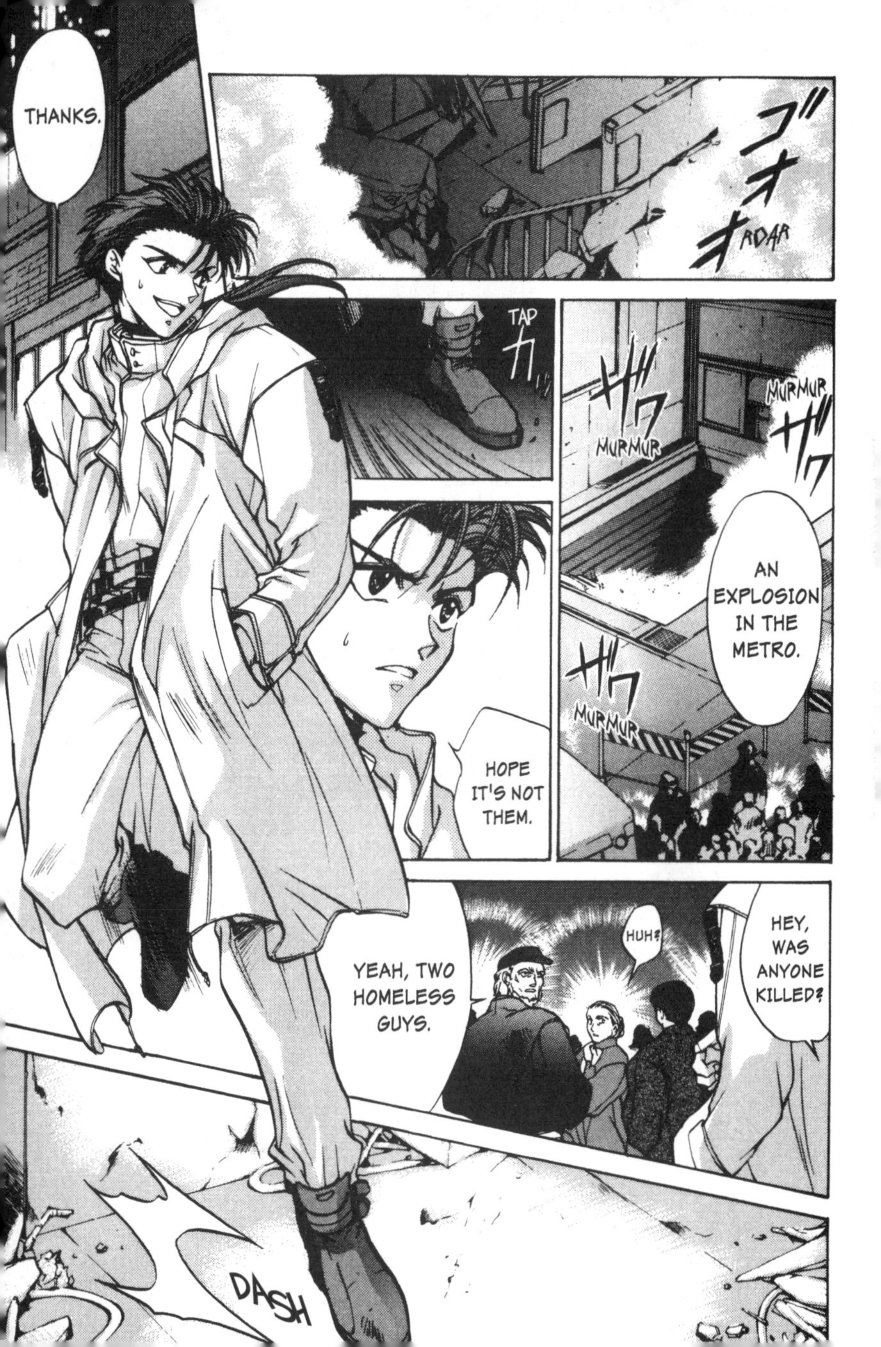
ゴオオ
ROAR
ザワ
MURMUR
ザワ
MURMUR
ザワ
MURMUR
AN EXPLOSION IN THE METRO.
カッ
TAP
HOPE IT'S NOT THEM.
HEY, WAS ANYONE KILLED?
HUH?
YEAH, TWO HOMELESS GUYS.
THANKS.
DASH

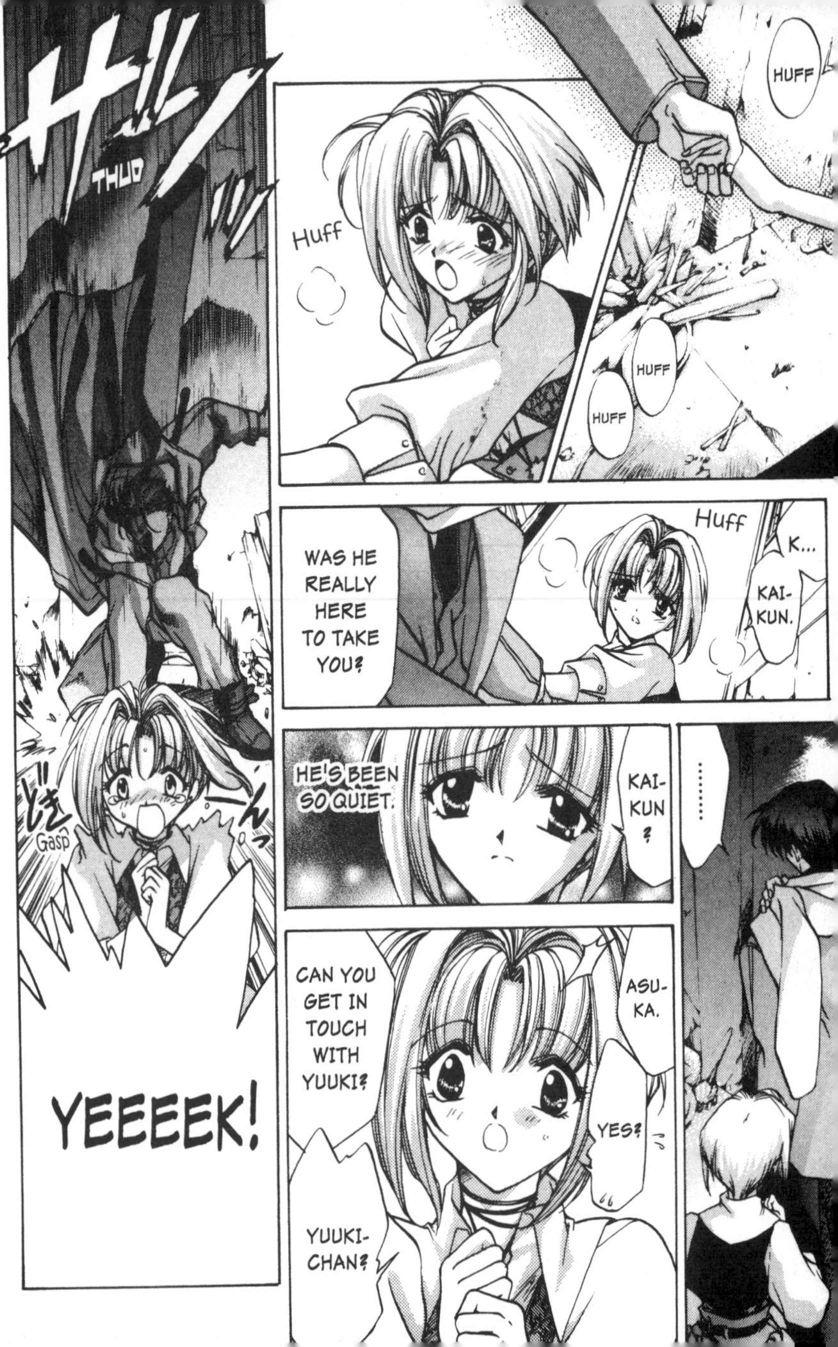
HUFF
HUFF
HUFF
Huff
Huff
K...
KAI-KUN.
WAS HE REALLY HERE TO TAKE YOU?
....
KAI-KUN?
HE'S BEEN SO QUIET.
ASU-KA.
CAN YOU GET IN TOUCH WITH YUUKI?
YES?
YUUKI-CHAN?
THUD
どき
Gasp
YEEEEK!

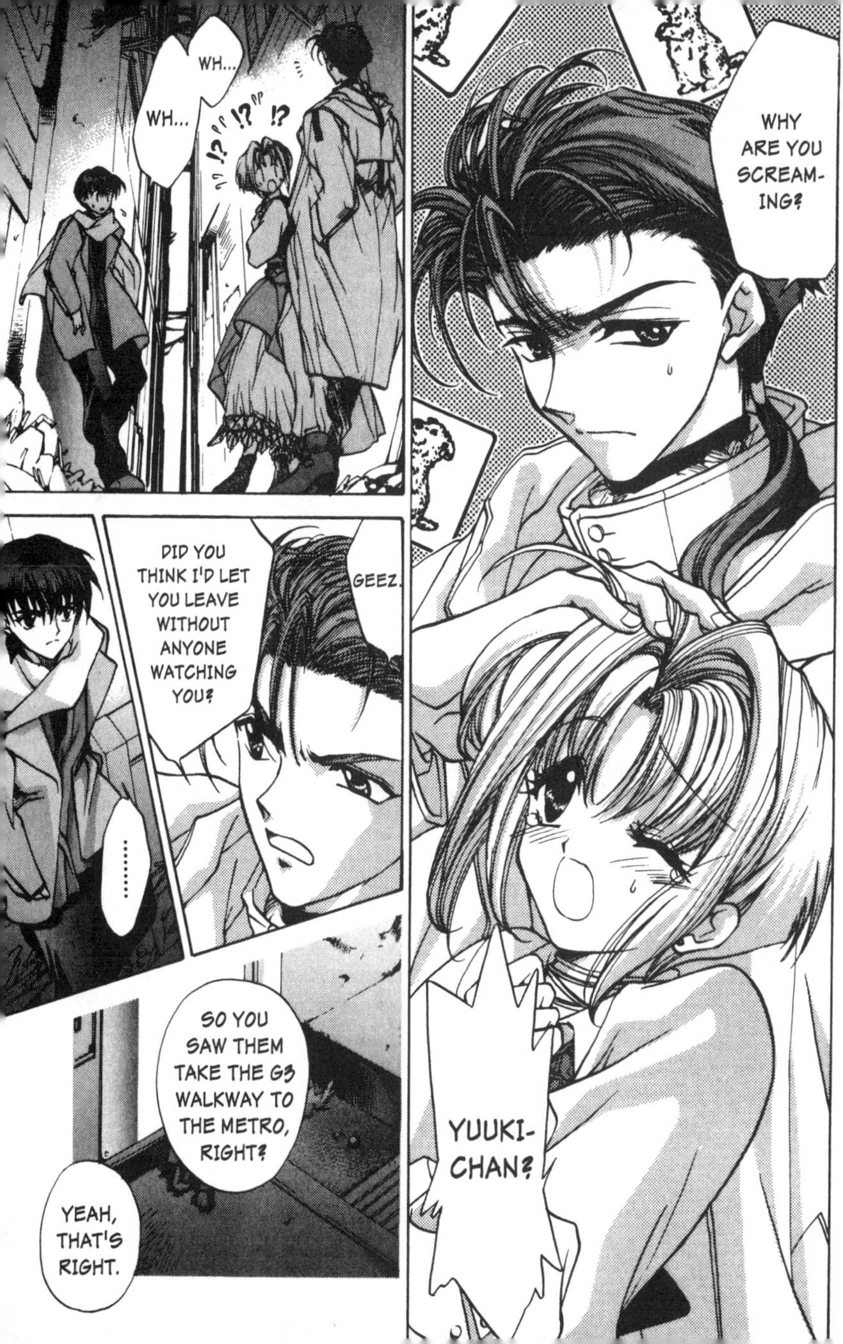
WHY ARE YOU SCREAMING?
YUUKI-CHAN?
WH...
WH...
!? !? !?
GEEZ.
DID YOU THINK I'D LET YOU LEAVE WITHOUT ANYONE WATCHING YOU?
....
SO YOU SAW THEM TAKE THE G3 WALKWAY TO THE METRO, RIGHT?
YEAH, THAT'S RIGHT.

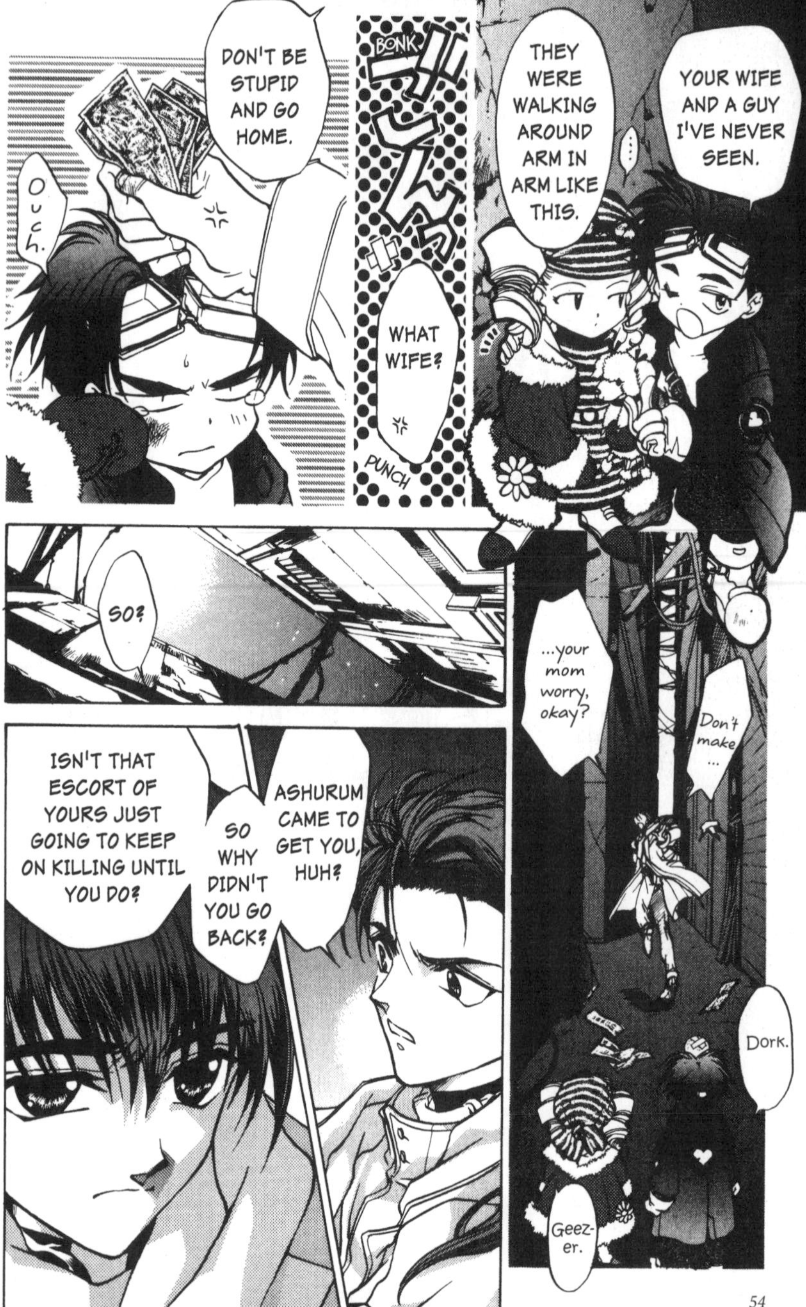
YOUR WIFE AND A GUY I'VE NEVER SEEN.
THEY WERE WALKING AROUND ARM IN ARM LIKE THIS.
...
BONK
WHAT WIFE?
PUNCH
DON'T BE STUPID AND GO HOME.
Ouch.
Don't make ...
...your mom worry, okay?
Dork.
Geez-er.
SO?
ASHURUM CAME TO GET YOU, HUH?
SO WHY DIDN'T YOU GO BACK?
ISN'T THAT ESCORT OF YOURS JUST GOING TO KEEP ON KILLING UNTIL YOU DO?

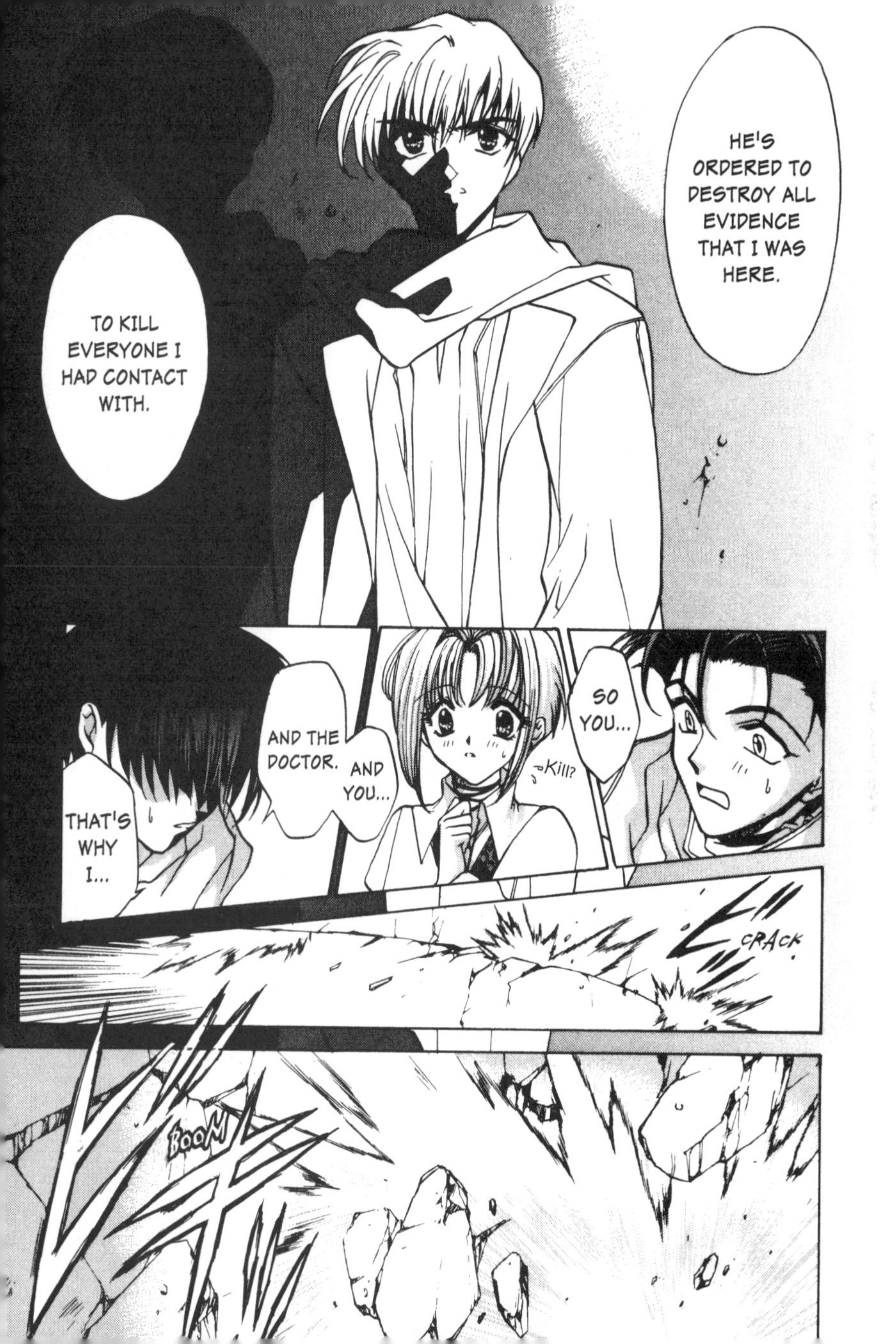
HE'S ORDERED TO DESTROY ALL EVIDENCE THAT I WAS HERE.
TO KILL EVERYONE I HAD CONTACT WITH.
SO YOU...
Kill?
AND YOU...
AND THE DOCTOR.
THAT'S WHY I...
CRACK
BOOM

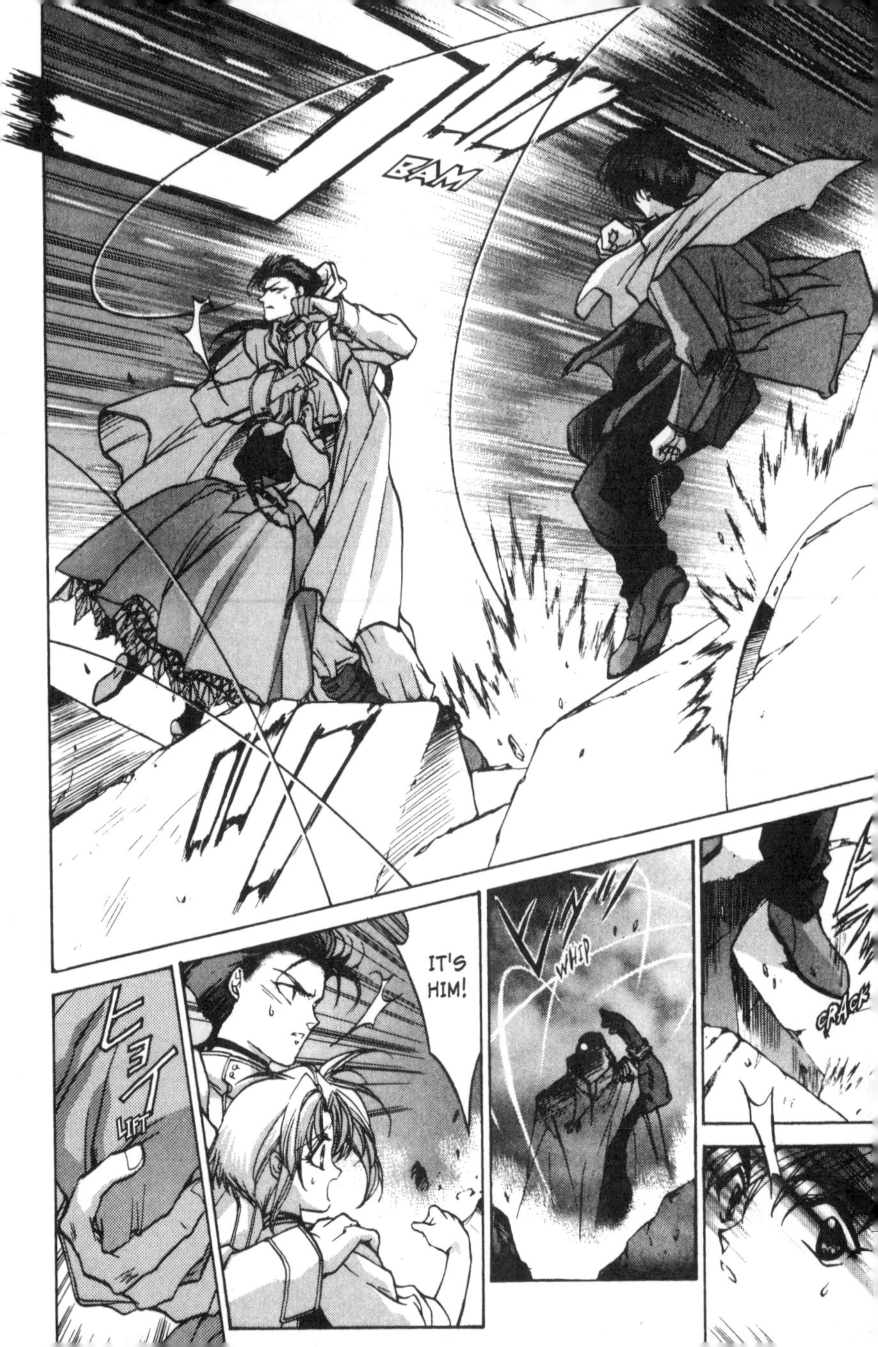
BAM
CRACK
WHIP
IT'S HIM!
ヒョイ
LIFT

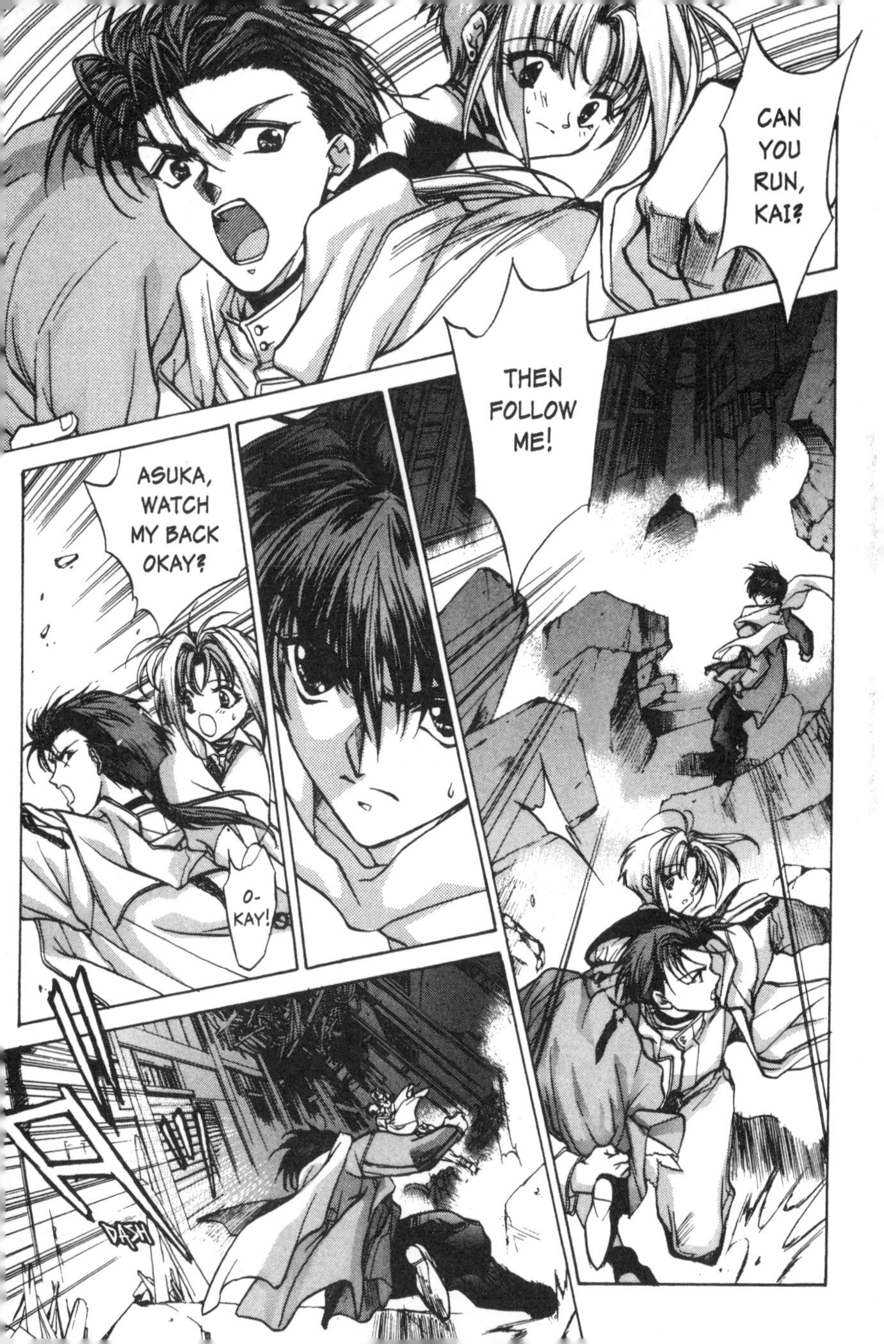
CAN YOU RUN, KAI?
THEN FOLLOW ME!
ASUKA, WATCH MY BACK OKAY?
O-KAY!
DASH

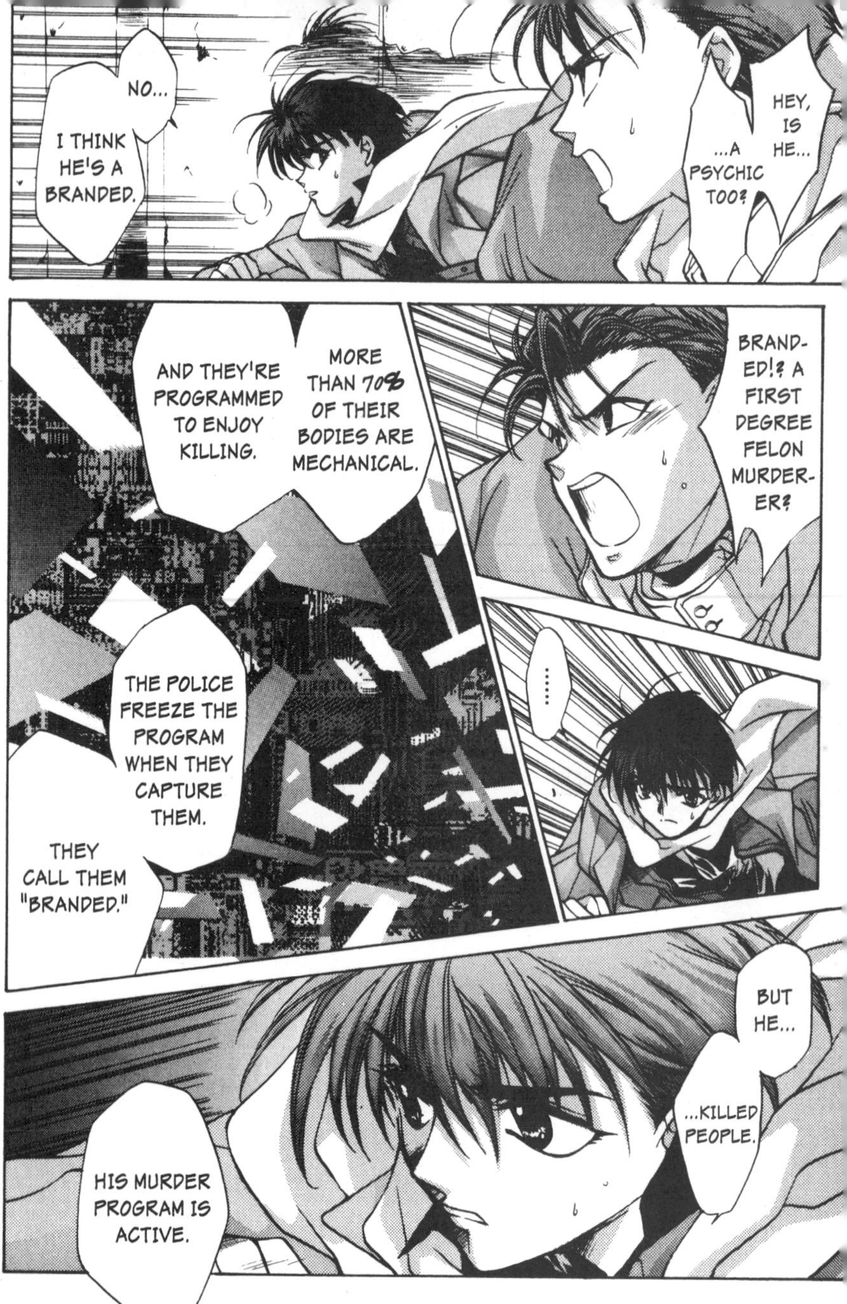
HEY, IS HE...
...A PSYCHIC TOO?
NO...
I THINK HE'S A BRANDED.
BRANDED!? A FIRST DEGREE FELON MURDERER?
......
MORE THAN 70% OF THEIR BODIES ARE MECHANICAL.
AND THEY'RE PROGRAMMED TO ENJOY KILLING.
THE POLICE FREEZE THE PROGRAM WHEN THEY CAPTURE THEM.
THEY CALL THEM "BRANDED."
BUT HE...
...KILLED PEOPLE.
HIS MURDER PROGRAM IS ACTIVE.

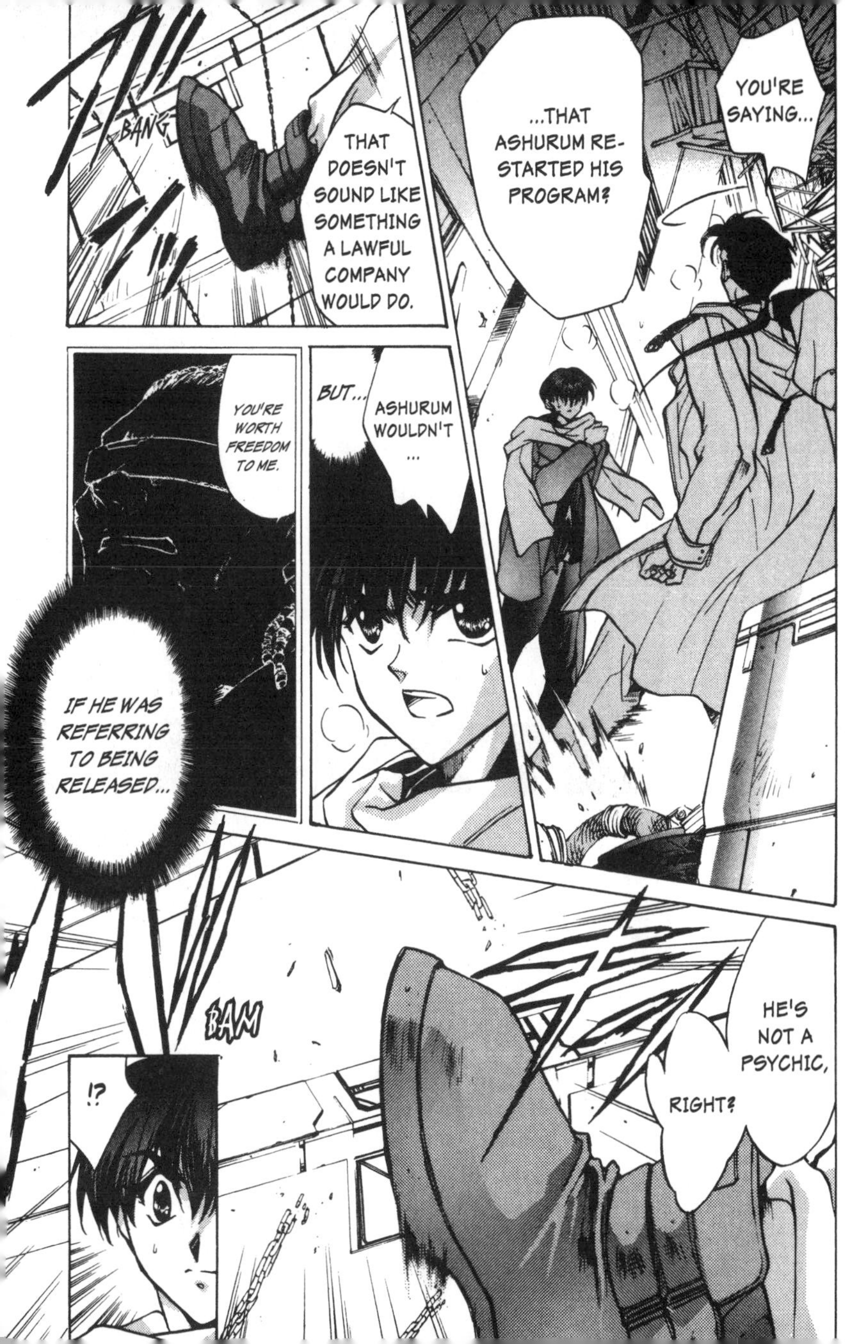
YOU'RE SAYING...
...THAT ASHURUM RE-STARTED HIS PROGRAM?
BANG
THAT DOESN'T SOUND LIKE SOMETHING A LAWFUL COMPANY WOULD DO.
BUT...
ASHURUM WOULDN'T ...
YOU'RE WORTH FREEDOM TO ME.
IF HE WAS REFERRING TO BEING RELEASED...
HE'S NOT A PSYCHIC,
RIGHT?
BAM
!?

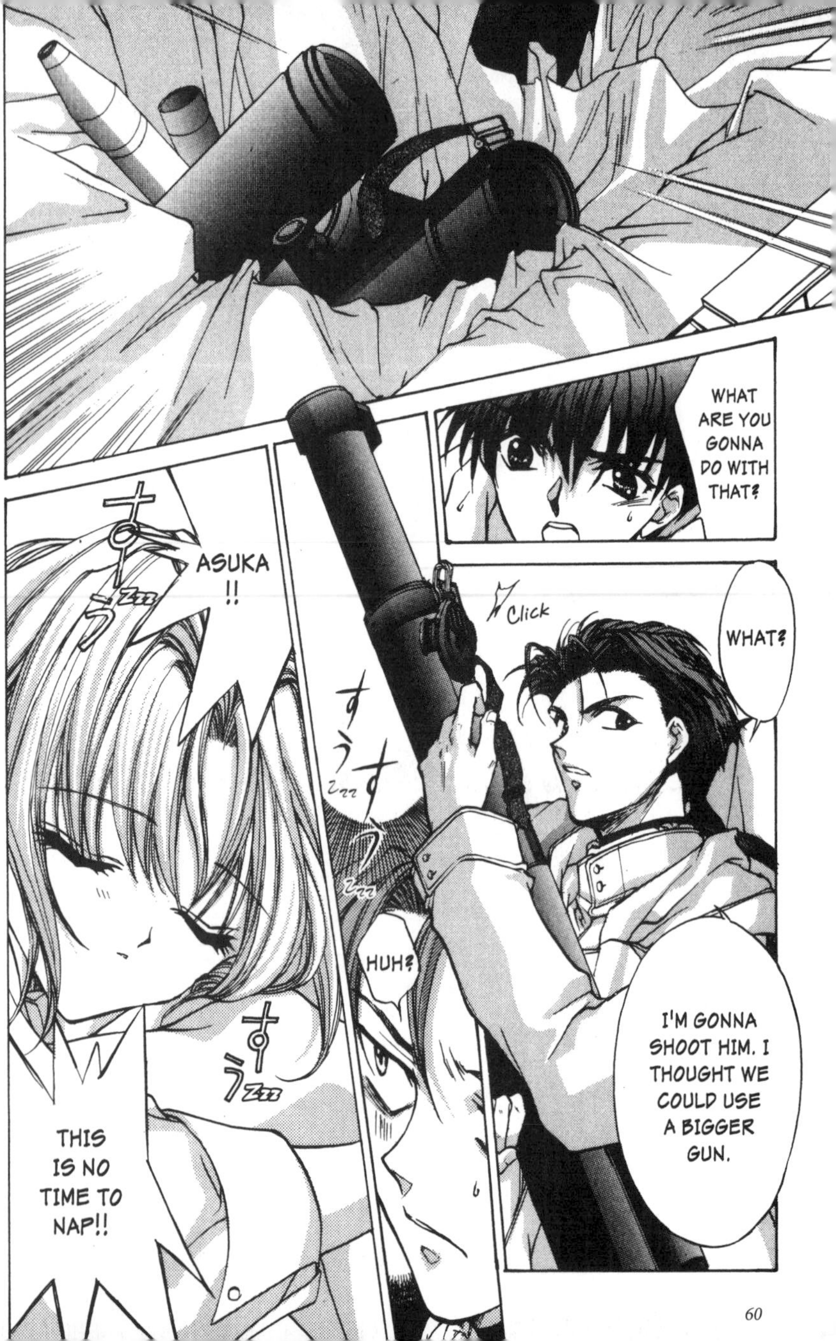
WHAT ARE YOU GONNA DO WITH THAT?
Click
WHAT?
I'M GONNA SHOOT HIM. I THOUGHT WE COULD USE A BIGGER GUN.
すぅ Zzz
すぅ Zzz
HUH?
すぅ Zzz
ASUKA !!
すぅ Zzz
THIS IS NO TIME TO NAP!!

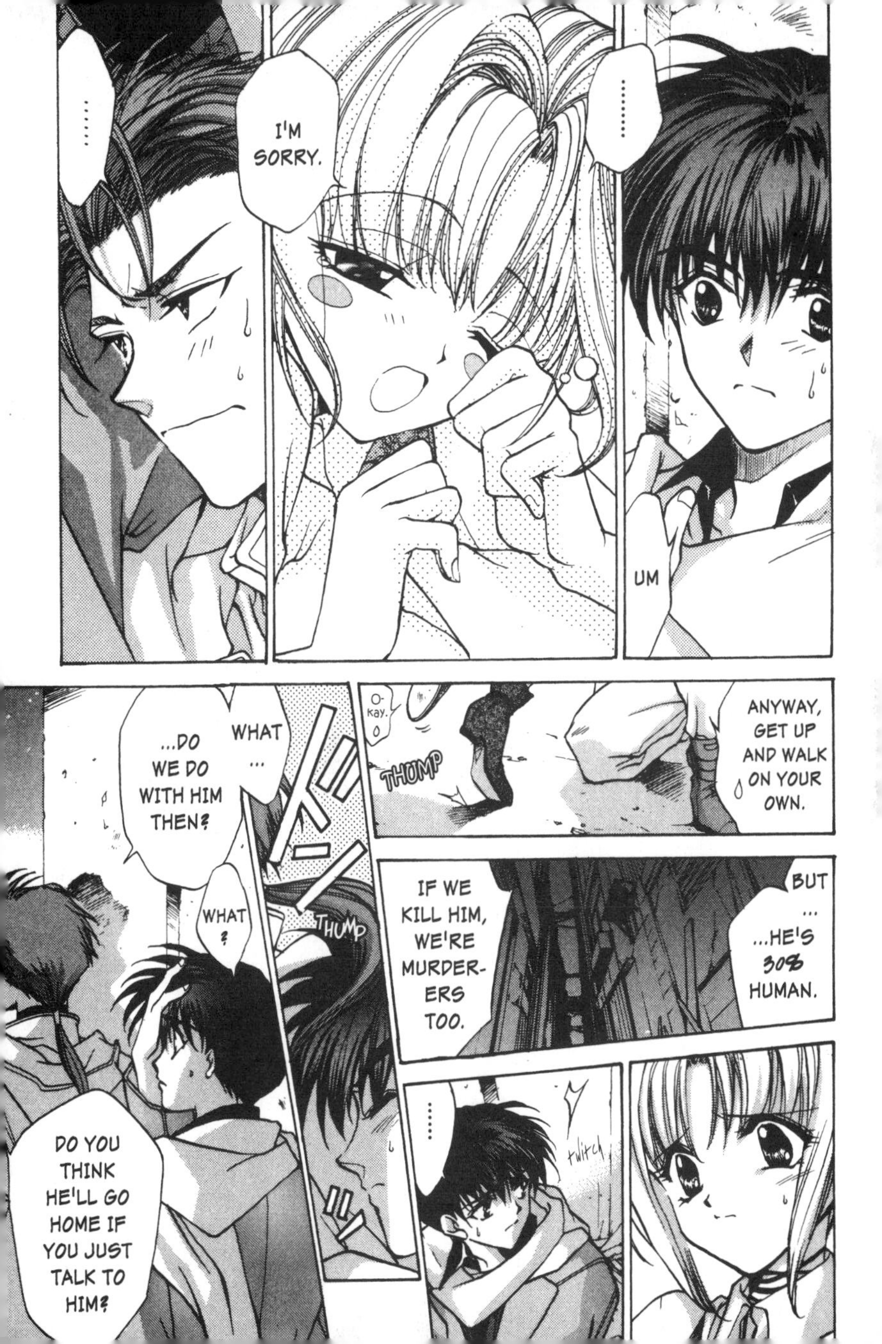
......
UM
I'M SORRY.
......
ANYWAY, GET UP AND WALK ON YOUR OWN.
O-kay.
THUMP
BUT ... ...HE'S 30% HUMAN.
IF WE KILL HIM, WE'RE MURDER-ERS TOO.
......
twitch
WHAT ...
...DO WE DO WITH HIM THEN?
WHAT?
THUMP
DO YOU THINK HE'LL GO HOME IF YOU JUST TALK TO HIM?

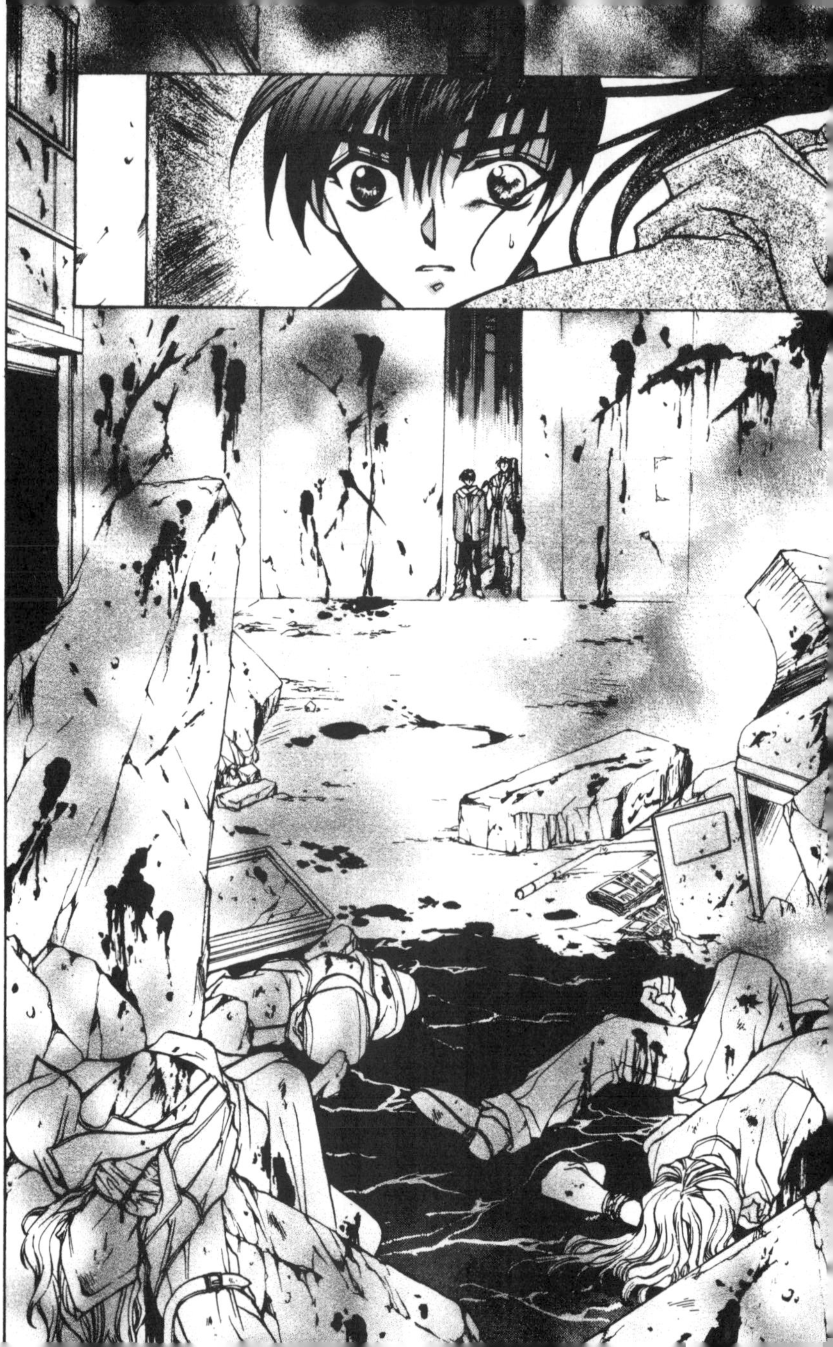

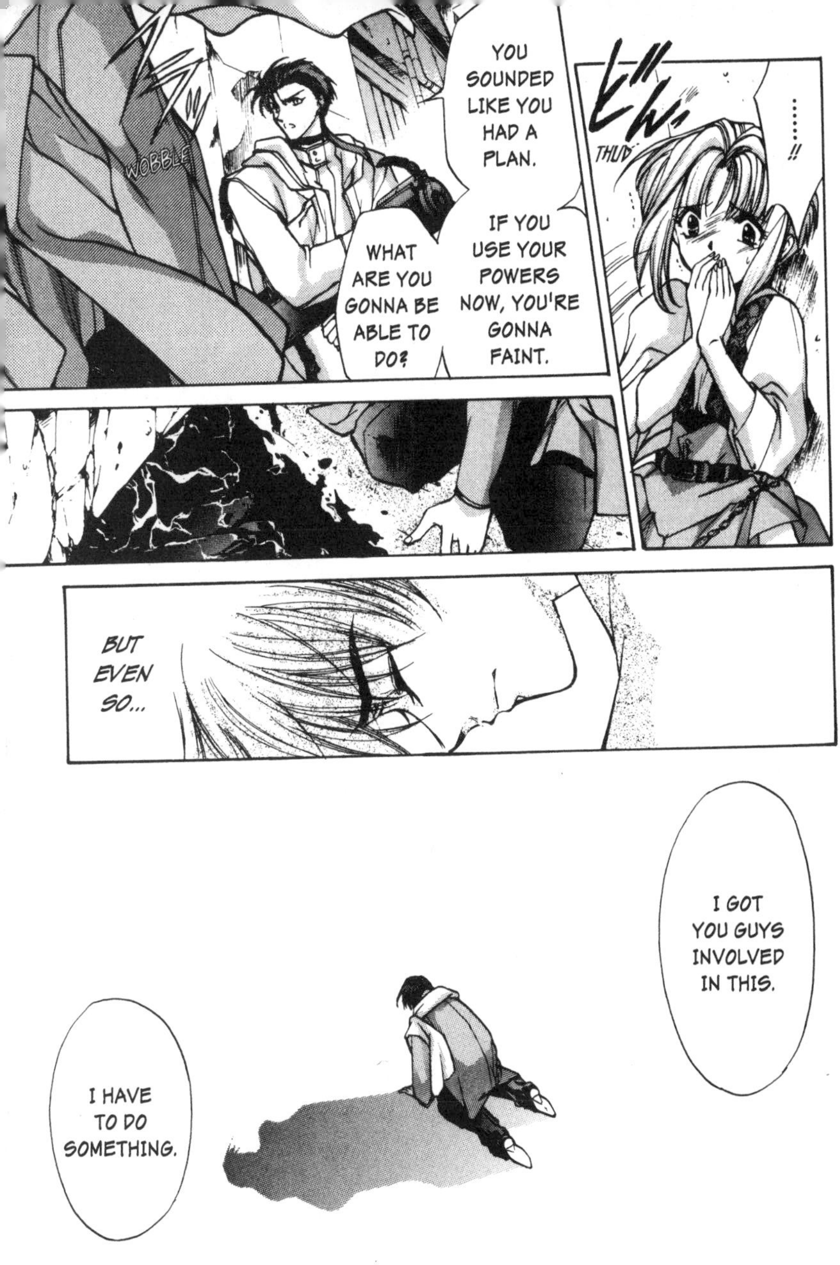
THUD
......!!
YOU SOUNDED LIKE YOU HAD A PLAN.
IF YOU USE YOUR POWERS NOW, YOU'RE GONNA FAINT.
WHAT ARE YOU GONNA BE ABLE TO DO?
WOBBLE
BUT EVEN SO...
I GOT YOU GUYS INVOLVED IN THIS.
I HAVE TO DO SOMETHING.

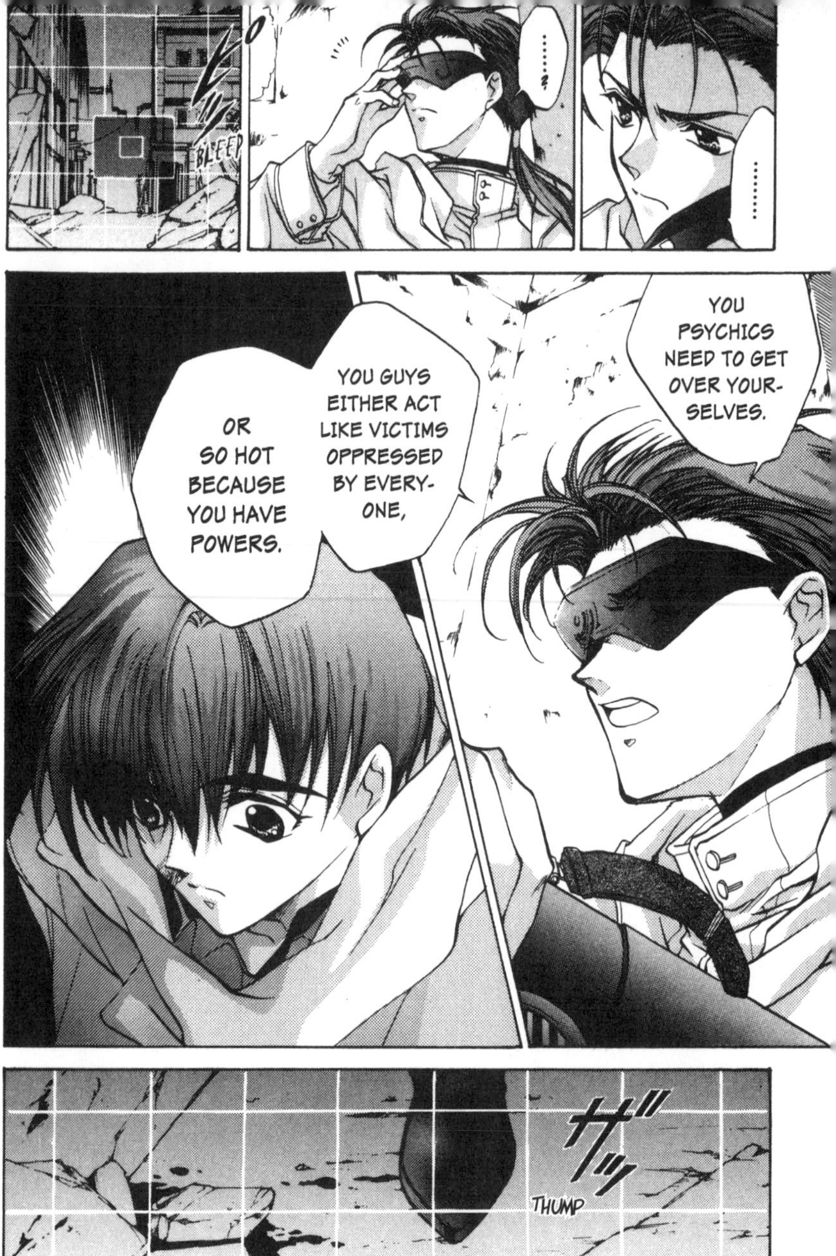
......
......?
BLEEP
YOU PSYCHICS NEED TO GET OVER YOUR-SELVES.
YOU GUYS EITHER ACT LIKE VICTIMS OPPRESSED BY EVERY-ONE,
OR SO HOT BECAUSE YOU HAVE POWERS.
ザッ
THUMP

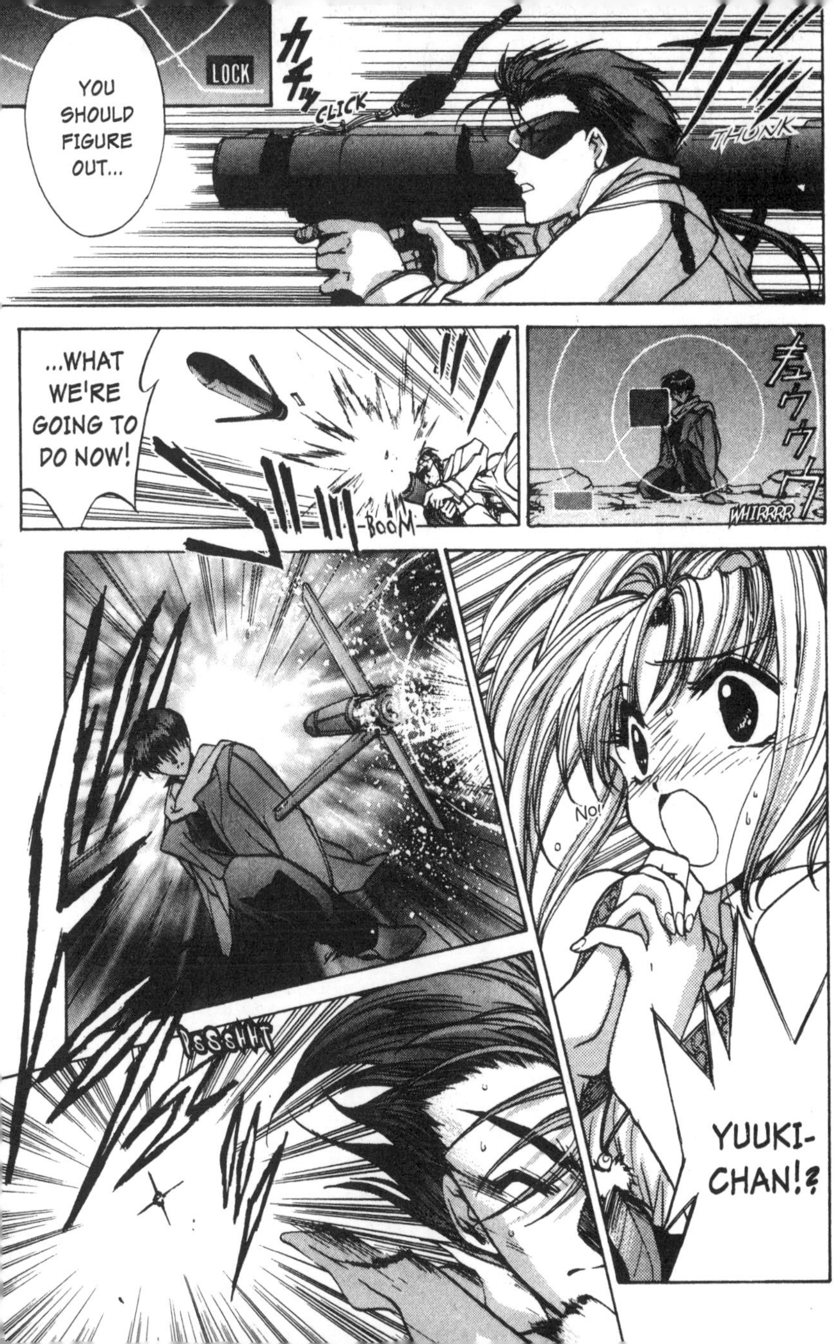
THUNK
カチッ
CLICK
LOCK
YOU SHOULD FIGURE OUT...
キュウウウ
WHIRRRR
...WHAT WE'RE GOING TO DO NOW!
BOOM
No!
YUUKI-CHAN!?
PSSSHHT

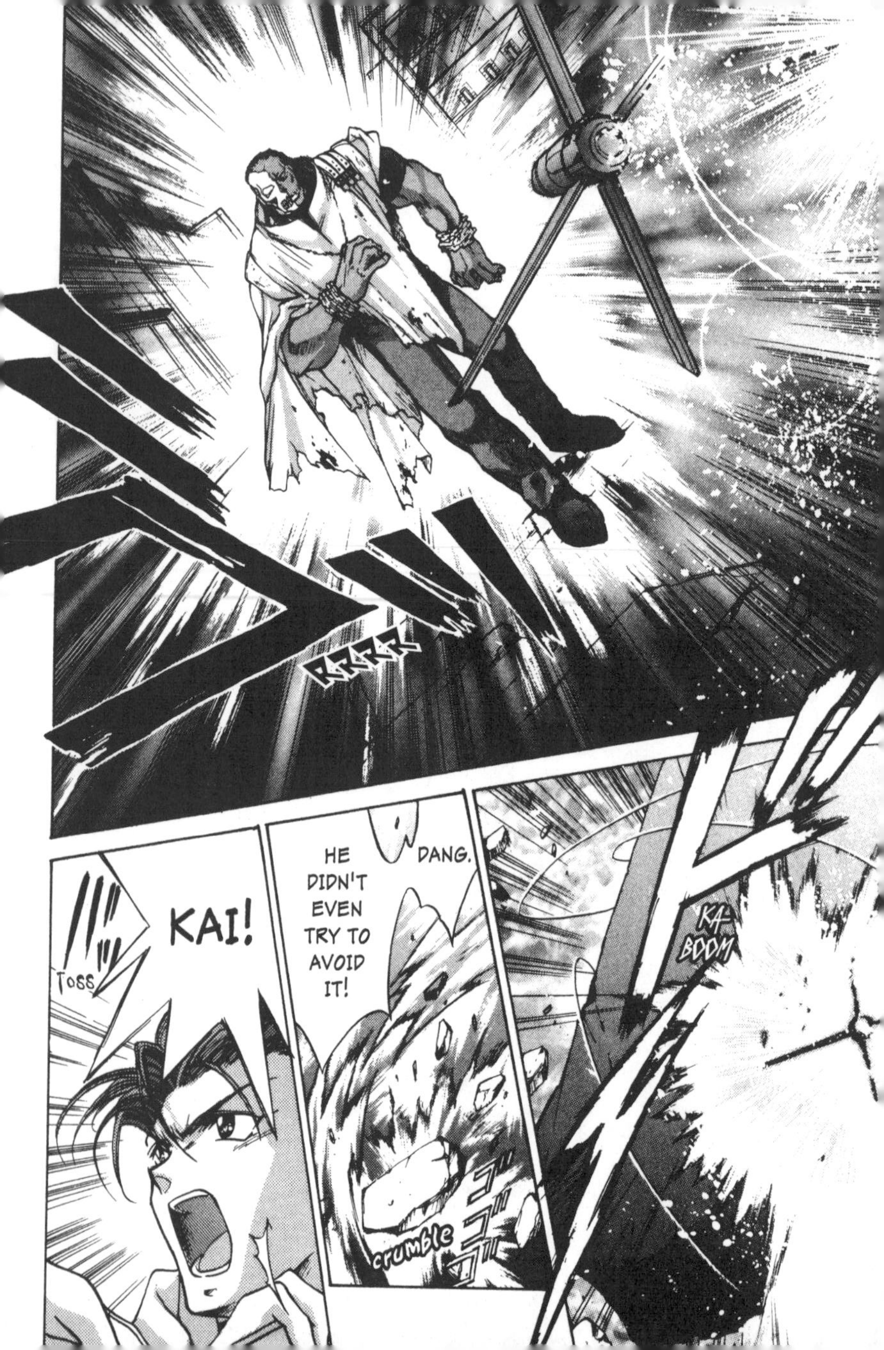
RRRRR
KA-BOOM
DANG.
HE DIDN'T EVEN TRY TO AVOID IT!
crumble
KAI!
Toss

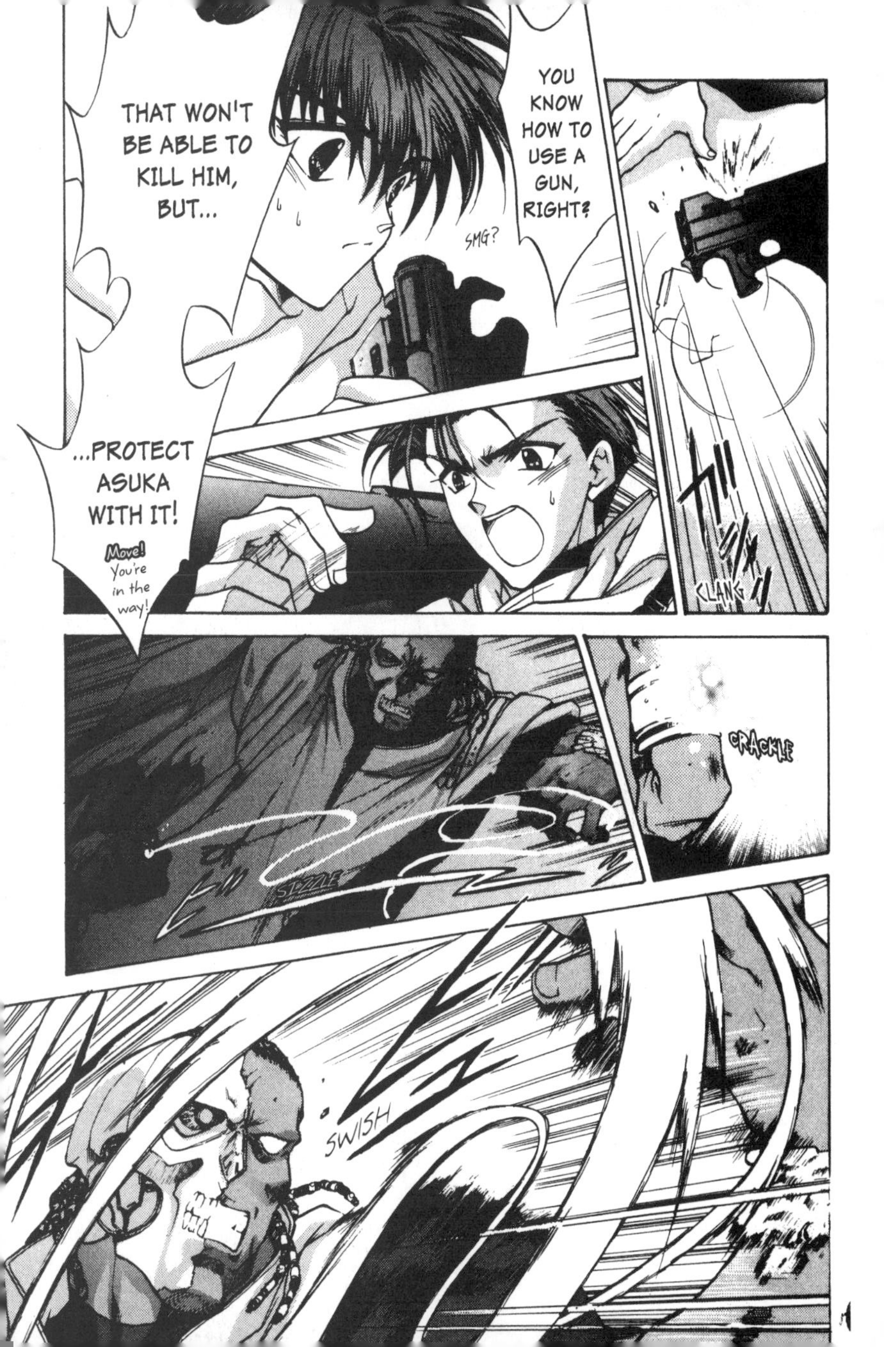
CLANG
YOU KNOW HOW TO USE A GUN, RIGHT?
SMG?
THAT WON'T BE ABLE TO KILL HIM, BUT...
...PROTECT ASUKA WITH IT!
Move! You're in the way!
CRACKLE
SIZZLE
SWISH

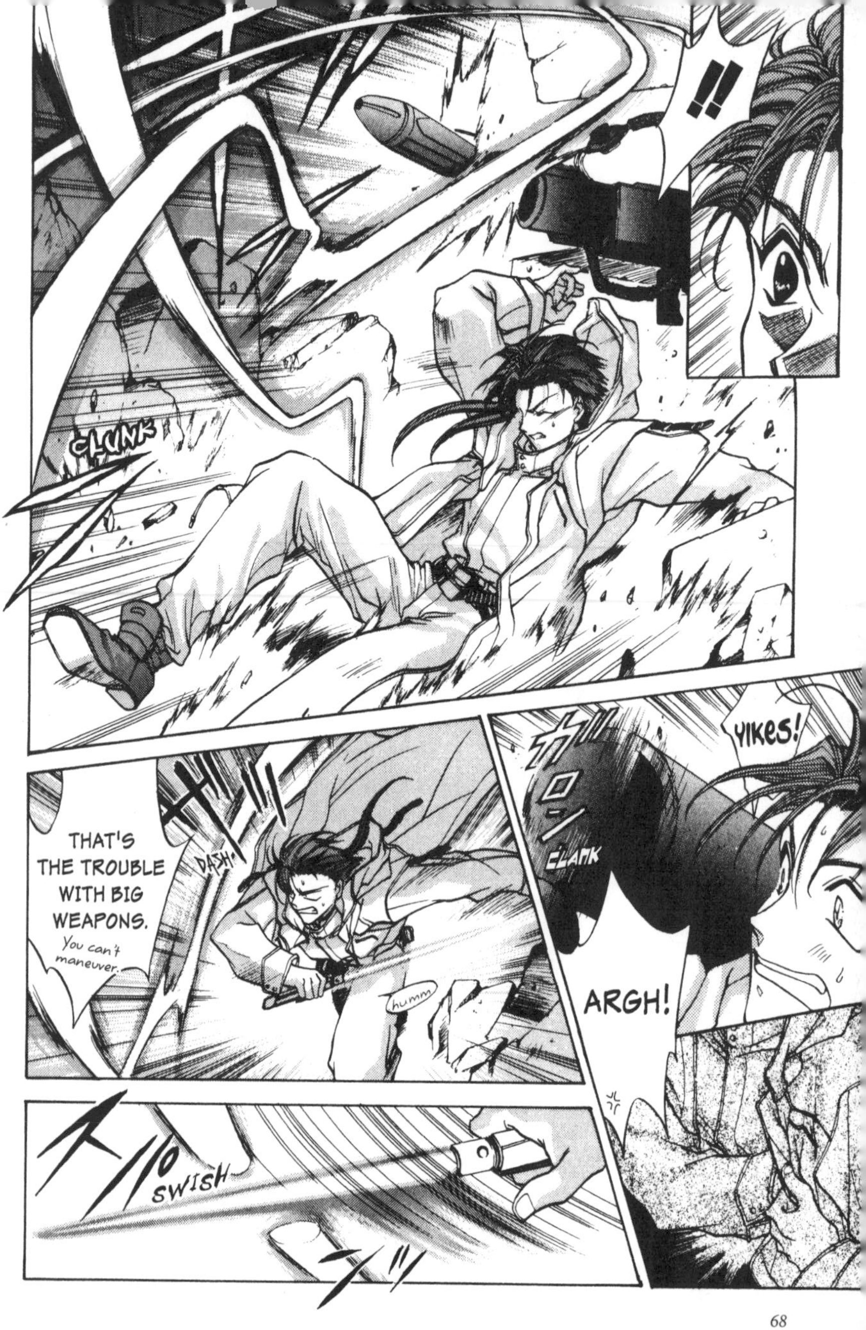
!!
CLUNK
YIKES!
CLANK
ARGH!
THAT'S THE TROUBLE WITH BIG WEAPONS.
You can't maneuver.
DASH
humm
SWISH

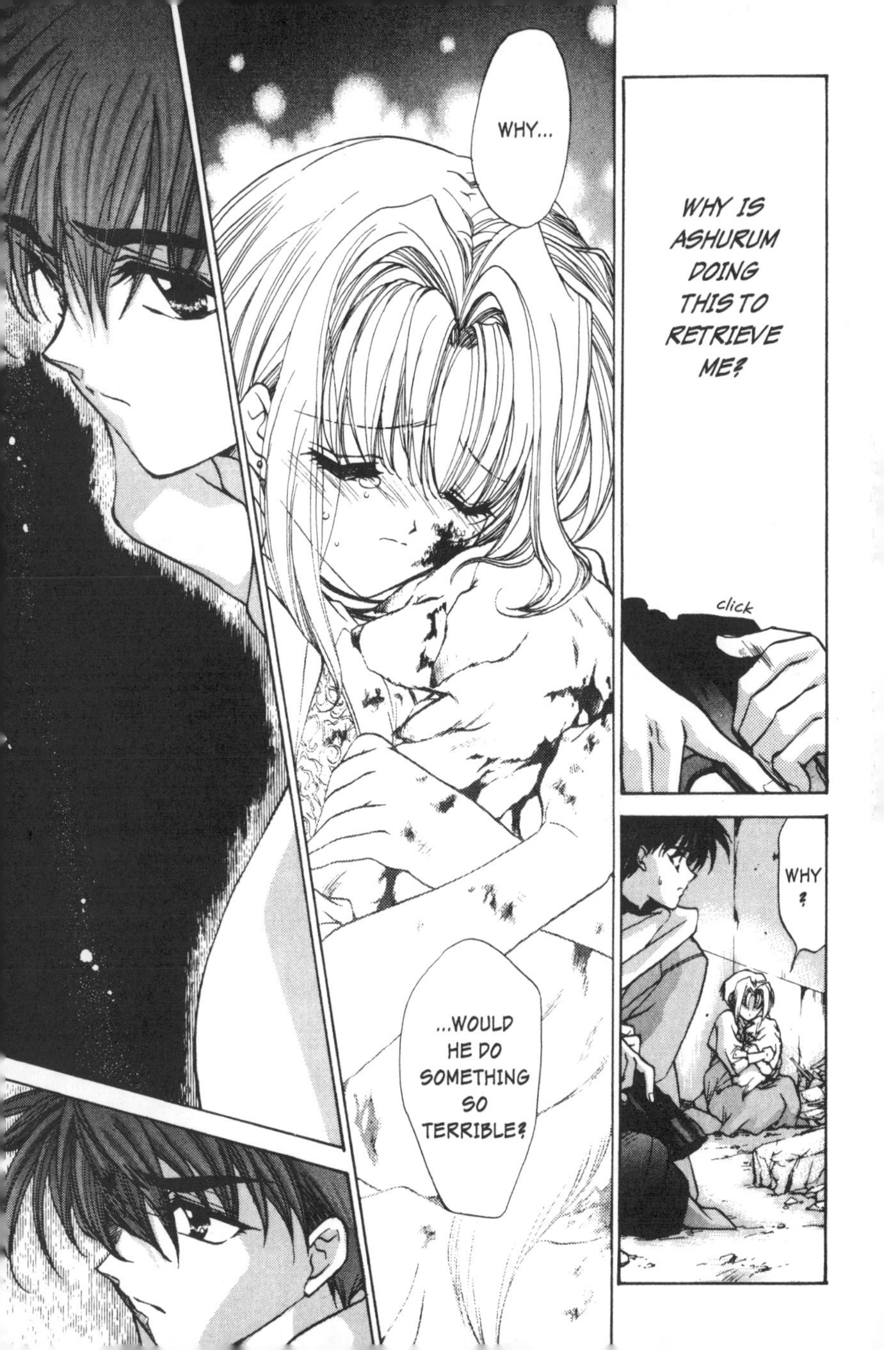
WHY IS ASHURUM DOING THIS TO RETRIEVE ME?
click
WHY?
WHY...
...WOULD HE DO SOMETHING SO TERRIBLE?

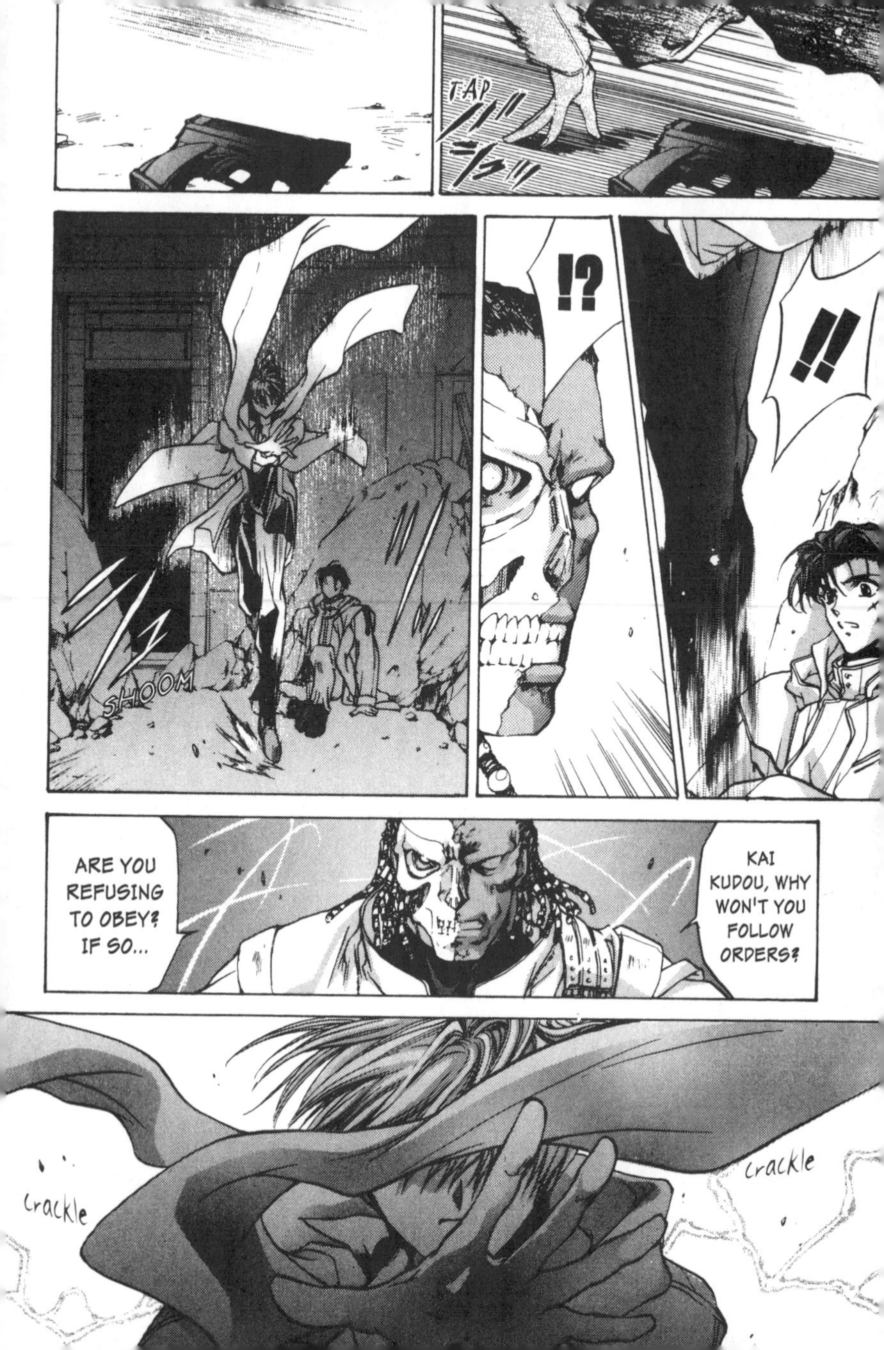
TAP
!!
!?
SHOOM
KAI KUDOU, WHY WON'T YOU FOLLOW ORDERS?
ARE YOU REFUSING TO OBEY? IF SO...
crackle
crackle

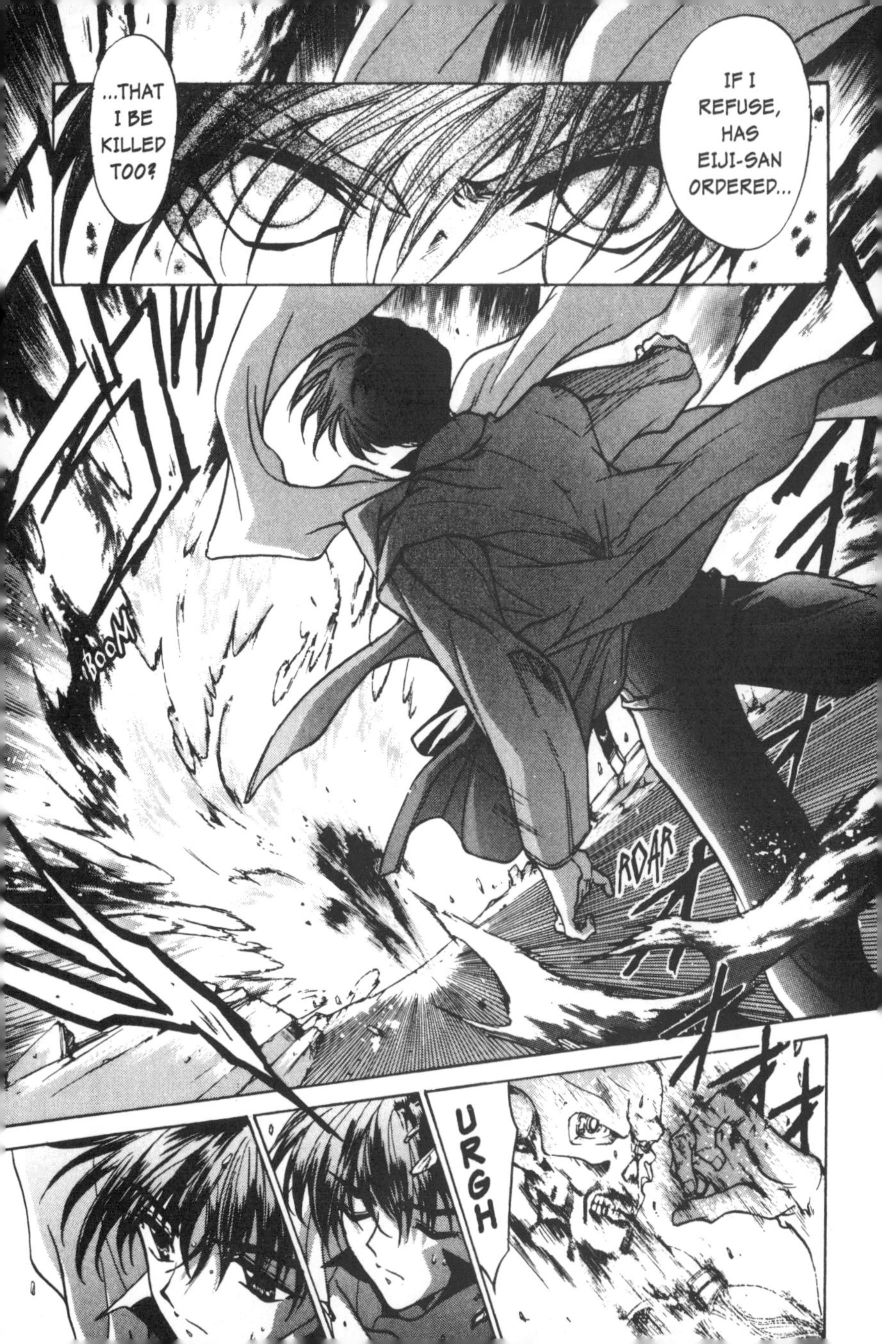
IF I REFUSE, HAS EIJI-SAN ORDERED...
...THAT I BE KILLED TOO?
ROAR
BOOM
URGH

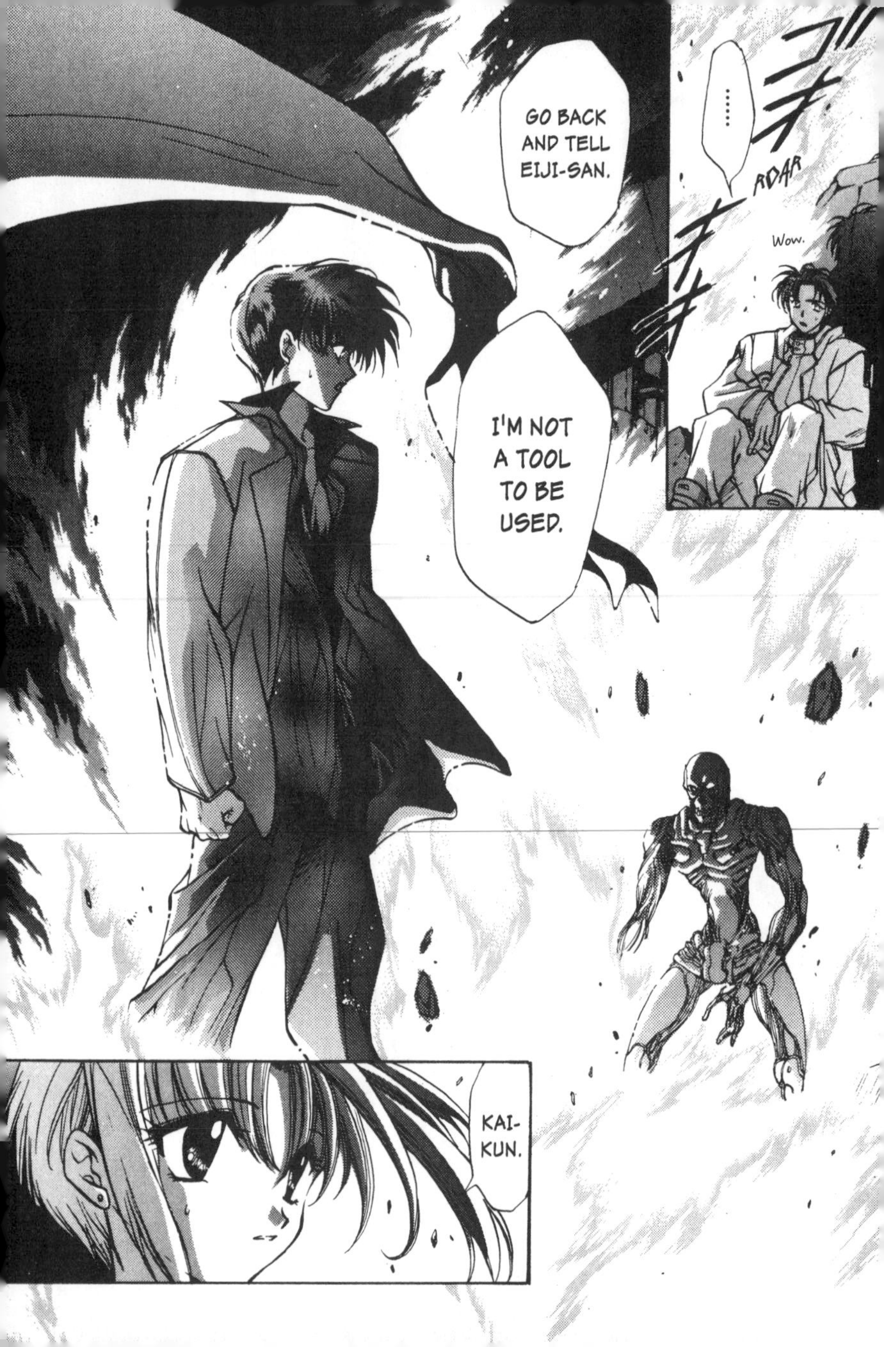
......
ROAR
Wow.
GO BACK AND TELL EIJI-SAN.
I'M NOT A TOOL TO BE USED.
KAI-KUN.

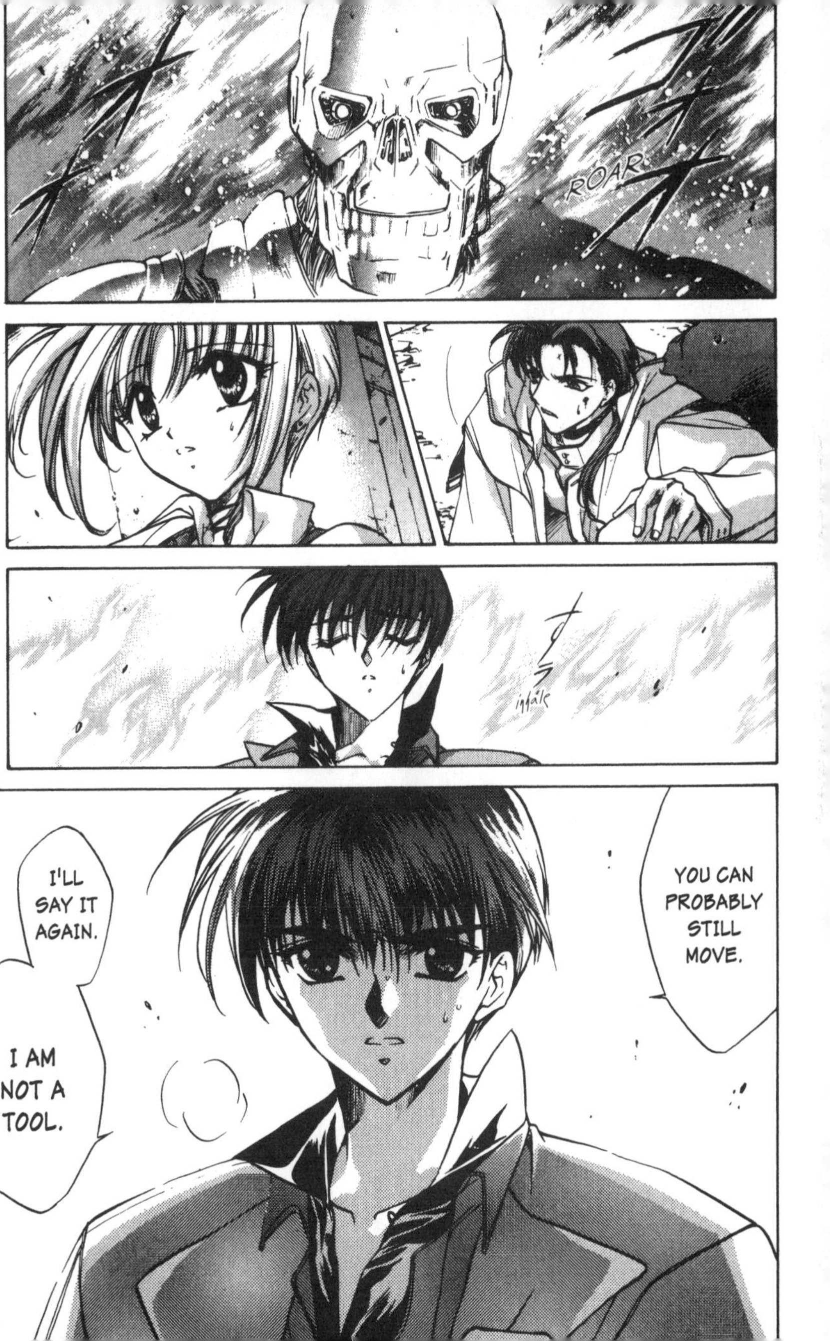
ROAR
inhale
YOU CAN PROBABLY STILL MOVE.
I'LL SAY IT AGAIN.
I AM NOT A TOOL.

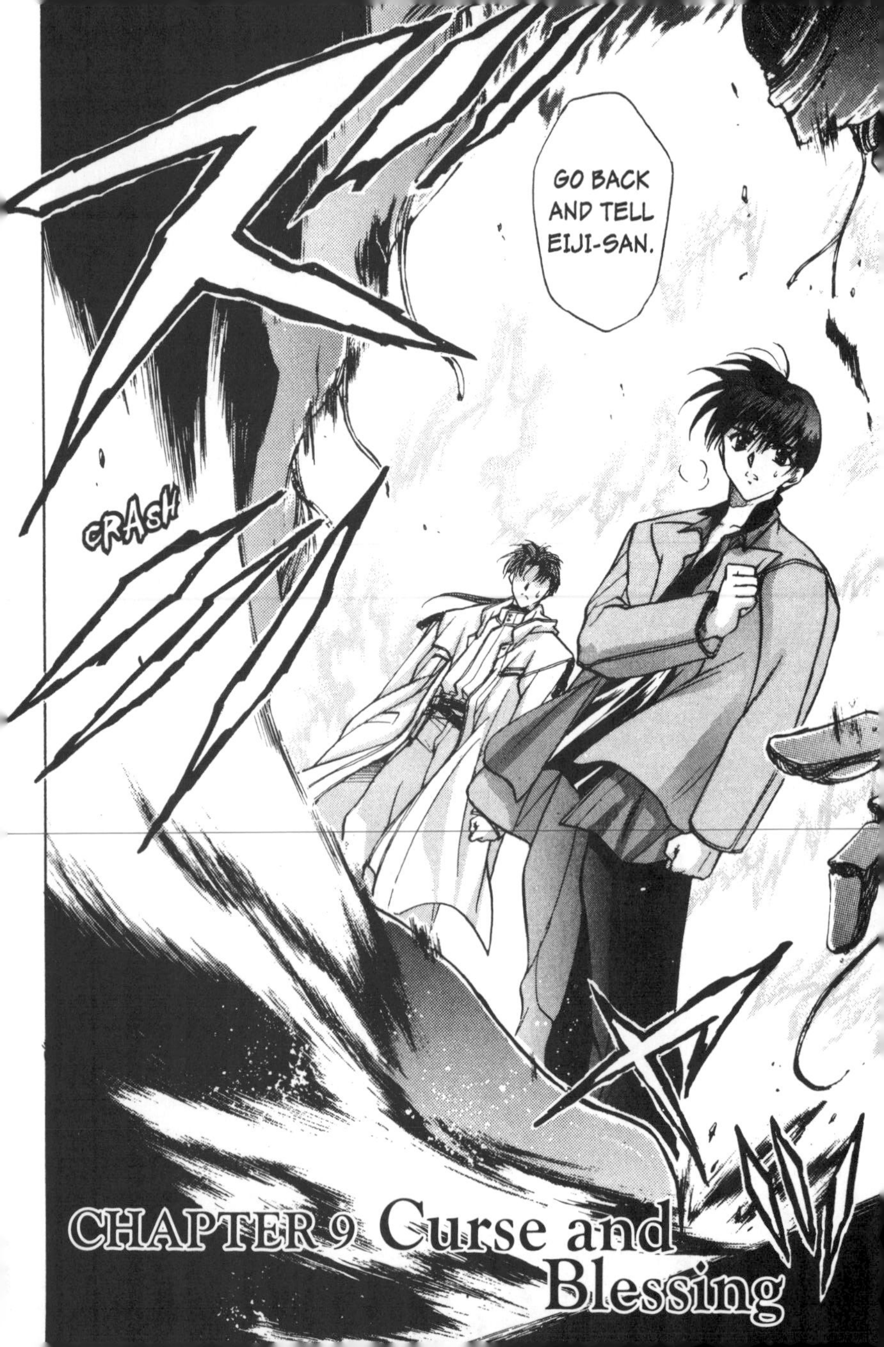
GO BACK AND TELL EIJI-SAN.
cRAsH

CHAPTER 9 Curse and Blessing

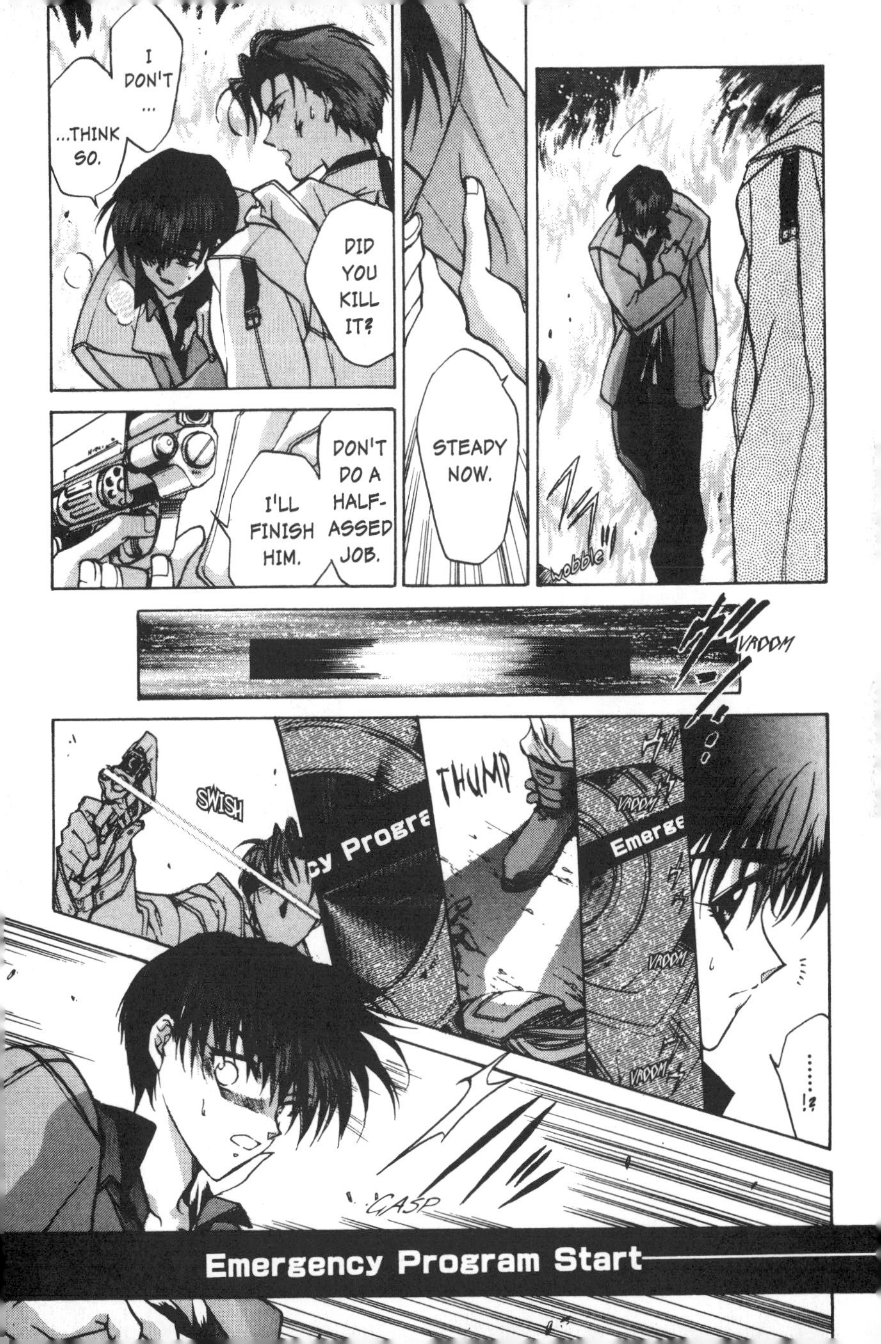
wobble
STEADY NOW.
DID YOU KILL IT?
I DON'T ... ...THINK SO.
DON'T DO A HALF-ASSED JOB.
I'LL FINISH HIM.
VROOM
Emerge
VROOM
VROOM
VROOM
......!?
THUMP
cy Progra
SWISH
GASP
Emergency Program Start

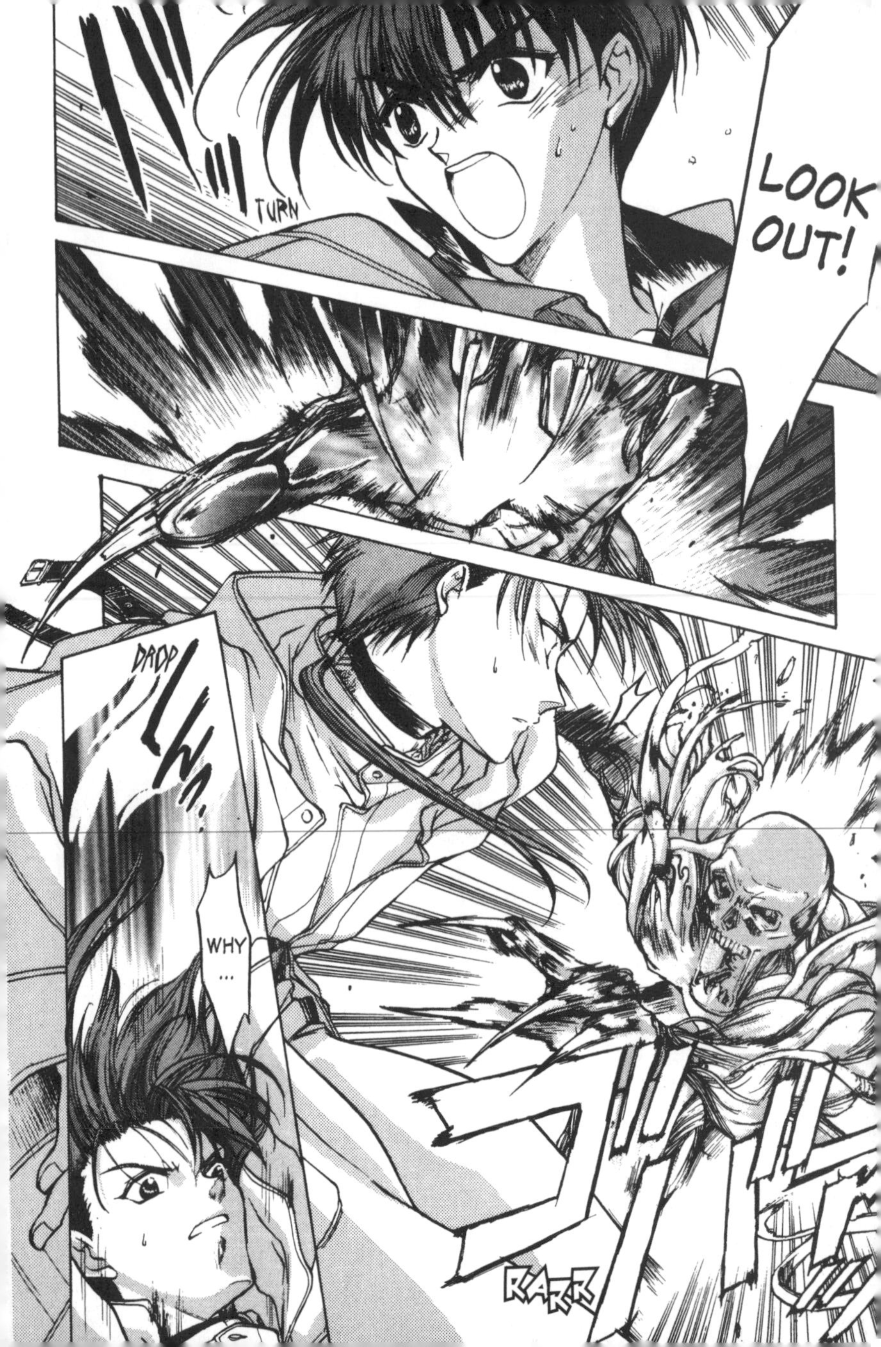

LOOK OUT!
TURN
RARR
DROP
WHY ...

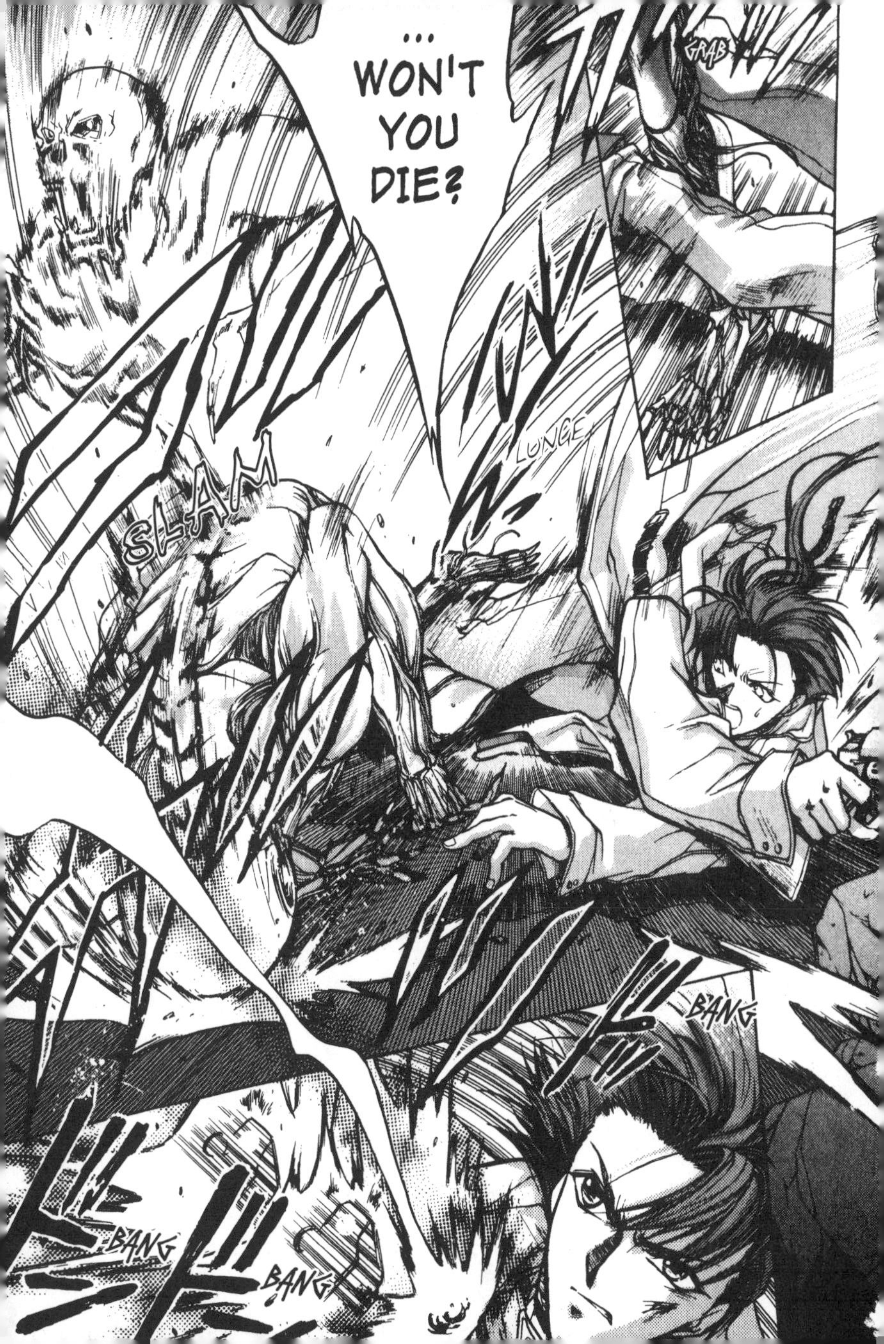
GRAB
... WON'T YOU DIE?
LUNGE
SLAM
BANG
BANG
BANG

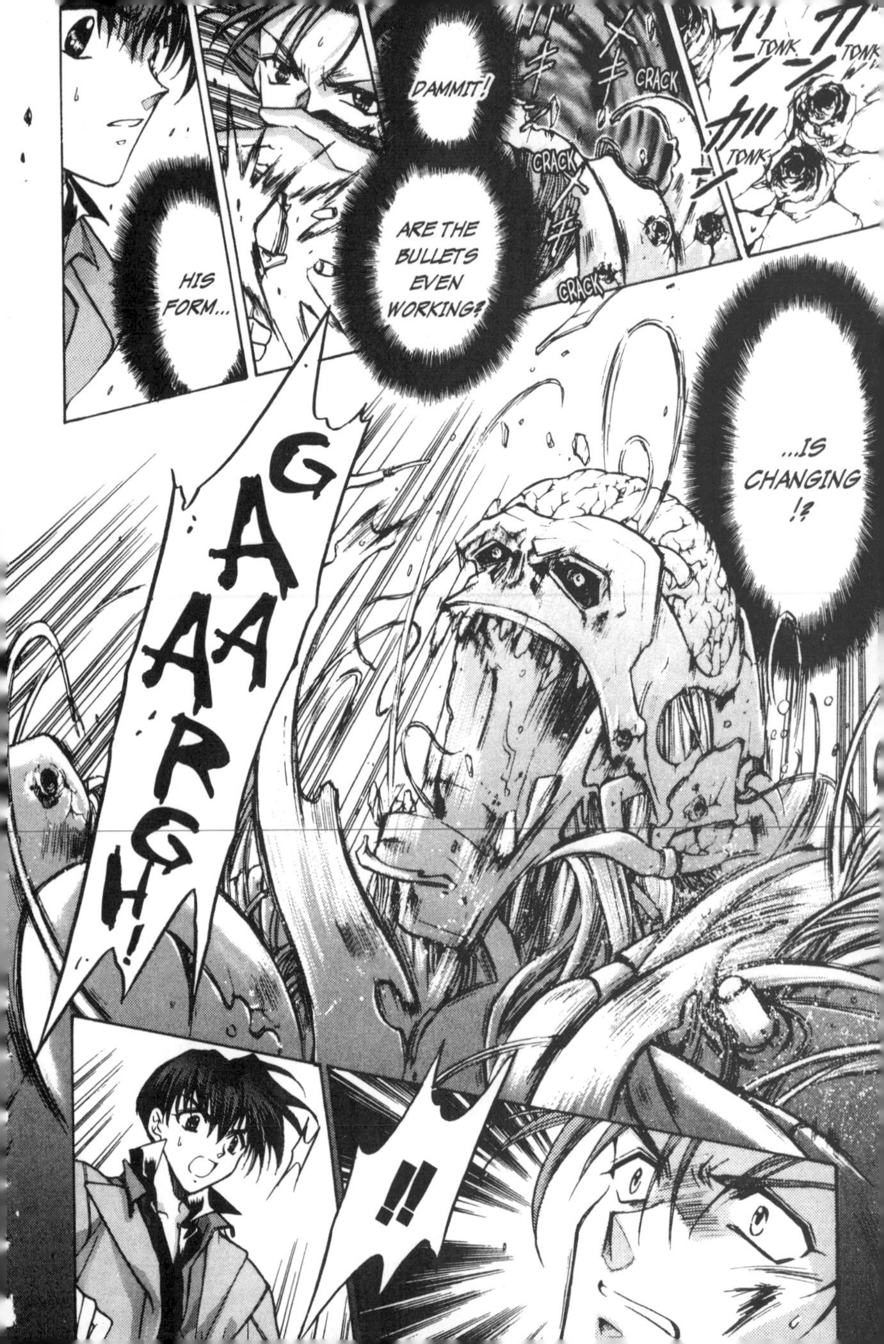

TONK
TONK
TONK
CRACK
CRACK
CRACK
DAMMIT!
ARE THE BULLETS EVEN WORKING?
HIS FORM...
...IS CHANGING !?
GAAARGH!
!!

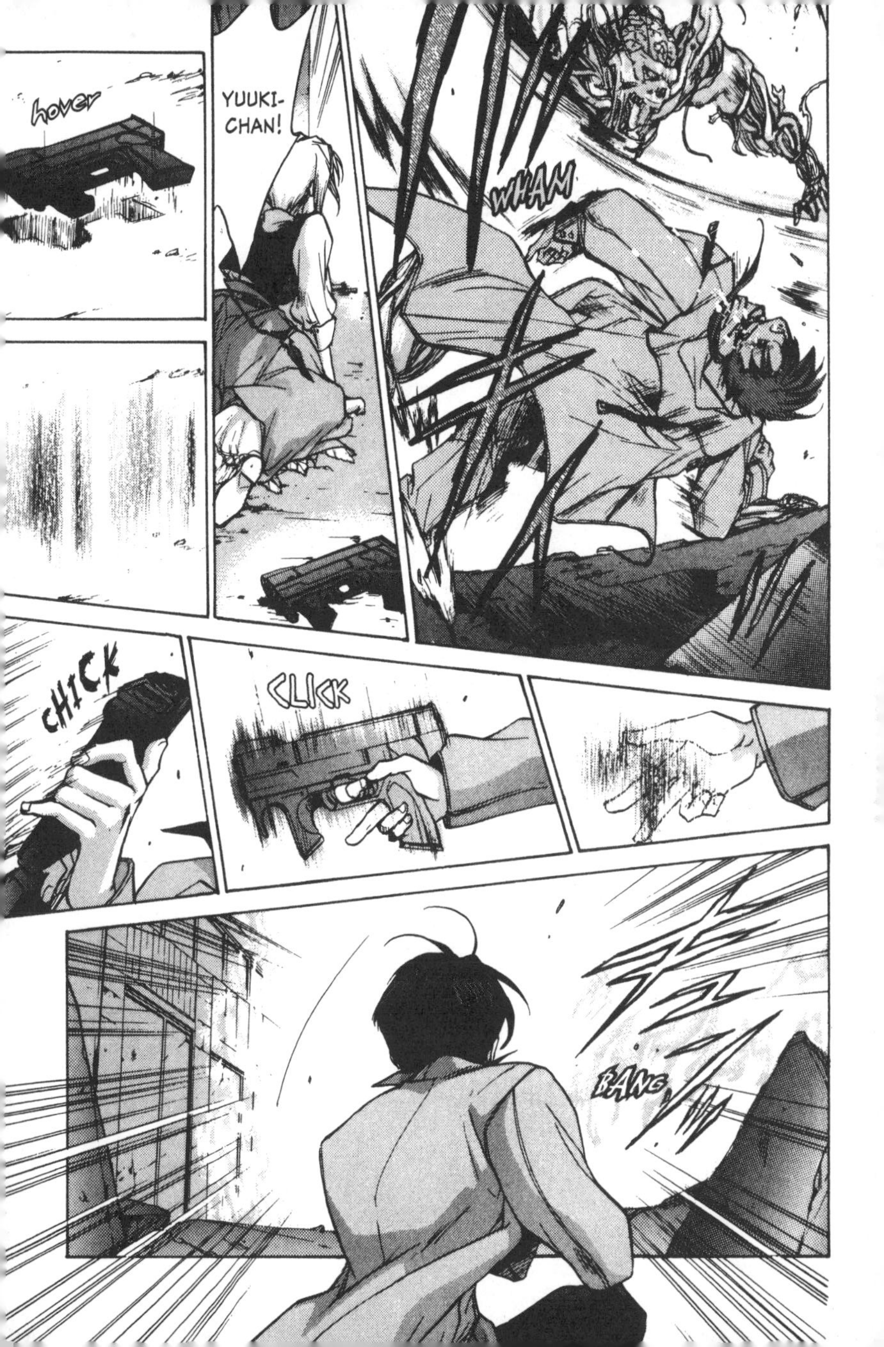
WHAM
YUUKI-CHAN!
hover
CLICK
CHICK
BANG

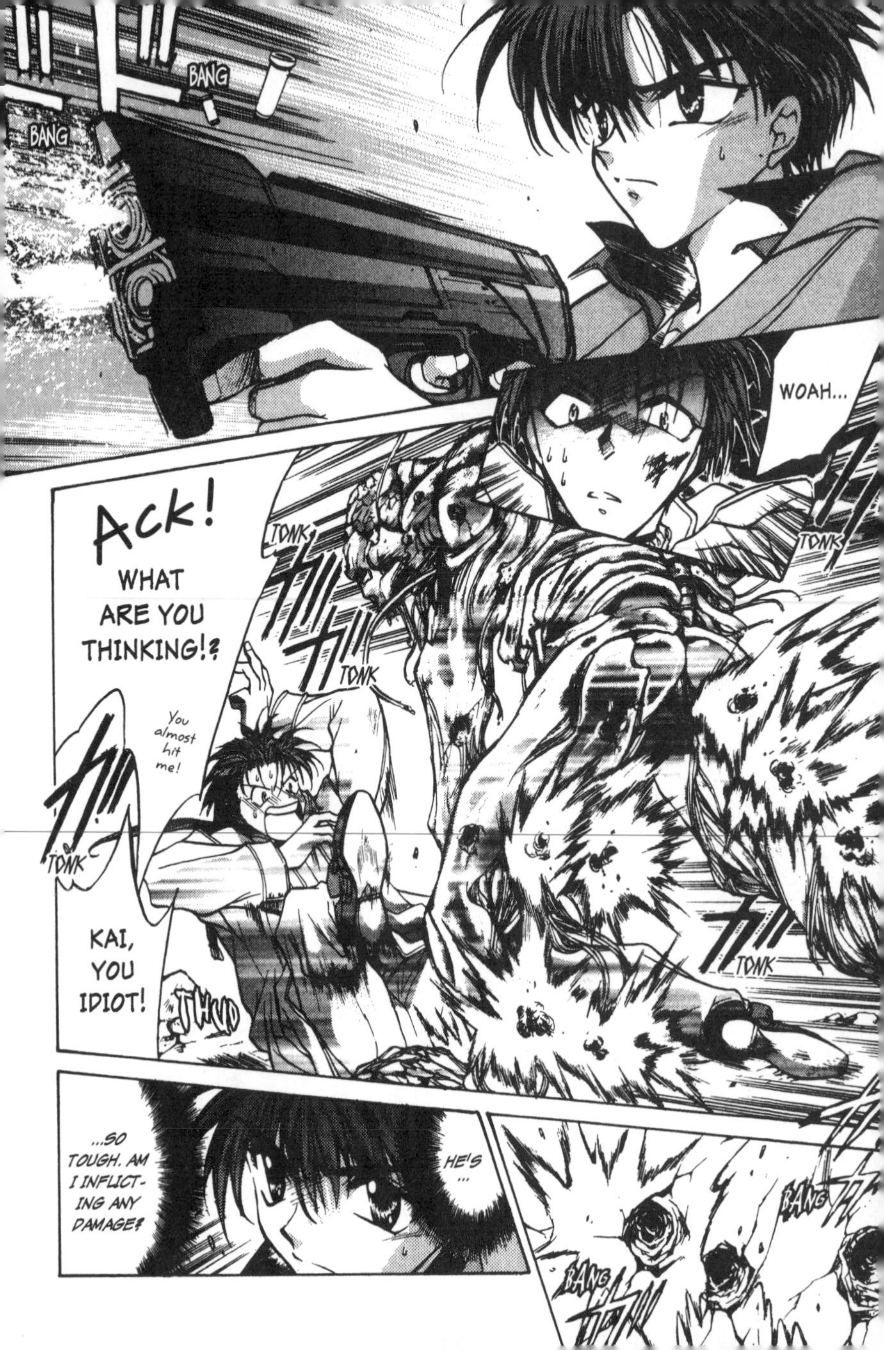
BANG
BANG
WOAH...
TONK
TONK
Ack! WHAT ARE YOU THINKING!?
TONK
You almost hit me!
TONK
TONK
KAI, YOU IDIOT!
THUD
BANG
BANG
HE'S ...
...SO TOUGH. AM I INFLICT-ING ANY DAMAGE?

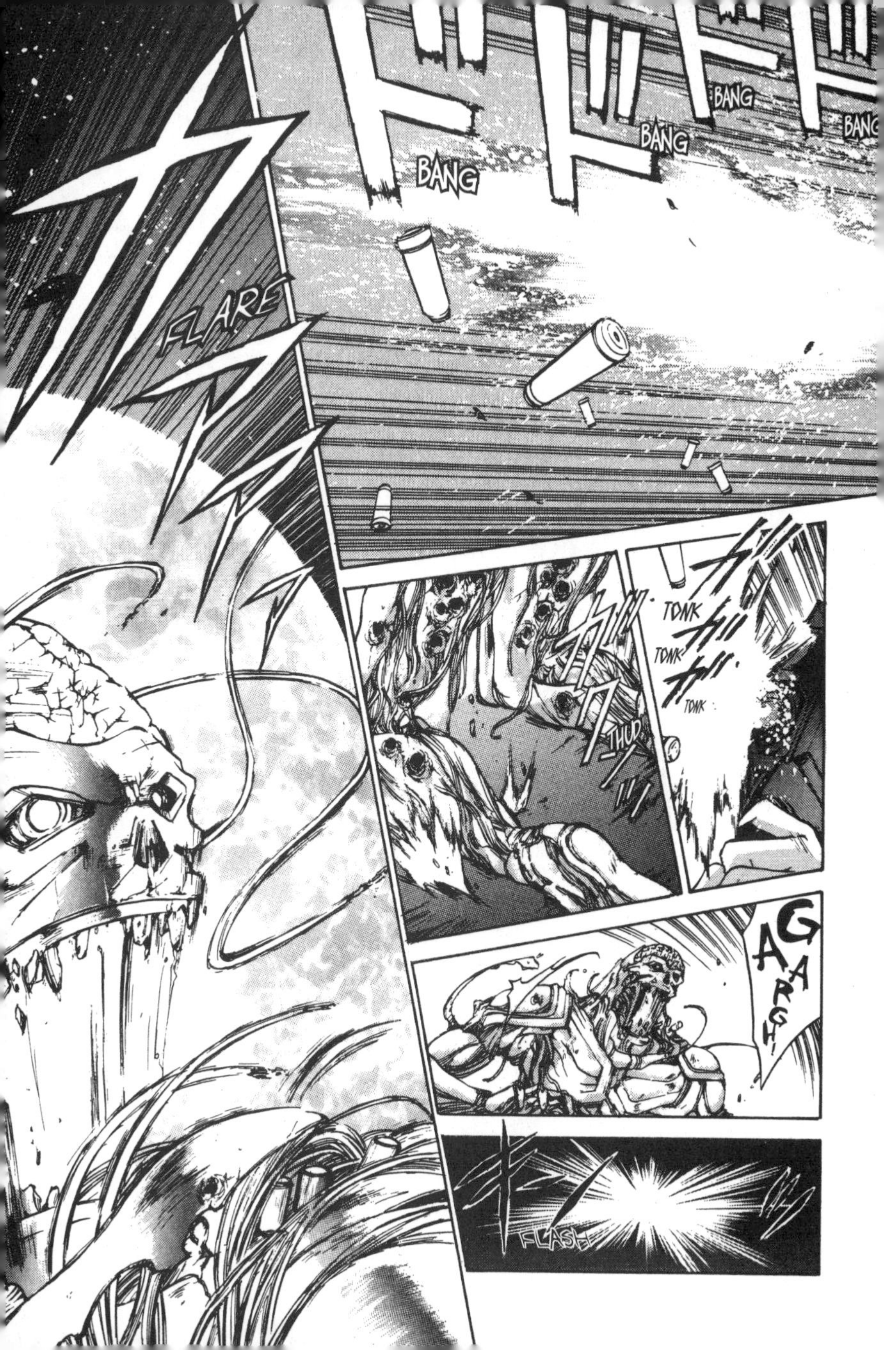
BANG
BANG
BANG
BANG
TONK
TONK
TONK
THUD
GARGH!
FLASH
FLARE

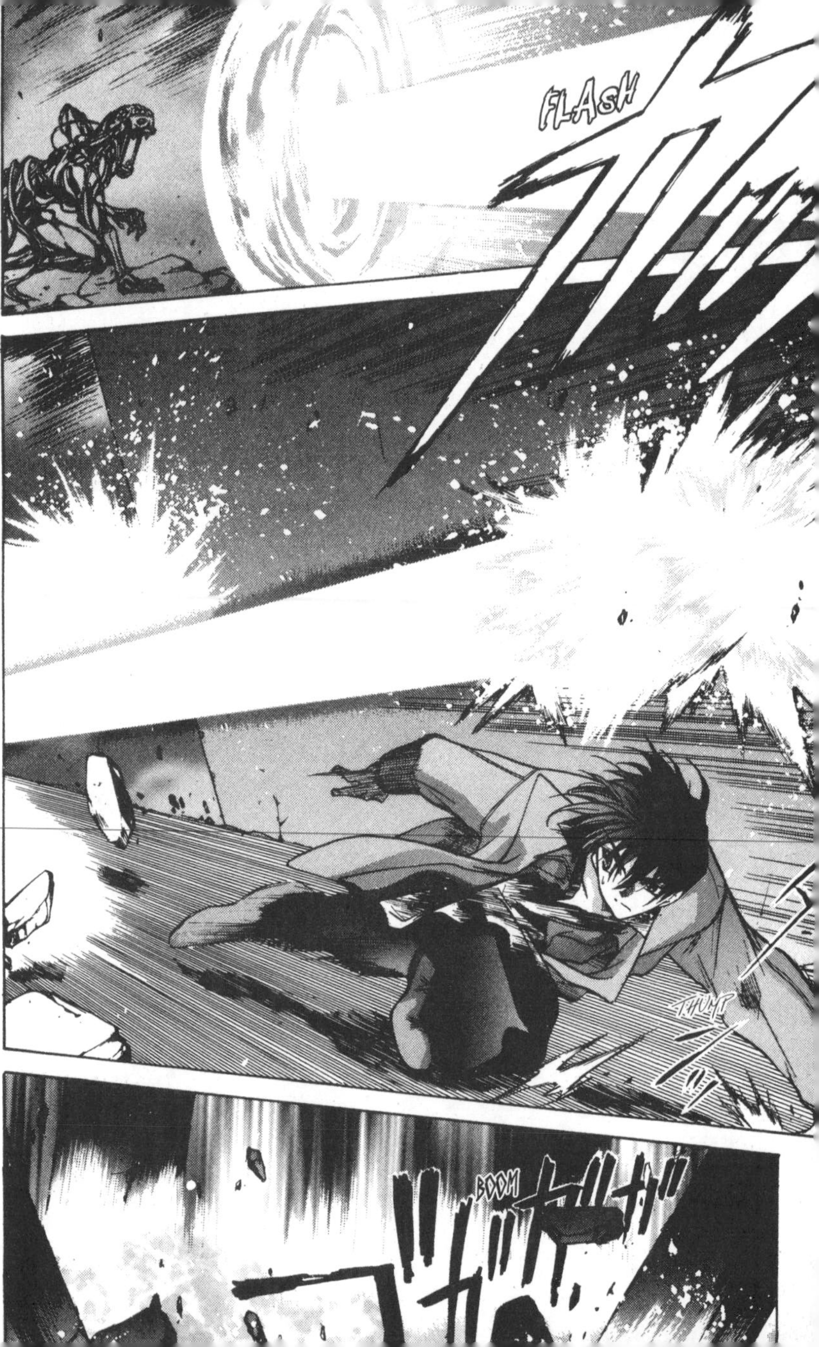
FLASH
THUMP
BOOM

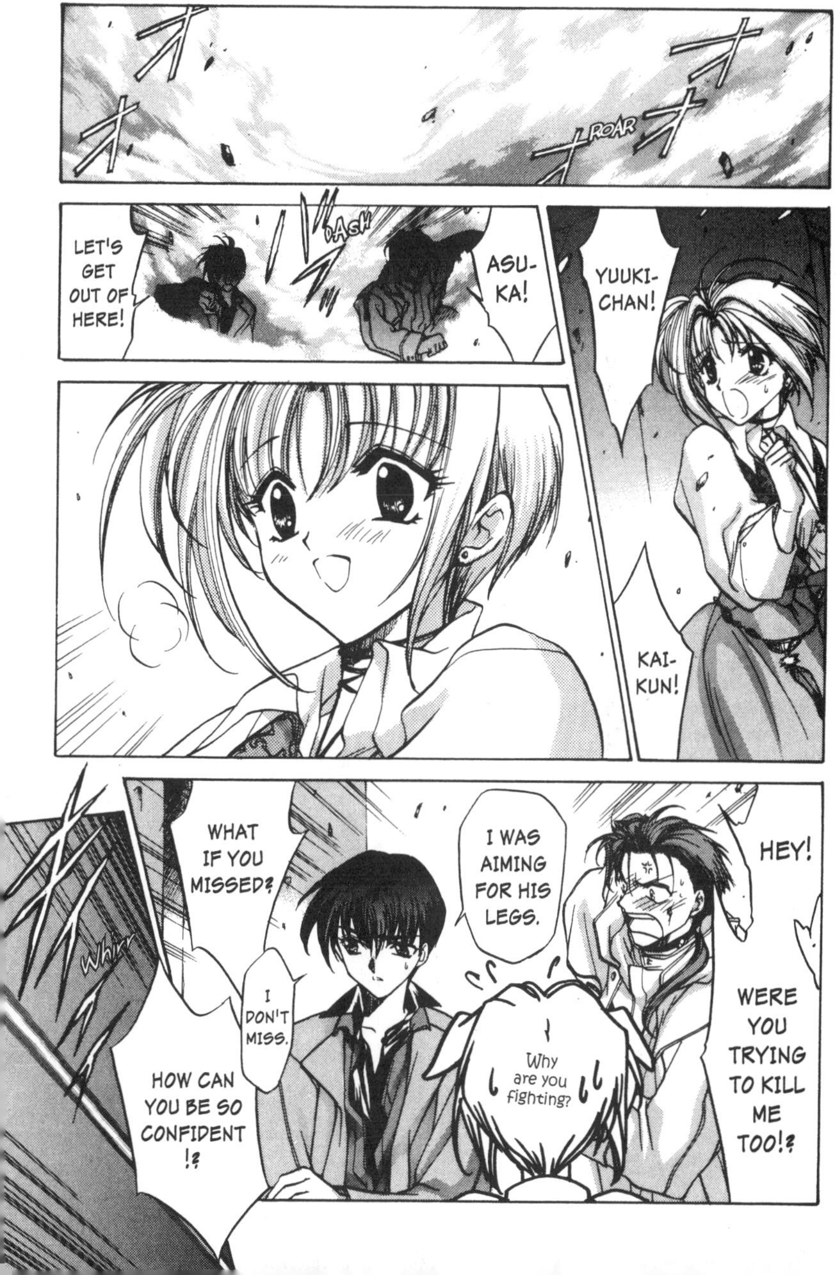
ROAR
YUUKI-CHAN!
KAI-KUN!
ASU-KA!
DASH
LET'S GET OUT OF HERE!
HEY!
WERE YOU TRYING TO KILL ME TOO!?
I WAS AIMING FOR HIS LEGS.
Why are you fighting?
WHAT IF YOU MISSED?
I DON'T MISS.
HOW CAN YOU BE SO CONFIDENT!?
Whirr

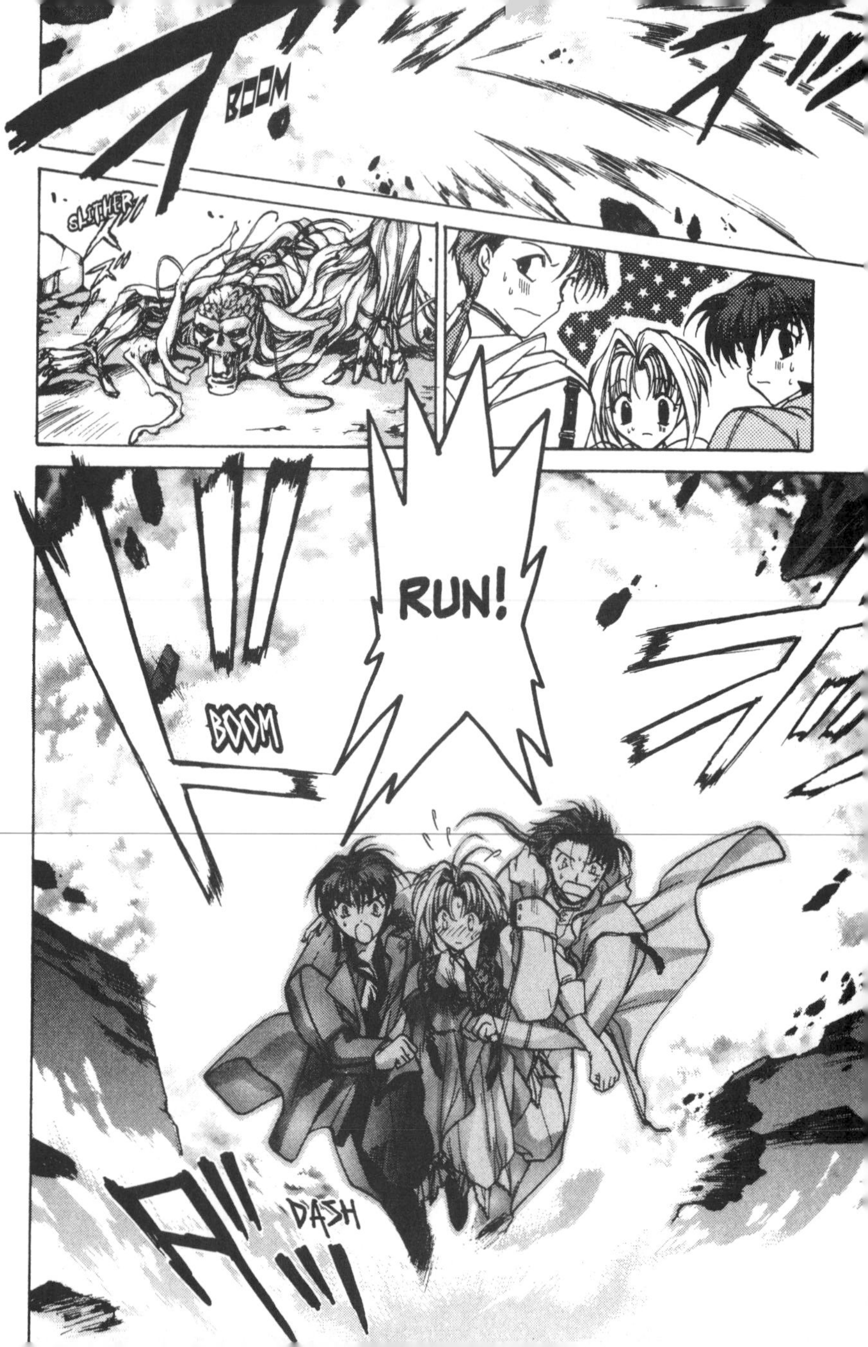
BOOM
SLITHER
RUN!
BOOM
DASH

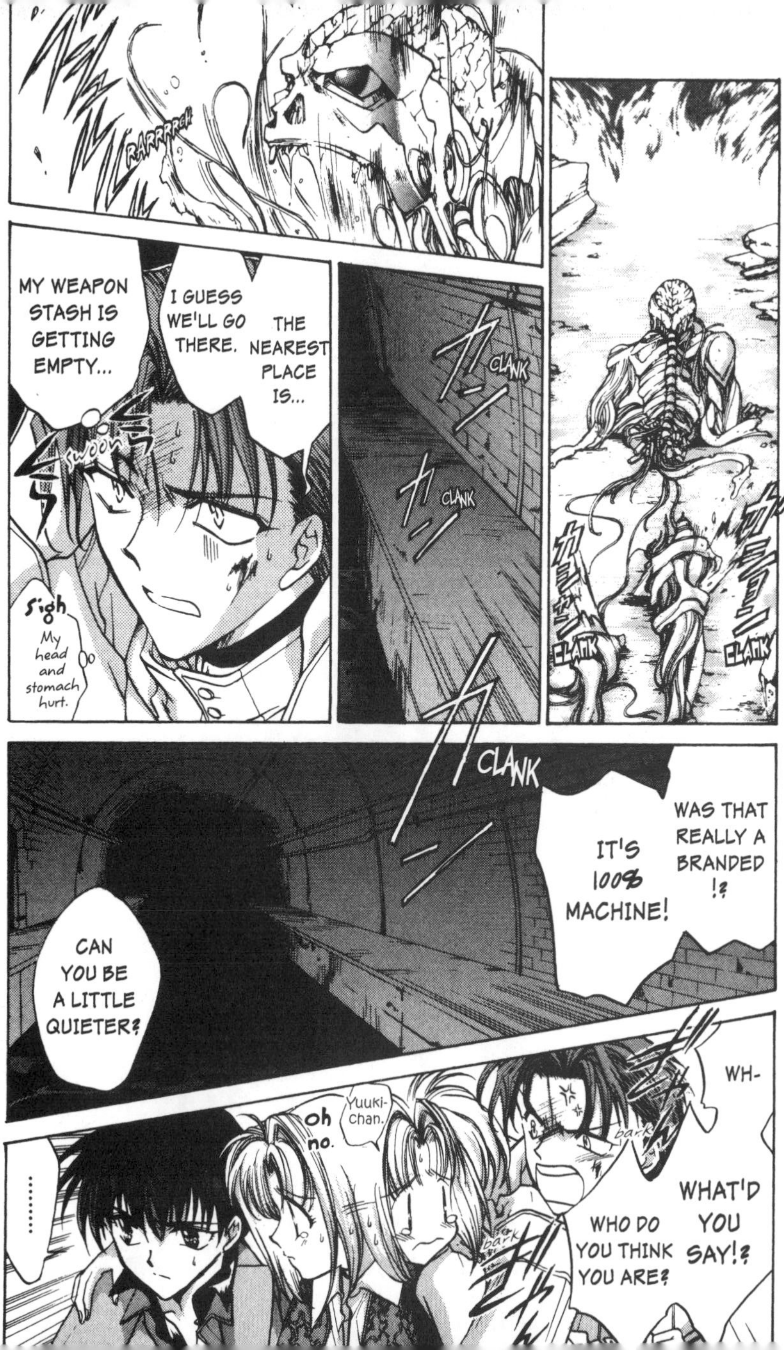
CLANK
CLANK
RARRRRGH
CLANK
CLANK
THE NEAREST PLACE IS...
I GUESS WE'LL GO THERE.
MY WEAPON STASH IS GETTING EMPTY...
swoon
Sigh
My head and stomach hurt.
CLANK
WAS THAT REALLY A BRANDED!?
IT'S 100% MACHINE!
CAN YOU BE A LITTLE QUIETER?
WH-
WHAT'D YOU SAY!?
WHO DO YOU THINK YOU ARE?
bark
bark
Yuuki-chan.
Oh no.
....

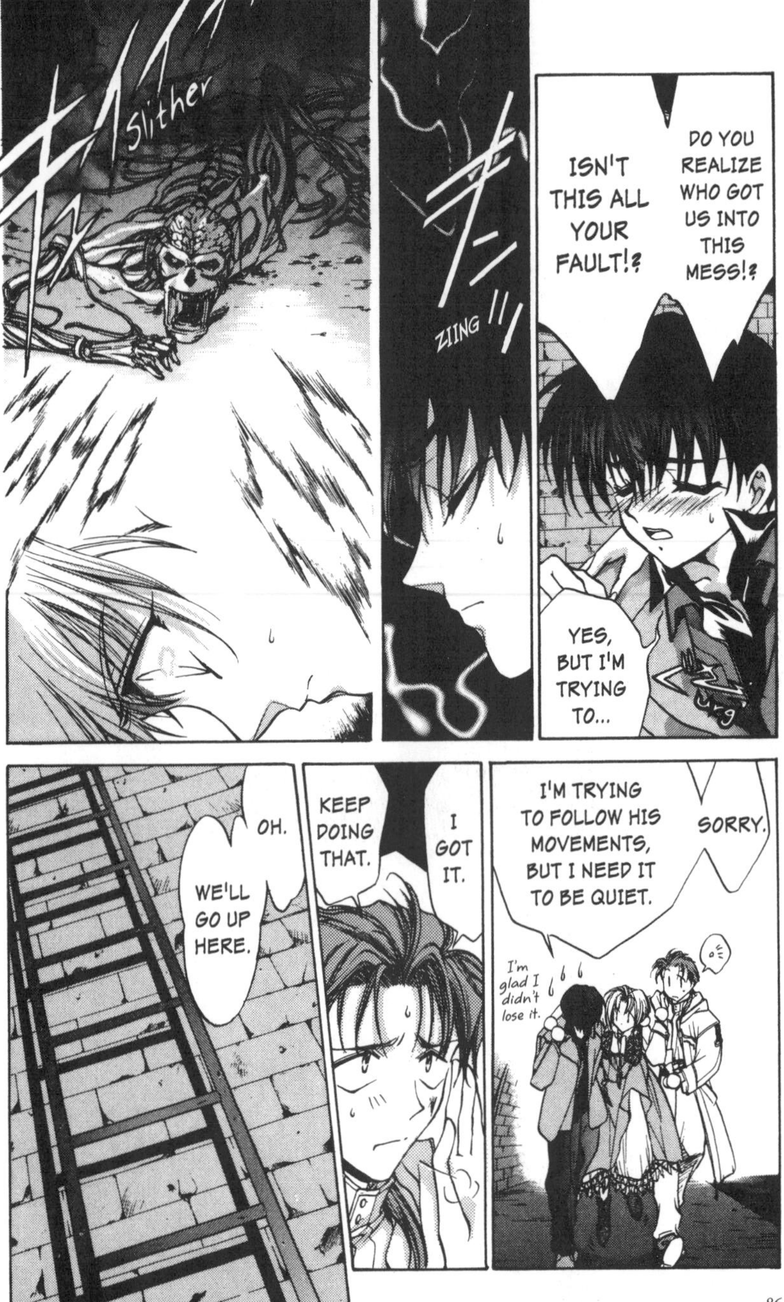
DO YOU REALIZE WHO GOT US INTO THIS MESS!?
ISN'T THIS ALL YOUR FAULT!?
YES, BUT I'M TRYING TO...
Urg
ZIING
Slither
SORRY.
I'M TRYING TO FOLLOW HIS MOVEMENTS, BUT I NEED IT TO BE QUIET.
I'm glad I didn't lose it.
I GOT IT.
KEEP DOING THAT.
OH.
WE'LL GO UP HERE.

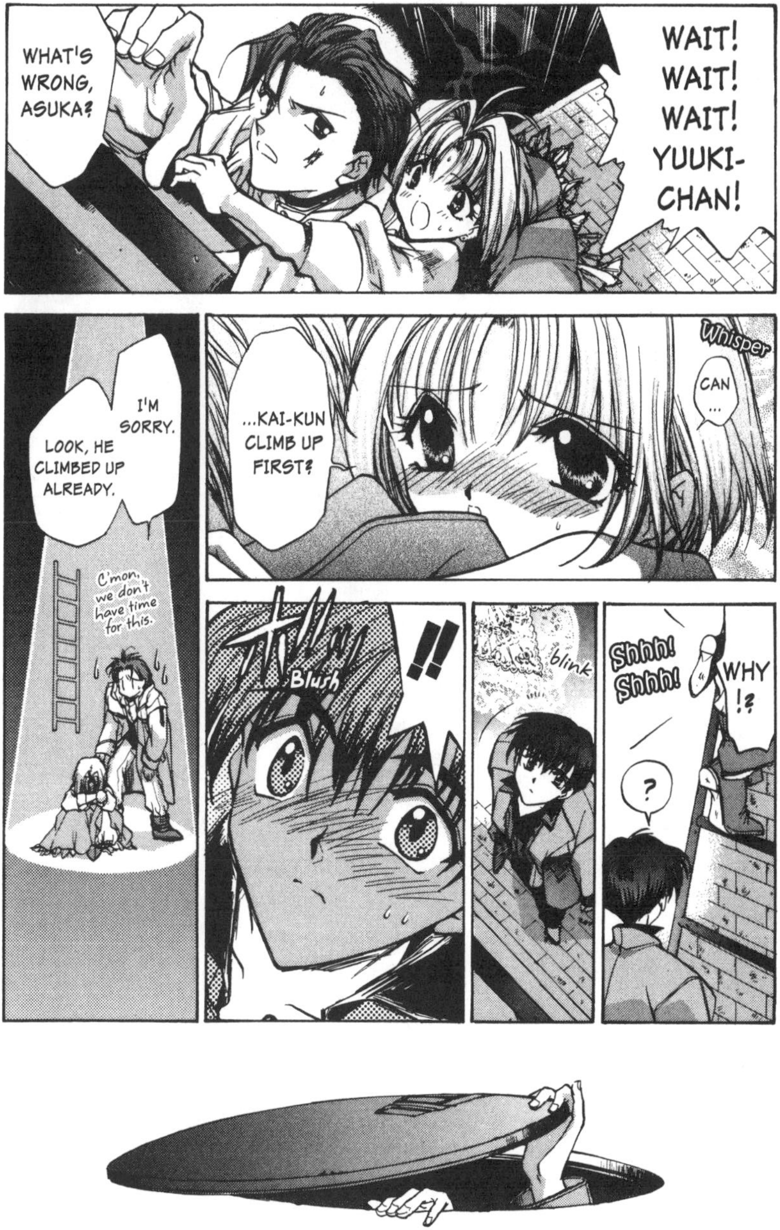
WAIT! WAIT! WAIT! YUUKI-CHAN!
WHAT'S WRONG, ASUKA?
Whisper
CAN ...
...KAI-KUN CLIMB UP FIRST?
WHY !?
Shhh! Shhh!
?
blink
!!
Blush
I'M SORRY.
LOOK, HE CLIMBED UP ALREADY.
C'mon, we don't have time for this.

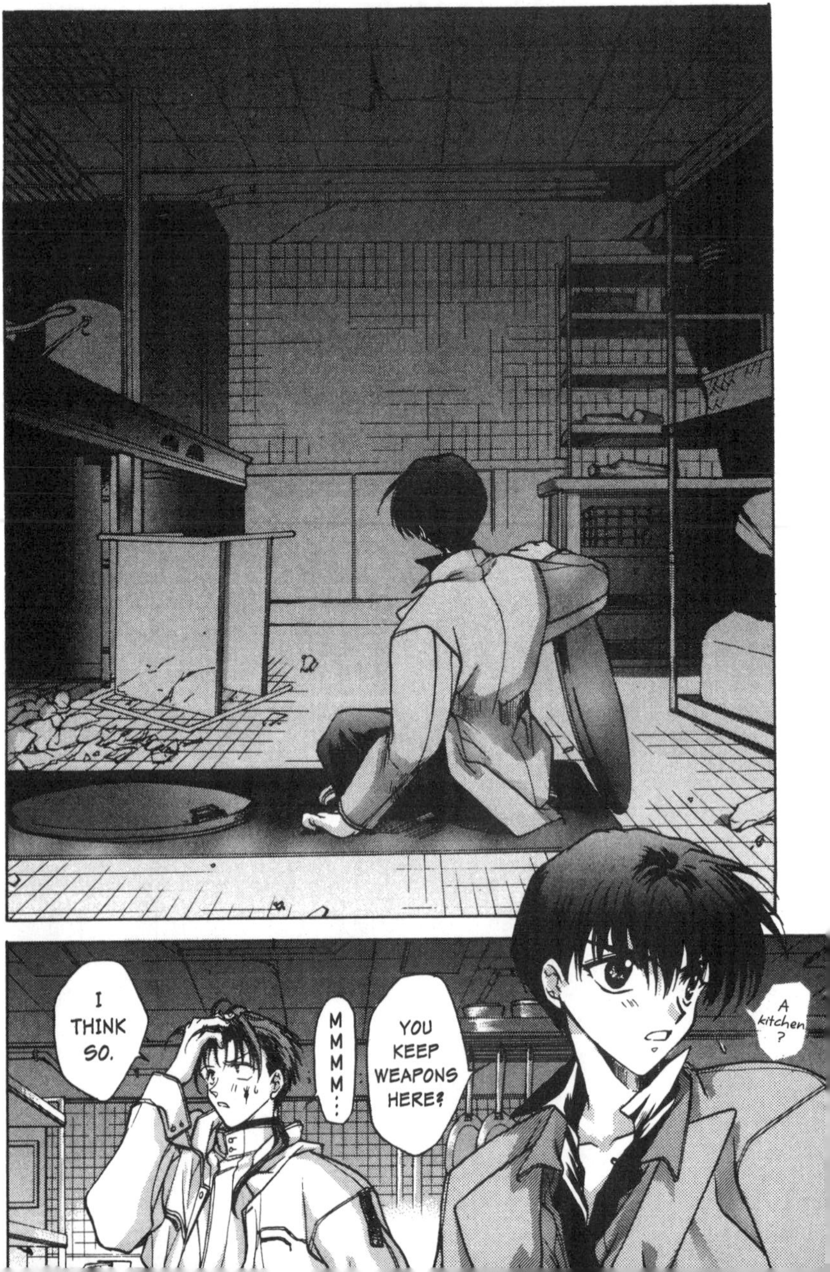
A kitchen?
YOU KEEP WEAPONS HERE?
MMMM...
I THINK SO.

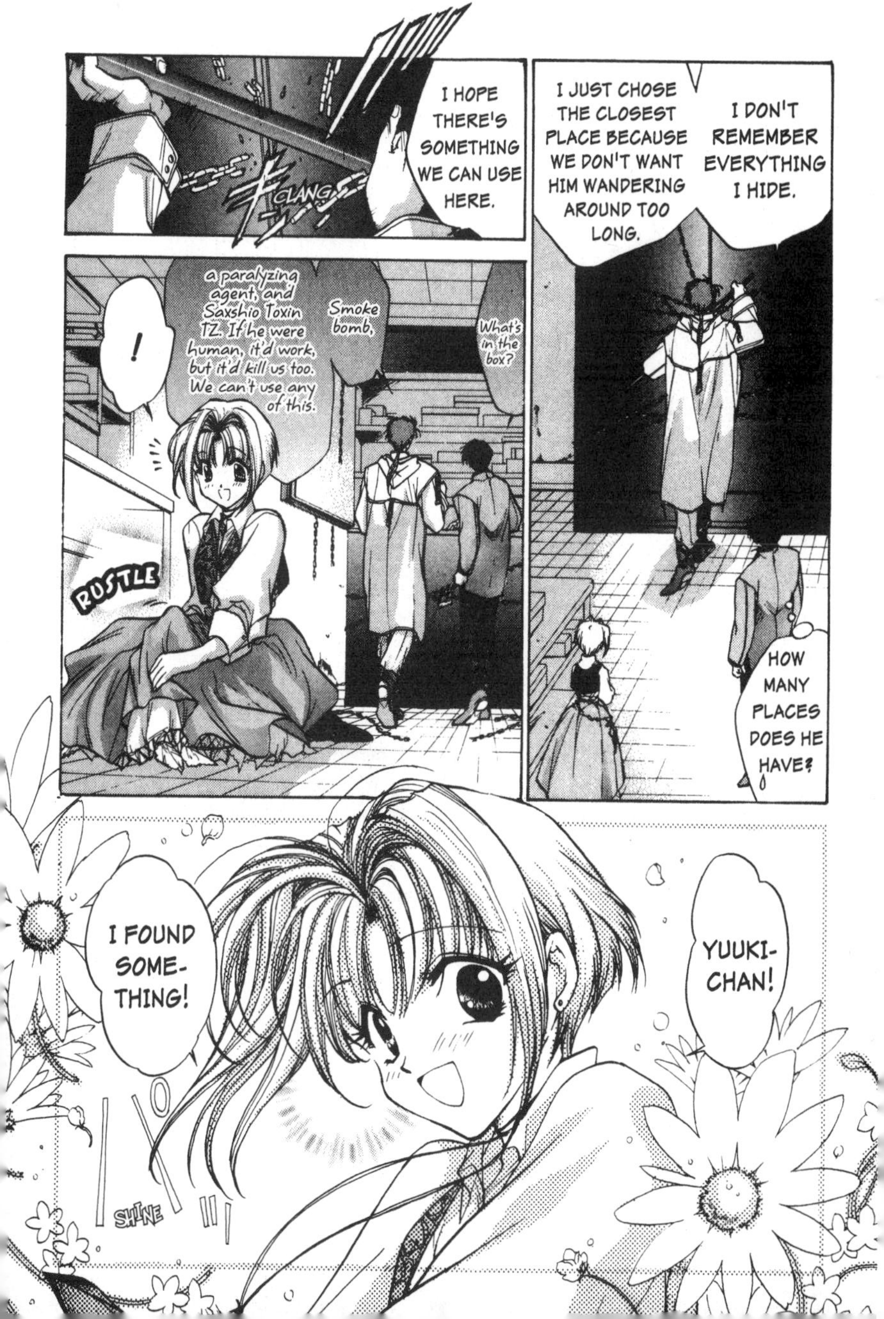
I DON'T REMEMBER EVERYTHING I HIDE.
I JUST CHOSE THE CLOSEST PLACE BECAUSE WE DON'T WANT HIM WANDERING AROUND TOO LONG.
HOW MANY PLACES DOES HE HAVE?
I HOPE THERE'S SOMETHING WE CAN USE HERE.
CLANG
What's in the box?
Smoke bomb,
a paralyzing agent, and Saxshio Toxin TZ. If he were human, it'd work, but it'd kill us too. We can't use any of this.
!
RUSTLE
YUUKI-CHAN!
I FOUND SOME-THING!
SHINE

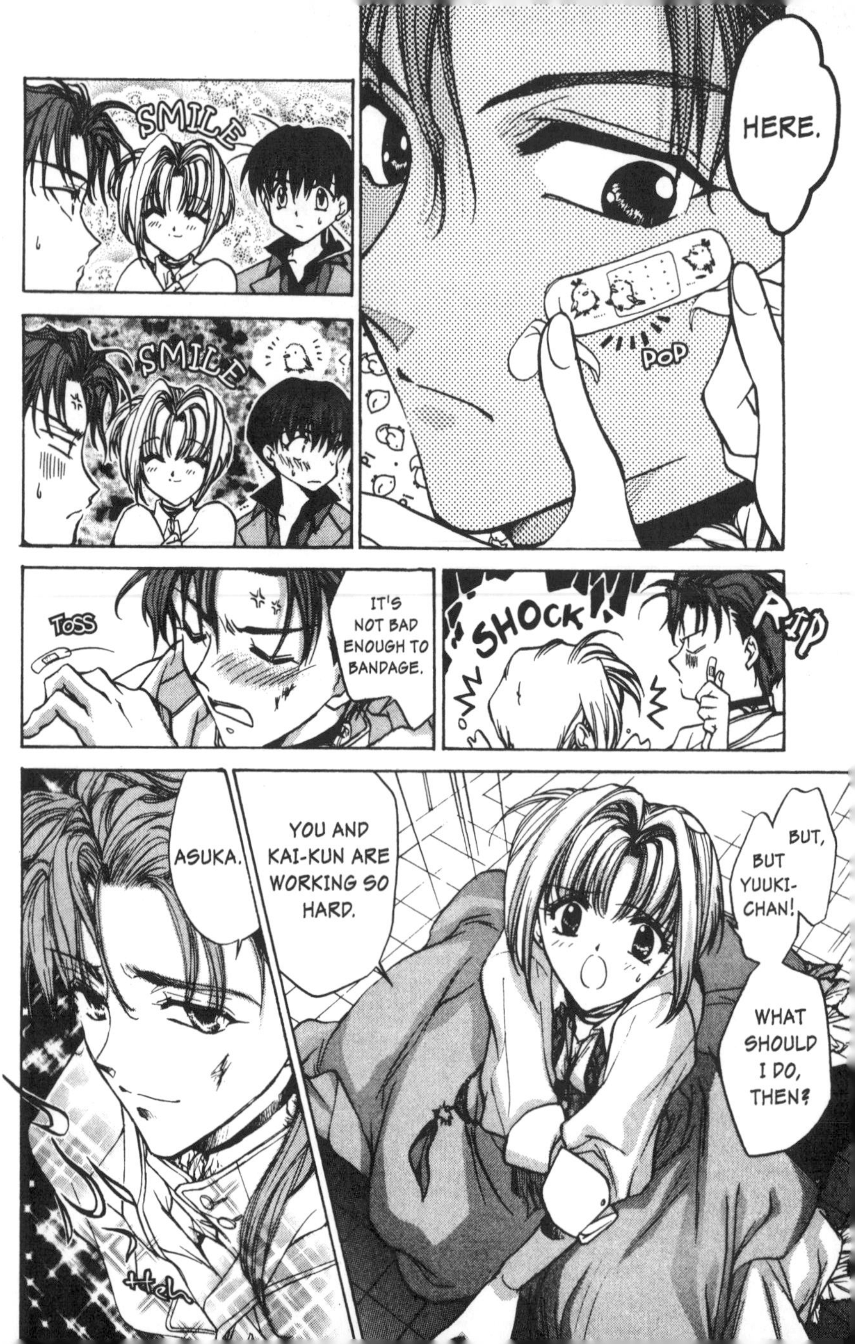
HERE.
POP
SMILE
SMILE
SHOCK
RIP
TOSS
IT'S NOT BAD ENOUGH TO BANDAGE.
BUT, BUT YUUKI-CHAN!
WHAT SHOULD I DO, THEN?
YOU AND KAI-KUN ARE WORKING SO HARD.
ASUKA.

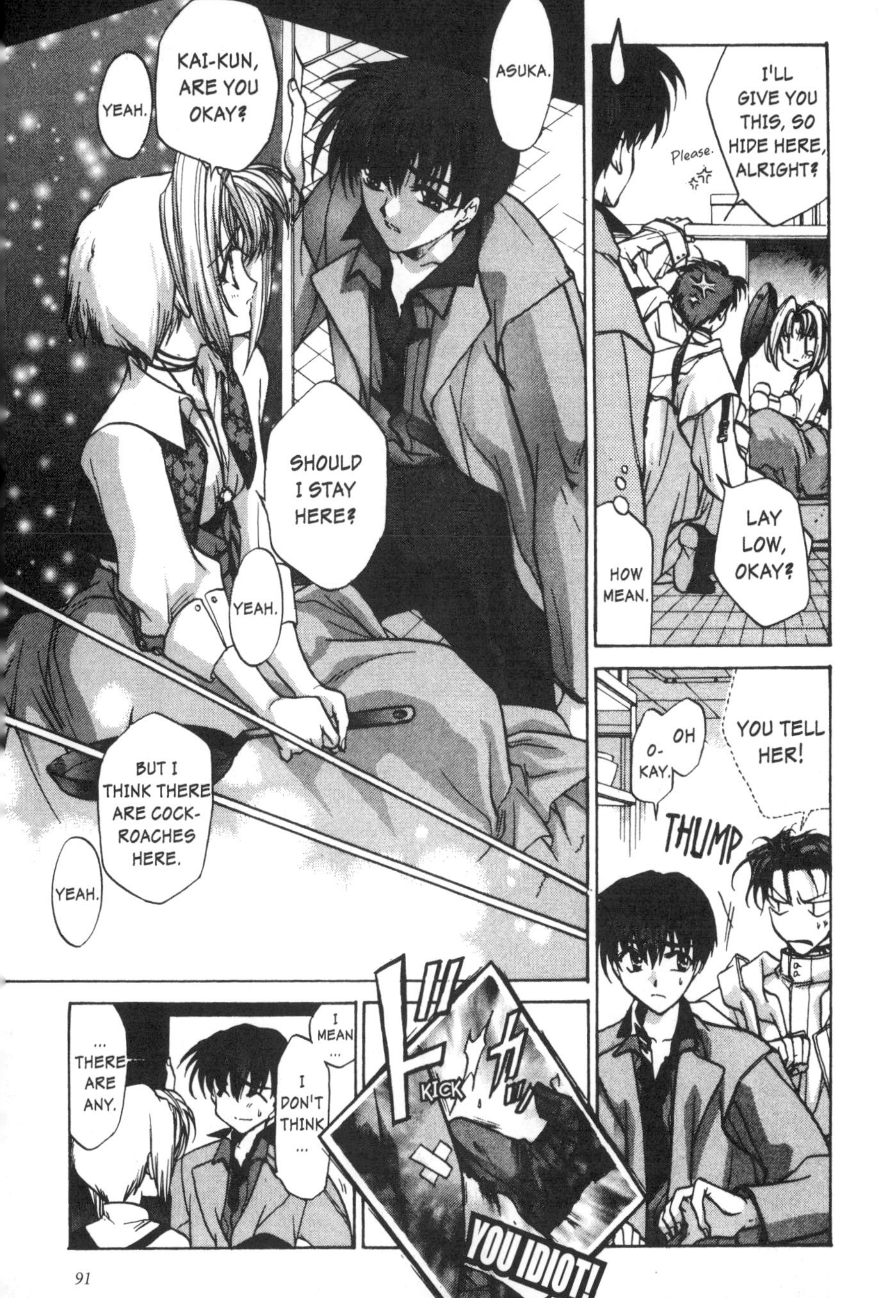
I'LL GIVE YOU THIS, SO HIDE HERE, ALRIGHT?
Please.
LAY LOW, OKAY?
HOW MEAN.
ASUKA.
KAI-KUN, ARE YOU OKAY?
YEAH.
SHOULD I STAY HERE?
YEAH.
BUT I THINK THERE ARE COCK-ROACHES HERE.
YEAH.
YOU TELL HER!
OH
O-KAY.
THUMP
KICK
YOU IDIOT!
I MEAN ...
I DON'T THINK ...
... THERE ARE ANY.

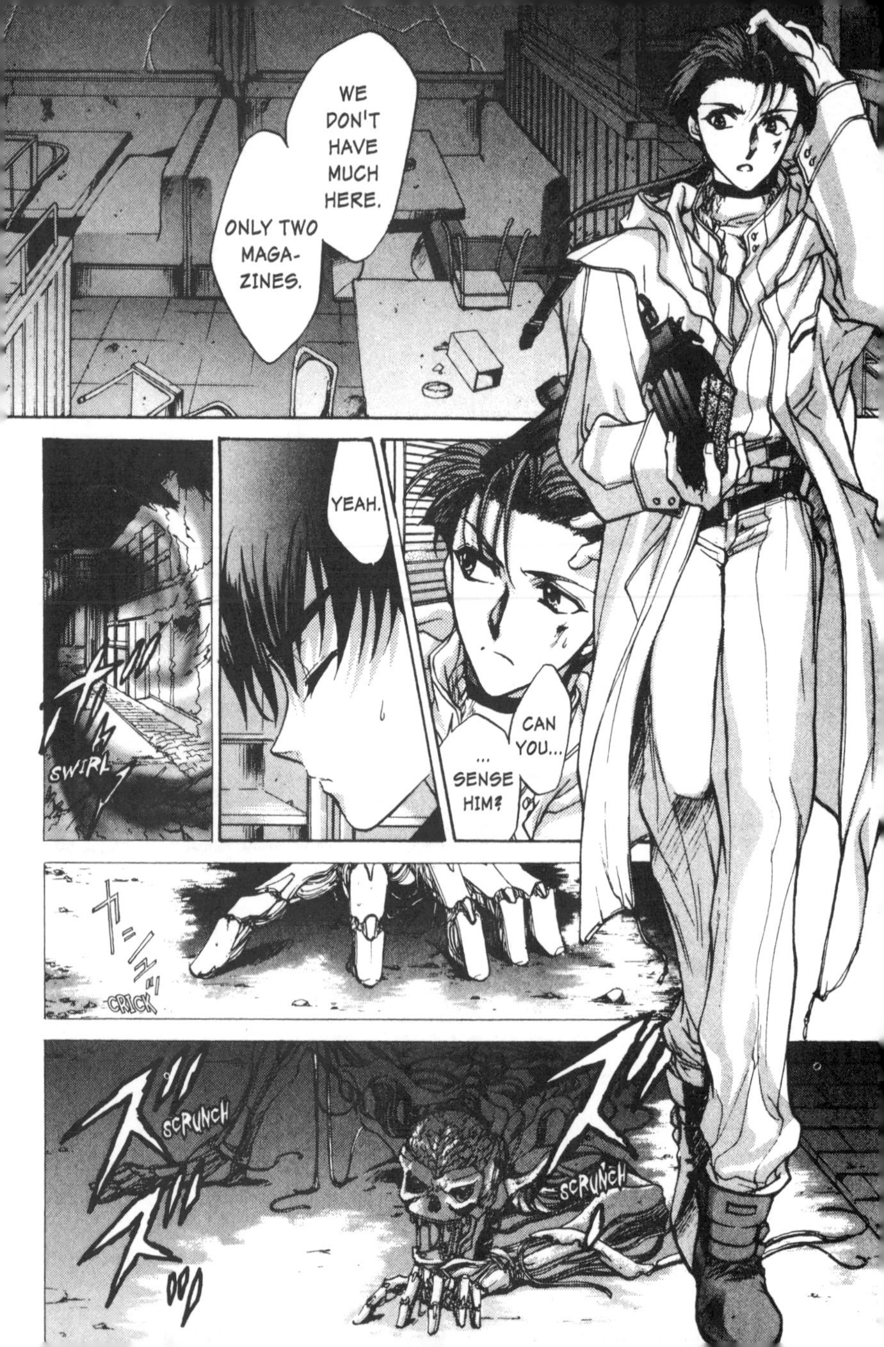
WE DON'T HAVE MUCH HERE.
ONLY TWO MAGAZINES.
CAN YOU...
...SENSE HIM?
YEAH.
SWIRL
CRICK
SCRUNCH
SCRUNCH

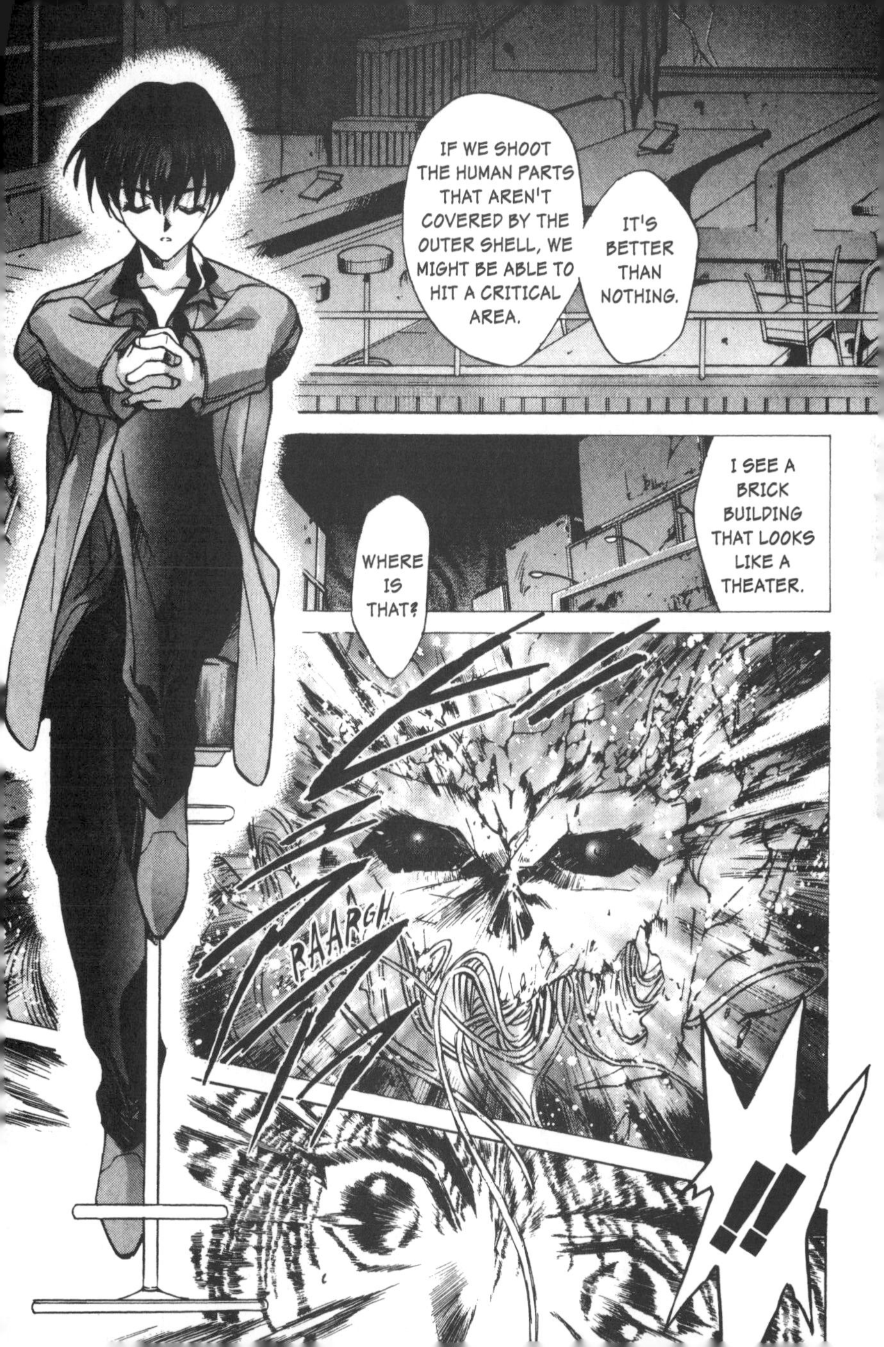
IT'S BETTER THAN NOTHING.
IF WE SHOOT THE HUMAN PARTS THAT AREN'T COVERED BY THE OUTER SHELL, WE MIGHT BE ABLE TO HIT A CRITICAL AREA.
I SEE A BRICK BUILDING THAT LOOKS LIKE A THEATER.
WHERE IS THAT?
RAARGH
!!

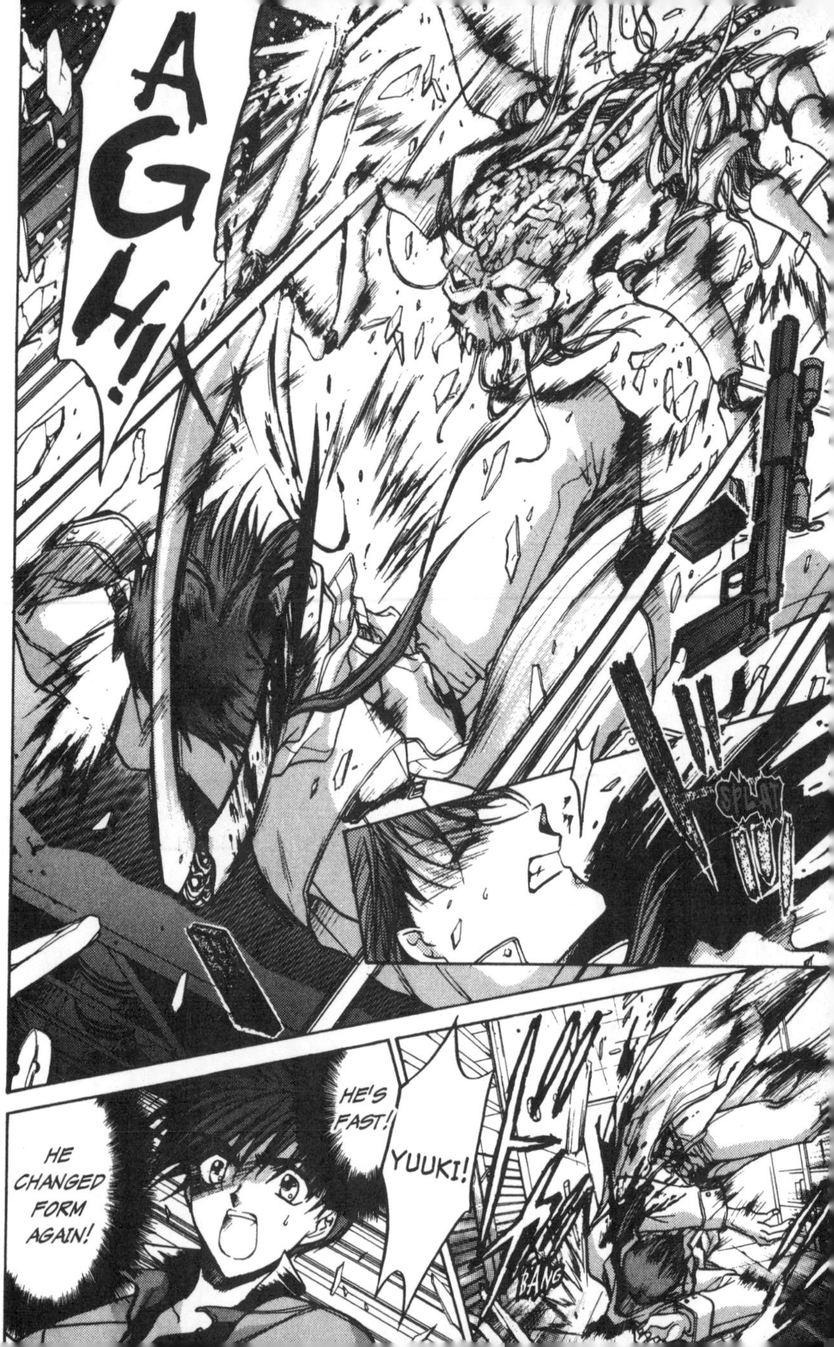
AGH!
SPLAT
HE'S FAST!
YUUKI!
HE CHANGED FORM AGAIN!
BANG

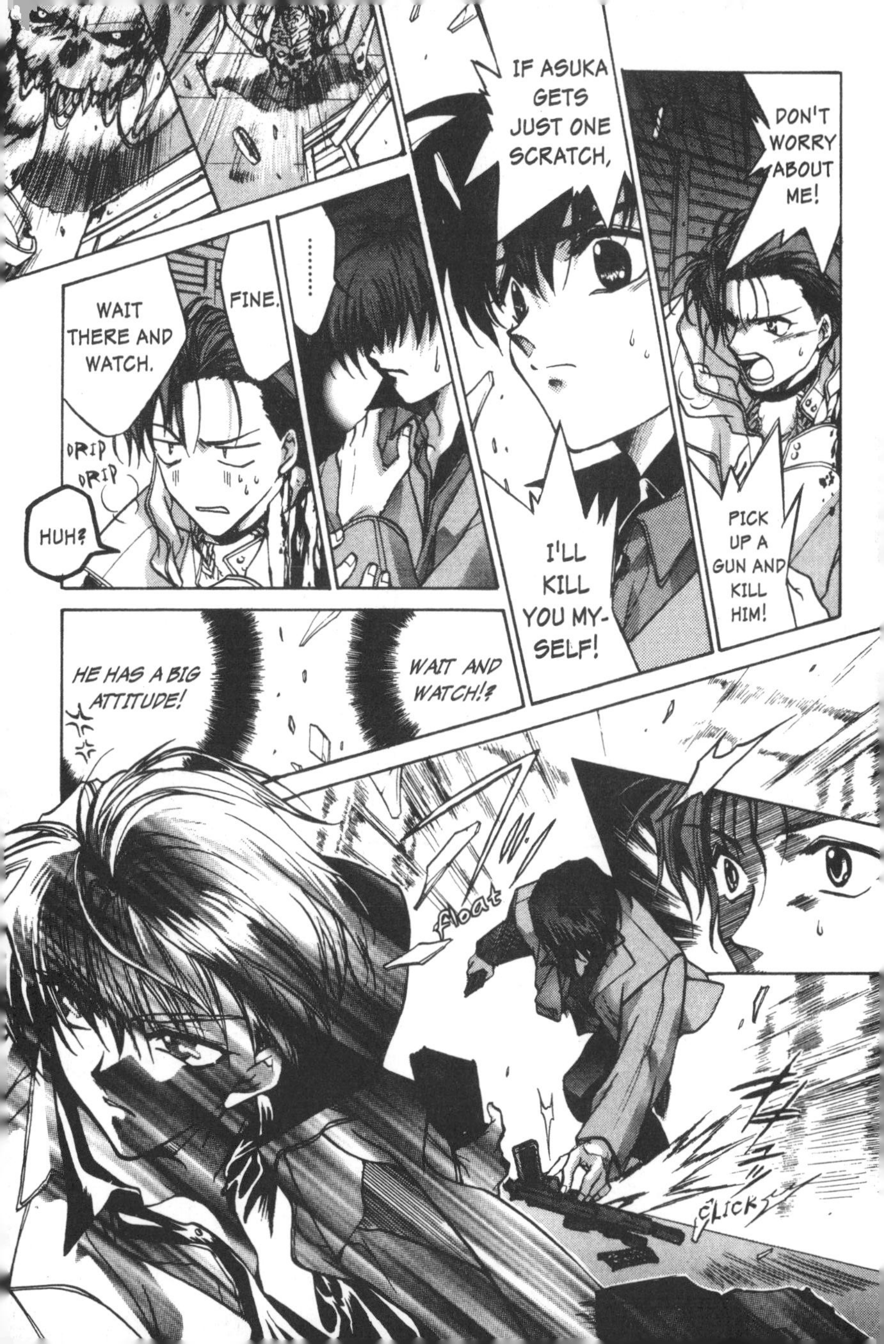
DON'T WORRY ABOUT ME!
PICK UP A GUN AND KILL HIM!
IF ASUKA GETS JUST ONE SCRATCH,
I'LL KILL YOU MY-SELF!
......
FINE.
WAIT THERE AND WATCH.
DRIP DRIP
HUH?
WAIT AND WATCH!?
HE HAS A BIG ATTITUDE!
float
CLICK

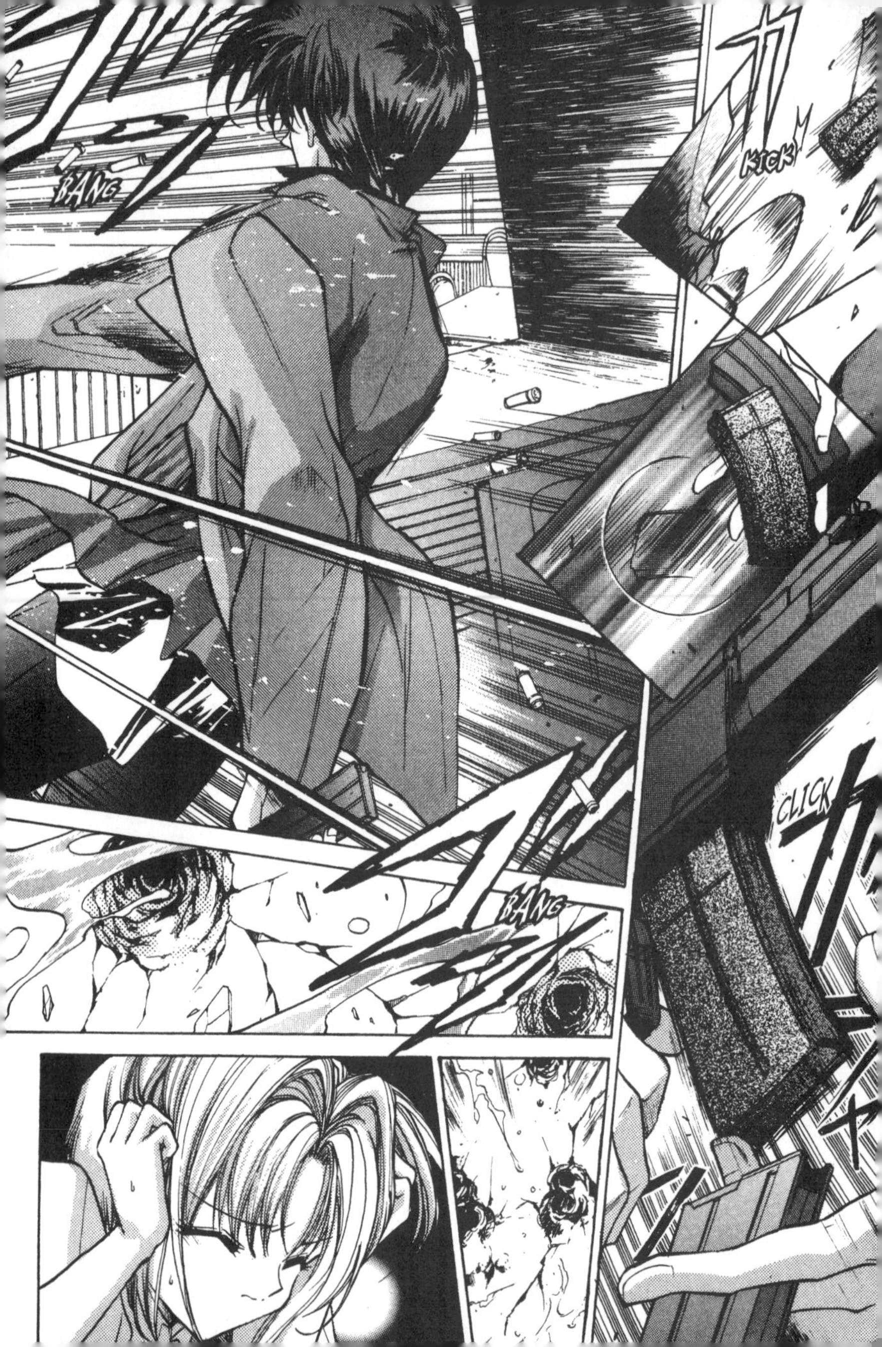
KICK
BANG
CLICK
BANG

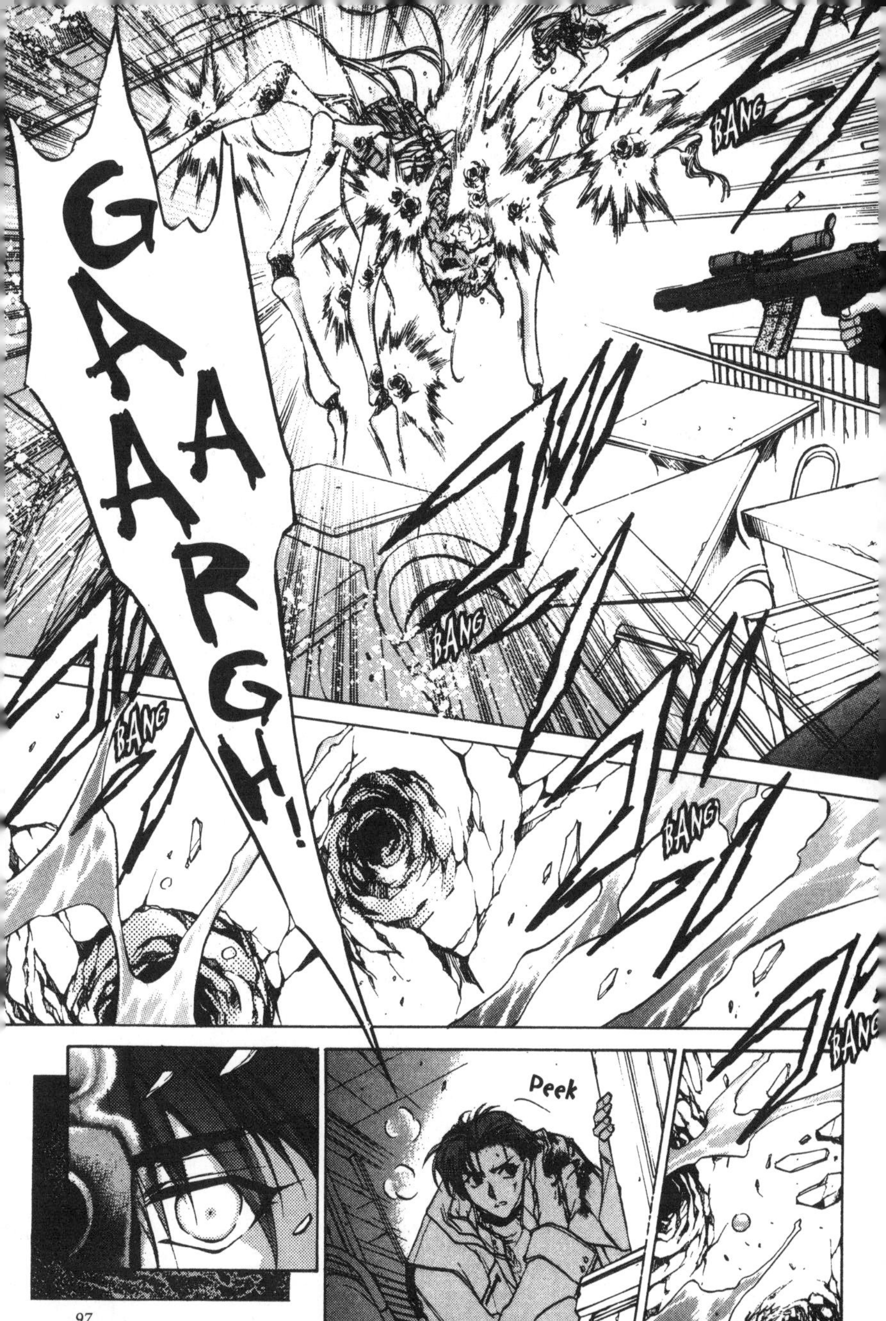

BANG
GAARGH!
BANG
BANG
BANG
BANG
Peek

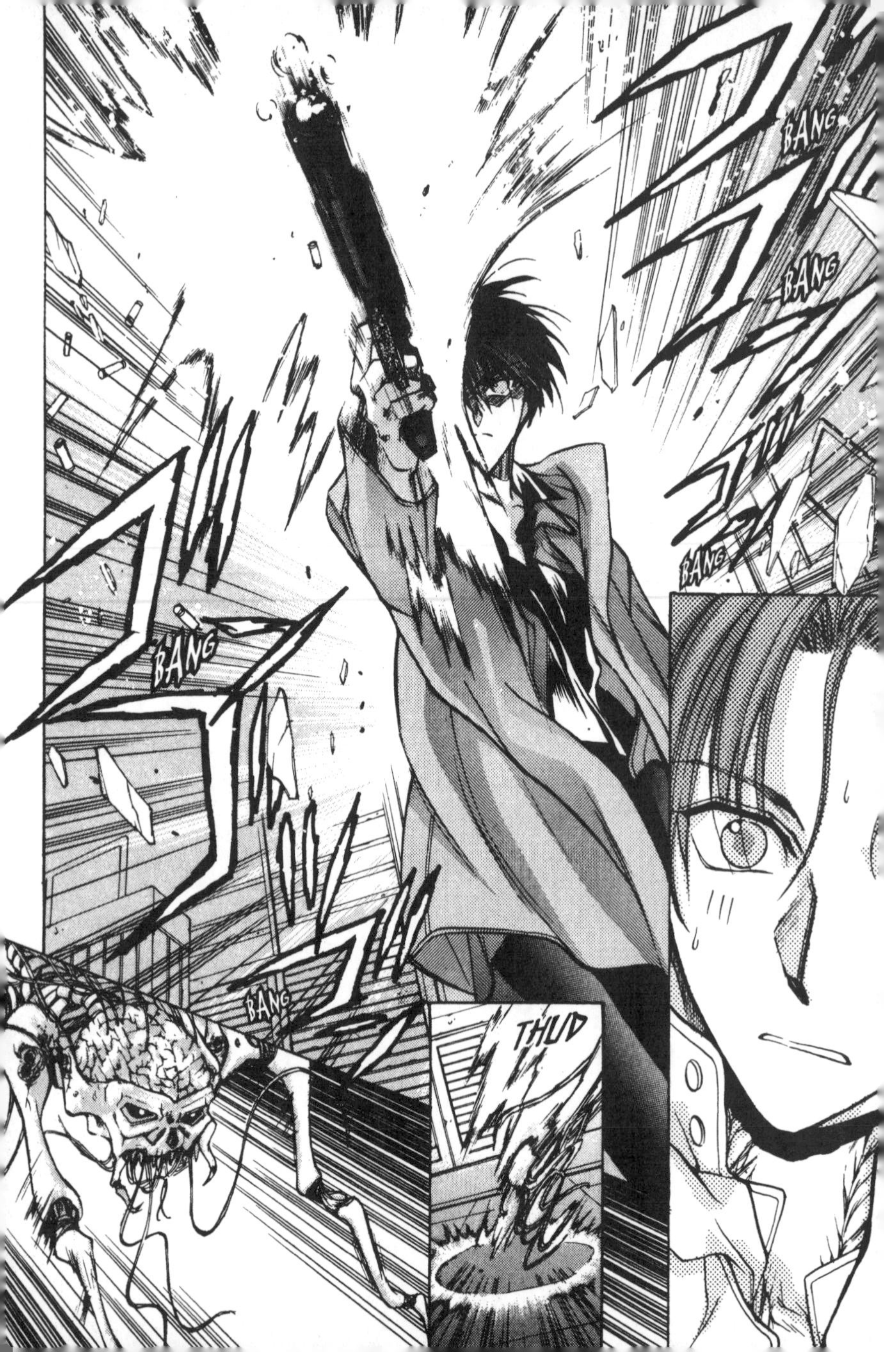
BANG
BANG
BANG
BANG
BANG
THUD

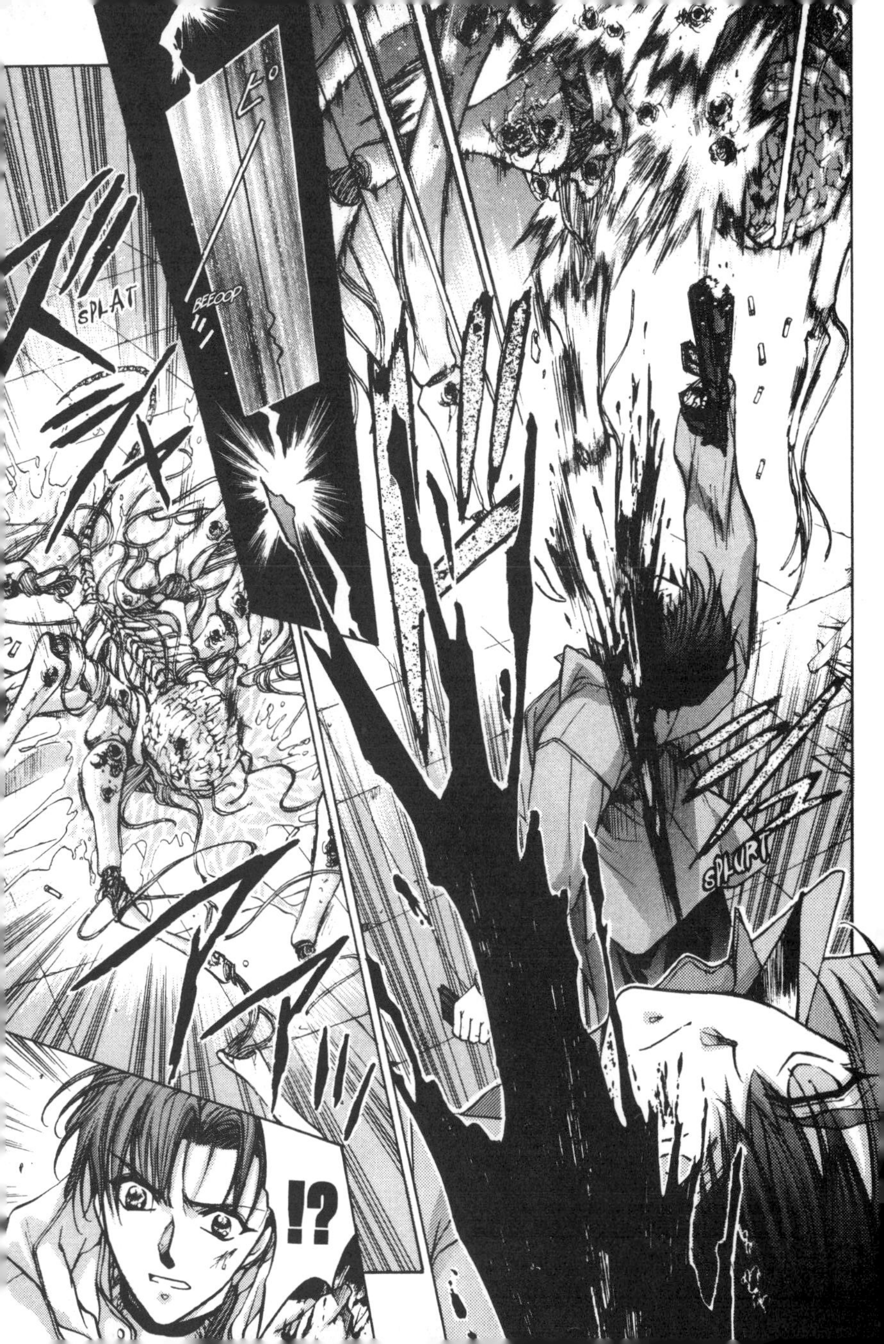
SPLURT
BEEOOP
SPLAT
!?

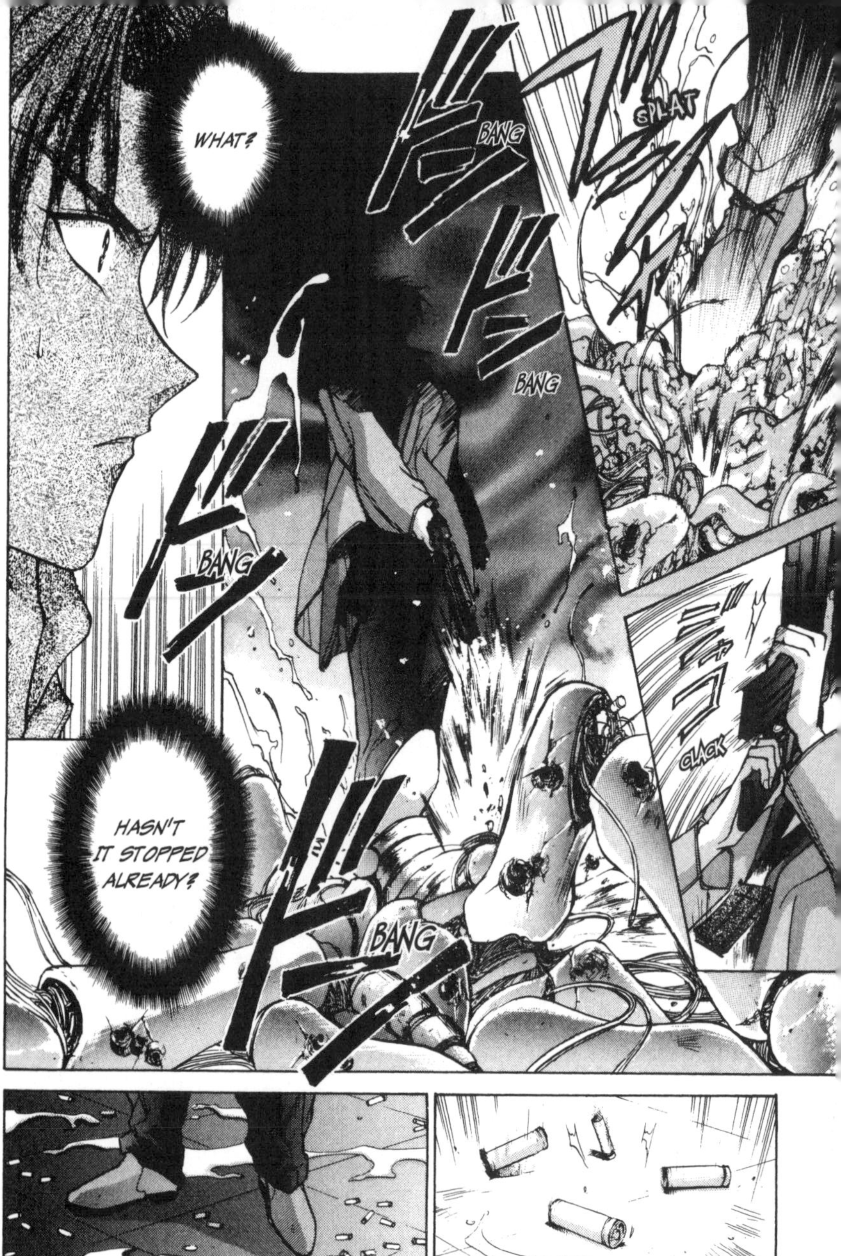
SPLAT
BANG
BANG
CLACK
WHAT?
BANG
HASN'T IT STOPPED ALREADY?
BANG

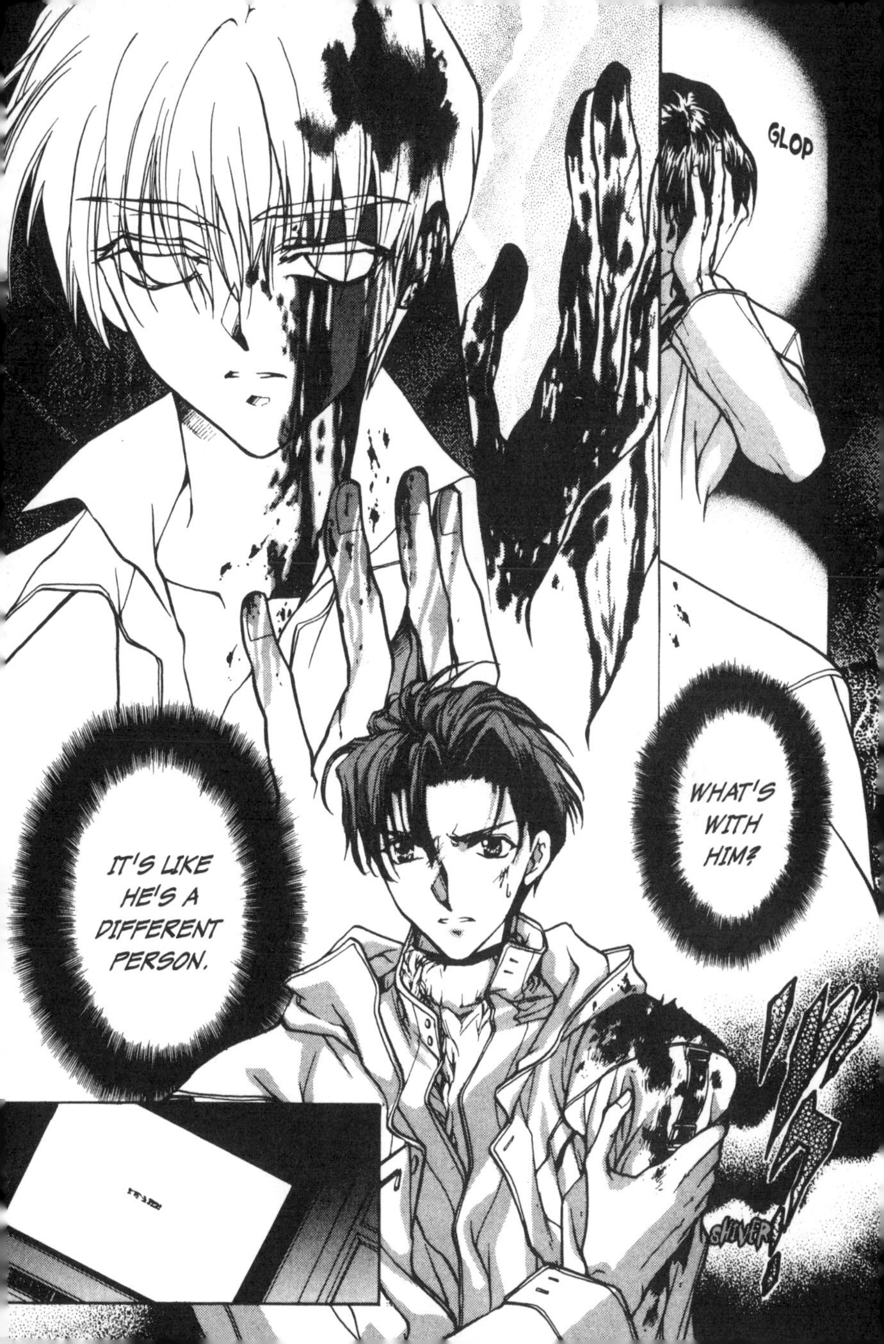
GLOP
WHAT'S WITH HIM?
IT'S LIKE HE'S A DIFFERENT PERSON.
SHIVER

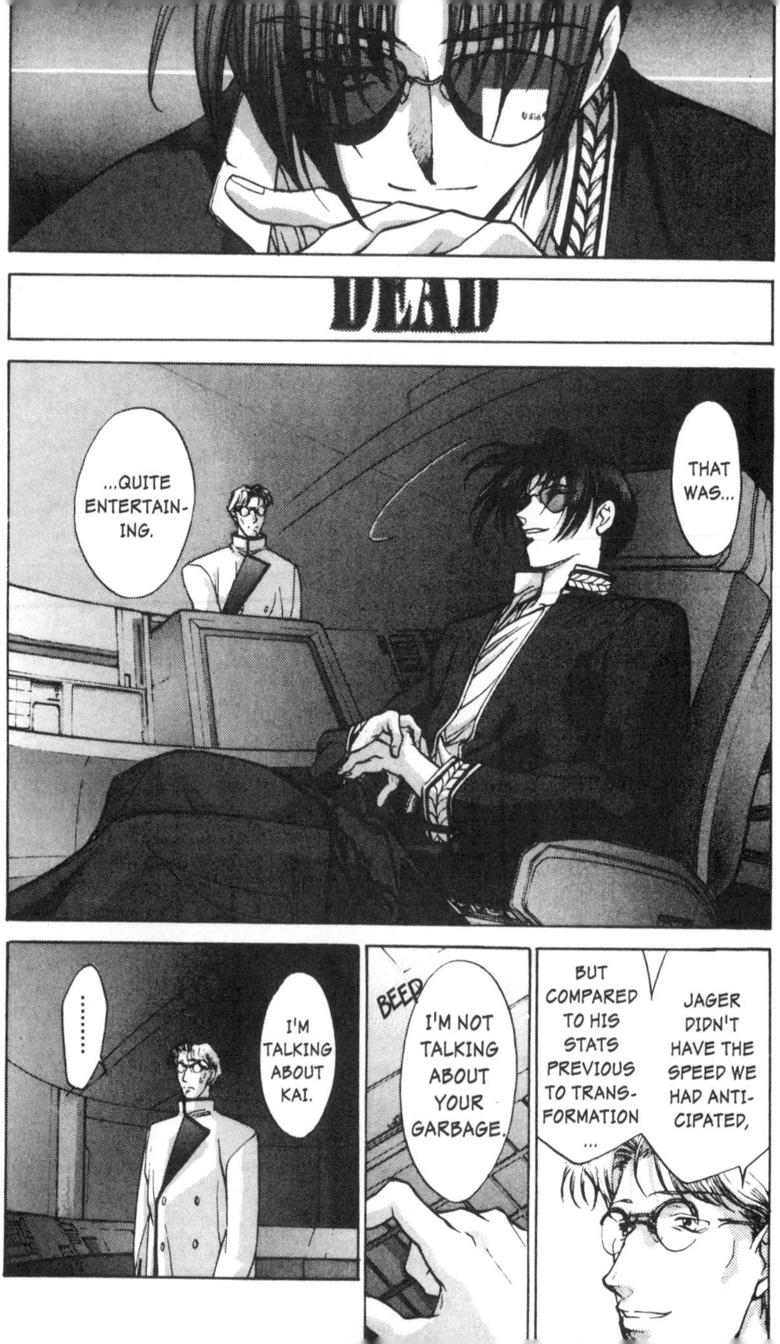
DEAD
THAT WAS...
...QUITE ENTERTAINING.
JAGER DIDN'T HAVE THE SPEED WE HAD ANTICIPATED,
BUT COMPARED TO HIS STATS PREVIOUS TO TRANSFORMATION ...
BEEP
I'M NOT TALKING ABOUT YOUR GARBAGE.
I'M TALKING ABOUT KAI.
....

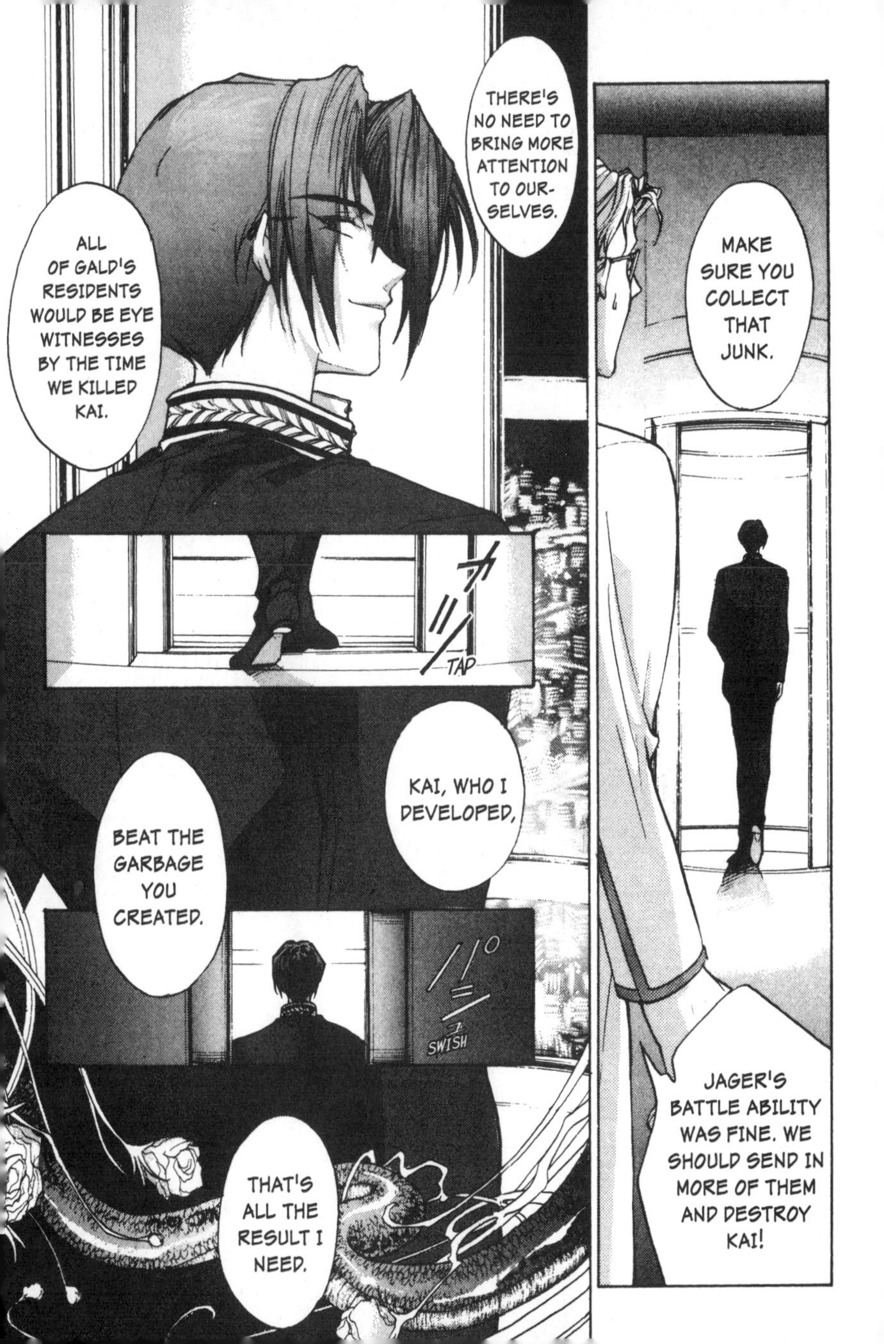
MAKE SURE YOU COLLECT THAT JUNK.
JAGER'S BATTLE ABILITY WAS FINE. WE SHOULD SEND IN MORE OF THEM AND DESTROY KAI!
THERE'S NO NEED TO BRING MORE ATTENTION TO OUR-SELVES.
ALL OF GALD'S RESIDENTS WOULD BE EYE WITNESSES BY THE TIME WE KILLED KAI.
TAP
KAI, WHO I DEVELOPED,
BEAT THE GARBAGE YOU CREATED.
SWISH
THAT'S ALL THE RESULT I NEED.

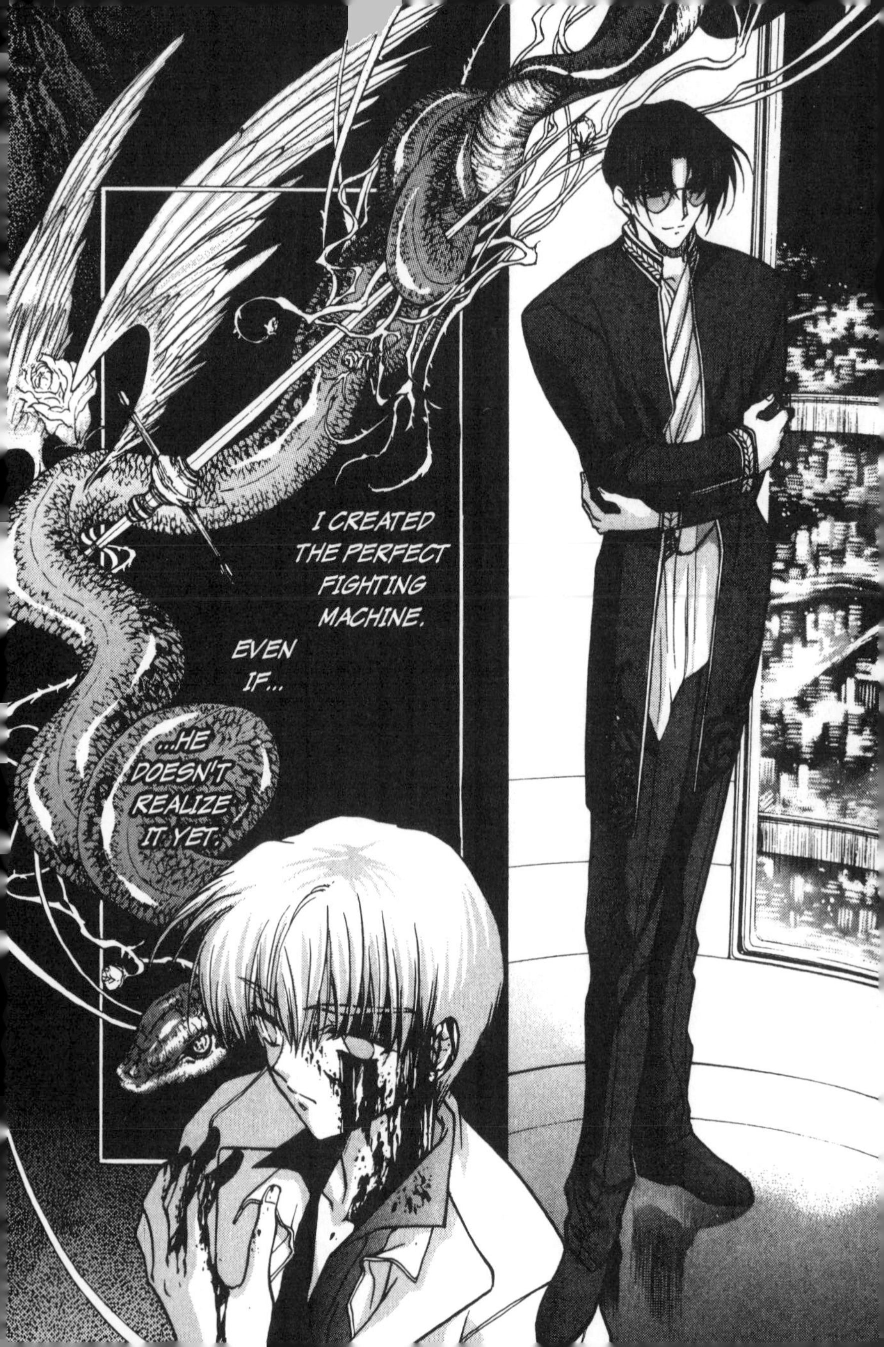
I CREATED THE PERFECT FIGHTING MACHINE.
EVEN IF...
...HE DOESN'T REALIZE IT YET.

CHAPTER 10 Buridan's Mule

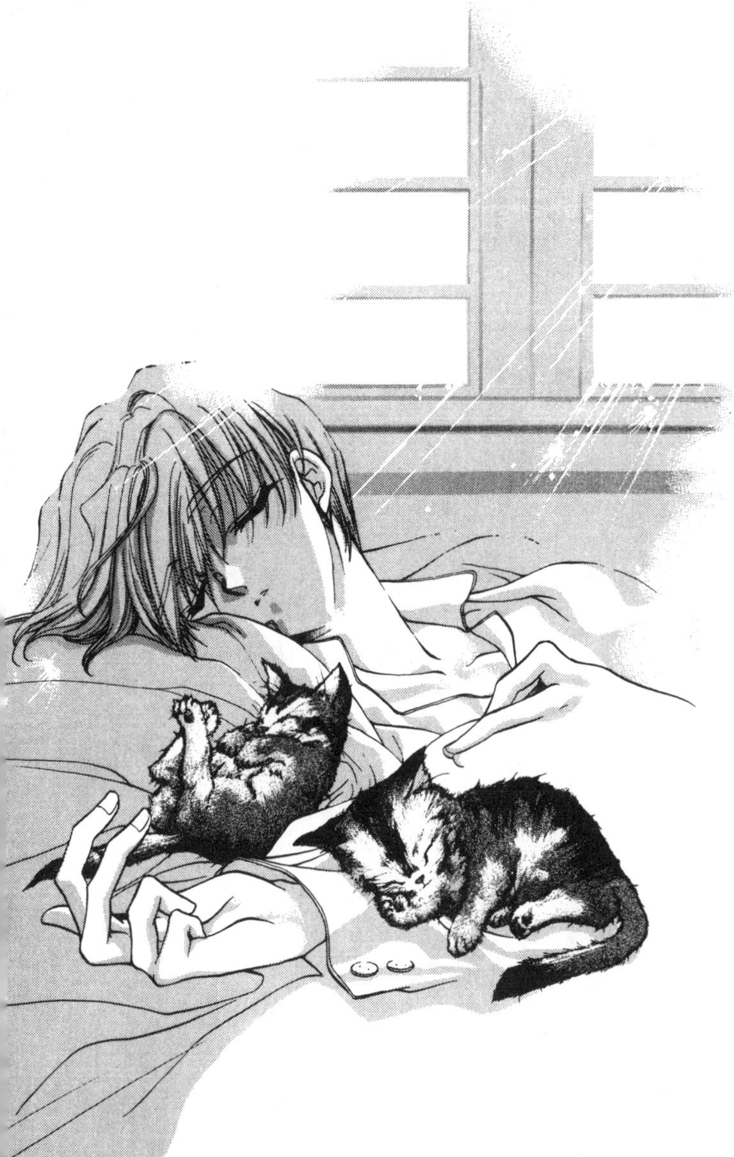

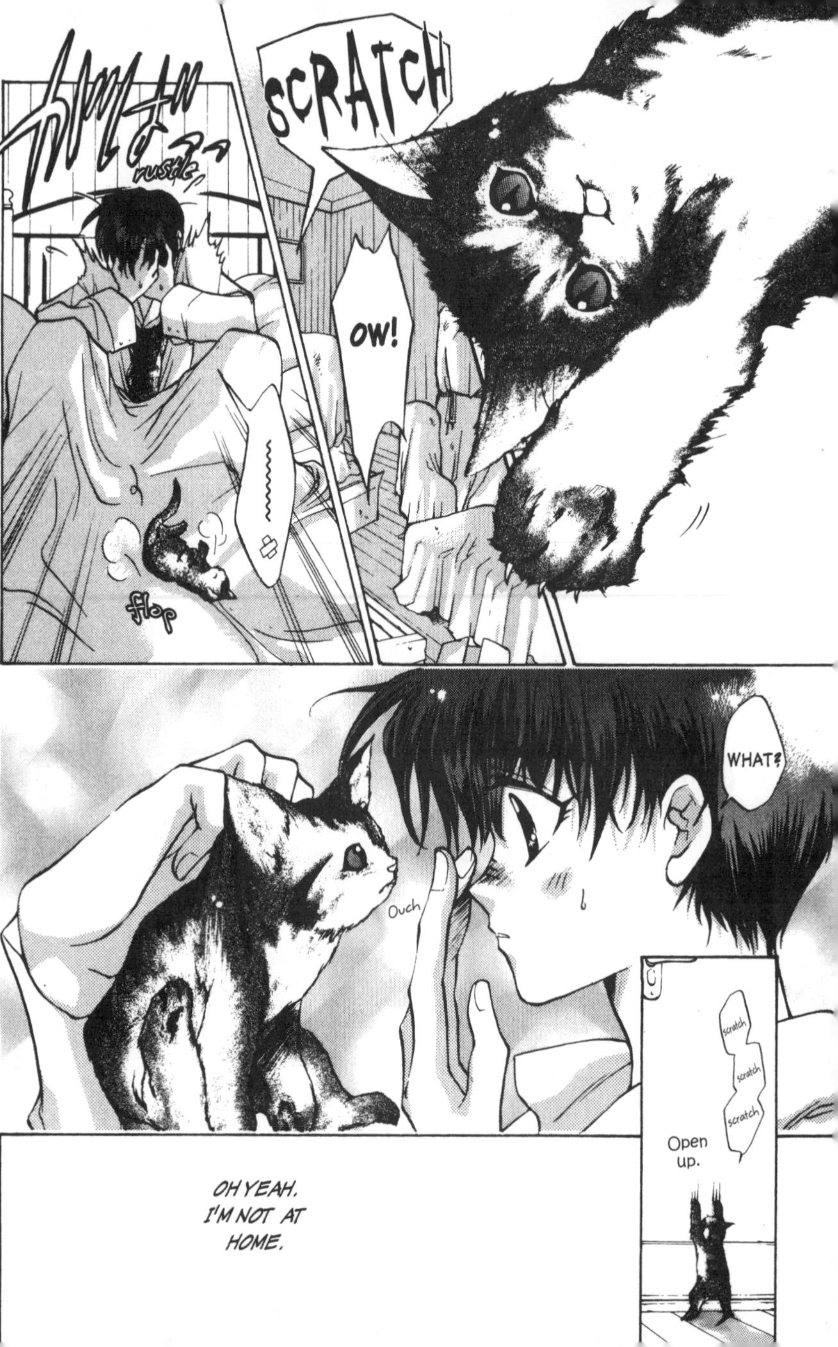
SCRATCH
OW!
rustle
flop
WHAT?
Ouch
scratch
scratch
scratch
Open up.
OH YEAH. I'M NOT AT HOME.

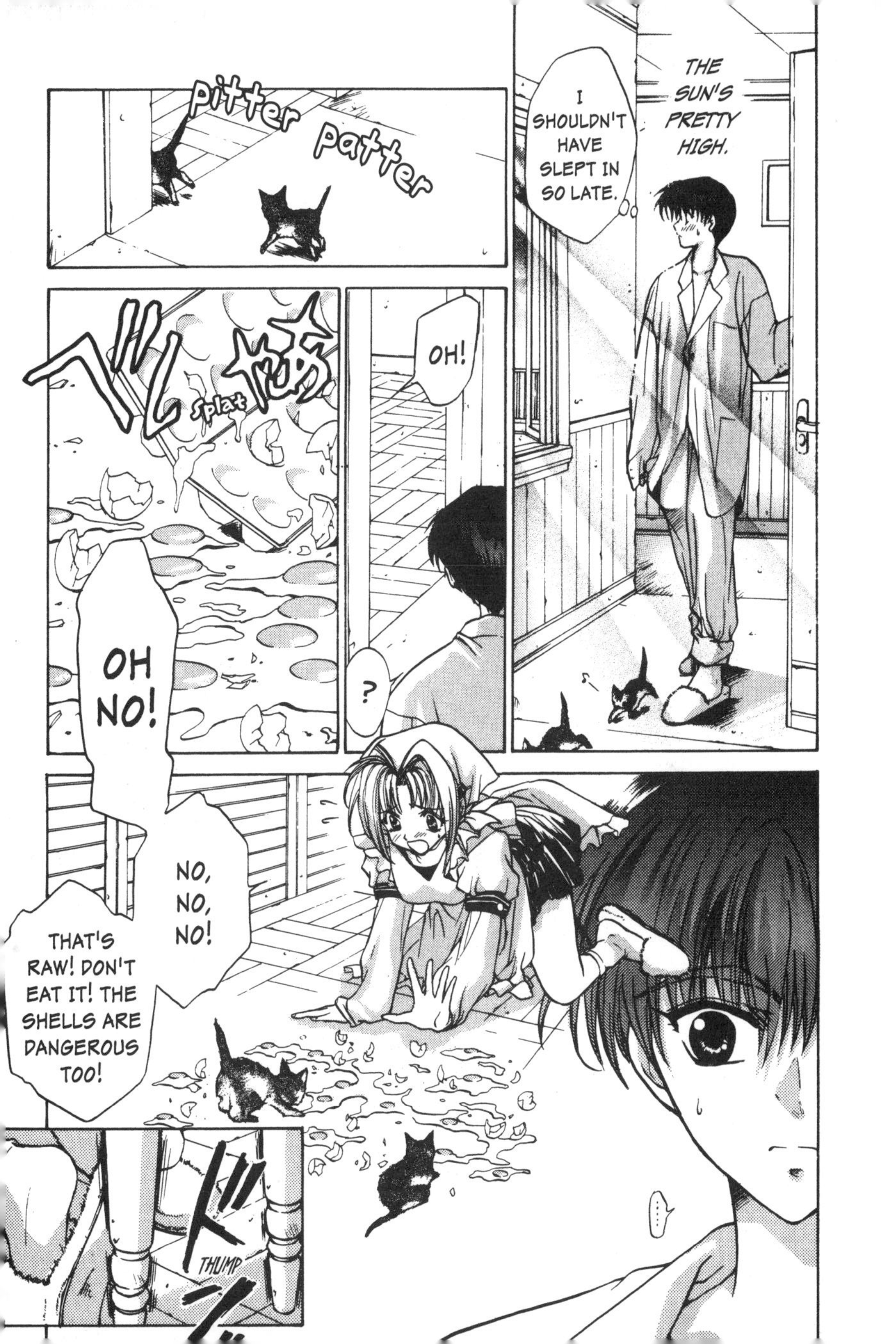
THE SUN'S PRETTY HIGH.
I SHOULDN'T HAVE SLEPT IN SO LATE.
pitter patter
OH!
?
splat
OH NO!
NO, NO, NO!
THAT'S RAW! DON'T EAT IT! THE SHELLS ARE DANGEROUS TOO!
...
THUMP

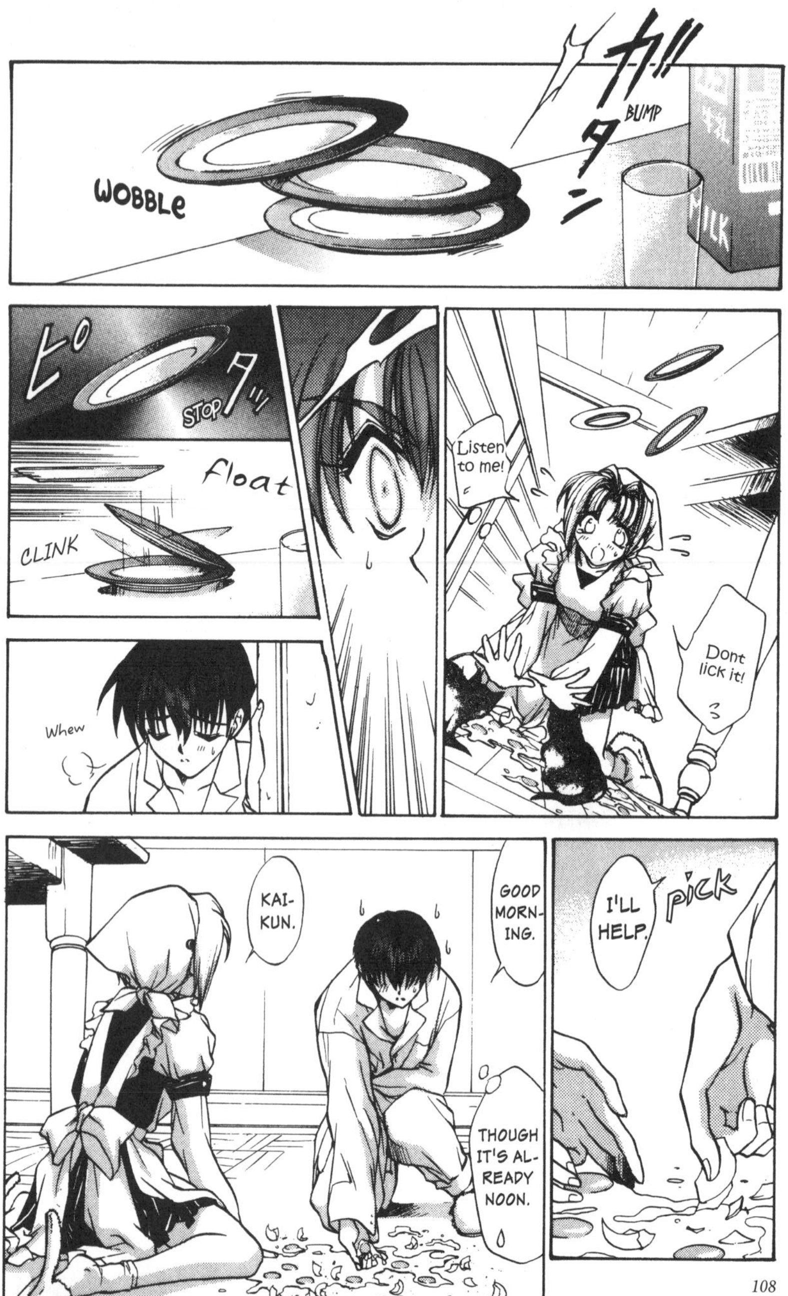
ガ!!タン
BUMP
WOBBLE
Listen to me!
Dont lick it!
ピタッ
STOP
float
CLINK
Whew
I'LL HELP.
pick
GOOD MORNING.
KAI-KUN.
THOUGH IT'S ALREADY NOON.

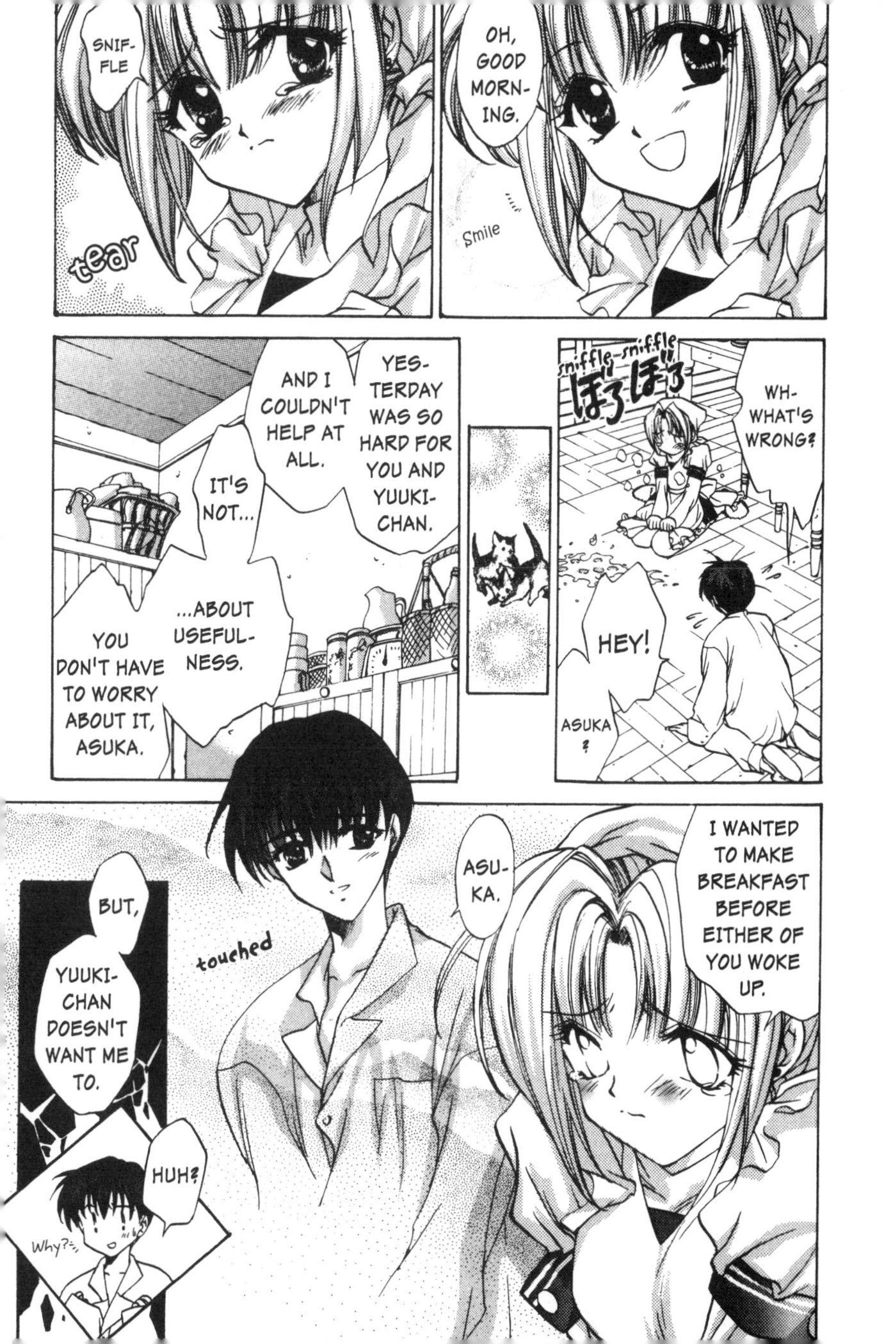
OH, GOOD MORN-ING.
Smile
SNIF-FLE
tear
sniffle-sniffle
ぼろぼろ
WH-WHAT'S WRONG?
HEY!
ASUKA?
YES-TERDAY WAS SO HARD FOR YOU AND YUUKI-CHAN.
AND I COULDN'T HELP AT ALL.
IT'S NOT...
...ABOUT USEFUL-NESS.
YOU DON'T HAVE TO WORRY ABOUT IT, ASUKA.
I WANTED TO MAKE BREAKFAST BEFORE EITHER OF YOU WOKE UP.
ASU-KA.
touched
BUT,
YUUKI-CHAN DOESN'T WANT ME TO.
HUH?
Why?

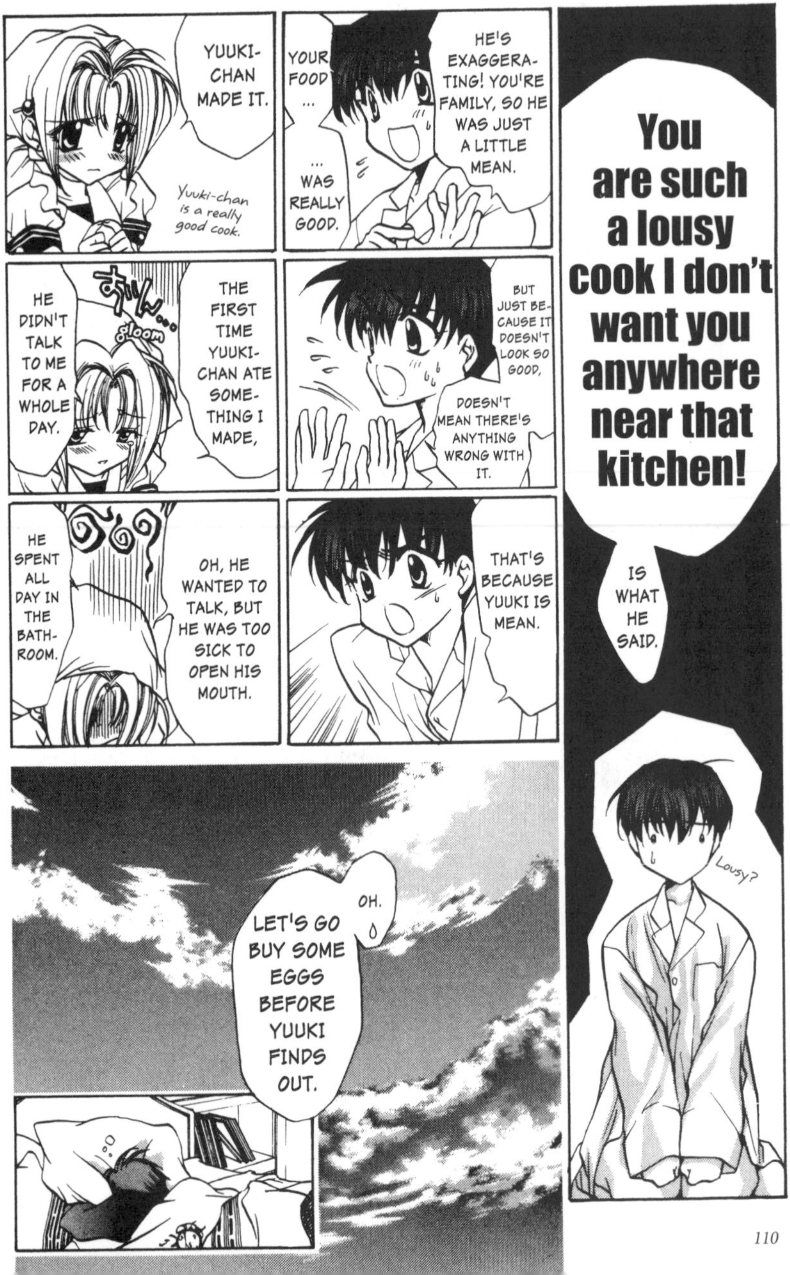
You are such a lousy cook I don't want you anywhere near that kitchen!
IS WHAT HE SAID.
Lousy?
HE'S EXAGGERATING! YOU'RE FAMILY, SO HE WAS JUST A LITTLE MEAN.
YOUR FOOD ...
... WAS REALLY GOOD.
YUUKI-CHAN MADE IT.
Yuuki-chan is a really good cook.
BUT JUST BECAUSE IT DOESN'T LOOK SO GOOD,
DOESN'T MEAN THERE'S ANYTHING WRONG WITH IT.
THE FIRST TIME YUUKI-CHAN ATE SOMETHING I MADE,
gloom
HE DIDN'T TALK TO ME FOR A WHOLE DAY.
THAT'S BECAUSE YUUKI IS MEAN.
OH, HE WANTED TO TALK, BUT HE WAS TOO SICK TO OPEN HIS MOUTH.
HE SPENT ALL DAY IN THE BATHROOM.
OH.
LET'S GO BUY SOME EGGS BEFORE YUUKI FINDS OUT.

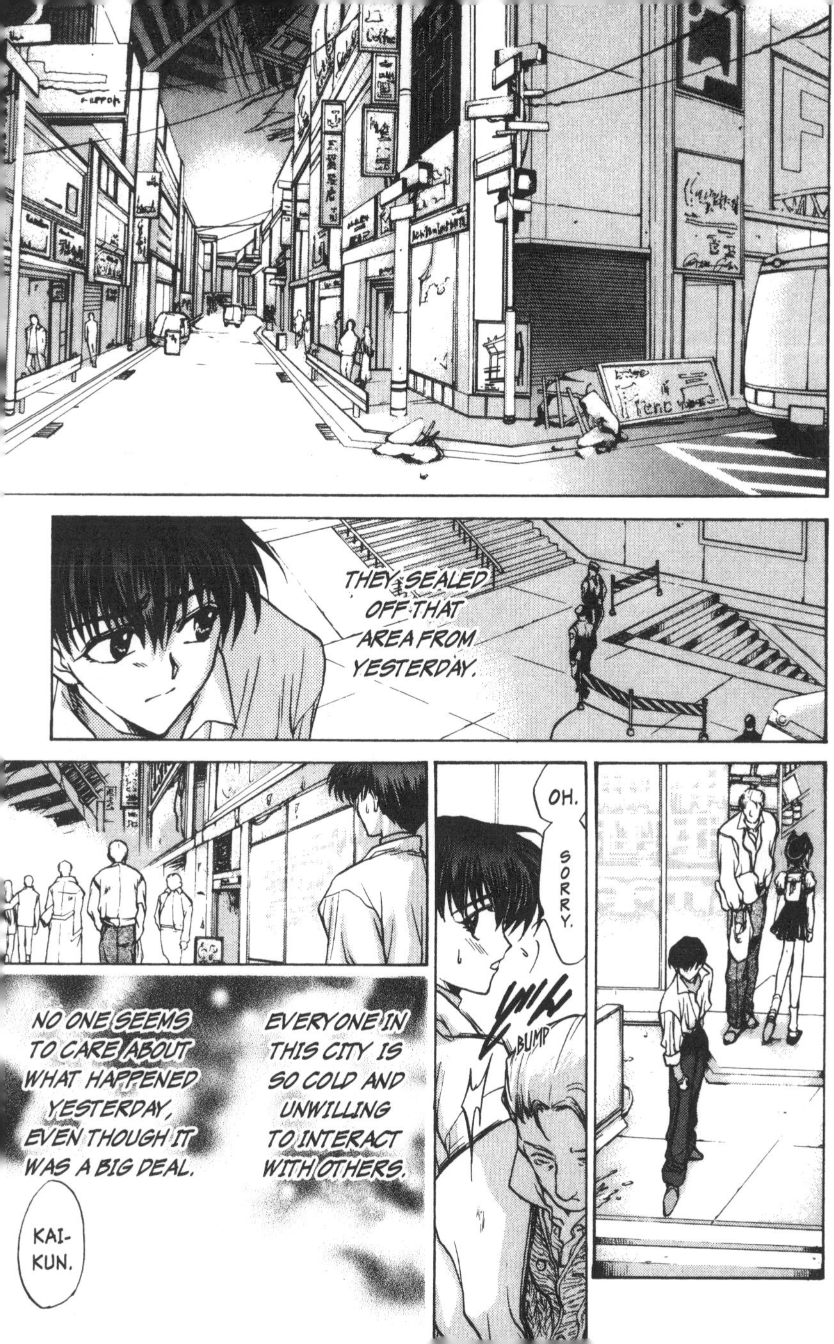
THEY SEALED OFF THAT AREA FROM YESTERDAY.
OH.
SORRY.
BUMP
EVERYONE IN THIS CITY IS SO COLD AND UNWILLING TO INTERACT WITH OTHERS.
NO ONE SEEMS TO CARE ABOUT WHAT HAPPENED YESTERDAY, EVEN THOUGH IT WAS A BIG DEAL.
KAI-KUN.

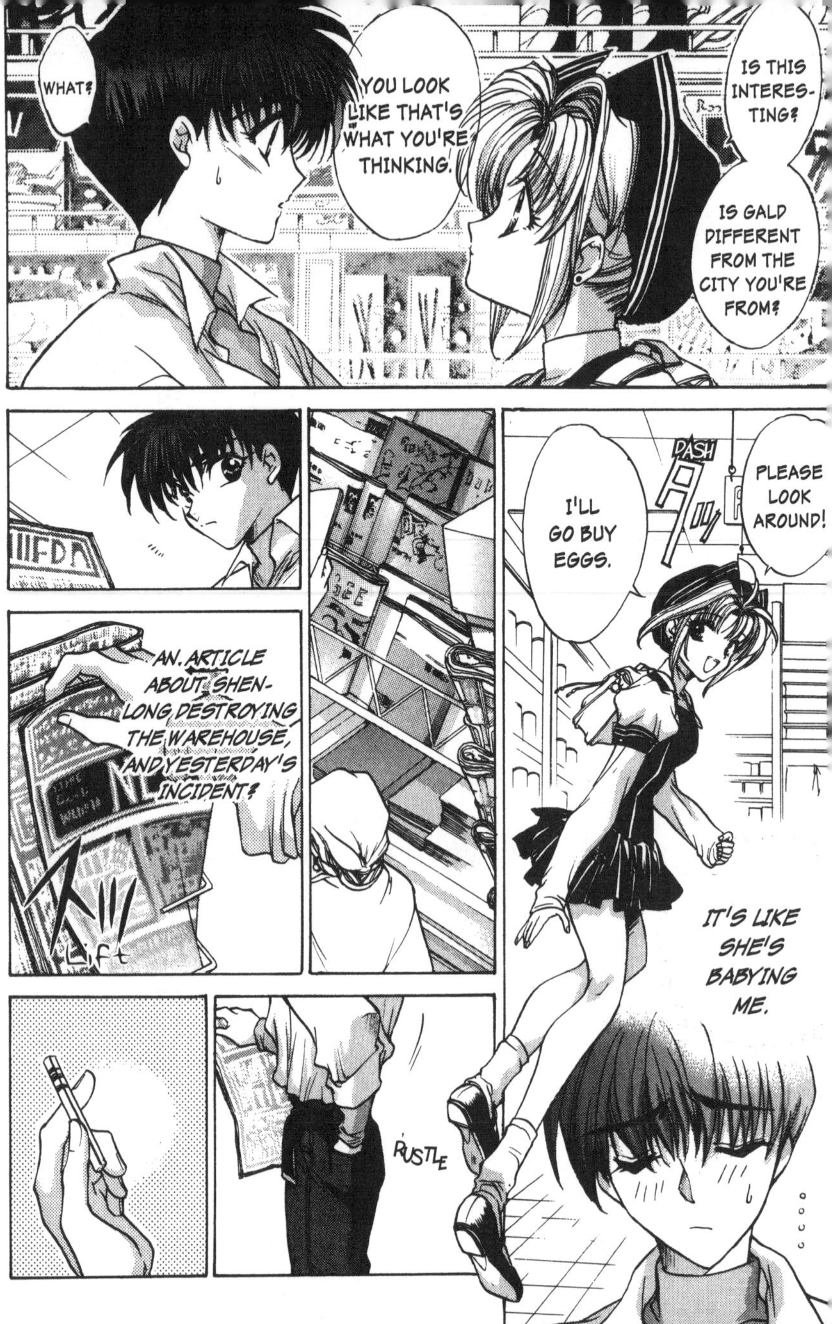
IS THIS INTERES-TING?
IS GALD DIFFERENT FROM THE CITY YOU'RE FROM?
YOU LOOK LIKE THAT'S WHAT YOU'RE THINKING.
WHAT?
PLEASE LOOK AROUND!
DASH
I'LL GO BUY EGGS.
IT'S LIKE SHE'S BABYING ME.
....
AN. ARTICLE ABOUT SHEN-LONG DESTROYING THE WAREHOUSE, ANDYESTERDAY'S INCIDENT?
Lift
RUSTLE

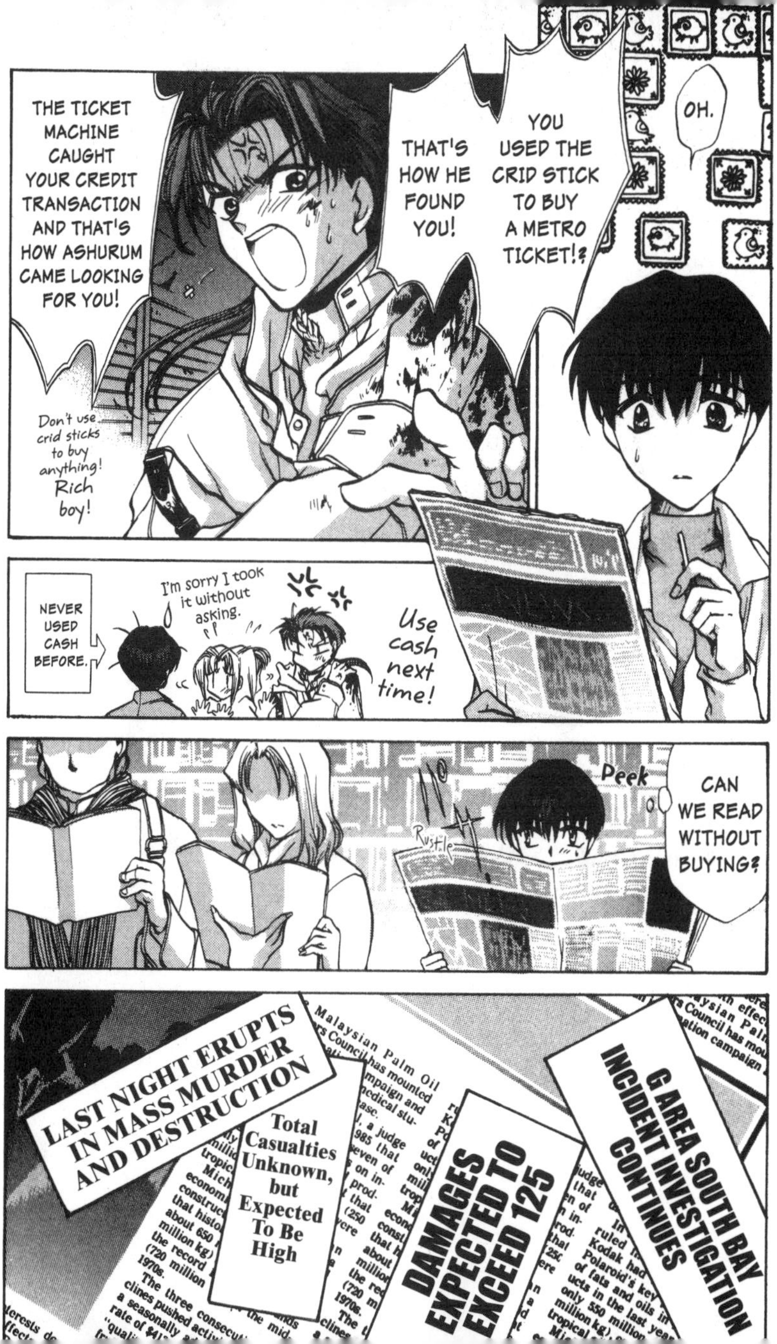
OH.
YOU USED THE CRID STICK TO BUY A METRO TICKET!?
THAT'S HOW HE FOUND YOU!
THE TICKET MACHINE CAUGHT YOUR CREDIT TRANSACTION AND THAT'S HOW ASHURUM CAME LOOKING FOR YOU!
Don't use crid sticks to buy anything! Rich boy!
Use cash next time!
I'm sorry I took it without asking.
NEVER USED CASH BEFORE.
CAN WE READ WITHOUT BUYING?
Peek
Rustle
G AREA SOUTH BAY INCIDENT INVESTIGATION CONTINUES
DAMAGES EXPECTED TO EXCEED 125
Total Casualties Unknown, but Expected To Be High
LAST NIGHT ERUPTS IN MASS MURDER AND DESTRUCTION

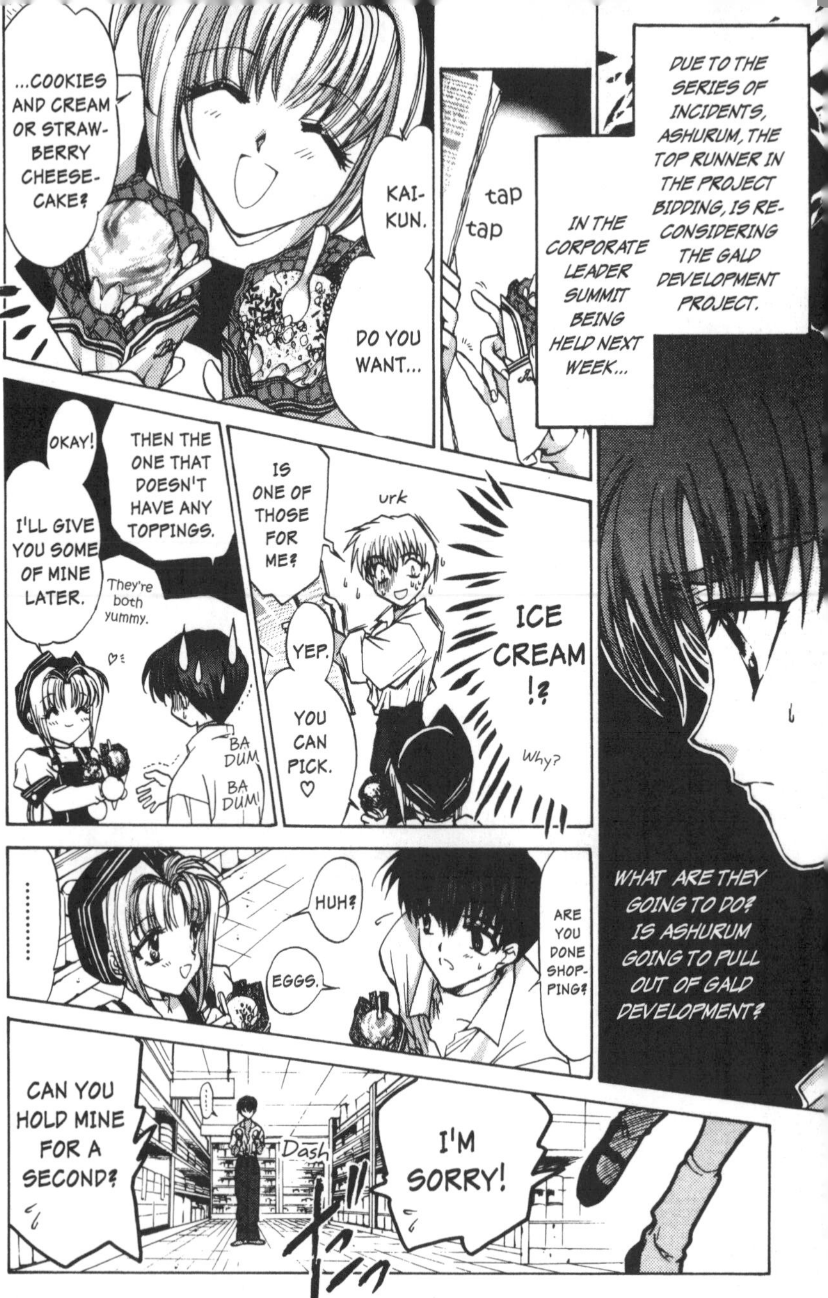
DUE TO THE SERIES OF INCIDENTS, ASHURUM, THE TOP RUNNER IN THE PROJECT BIDDING, IS RECONSIDERING THE GALD DEVELOPMENT PROJECT.
IN THE CORPORATE LEADER SUMMIT BEING HELD NEXT WEEK...
WHAT ARE THEY GOING TO DO? IS ASHURUM GOING TO PULL OUT OF GALD DEVELOPMENT?
tap
tap
KAI-KUN.
DO YOU WANT...
...COOKIES AND CREAM OR STRAWBERRY CHEESECAKE?
ICE CREAM!?
urk
IS ONE OF THOSE FOR ME?
YEP.
YOU CAN PICK. ♡
Why?
THEN THE ONE THAT DOESN'T HAVE ANY TOPPINGS.
OKAY!
I'LL GIVE YOU SOME OF MINE LATER.
They're both yummy.
BA DUM
BA DUM
ARE YOU DONE SHOPPING?
HUH?
EGGS.
....
I'M SORRY!
Dash
CAN YOU HOLD MINE FOR A SECOND?

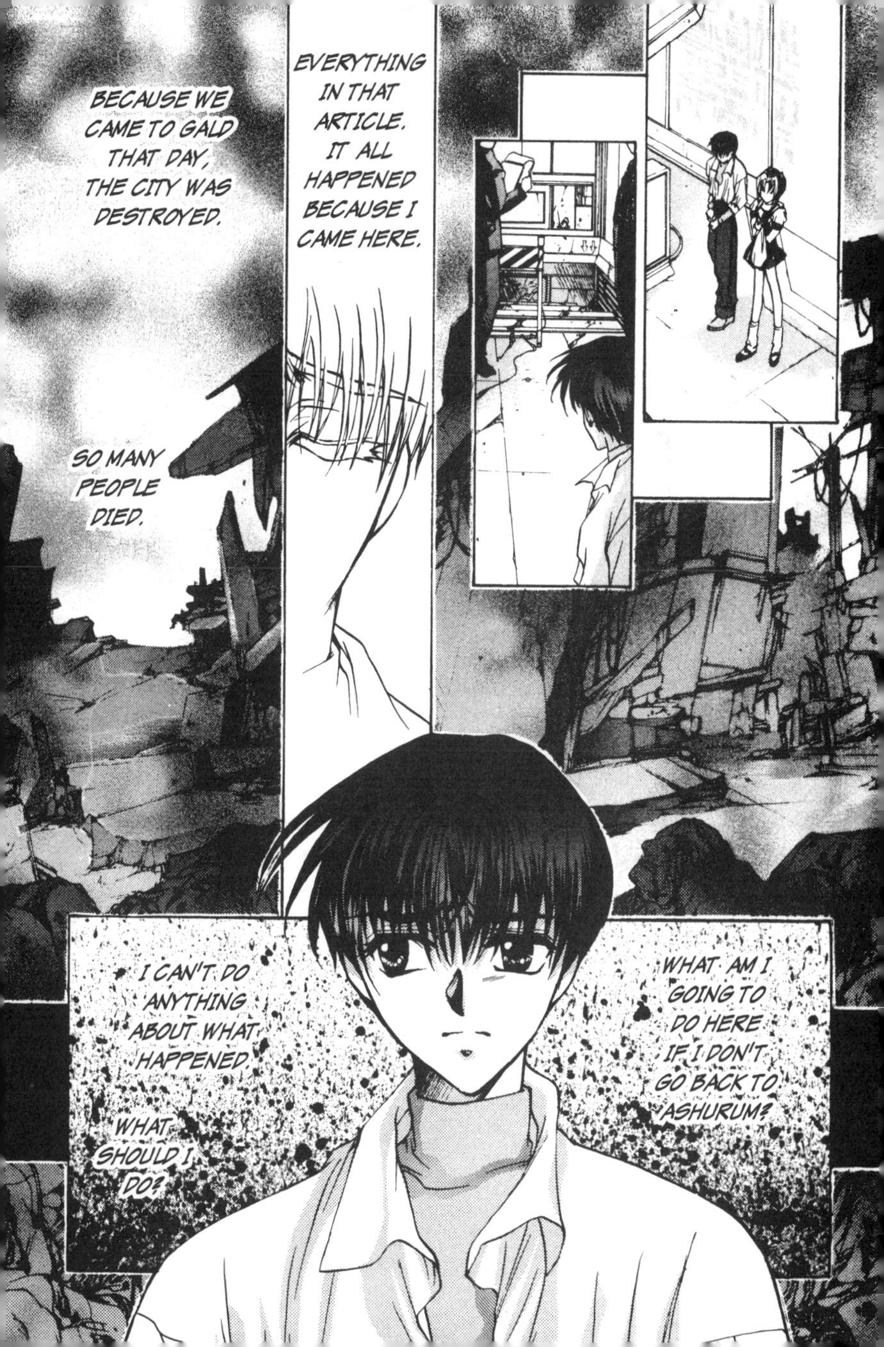
EVERYTHING IN THAT ARTICLE. IT ALL HAPPENED BECAUSE I CAME HERE.
BECAUSE WE CAME TO GALD THAT DAY, THE CITY WAS DESTROYED.
SO MANY PEOPLE DIED.
WHAT AM I GOING TO DO HERE IF I DON'T GO BACK TO ASHURUM?
I CAN'T DO ANYTHING ABOUT WHAT HAPPENED.
WHAT SHOULD I DO?

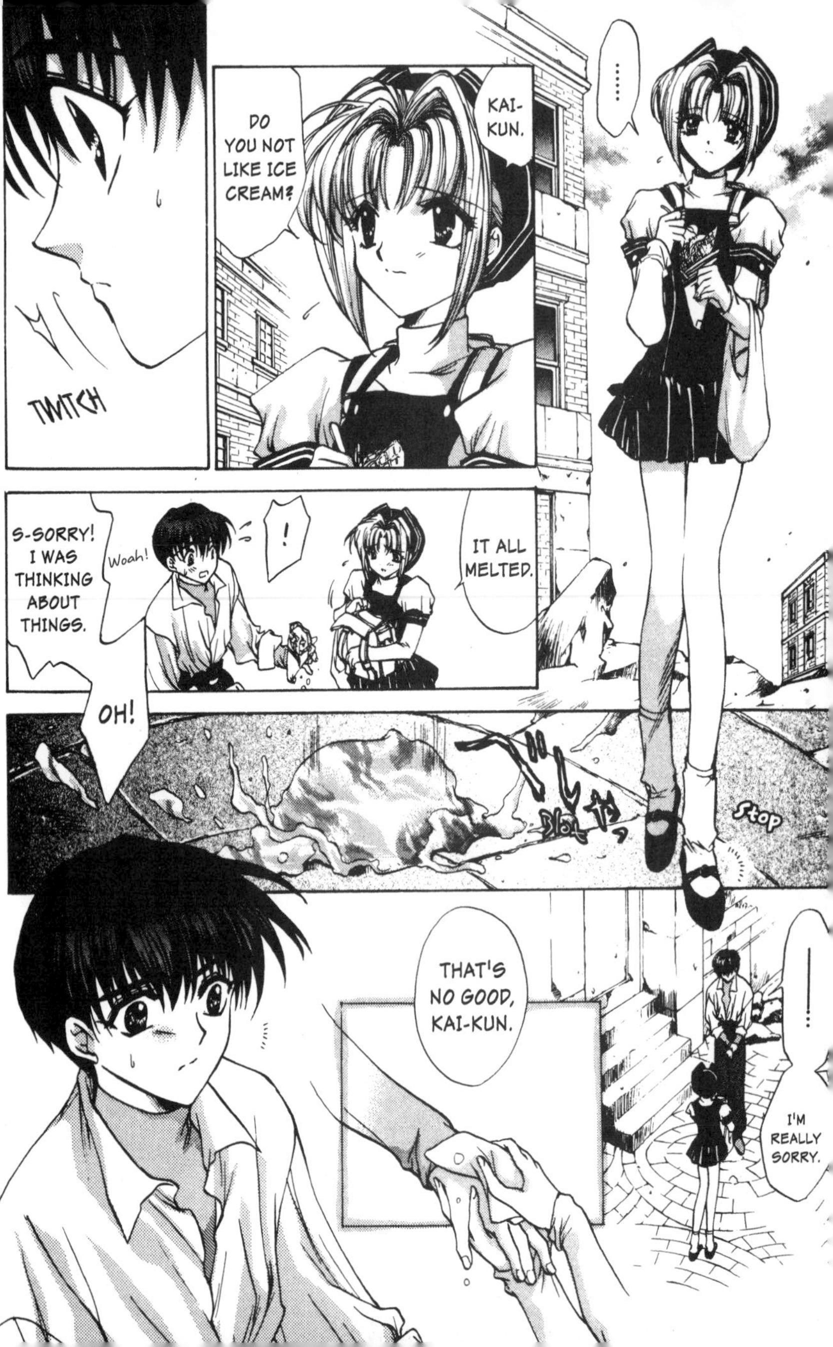
......
Stop
KAI-KUN.
DO YOU NOT LIKE ICE CREAM?
TWITCH
IT ALL MELTED.
!
S-SORRY! I WAS THINKING ABOUT THINGS.
Woah!
OH!
......
I'M REALLY SORRY.
THAT'S NO GOOD, KAI-KUN.

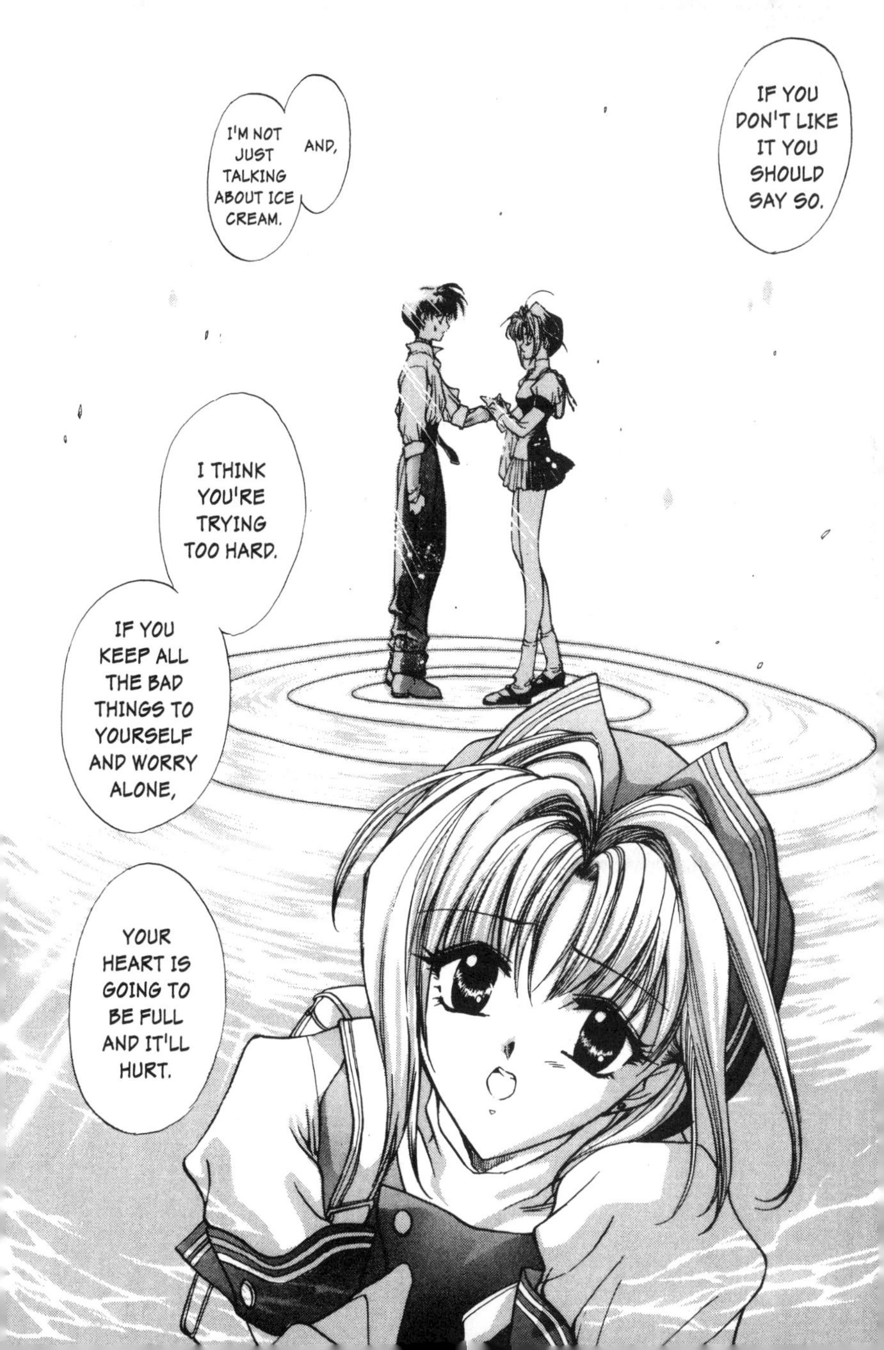
IF YOU DON'T LIKE IT YOU SHOULD SAY SO.
AND,
I'M NOT JUST TALKING ABOUT ICE CREAM.
I THINK YOU'RE TRYING TOO HARD.
IF YOU KEEP ALL THE BAD THINGS TO YOURSELF AND WORRY ALONE,
YOUR HEART IS GOING TO BE FULL AND IT'LL HURT.

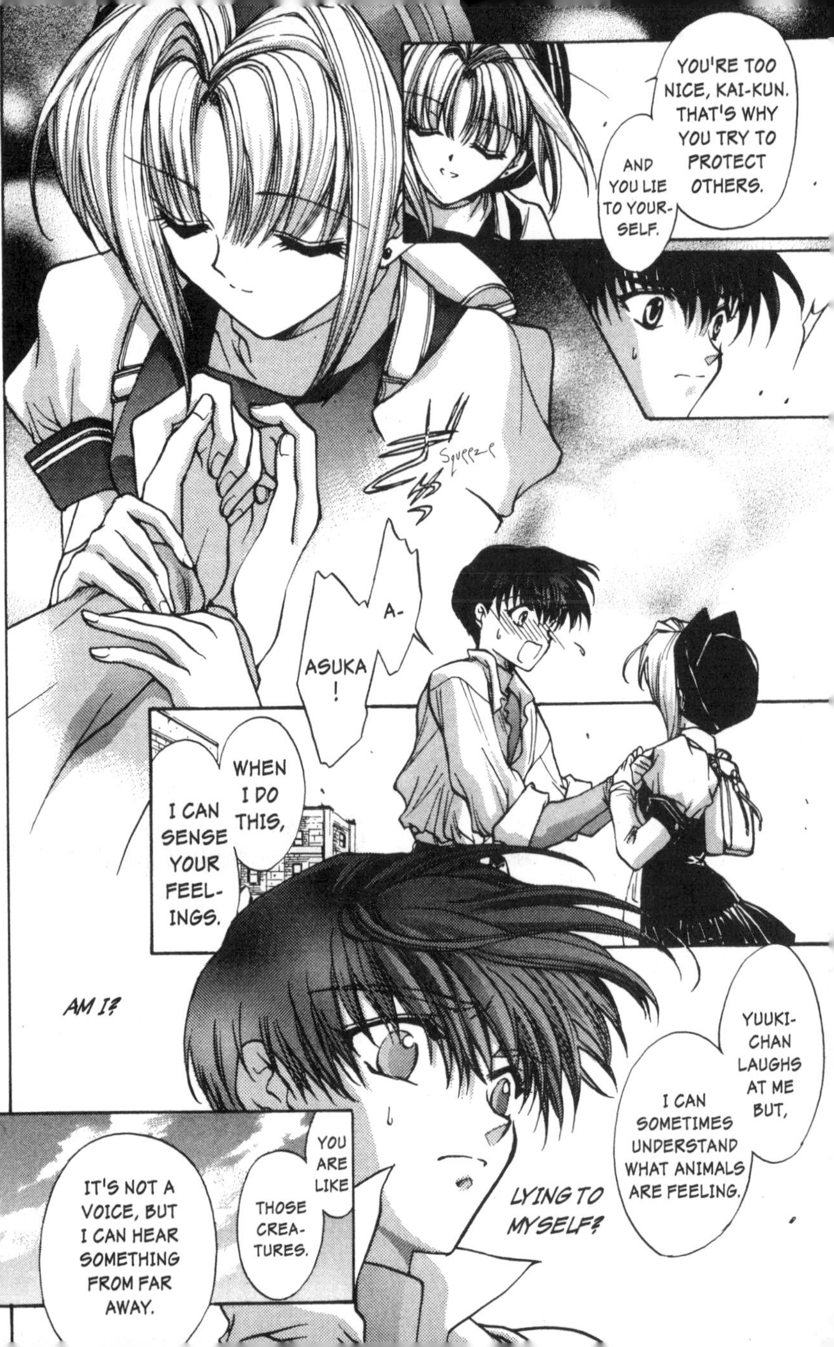
YOU'RE TOO NICE, KAI-KUN. THAT'S WHY YOU TRY TO PROTECT OTHERS.
AND YOU LIE TO YOURSELF.
Squeeze
A- ASUKA!
WHEN I DO THIS, I CAN SENSE YOUR FEELINGS.
YUUKI-CHAN LAUGHS AT ME BUT, I CAN SOMETIMES UNDERSTAND WHAT ANIMALS ARE FEELING.
LYING TO MYSELF?
AM I?
YOU ARE LIKE THOSE CREATURES.
IT'S NOT A VOICE, BUT I CAN HEAR SOMETHING FROM FAR AWAY.

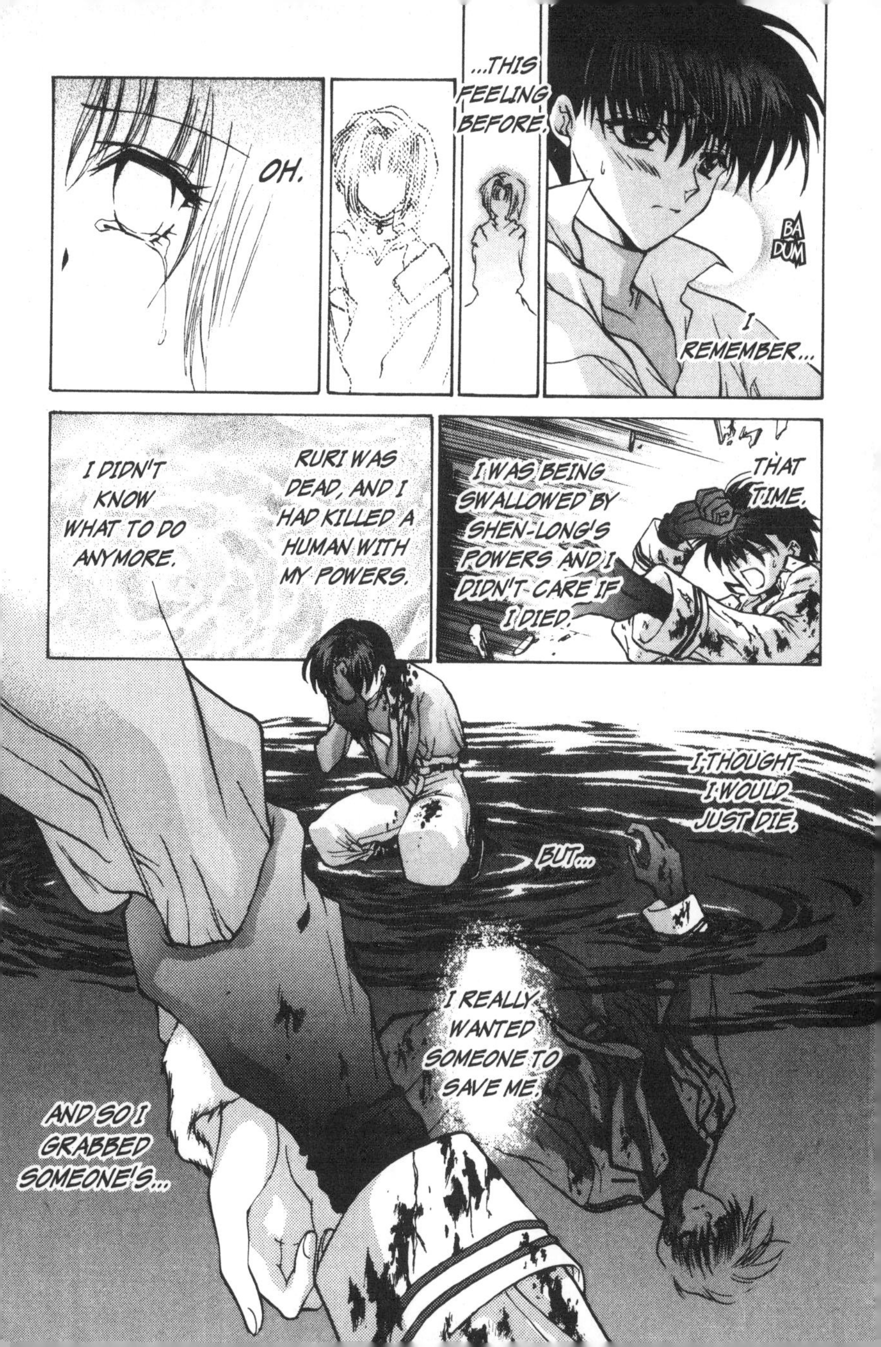
BA DUM
I REMEMBER...
...THIS FEELING BEFORE.
OH.
THAT TIME.
I WAS BEING SWALLOWED BY SHEN-LONG'S POWERS AND I DIDN'T CARE IF I DIED.
RURI WAS DEAD, AND I HAD KILLED A HUMAN WITH MY POWERS.
I DIDN'T KNOW WHAT TO DO ANYMORE.
I THOUGHT I WOULD JUST DIE.
BUT...
I REALLY WANTED SOMEONE TO SAVE ME.
AND SO I GRABBED SOMEONE'S...

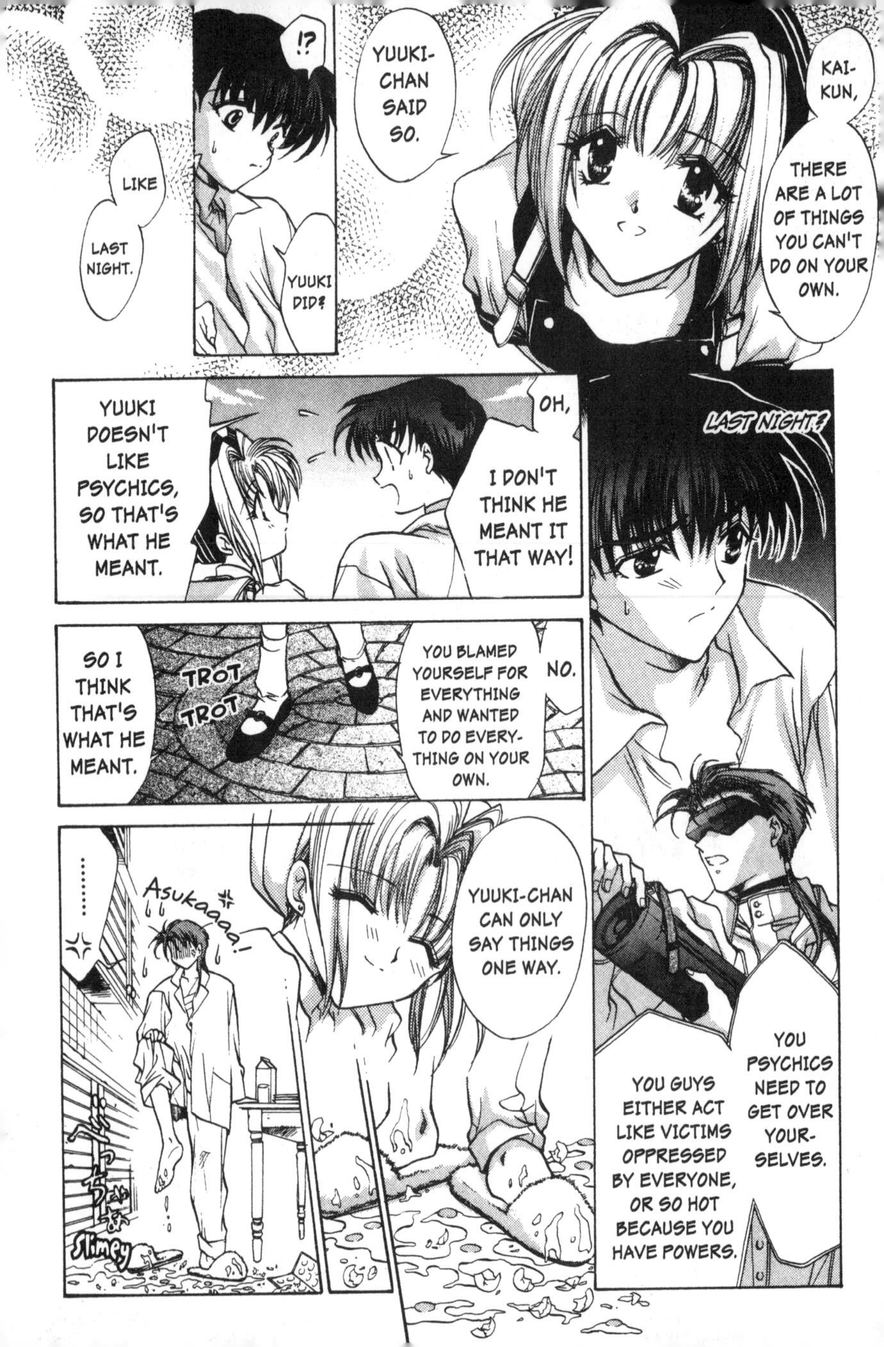
KAI-KUN,
THERE ARE A LOT OF THINGS YOU CAN'T DO ON YOUR OWN.
YUUKI-CHAN SAID SO.
!?
YUUKI DID?
LIKE
LAST NIGHT.
LAST NIGHT?
YOU PSYCHICS NEED TO GET OVER YOUR-SELVES.
YOU GUYS EITHER ACT LIKE VICTIMS OPPRESSED BY EVERYONE, OR SO HOT BECAUSE YOU HAVE POWERS.
OH,
I DON'T THINK HE MEANT IT THAT WAY!
YUUKI DOESN'T LIKE PSYCHICS, SO THAT'S WHAT HE MEANT.
NO.
YOU BLAMED YOURSELF FOR EVERYTHING AND WANTED TO DO EVERY-THING ON YOUR OWN.
TROT TROT
SO I THINK THAT'S WHAT HE MEANT.
YUUKI-CHAN CAN ONLY SAY THINGS ONE WAY.
Asukaaaa!
....
Slimey

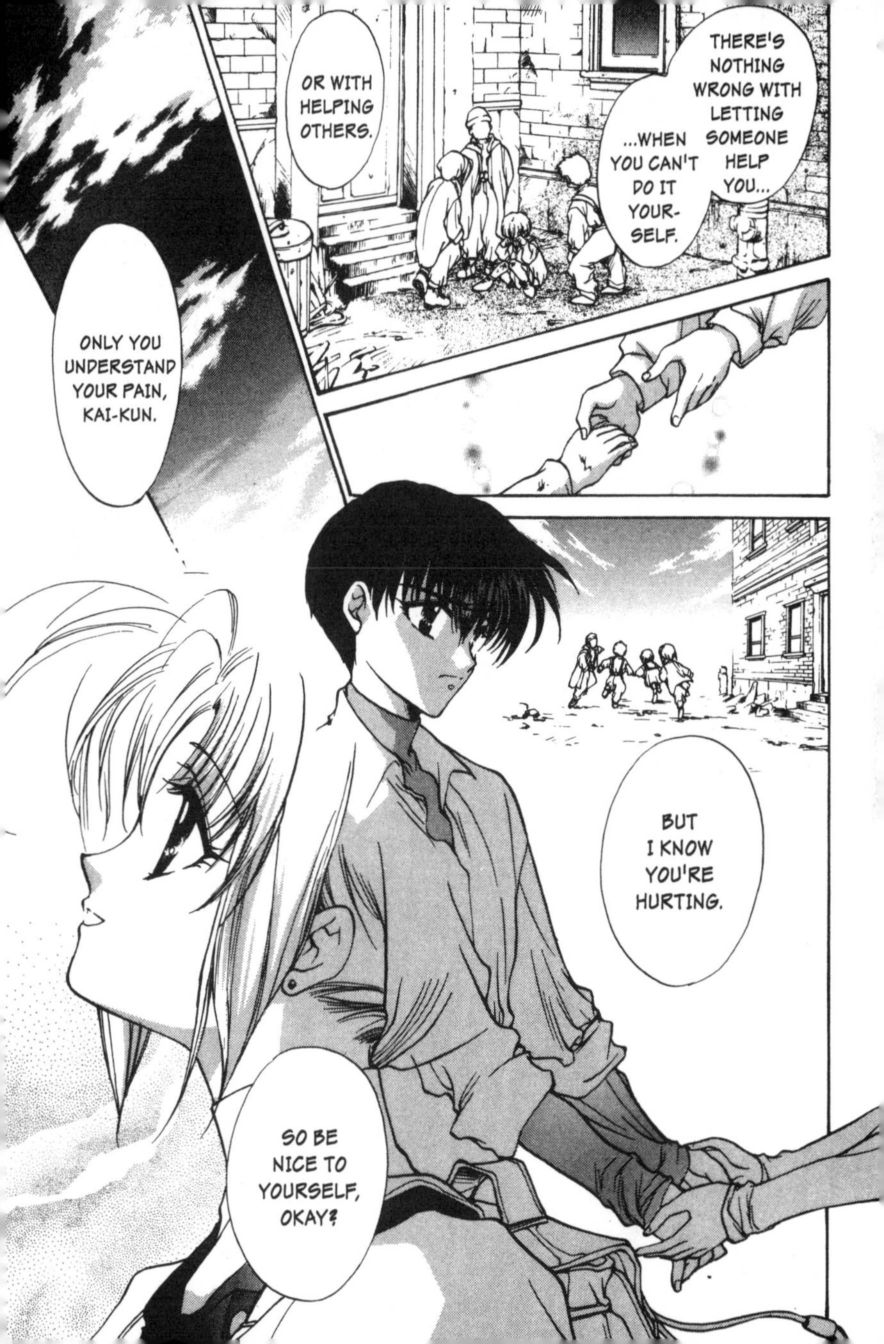
THERE'S NOTHING WRONG WITH LETTING SOMEONE HELP YOU...
...WHEN YOU CAN'T DO IT YOUR-SELF.
OR WITH HELPING OTHERS.
ONLY YOU UNDERSTAND YOUR PAIN, KAI-KUN.
BUT I KNOW YOU'RE HURTING.
SO BE NICE TO YOURSELF, OKAY?

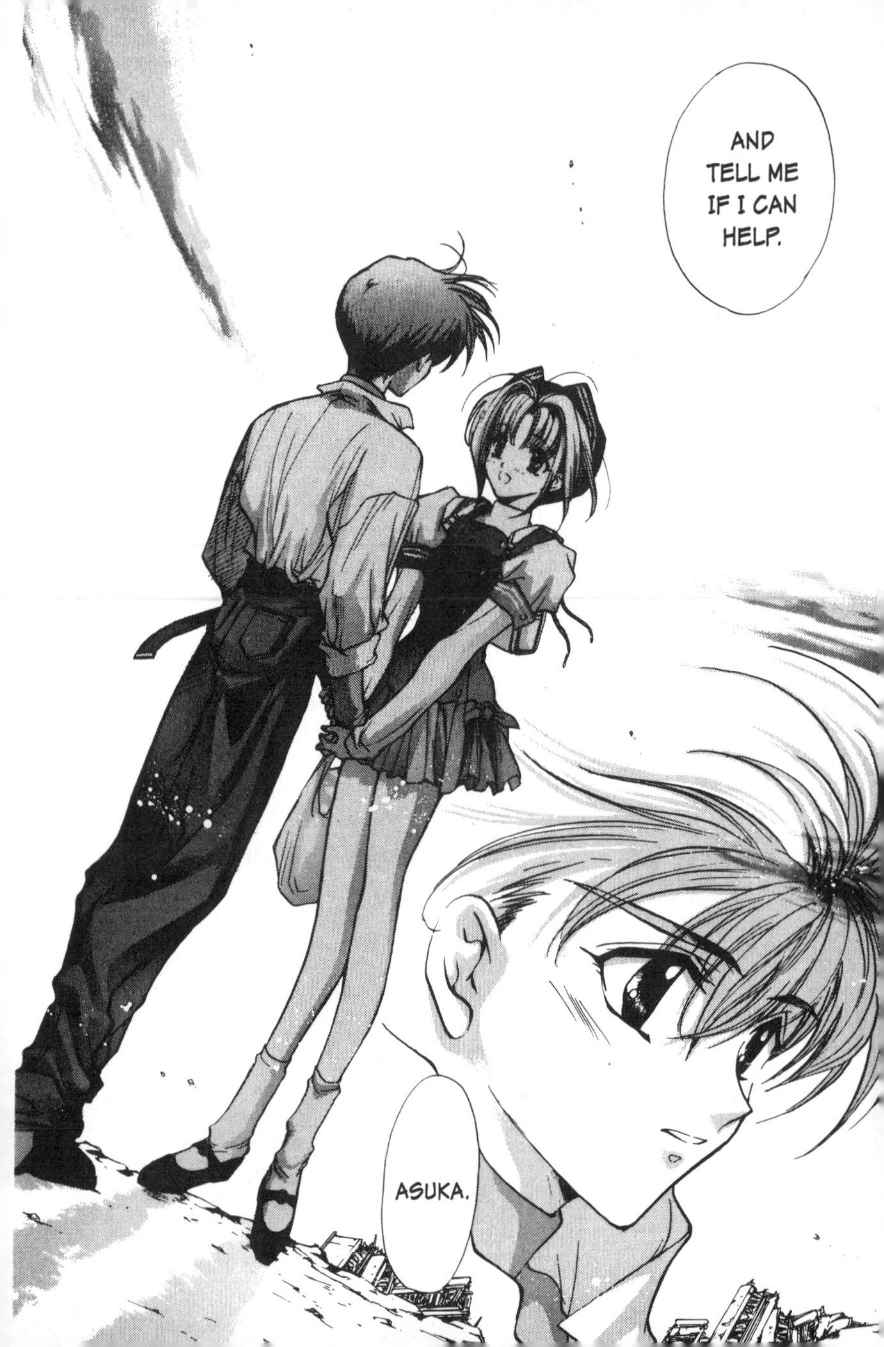
AND TELL ME IF I CAN HELP.
ASUKA.

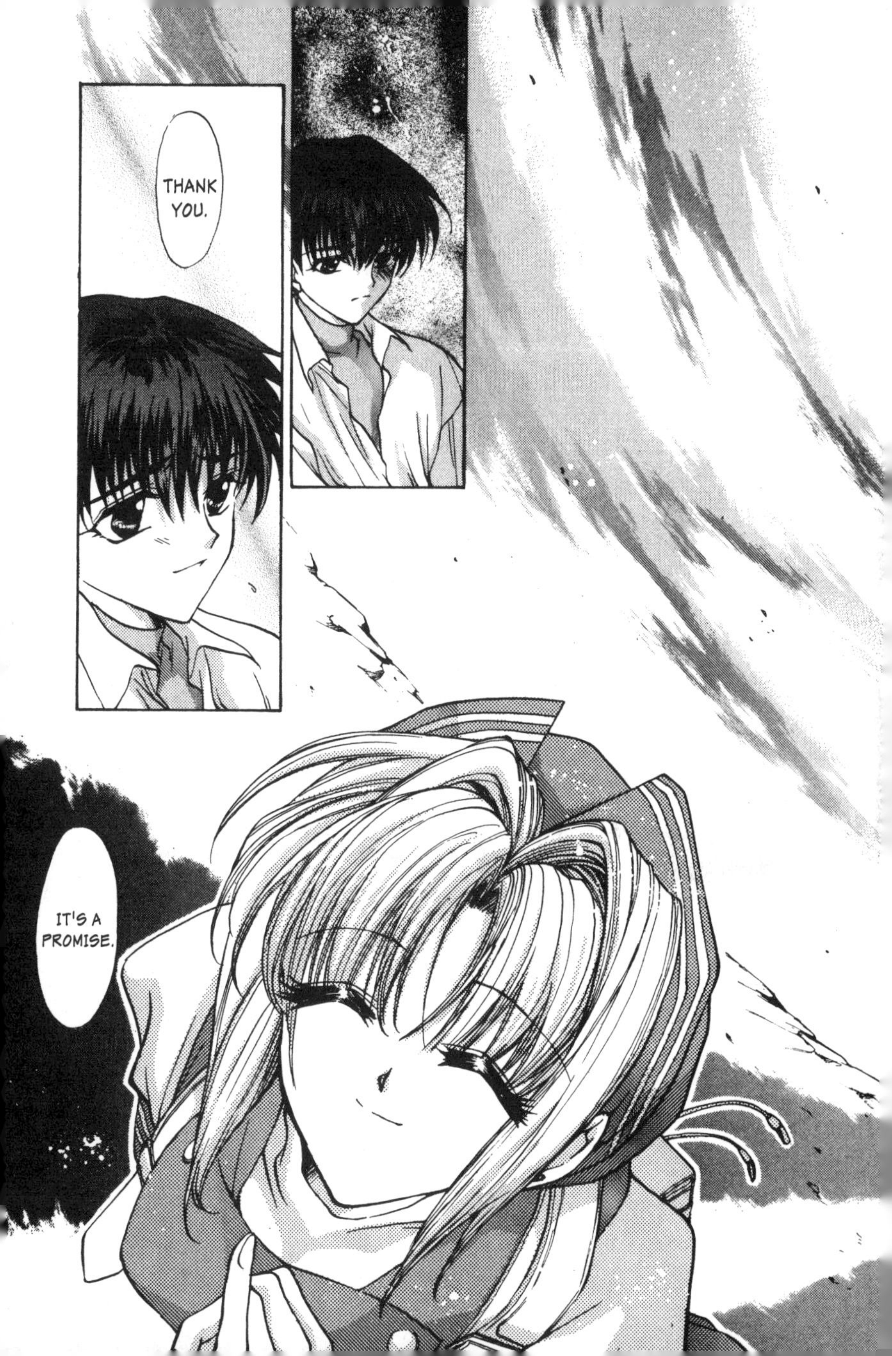
THANK YOU.
IT'S A PROMISE.

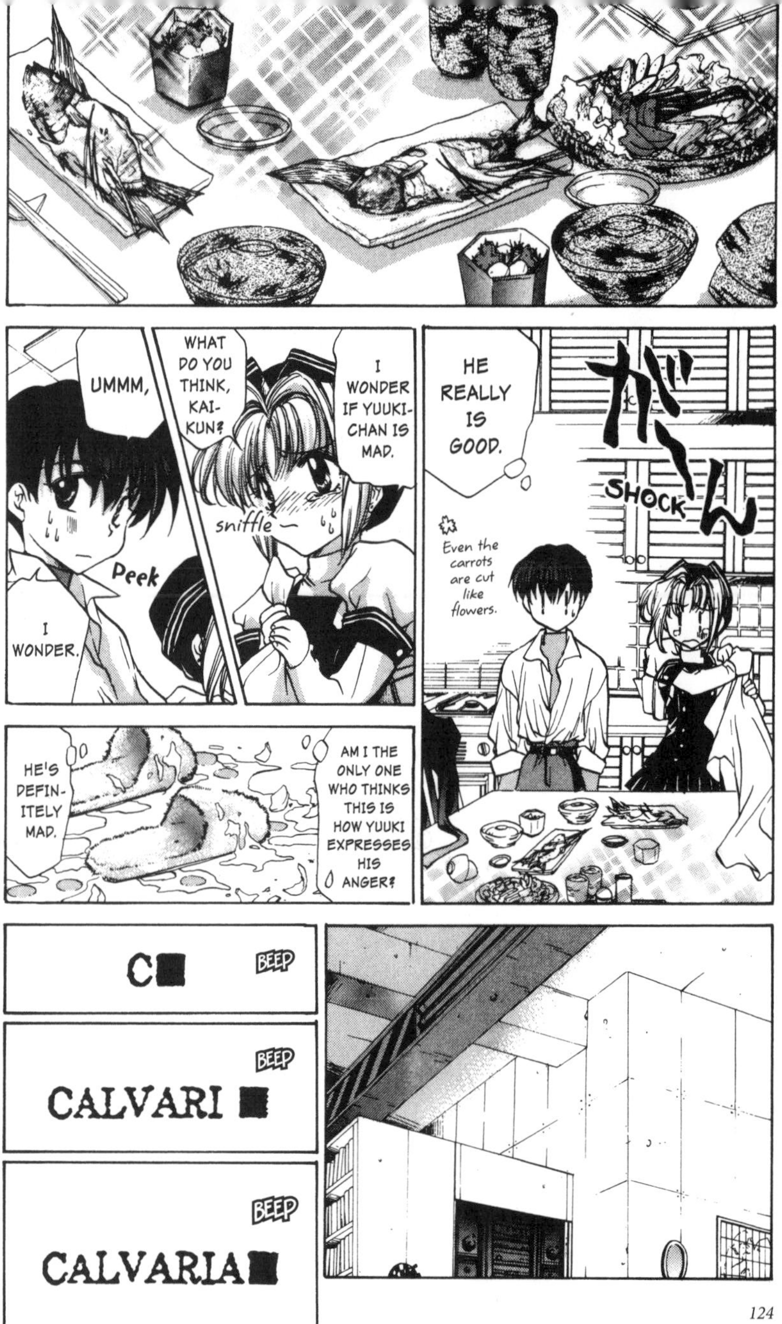
HE REALLY IS GOOD.
がーん
SHOCK
Even the carrots are cut like flowers.
I WONDER IF YUUKI-CHAN IS MAD.
WHAT DO YOU THINK, KAI-KUN?
sniffle
UMMM,
Peek
I WONDER.
AM I THE ONLY ONE WHO THINKS THIS IS HOW YUUKI EXPRESSES HIS ANGER?
HE'S DEFIN-ITELY MAD.
BEEP
C■
BEEP
CALVARI■
BEEP
CALVARIA■

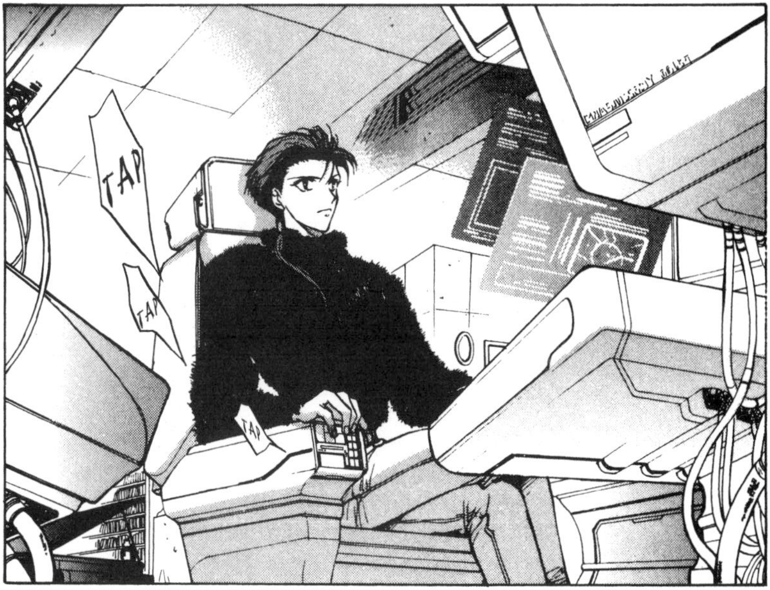
TAP
TAP
TAP

CALVARIA … ① Hill near Jerusalem that Christ was crucified at.
② Cross figure with Christ on it.
③ Relic.

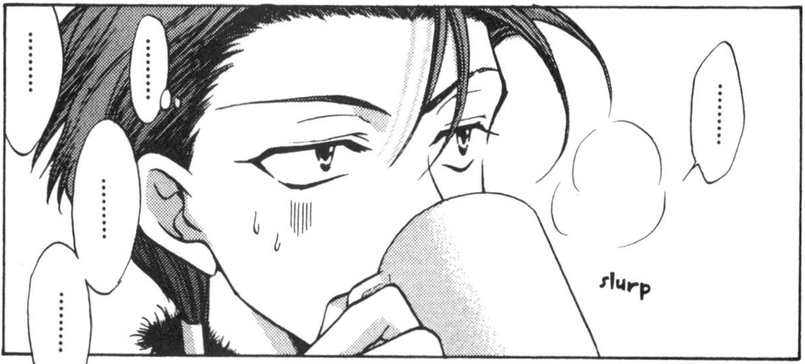
……
……
……
……
……
slurp

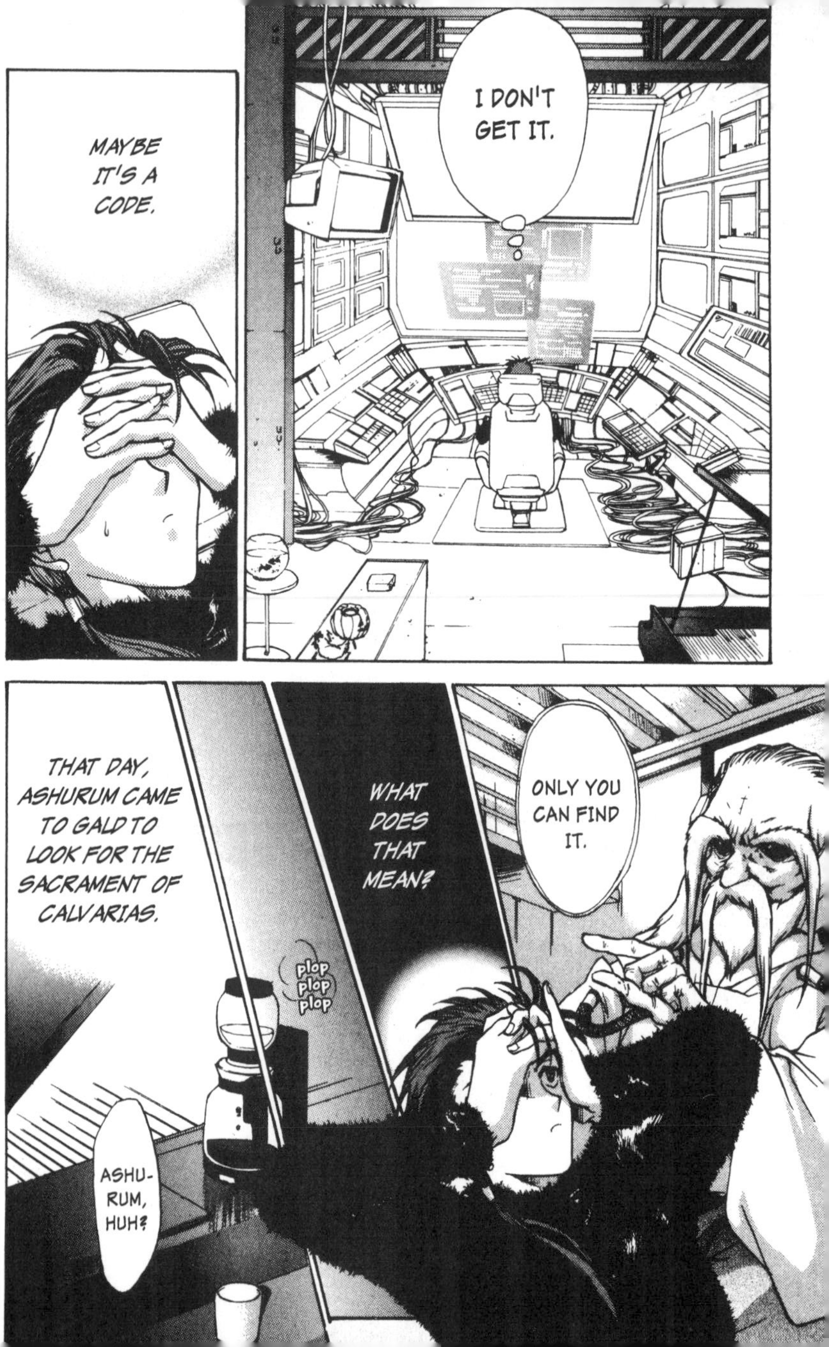
I DON'T GET IT.
MAYBE IT'S A CODE.
ONLY YOU CAN FIND IT.
WHAT DOES THAT MEAN?
THAT DAY, ASHURUM CAME TO GALD TO LOOK FOR THE SACRAMENT OF CALVARIAS.
plop plop plop
ASHURUM, HUH?

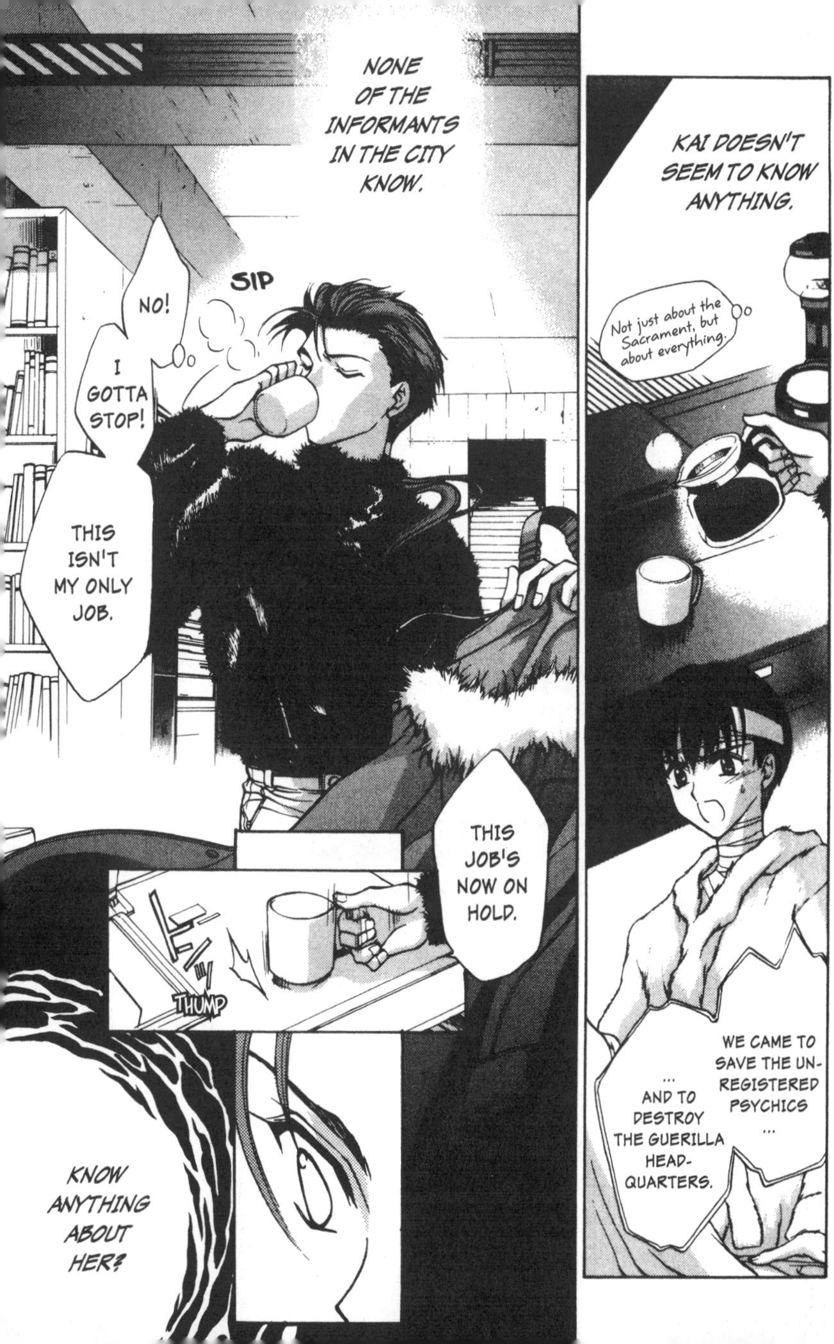
KAI DOESN'T SEEM TO KNOW ANYTHING.
Not just about the Sacrament, but about everything.
WE CAME TO SAVE THE UN-REGISTERED PSYCHICS ...
... AND TO DESTROY THE GUERILLA HEAD-QUARTERS.
NONE OF THE INFORMANTS IN THE CITY KNOW.
SIP
NO!
I GOTTA STOP!
THIS ISN'T MY ONLY JOB.
THIS JOB'S NOW ON HOLD.
THUMP
KNOW ANYTHING ABOUT HER?

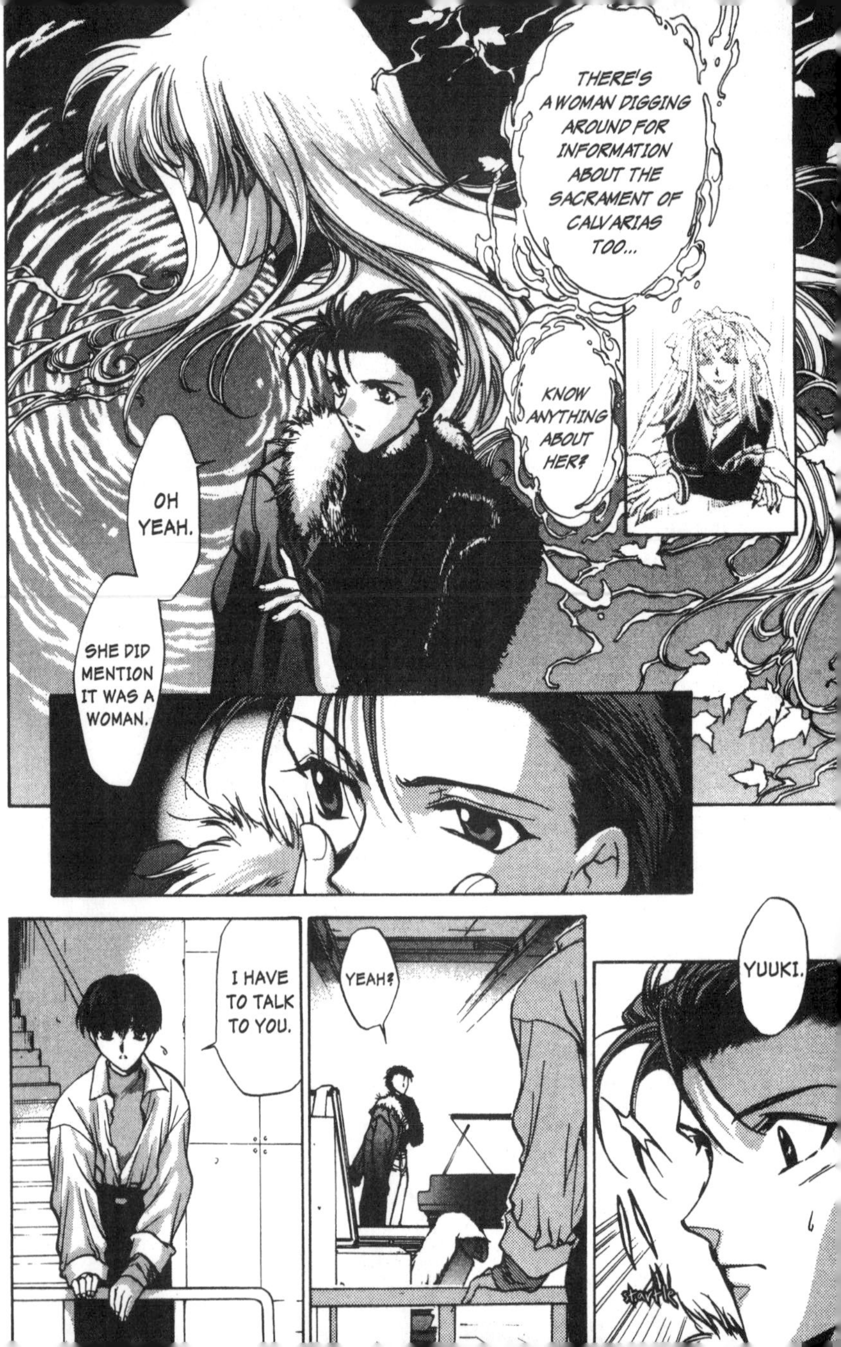
THERE'S A WOMAN DIGGING AROUND FOR INFORMATION ABOUT THE SACRAMENT OF CALVARIAS TOO...
KNOW ANYTHING ABOUT HER?
OH YEAH.
SHE DID MENTION IT WAS A WOMAN.
YUUKI.
startle
YEAH?
I HAVE TO TALK TO YOU.

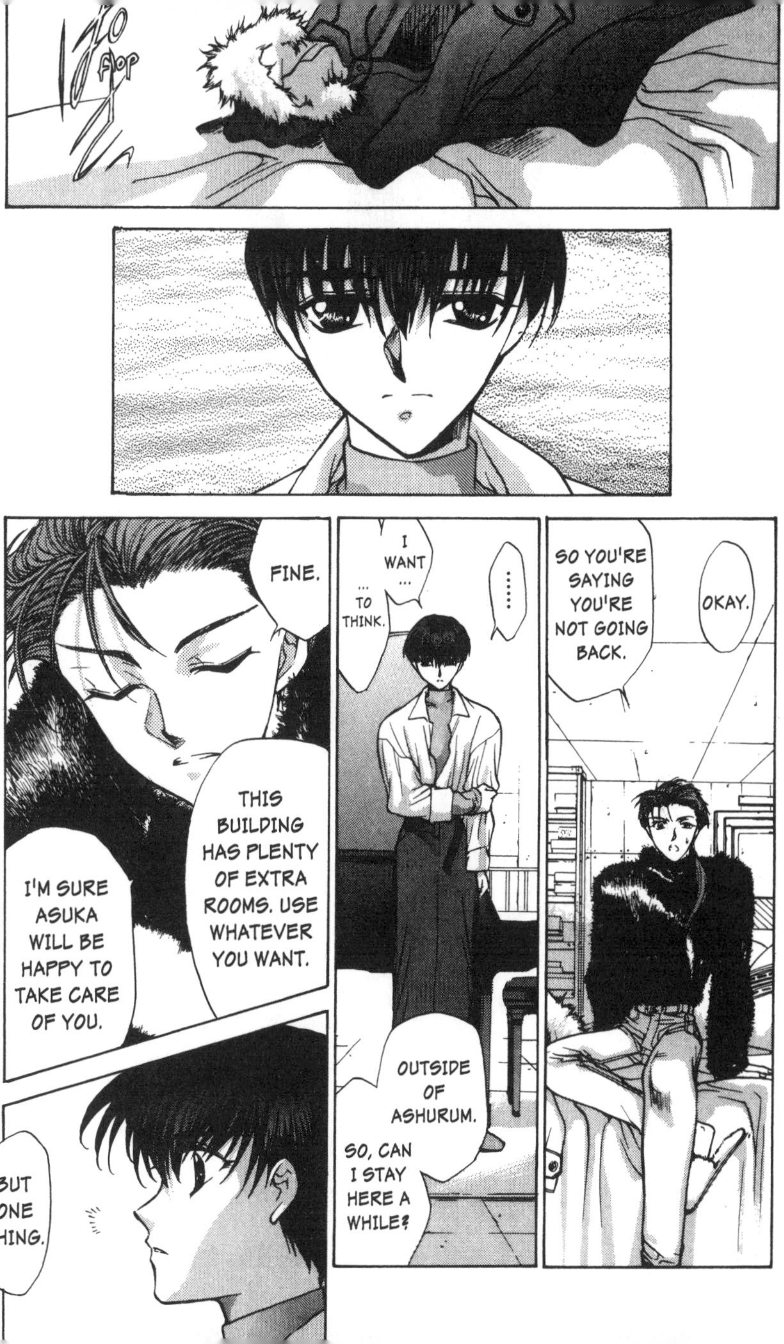

FLOP
OKAY.
SO YOU'RE SAYING YOU'RE NOT GOING BACK.
......
I WANT ...
... TO THINK.
OUTSIDE OF ASHURUM.
SO, CAN I STAY HERE A WHILE?
FINE.
THIS BUILDING HAS PLENTY OF EXTRA ROOMS. USE WHATEVER YOU WANT.
I'M SURE ASUKA WILL BE HAPPY TO TAKE CARE OF YOU.
BUT ONE THING.

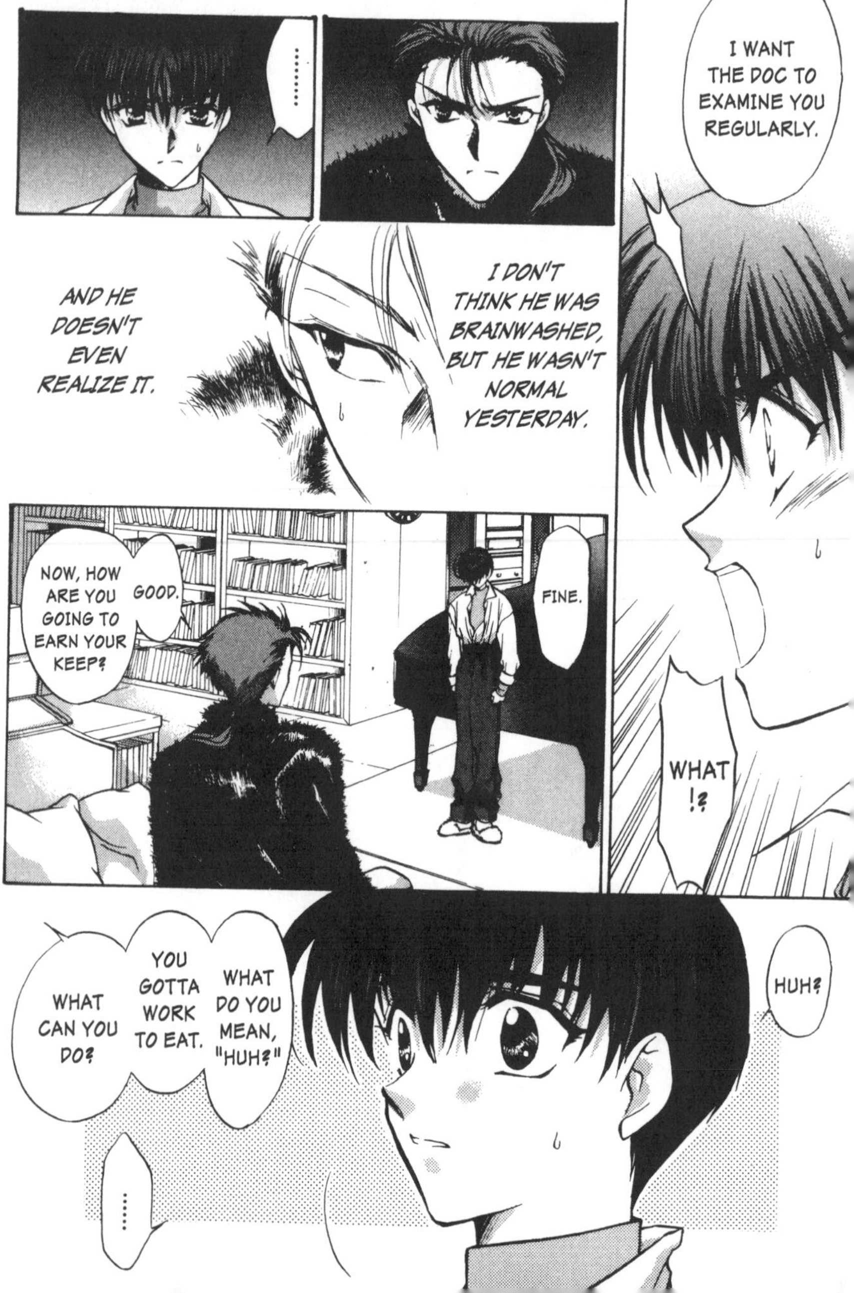
I WANT THE DOC TO EXAMINE YOU REGULARLY.
WHAT!?
......
I DON'T THINK HE WAS BRAINWASHED, BUT HE WASN'T NORMAL YESTERDAY.
AND HE DOESN'T EVEN REALIZE IT.
FINE.
GOOD.
NOW, HOW ARE YOU GOING TO EARN YOUR KEEP?
HUH?
WHAT DO YOU MEAN, "HUH?"
YOU GOTTA WORK TO EAT.
WHAT CAN YOU DO?
......

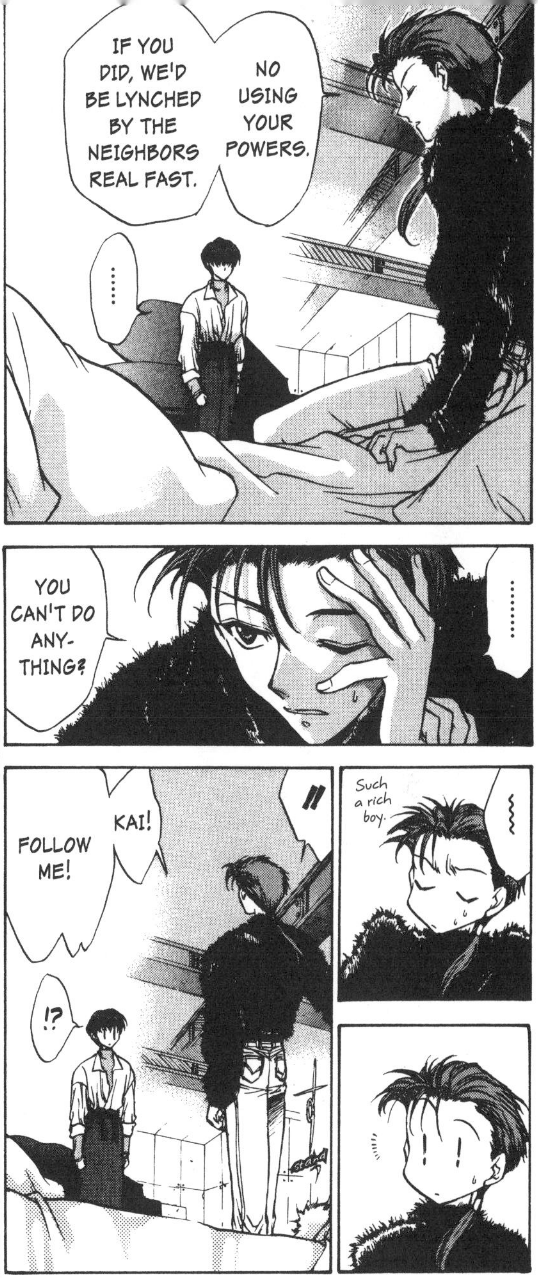
NO USING YOUR POWERS.
IF YOU DID, WE'D BE LYNCHED BY THE NEIGHBORS REAL FAST.
......
....
YOU CAN'T DO ANY-THING?
Such a rich boy.
!!
KAI!
FOLLOW ME!
!?
stand

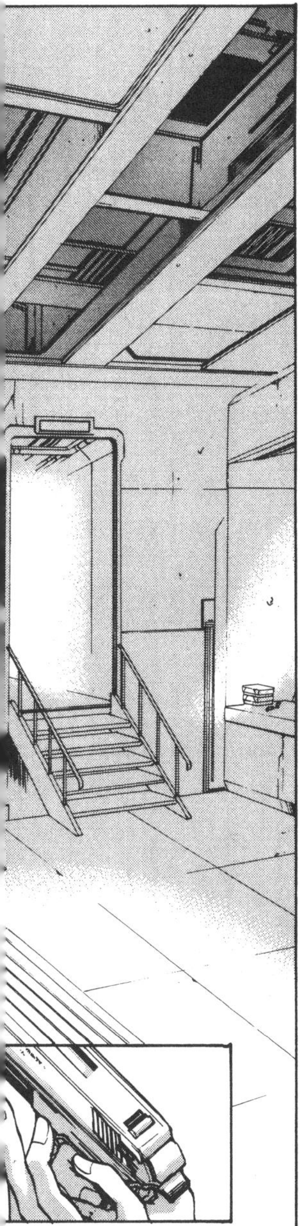

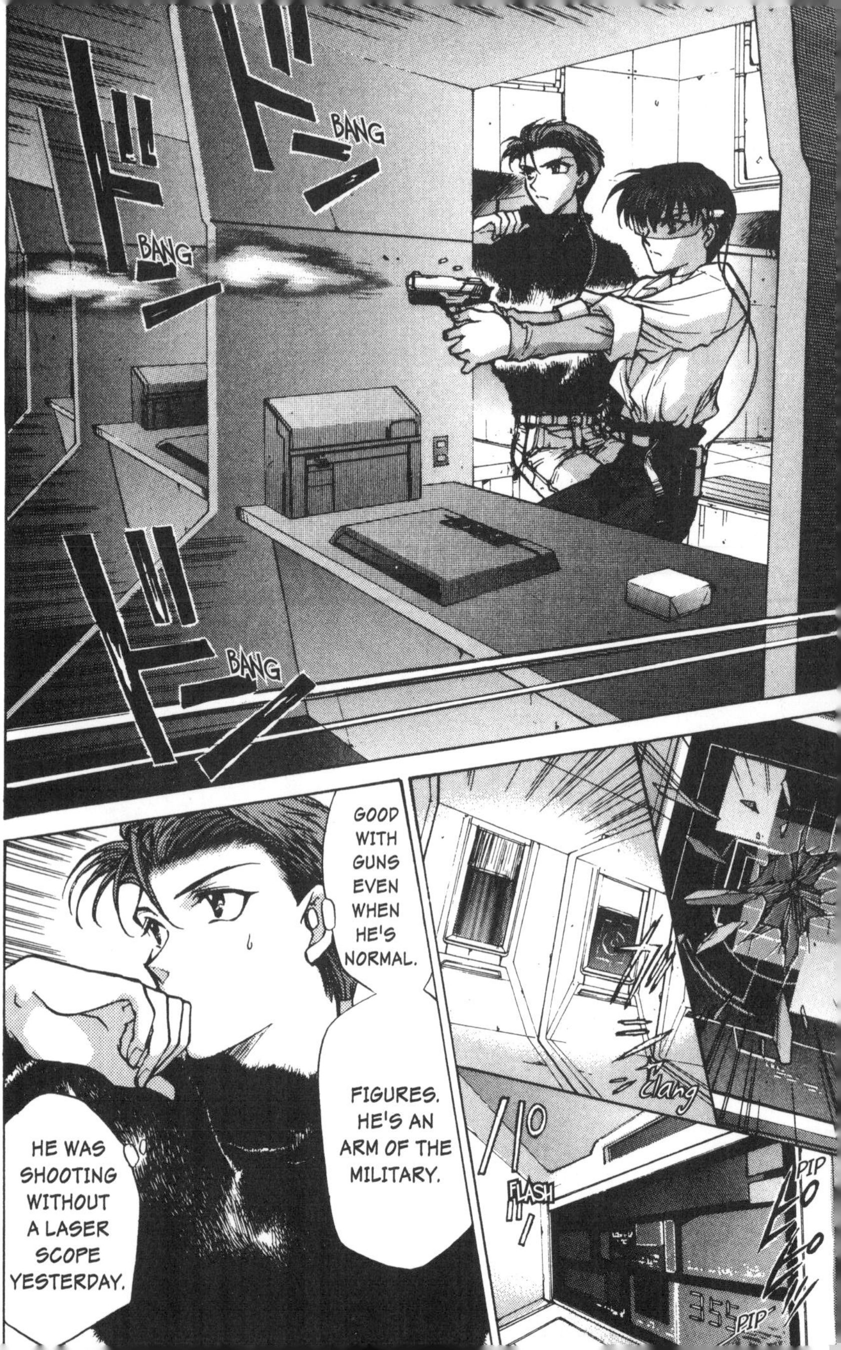
BANG
BANG
BANG
Clang
FLASH
PIP
355
PIP
GOOD WITH GUNS EVEN WHEN HE'S NORMAL.
FIGURES. HE'S AN ARM OF THE MILITARY.
HE WAS SHOOTING WITHOUT A LASER SCOPE YESTERDAY.

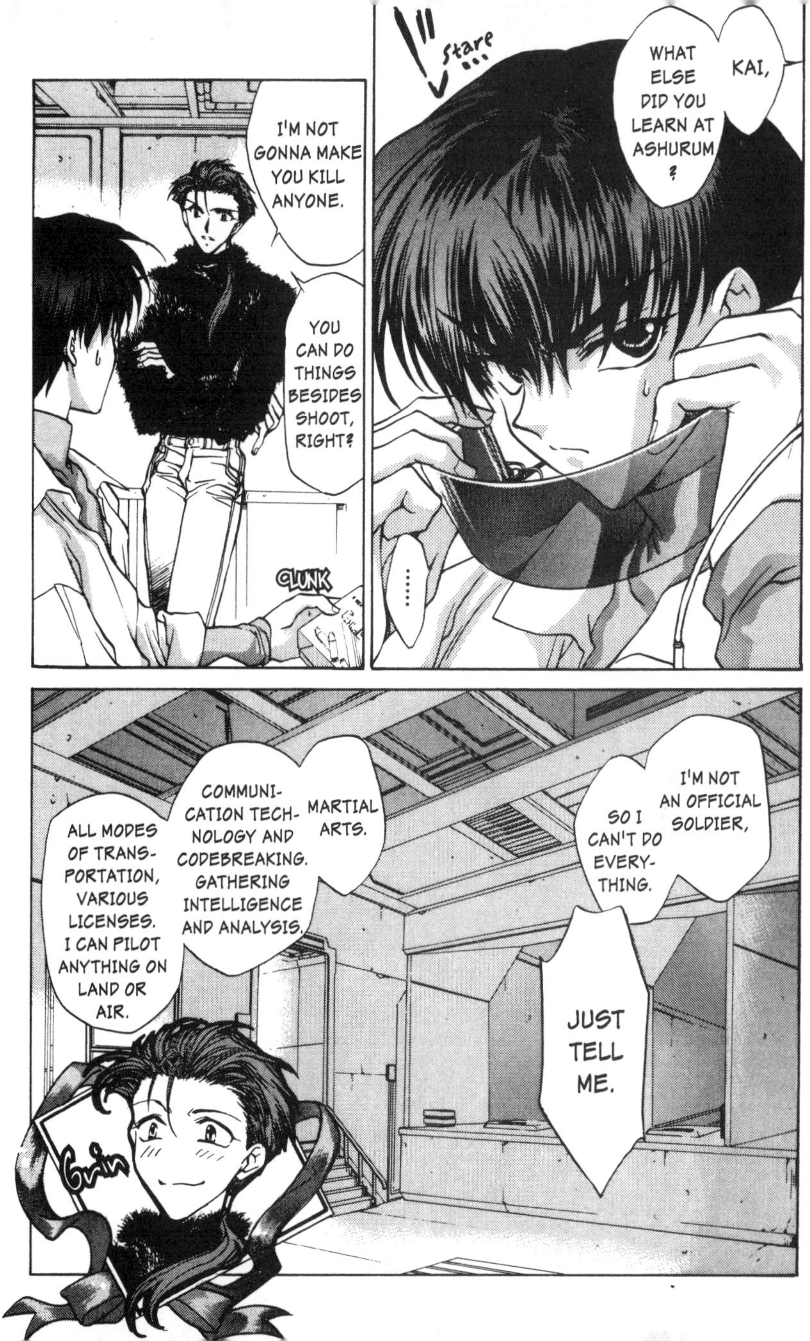
KAI,
WHAT ELSE DID YOU LEARN AT ASHURUM?
Stare...
......
I'M NOT GONNA MAKE YOU KILL ANYONE.
YOU CAN DO THINGS BESIDES SHOOT, RIGHT?
CLUNK
I'M NOT AN OFFICIAL SOLDIER,
SO I CAN'T DO EVERYTHING.
JUST TELL ME.
MARTIAL ARTS.
COMMUNICATION TECHNOLOGY AND CODEBREAKING. GATHERING INTELLIGENCE AND ANALYSIS.
ALL MODES OF TRANSPORTATION, VARIOUS LICENSES. I CAN PILOT ANYTHING ON LAND OR AIR.
Grin

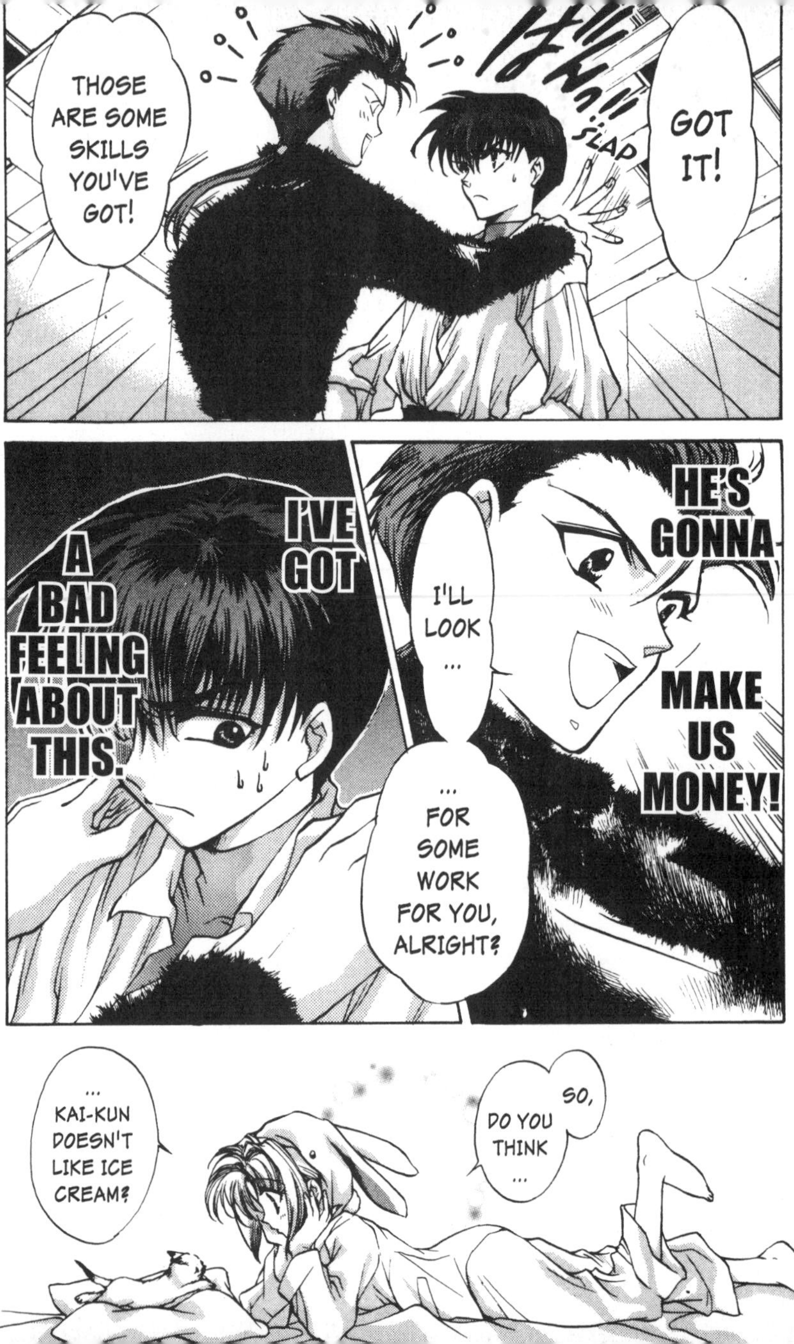
GOT IT!
SLAP
THOSE ARE SOME SKILLS YOU'VE GOT!
HE'S GONNA MAKE US MONEY!
I'LL LOOK ...
... FOR SOME WORK FOR YOU, ALRIGHT?
I'VE GOT A BAD FEELING ABOUT THIS.
SO, DO YOU THINK ...
... KAI-KUN DOESN'T LIKE ICE CREAM?

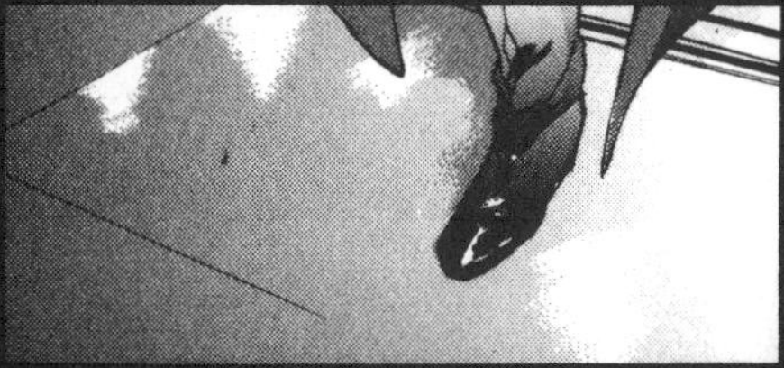

CHAPTER 11 Potential Energy

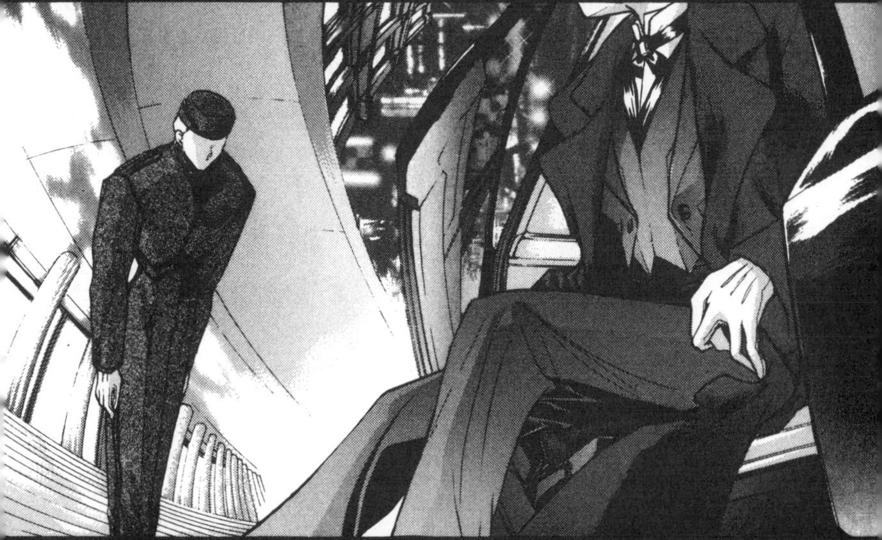

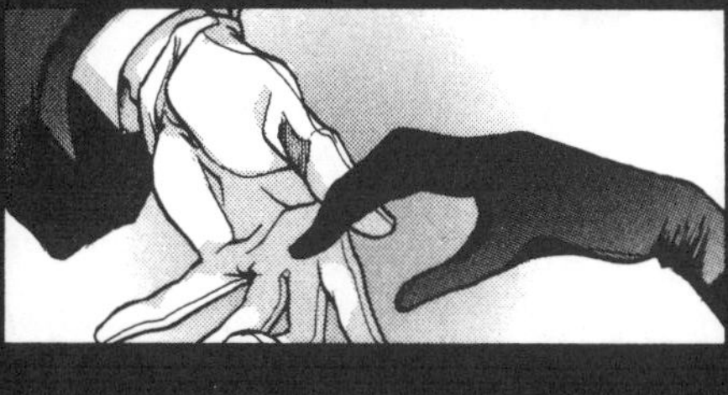

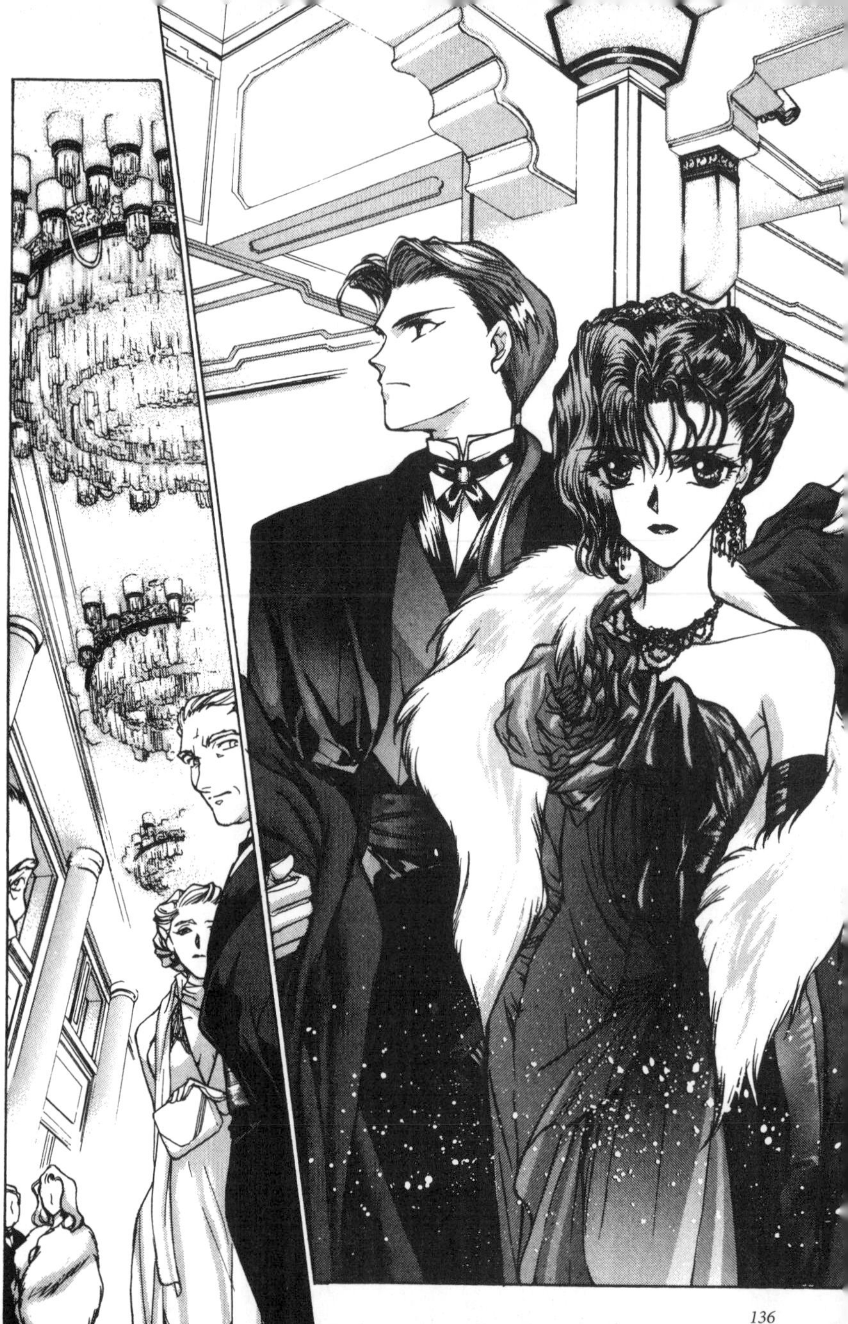

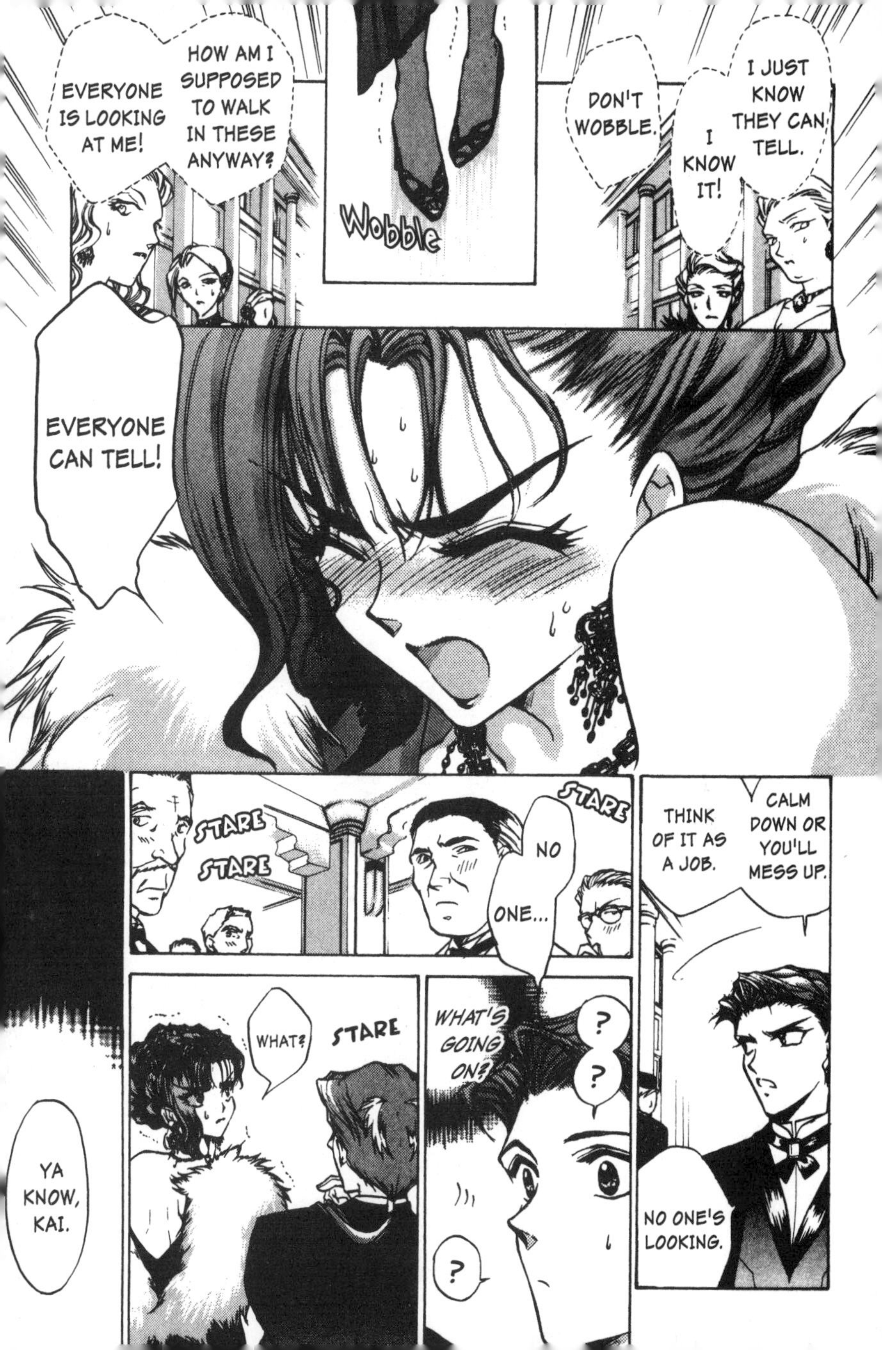
I JUST KNOW THEY CAN TELL.
I KNOW IT!
DON'T WOBBLE.
Wobble
HOW AM I SUPPOSED TO WALK IN THESE ANYWAY?
EVERYONE IS LOOKING AT ME!
EVERYONE CAN TELL!
CALM DOWN OR YOU'LL MESS UP.
THINK OF IT AS A JOB.
NO ONE'S LOOKING.
STARE
NO ONE...
STARE
STARE
WHAT'S GOING ON?
?
?
?
STARE
WHAT?
YA KNOW, KAI.

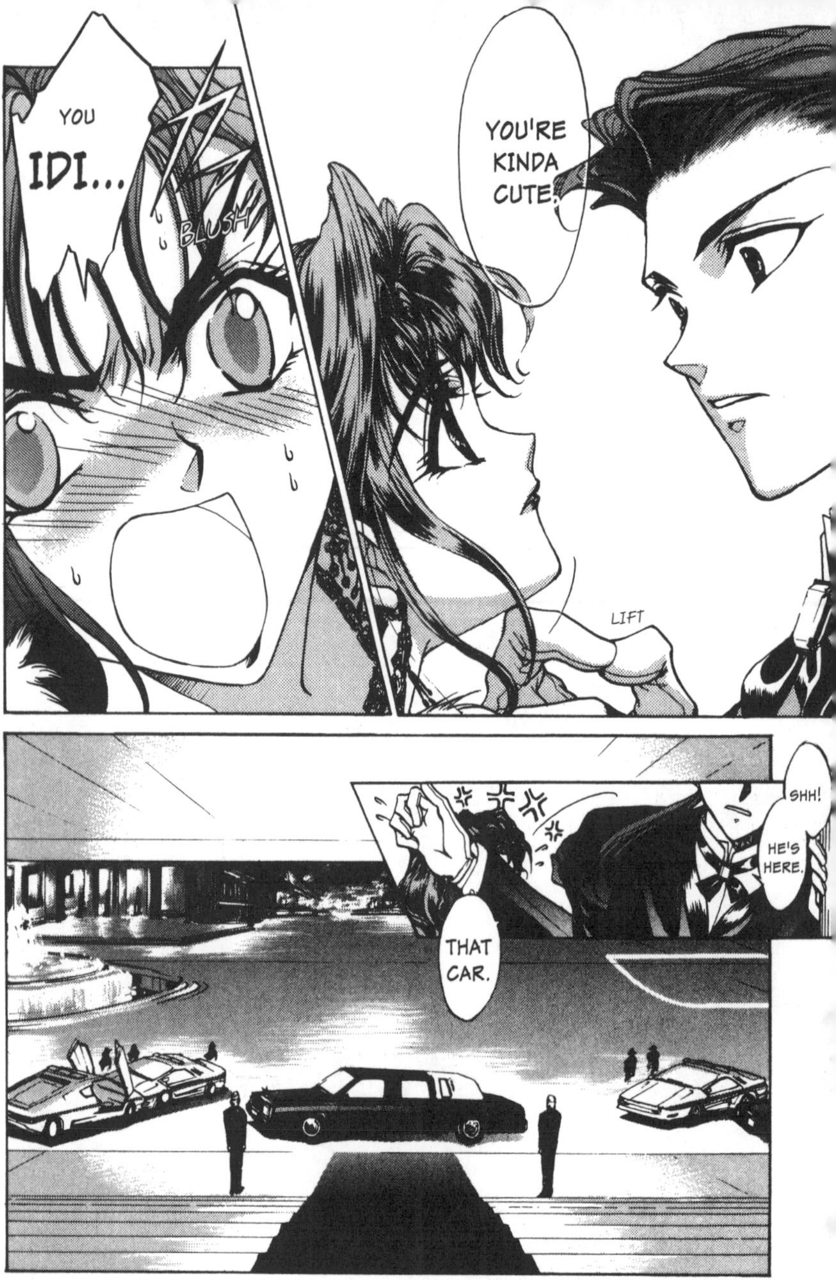

YOU'RE KINDA CUTE.
LIFT
YOU IDI...
BLUSH
SHH!
HE'S HERE.
THAT CAR.

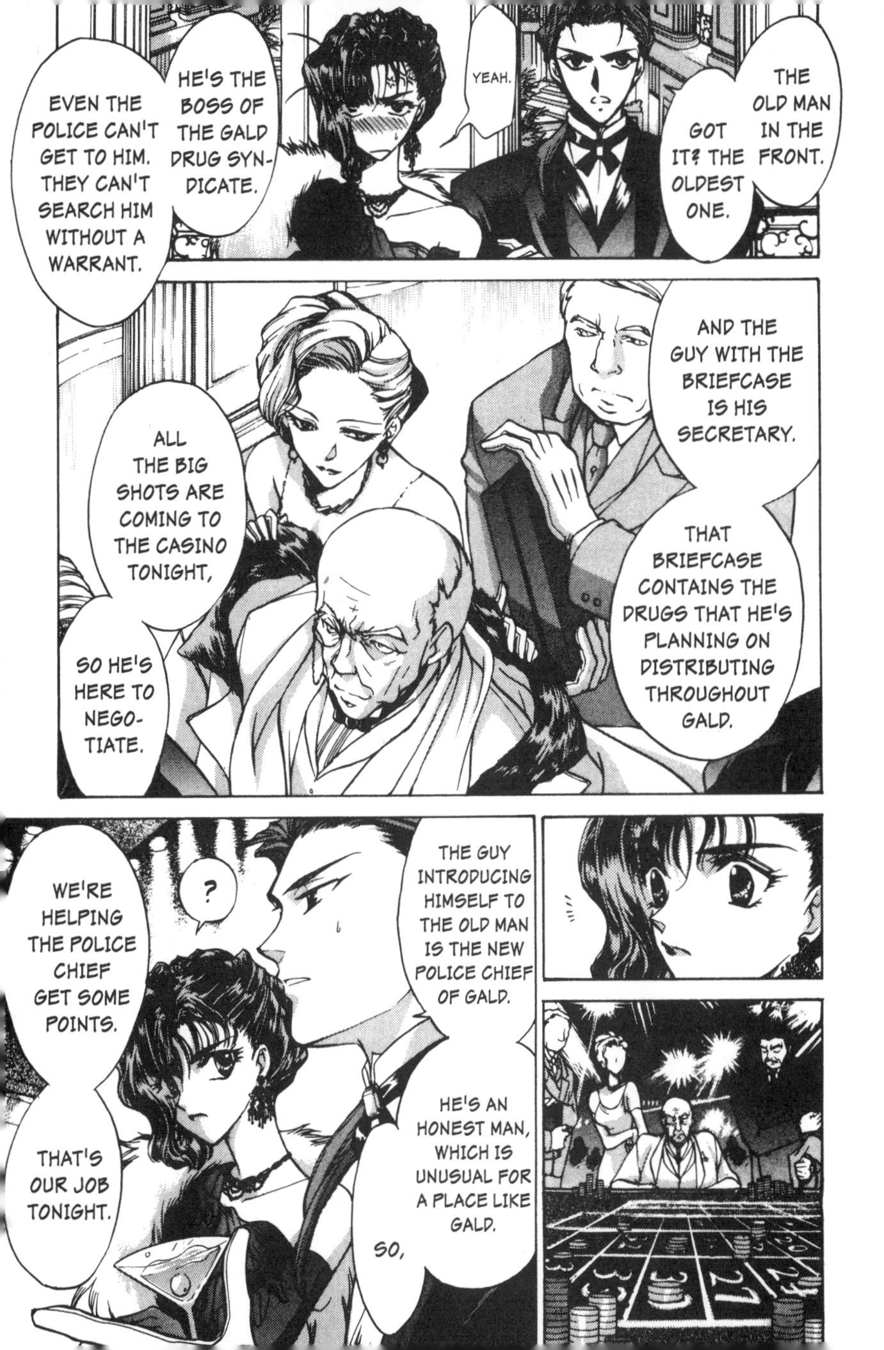
THE OLD MAN IN THE FRONT.
GOT IT? THE OLDEST ONE.
YEAH.
HE'S THE BOSS OF THE GALD DRUG SYNDICATE.
EVEN THE POLICE CAN'T GET TO HIM. THEY CAN'T SEARCH HIM WITHOUT A WARRANT.
AND THE GUY WITH THE BRIEFCASE IS HIS SECRETARY.
THAT BRIEFCASE CONTAINS THE DRUGS THAT HE'S PLANNING ON DISTRIBUTING THROUGHOUT GALD.
ALL THE BIG SHOTS ARE COMING TO THE CASINO TONIGHT,
SO HE'S HERE TO NEGOTIATE.
THE GUY INTRODUCING HIMSELF TO THE OLD MAN IS THE NEW POLICE CHIEF OF GALD.
HE'S AN HONEST MAN, WHICH IS UNUSUAL FOR A PLACE LIKE GALD.
SO,
?
WE'RE HELPING THE POLICE CHIEF GET SOME POINTS.
THAT'S OUR JOB TONIGHT.

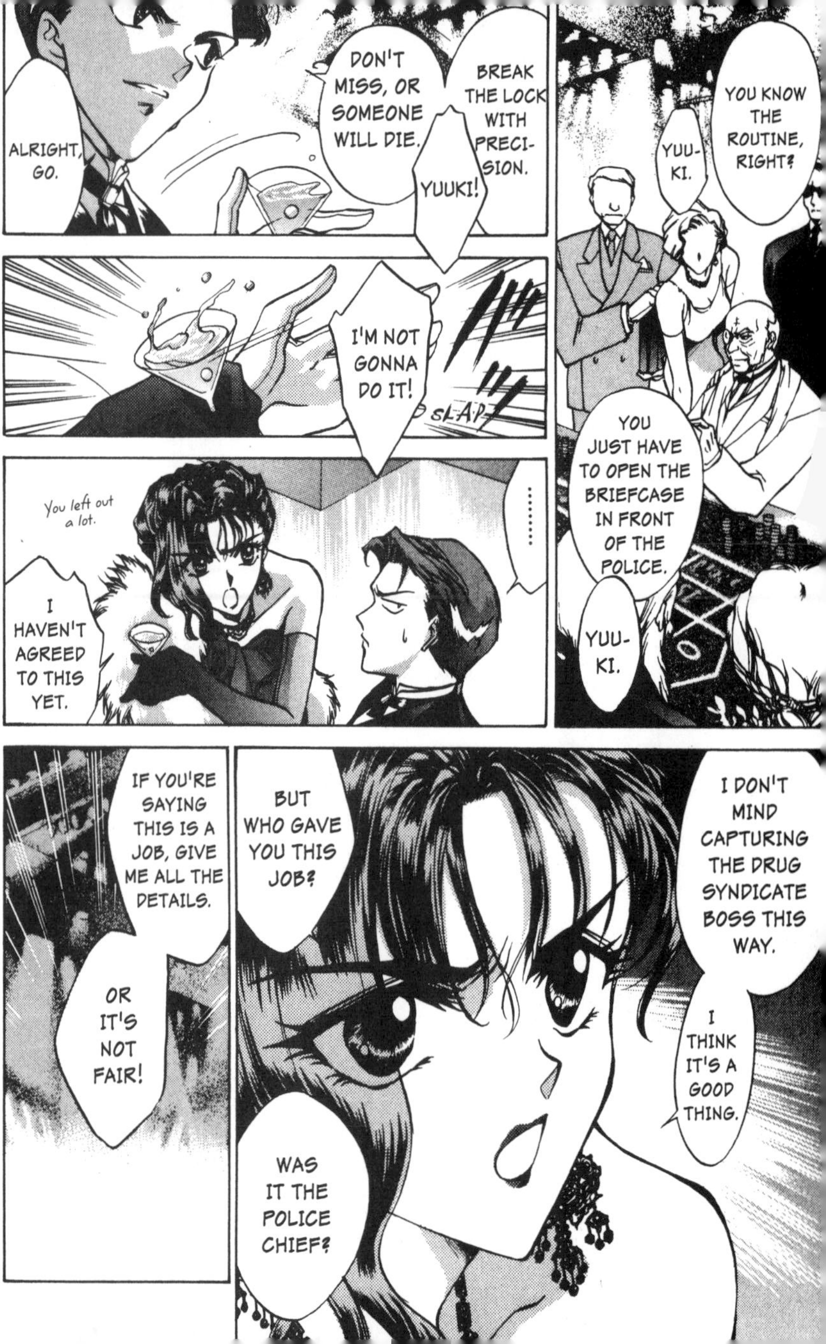
YOU KNOW THE ROUTINE, RIGHT?
YUU-KI.
YOU JUST HAVE TO OPEN THE BRIEFCASE IN FRONT OF THE POLICE.
YUU-KI.
BREAK THE LOCK WITH PRECISION.
DON'T MISS, OR SOMEONE WILL DIE.
ALRIGHT, GO.
YUUKI!
I'M NOT GONNA DO IT!
SLAP
....
I HAVEN'T AGREED TO THIS YET.
You left out a lot.
I DON'T MIND CAPTURING THE DRUG SYNDICATE BOSS THIS WAY.
I THINK IT'S A GOOD THING.
BUT WHO GAVE YOU THIS JOB?
WAS IT THE POLICE CHIEF?
IF YOU'RE SAYING THIS IS A JOB, GIVE ME ALL THE DETAILS.
OR IT'S NOT FAIR!

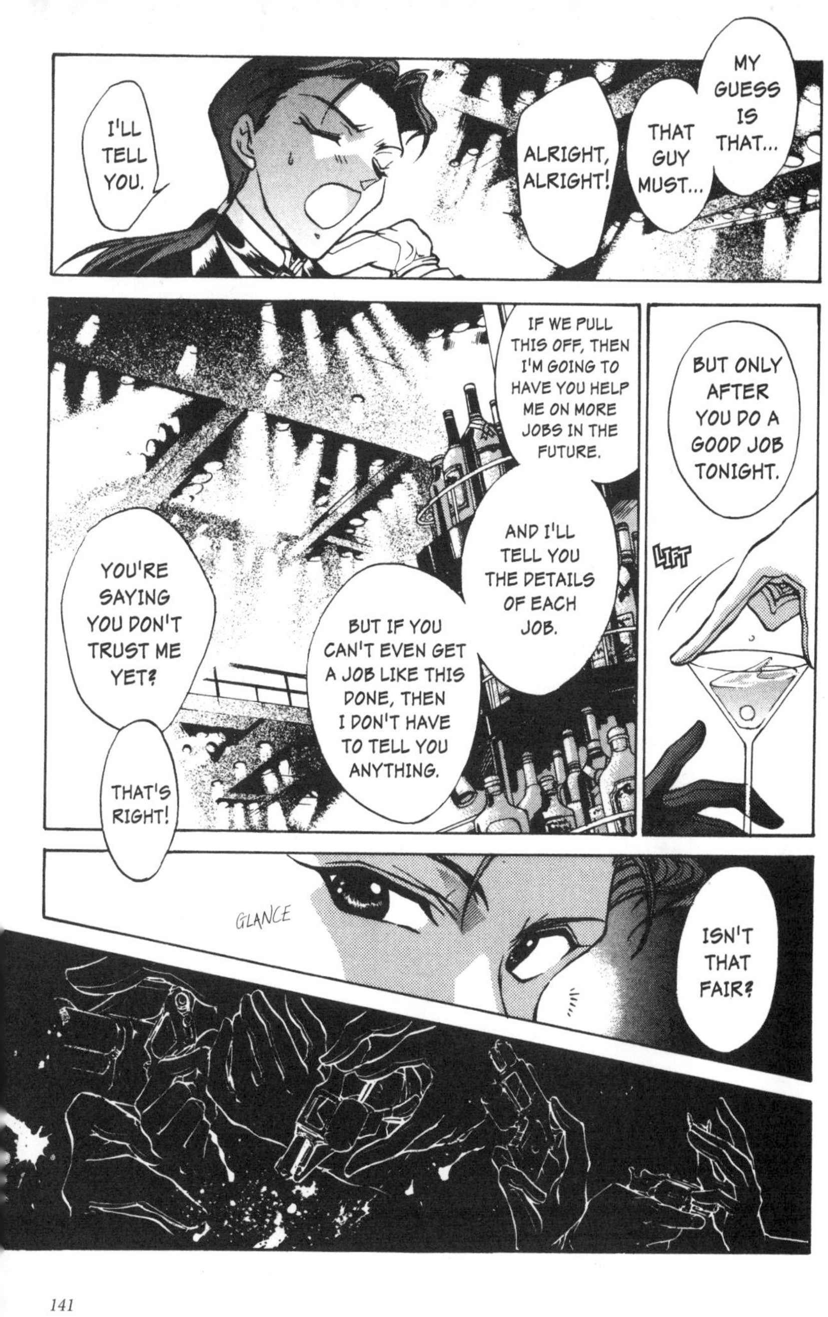
MY GUESS IS THAT...
THAT GUY MUST...
ALRIGHT, ALRIGHT!
I'LL TELL YOU.
BUT ONLY AFTER YOU DO A GOOD JOB TONIGHT.
LIFT
IF WE PULL THIS OFF, THEN I'M GOING TO HAVE YOU HELP ME ON MORE JOBS IN THE FUTURE.
AND I'LL TELL YOU THE DETAILS OF EACH JOB.
BUT IF YOU CAN'T EVEN GET A JOB LIKE THIS DONE, THEN I DON'T HAVE TO TELL YOU ANYTHING.
YOU'RE SAYING YOU DON'T TRUST ME YET?
THAT'S RIGHT!
ISN'T THAT FAIR?
GLANCE

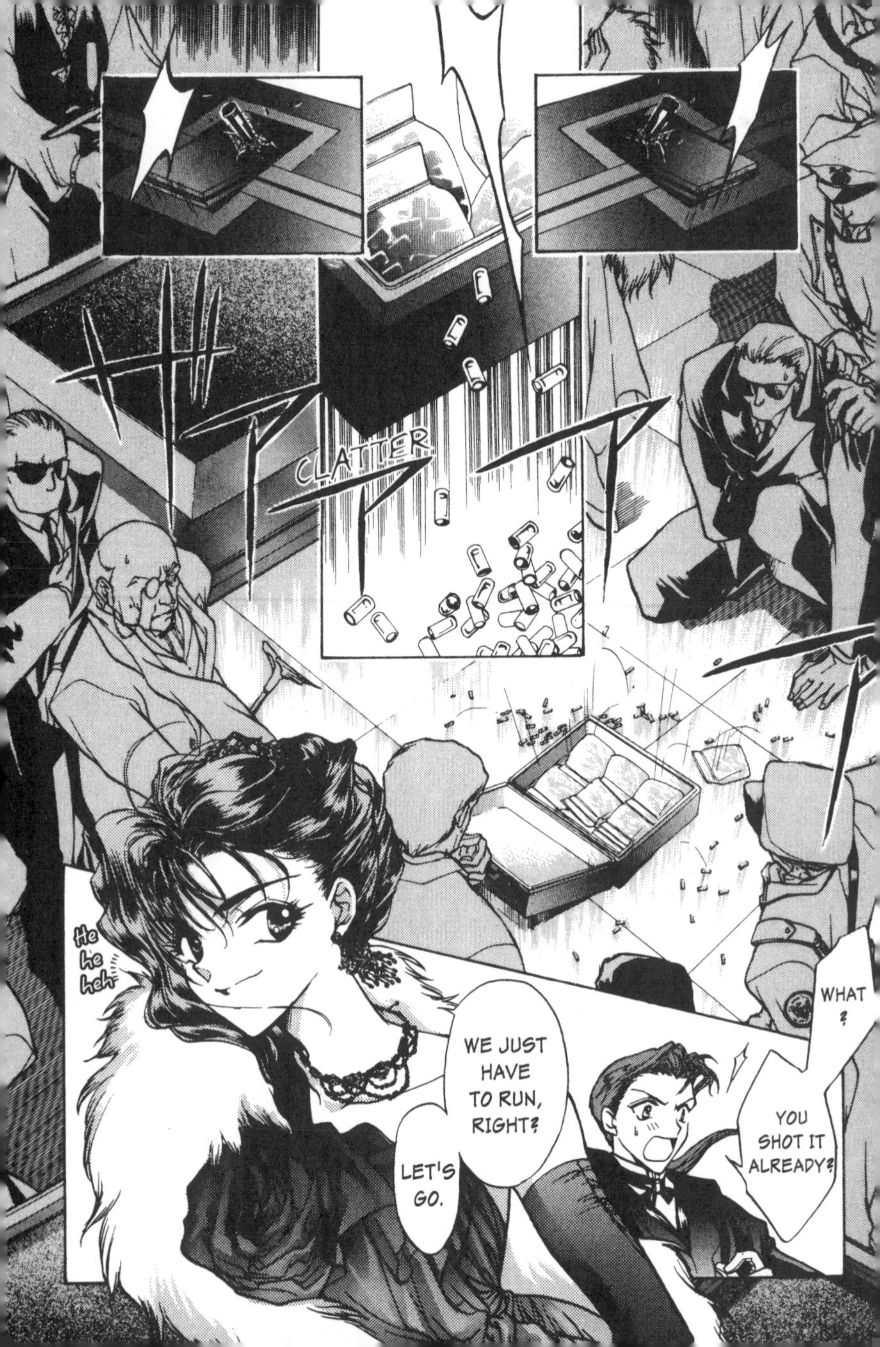
CLATTER
WHAT?
YOU SHOT IT ALREADY?
He he heh
WE JUST HAVE TO RUN, RIGHT?
LET'S GO.

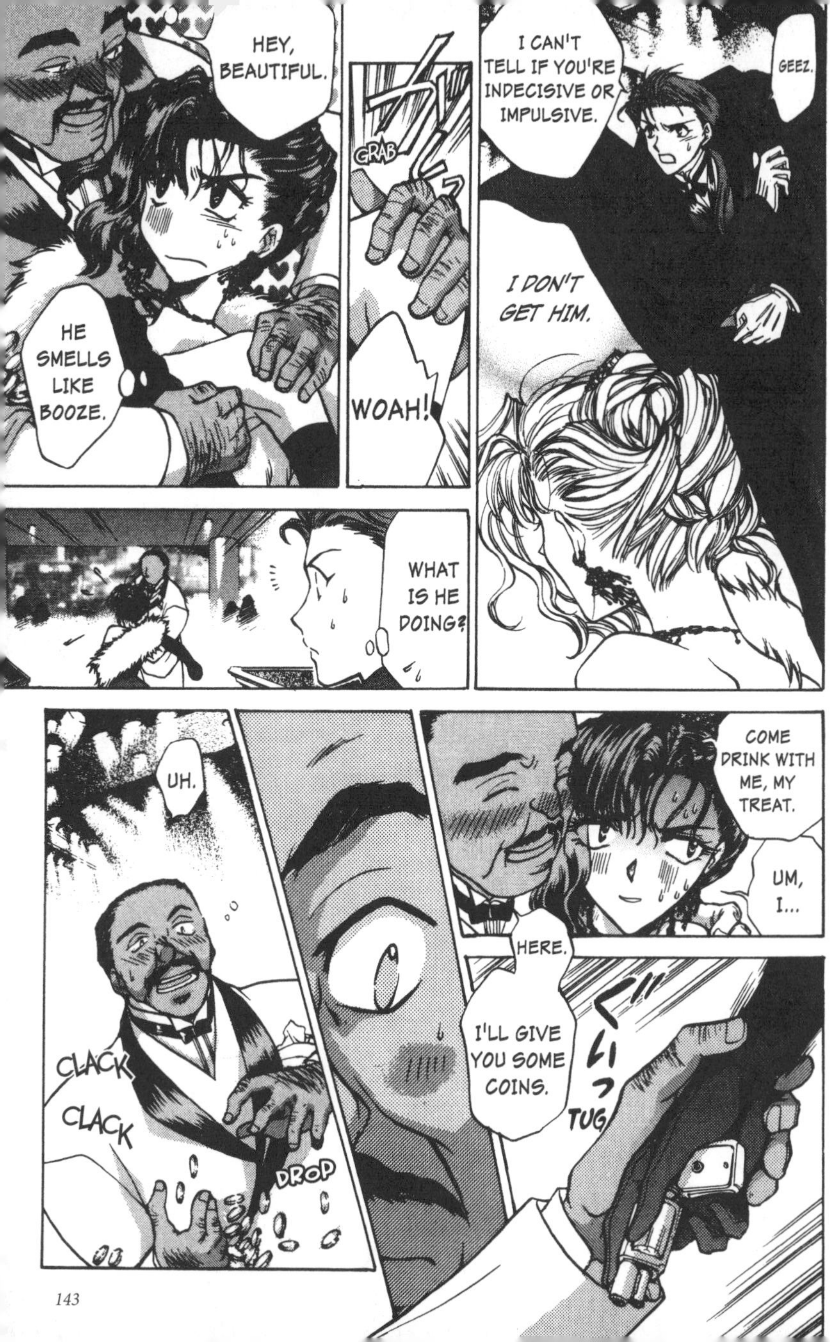
GEEZ.
I CAN'T TELL IF YOU'RE INDECISIVE OR IMPULSIVE.
I DON'T GET HIM.
GRAB
WOAH!
HEY, BEAUTIFUL.
HE SMELLS LIKE BOOZE.
WHAT IS HE DOING?
COME DRINK WITH ME, MY TREAT.
UM, I...
HERE.
I'LL GIVE YOU SOME COINS.
TUG
UH.
CLACK
CLACK
DROP

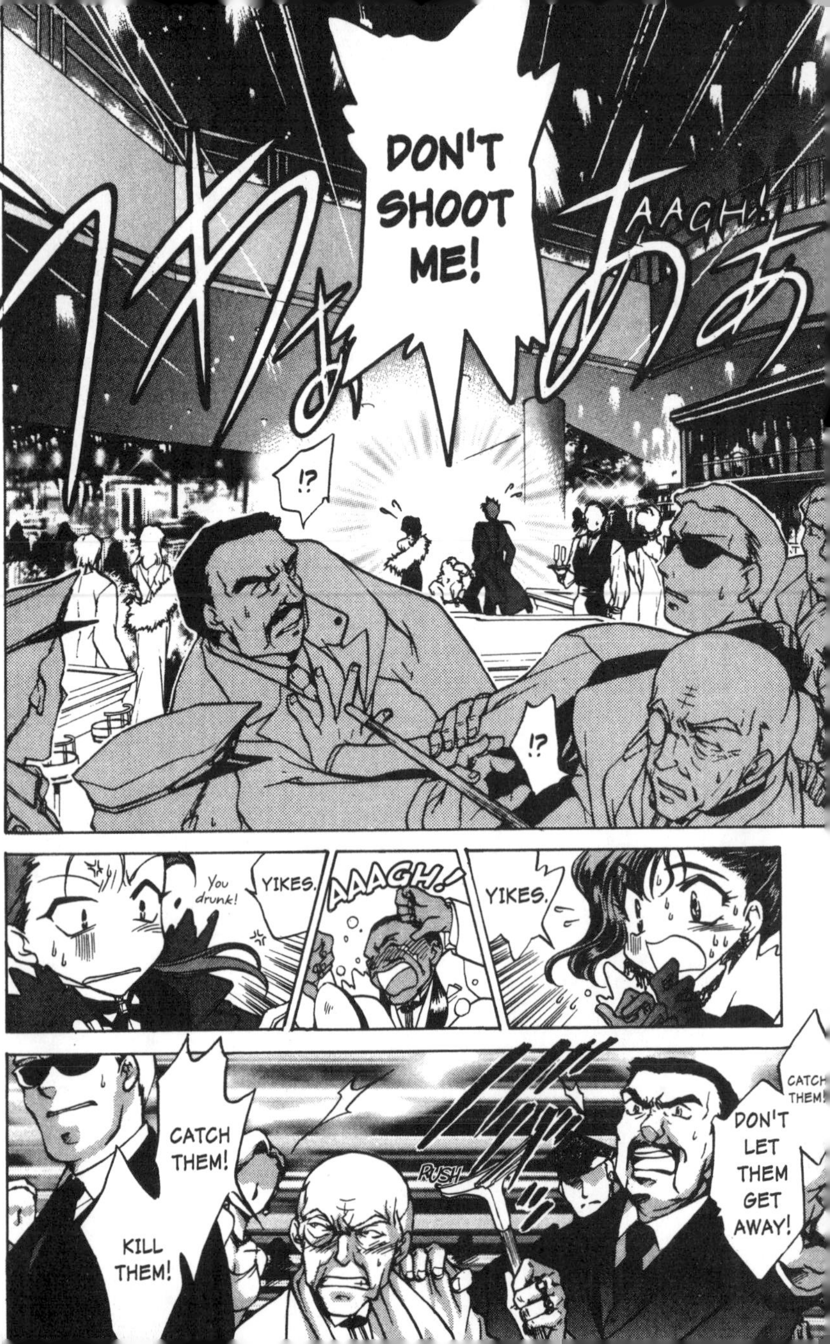

AAGH!
DON'T SHOOT ME!
!?
!?
YIKES.
AAAGH!
YIKES.
You drunk!
CATCH THEM!
DON'T LET THEM GET AWAY!
RUSH
CATCH THEM!
KILL THEM!

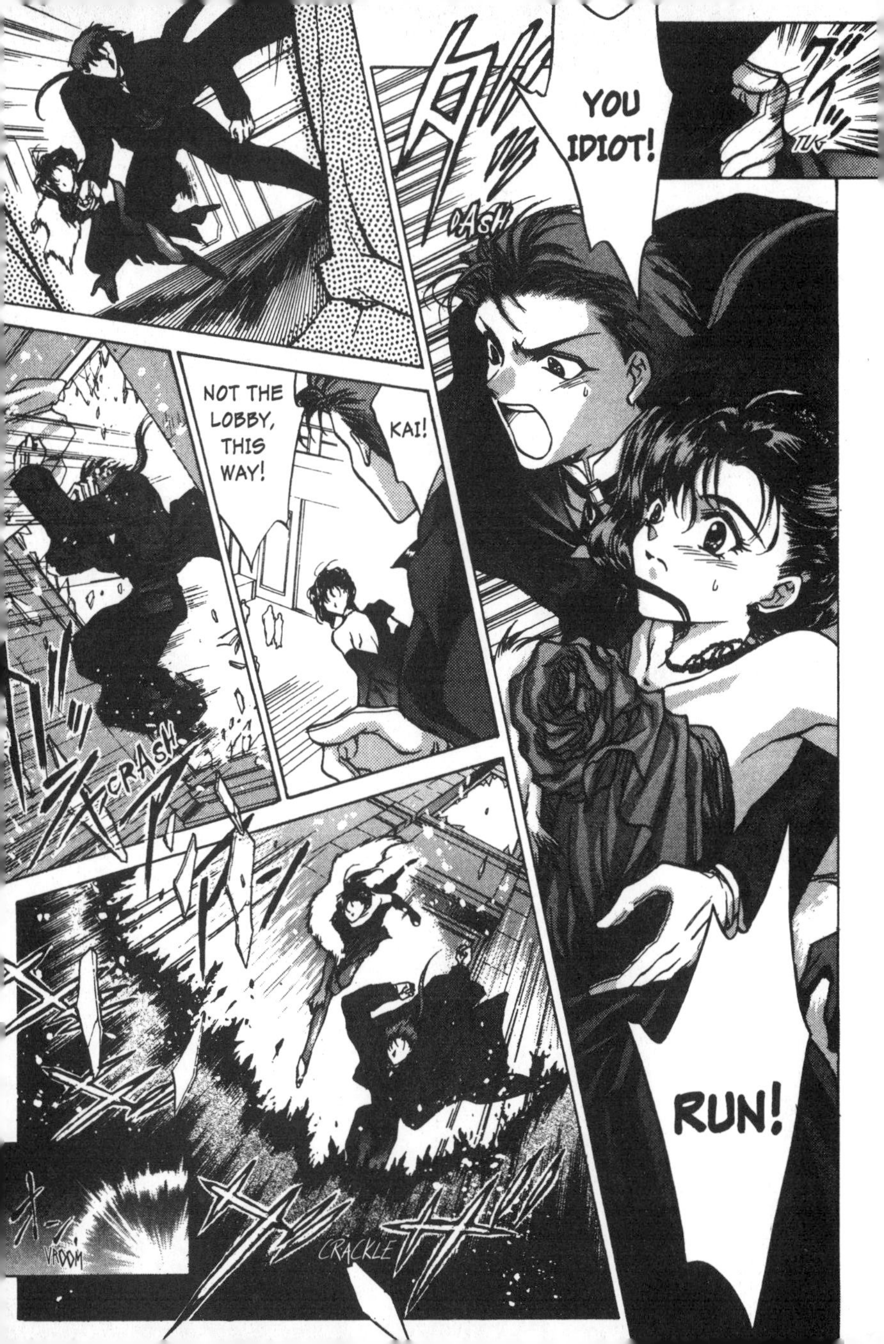
TUG
YOU IDIOT!
DASH
RUN!
KAI!
NOT THE LOBBY, THIS WAY!
CRASH
CRACKLE
VROOM

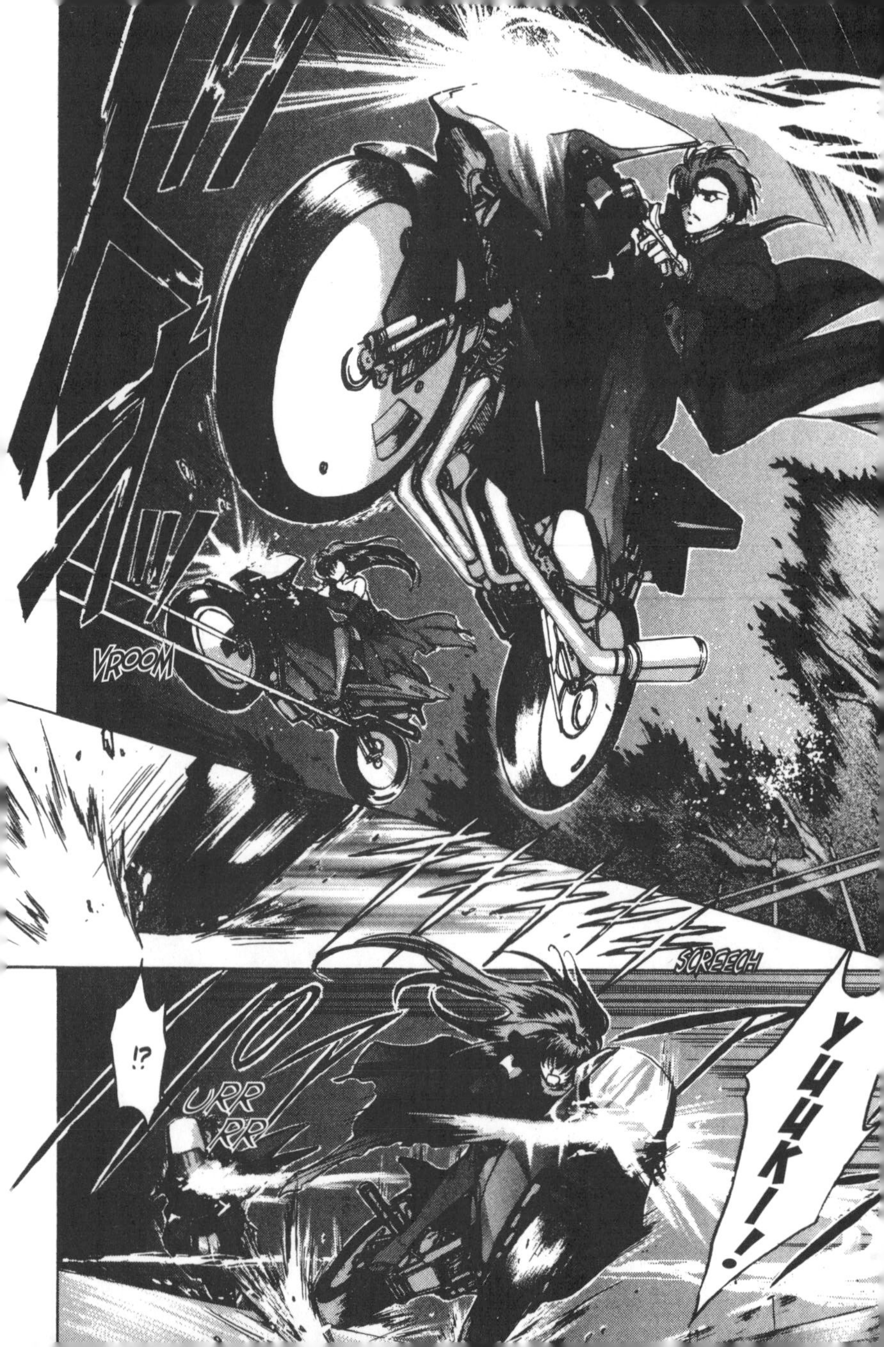
VROOM
SCREEECH
YUUKI!!!
!?
URR
RR

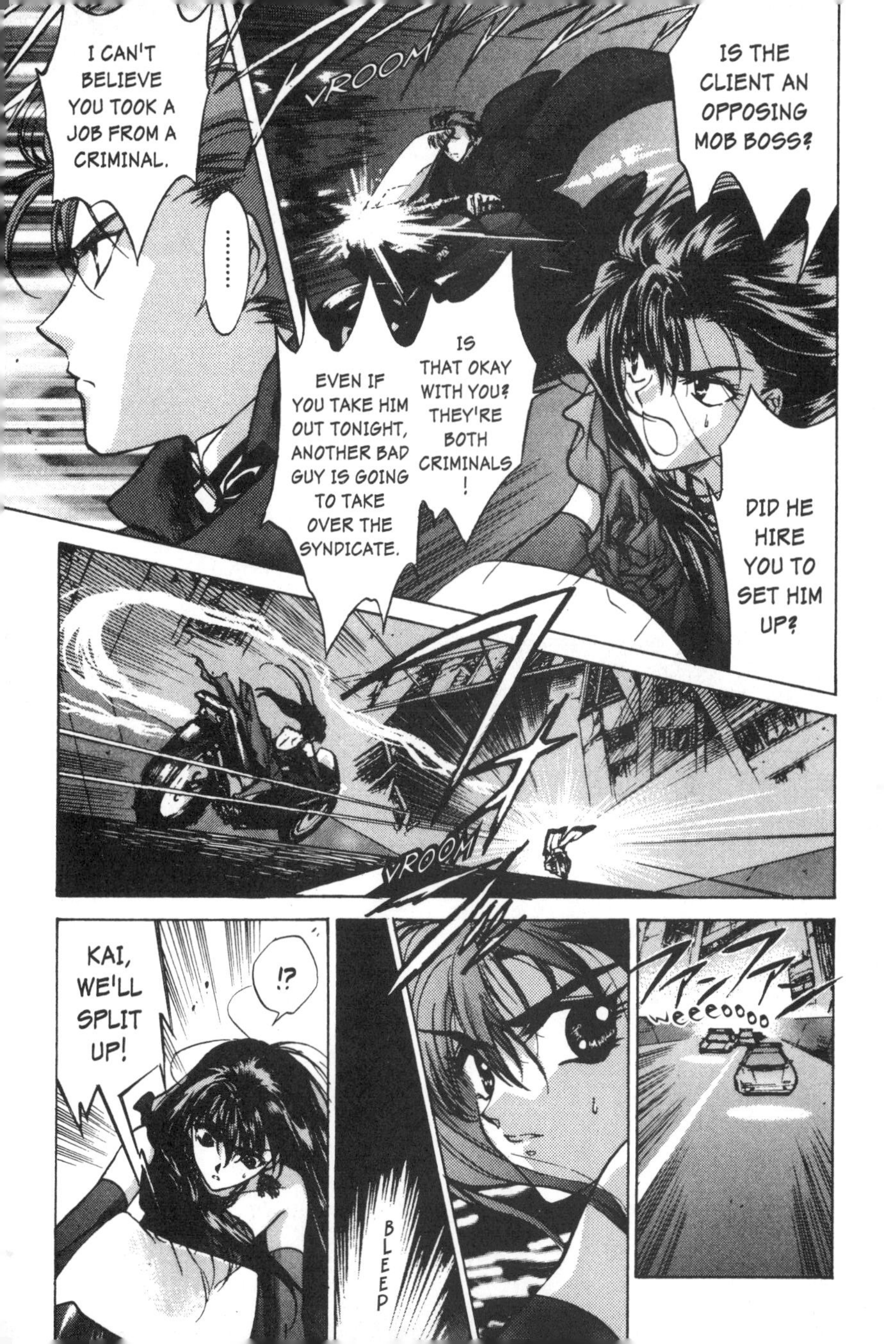
VROOM
IS THE CLIENT AN OPPOSING MOB BOSS?
DID HE HIRE YOU TO SET HIM UP?
IS THAT OKAY WITH YOU? THEY'RE BOTH CRIMINALS!
I CAN'T BELIEVE YOU TOOK A JOB FROM A CRIMINAL.
......
EVEN IF YOU TAKE HIM OUT TONIGHT, ANOTHER BAD GUY IS GOING TO TAKE OVER THE SYNDICATE.
VROOM
weeeoooo
BLEEP
KAI, WE'LL SPLIT UP!
!?

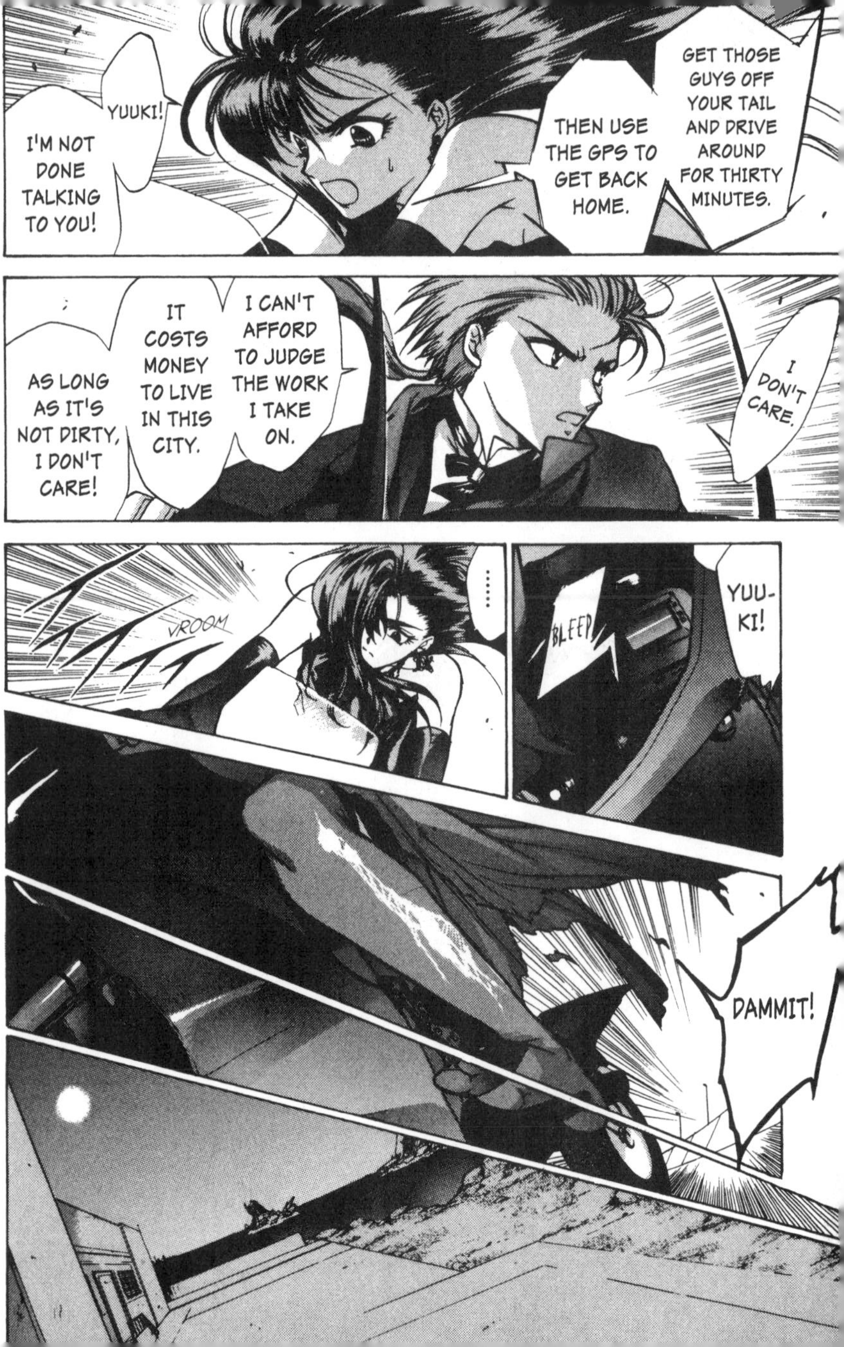
GET THOSE GUYS OFF YOUR TAIL AND DRIVE AROUND FOR THIRTY MINUTES.
THEN USE THE GPS TO GET BACK HOME.
YUUKI!
I'M NOT DONE TALKING TO YOU!
I DON'T CARE.
I CAN'T AFFORD TO JUDGE THE WORK I TAKE ON.
IT COSTS MONEY TO LIVE IN THIS CITY.
AS LONG AS IT'S NOT DIRTY, I DON'T CARE!
YUU-KI!
BLEEP
......
VROOM
DAMMIT!

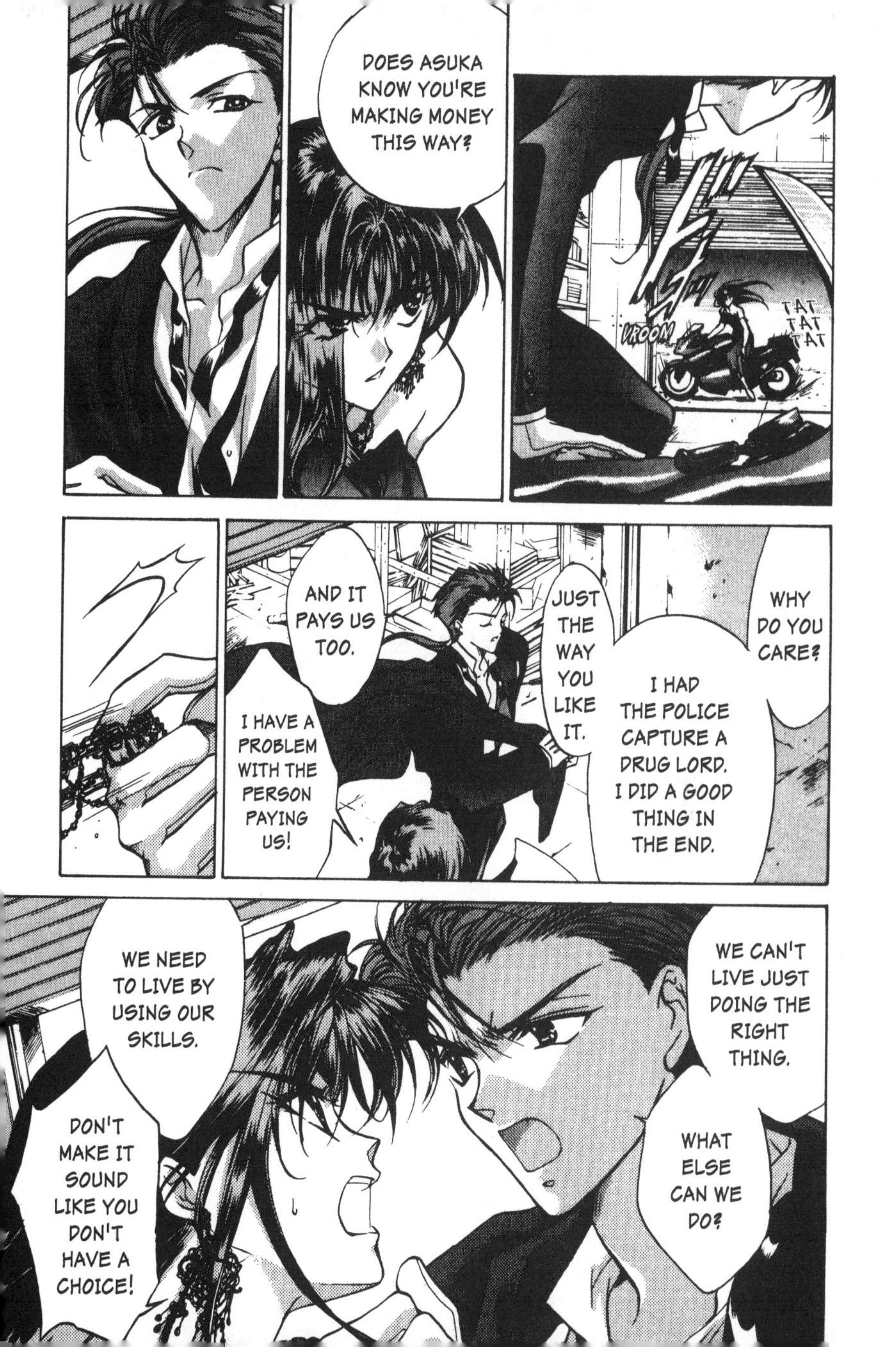
TAT TAT TAT
VROOM
DOES ASUKA KNOW YOU'RE MAKING MONEY THIS WAY?
WHY DO YOU CARE?
I HAD THE POLICE CAPTURE A DRUG LORD. I DID A GOOD THING IN THE END.
JUST THE WAY YOU LIKE IT.
AND IT PAYS US TOO.
I HAVE A PROBLEM WITH THE PERSON PAYING US!
WE CAN'T LIVE JUST DOING THE RIGHT THING.
WE NEED TO LIVE BY USING OUR SKILLS.
WHAT ELSE CAN WE DO?
DON'T MAKE IT SOUND LIKE YOU DON'T HAVE A CHOICE!

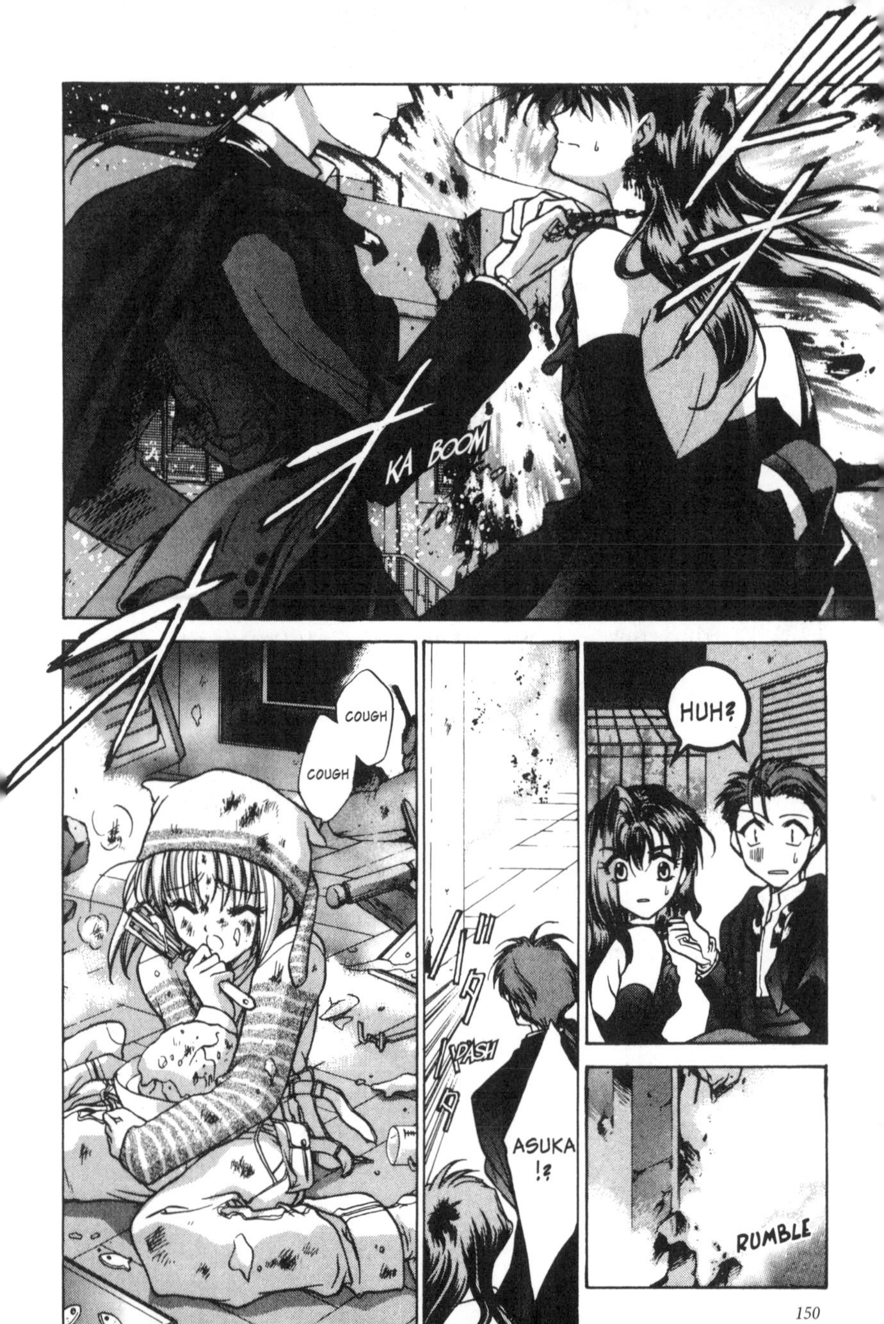
KA BOOM
HUH?
RUMBLE
PASH
ASUKA !?
COUGH
COUGH

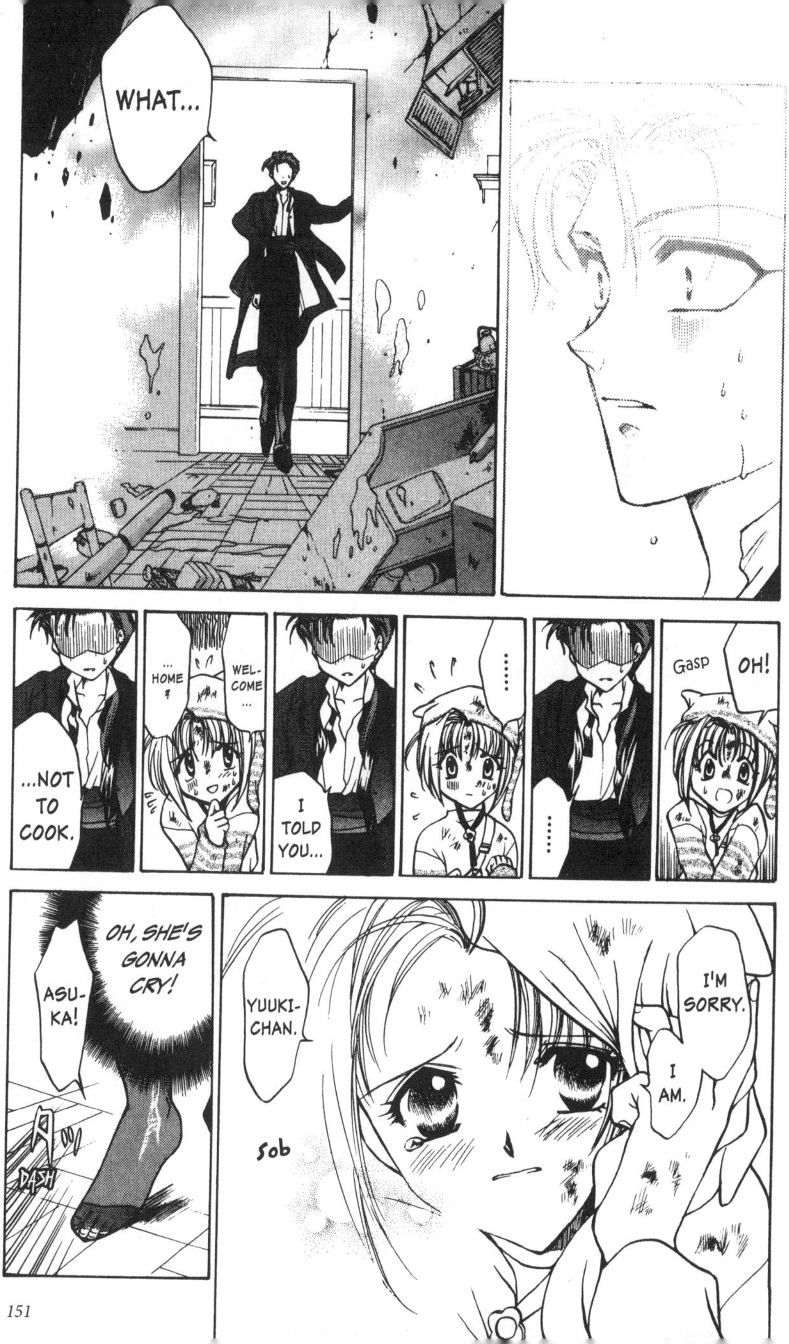
WHAT...
OH!
Gasp
......
......
I TOLD YOU...
WEL-COME...
...HOME?
...NOT TO COOK.
I'M SORRY.
I AM.
YUUKI-CHAN.
Sob
OH, SHE'S GONNA CRY!
ASU-KA!
DASH

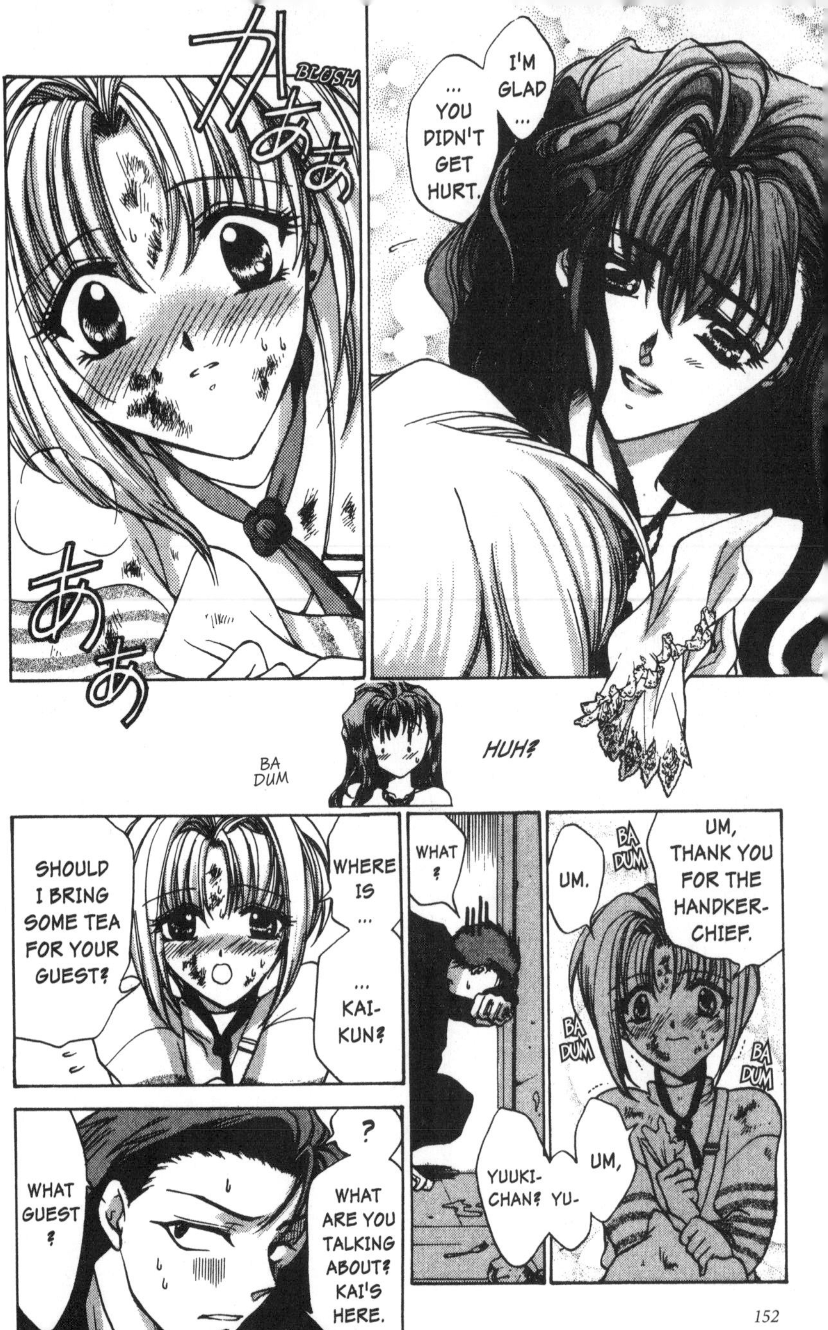
I'M GLAD ...
... YOU DIDN'T GET HURT.
カあああ
BLUSH
ああ
HUH?
BA DUM
UM, THANK YOU FOR THE HANDKER-CHIEF.
BA DUM
UM.
BA DUM
BA DUM
UM, YU-
YUUKI-CHAN?
WHAT?
WHERE IS ... ... KAI-KUN?
SHOULD I BRING SOME TEA FOR YOUR GUEST?
?
WHAT ARE YOU TALKING ABOUT? KAI'S HERE.
WHAT GUEST?

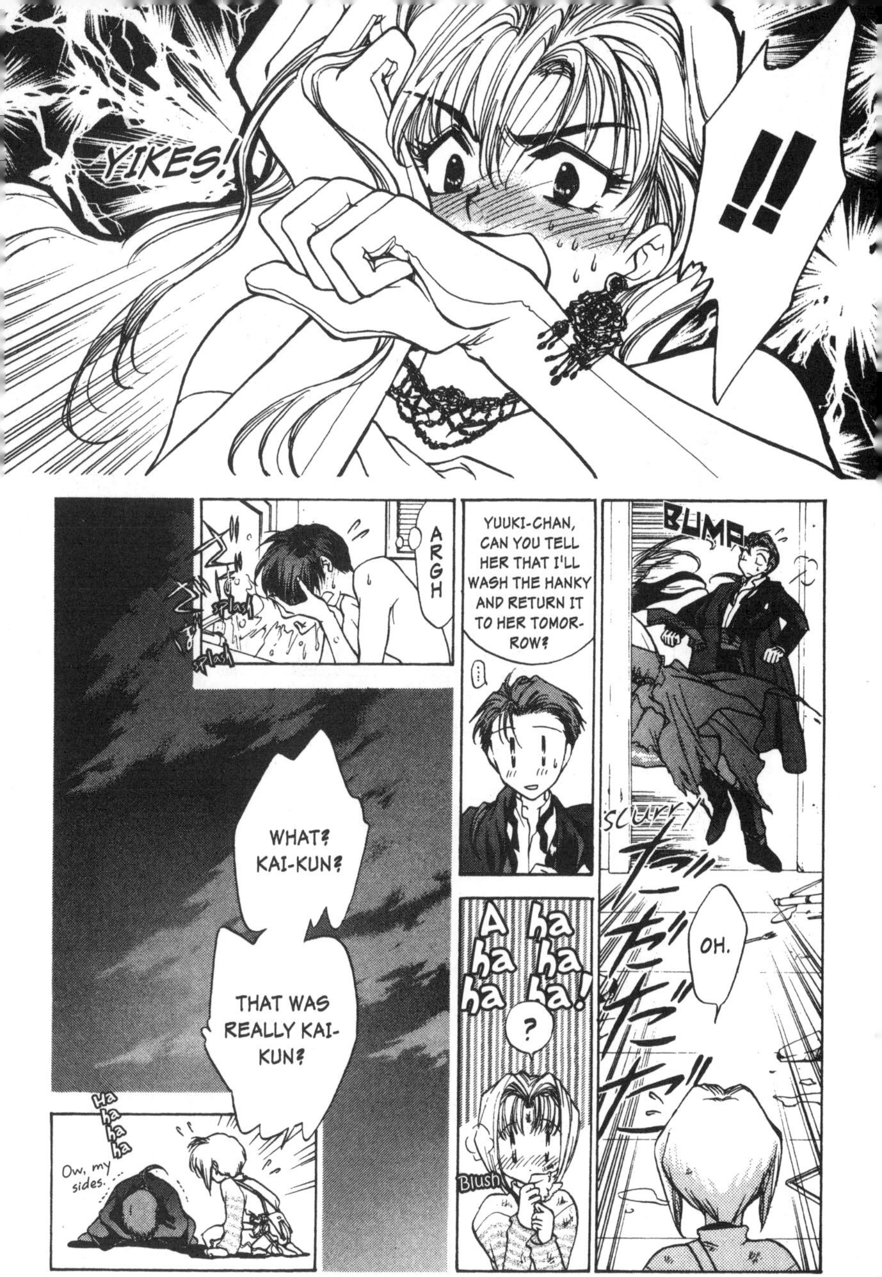
!!
YIKES!
BUMP
SCURRY
YUUKI-CHAN, CAN YOU TELL HER THAT I'LL WASH THE HANKY AND RETURN IT TO HER TOMORROW?
...
ARGH
splash
splash
OH.
A ha ha ha ha ha ha!
?
Blush
WHAT? KAI-KUN?
THAT WAS REALLY KAI-KUN?
Ha ha ha ha
Ow, my sides...

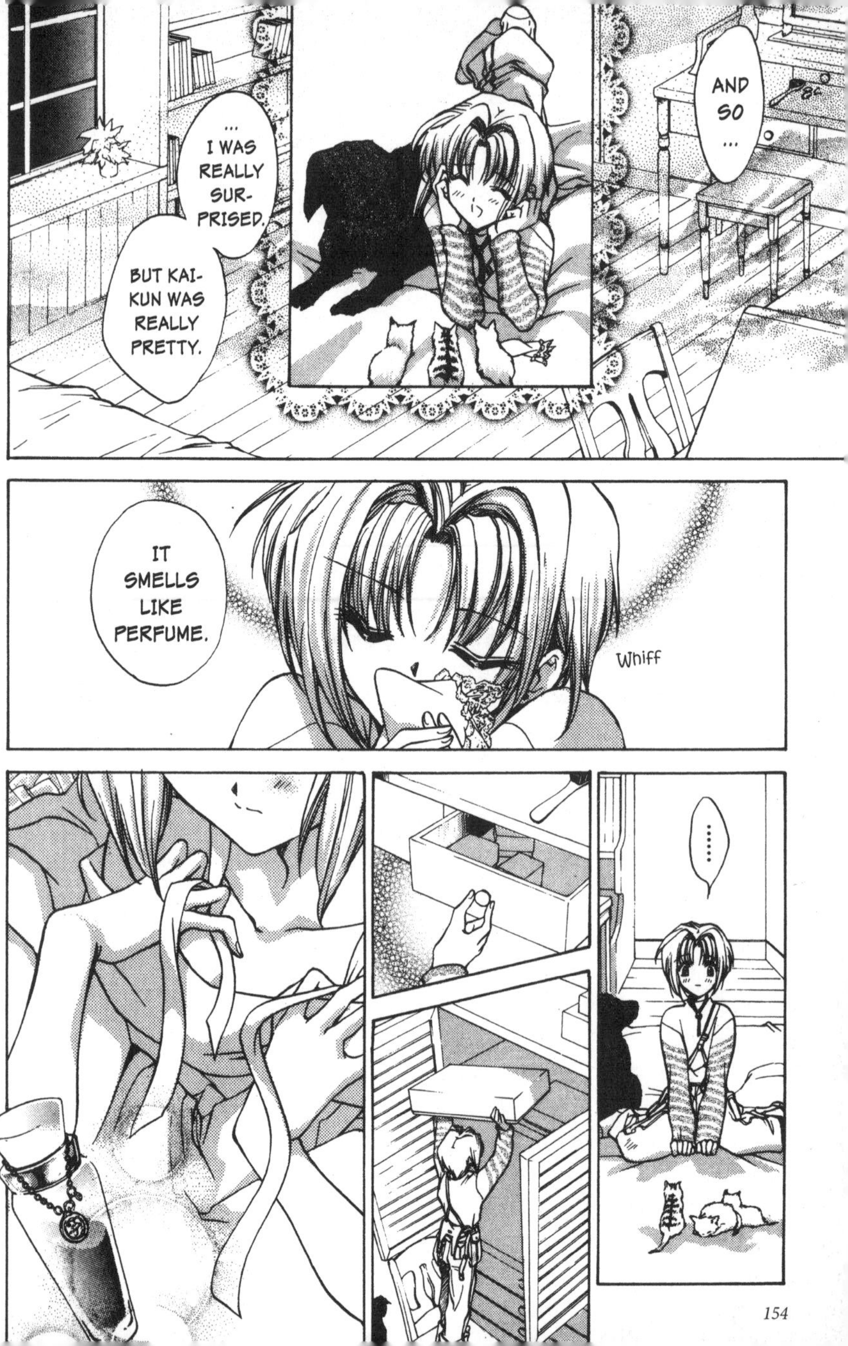
AND SO ...
... I WAS REALLY SUR-PRISED.
BUT KAI-KUN WAS REALLY PRETTY.
IT SMELLS LIKE PERFUME.
Whiff
......

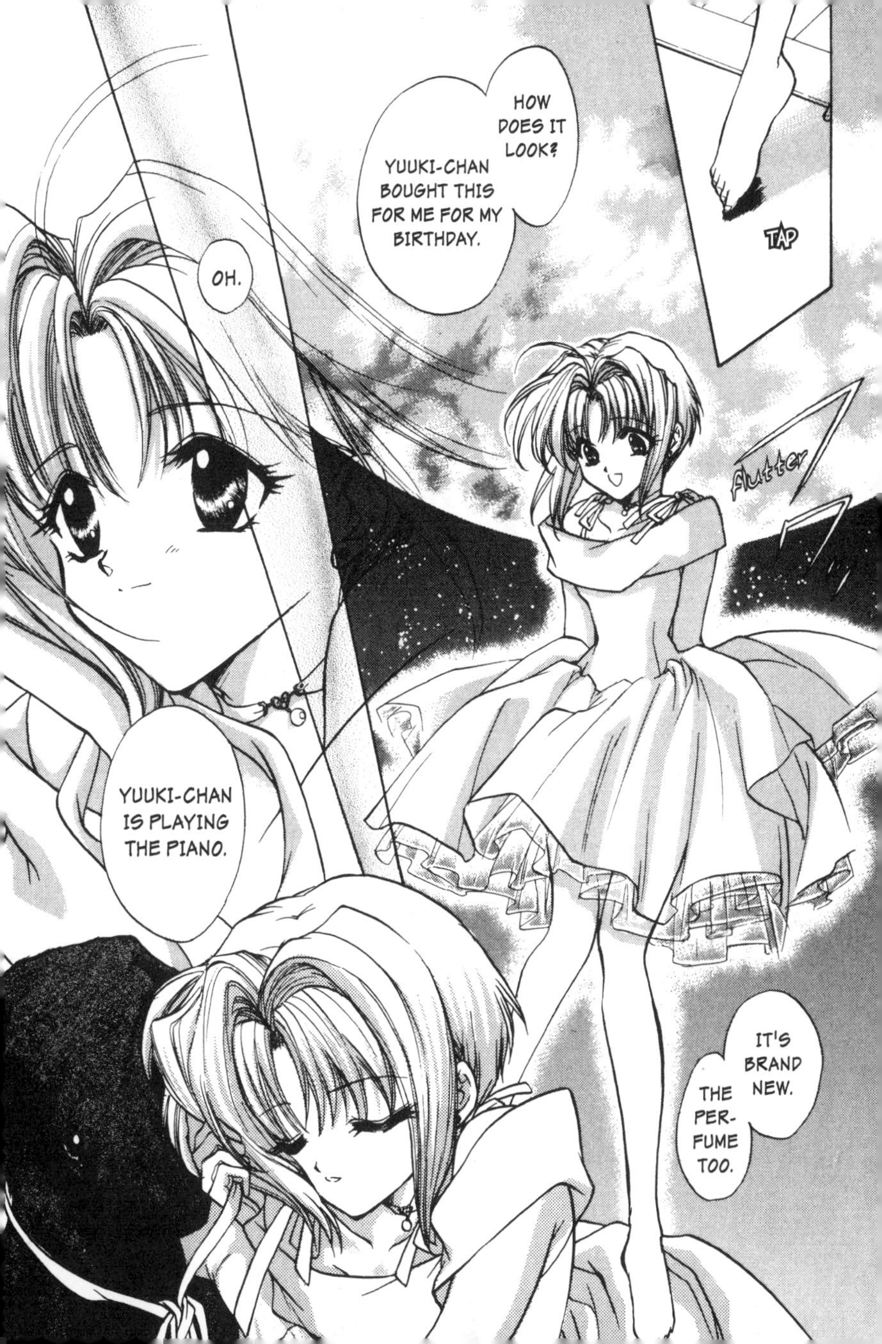
TAP
HOW DOES IT LOOK?
YUUKI-CHAN BOUGHT THIS FOR ME FOR MY BIRTHDAY.
flutter
IT'S BRAND NEW.
THE PER-FUME TOO.
OH.
YUUKI-CHAN IS PLAYING THE PIANO.

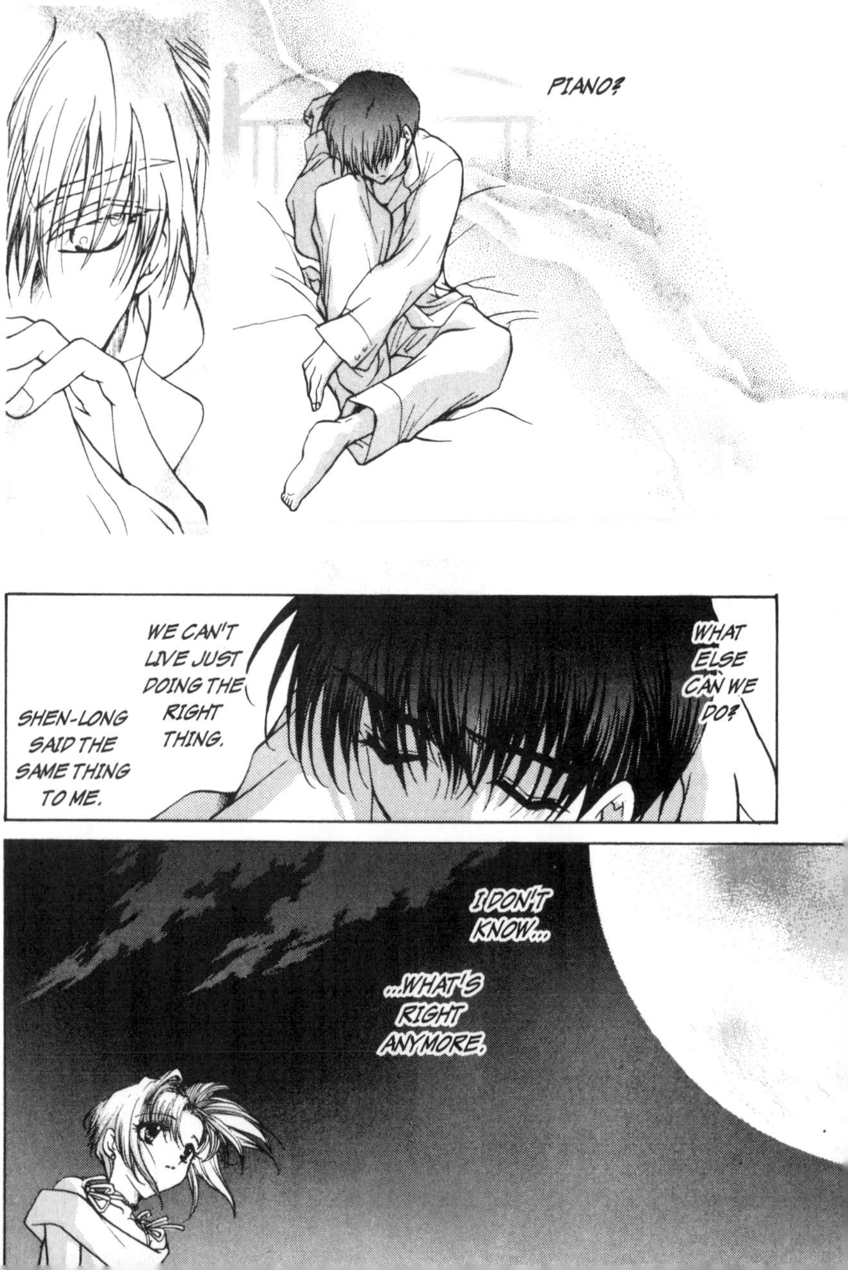
PIANO?
WHAT ELSE CAN WE DO?
WE CAN'T LIVE JUST DOING THE RIGHT THING.
SHEN-LONG SAID THE SAME THING TO ME.
I DON'T KNOW...
...WHAT'S RIGHT ANYMORE.

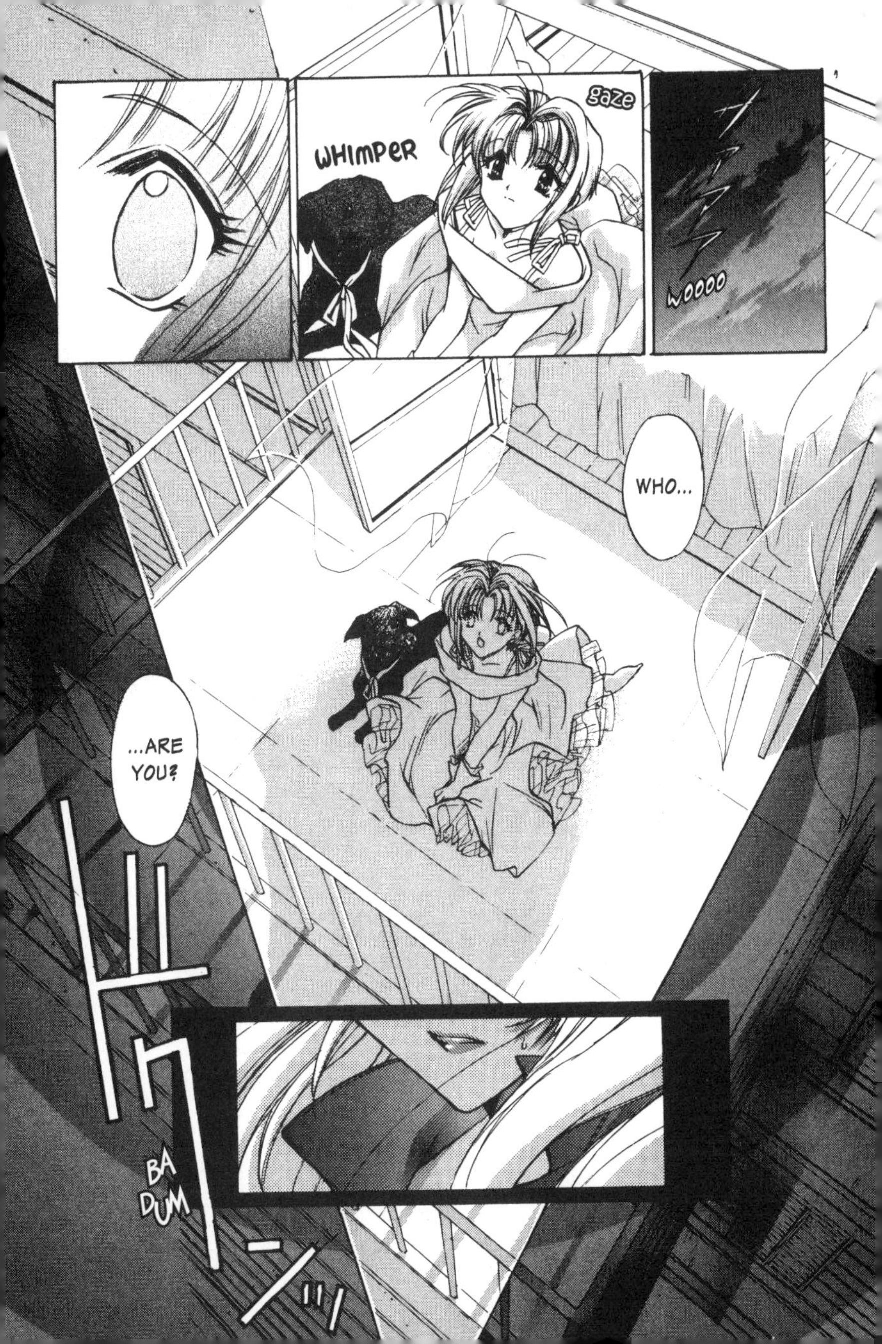
WOOOO
gaze
WHIMPER
WHO...
...ARE YOU?
BA DUM

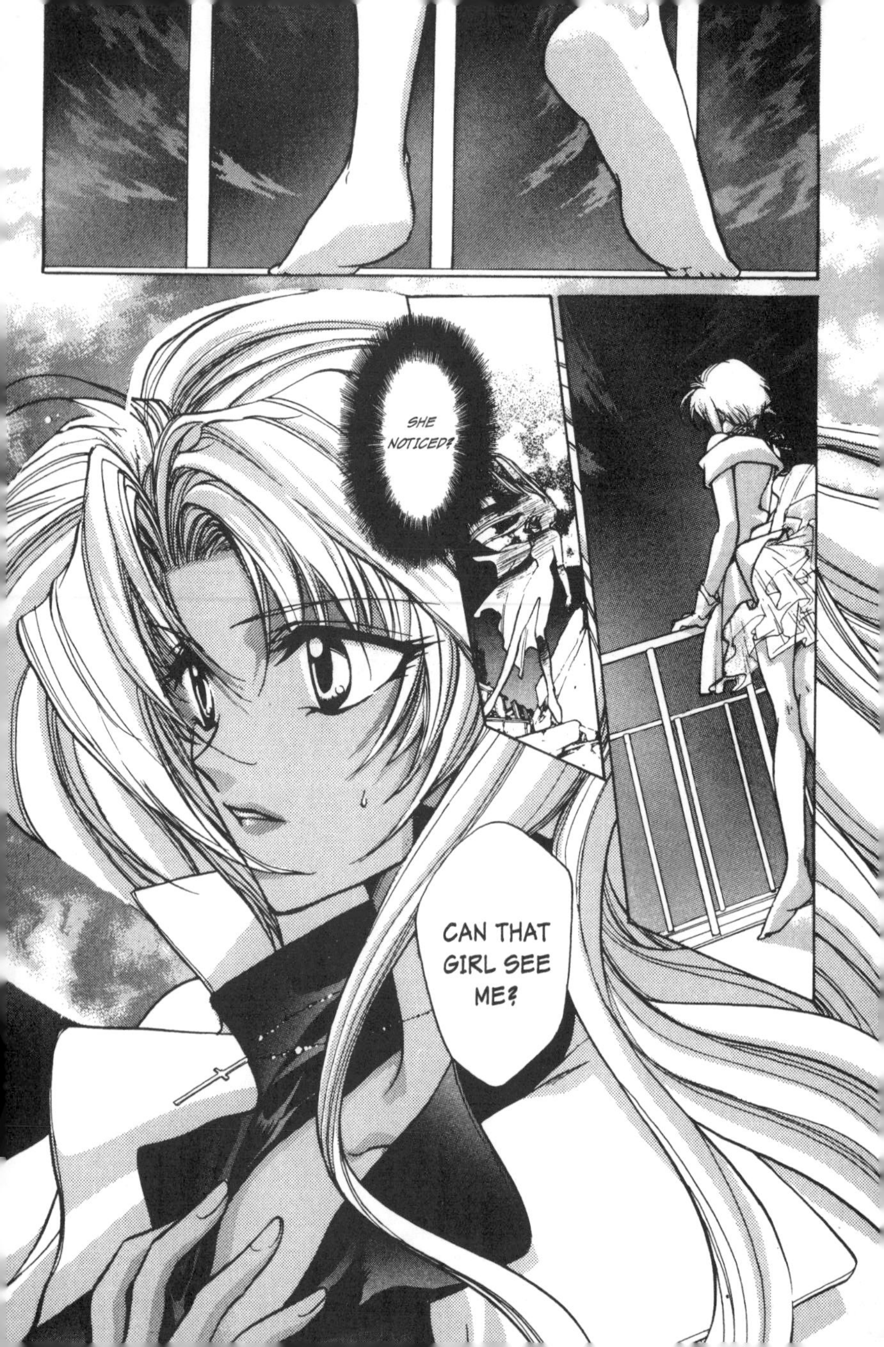
SHE NOTICED?
CAN THAT GIRL SEE ME?

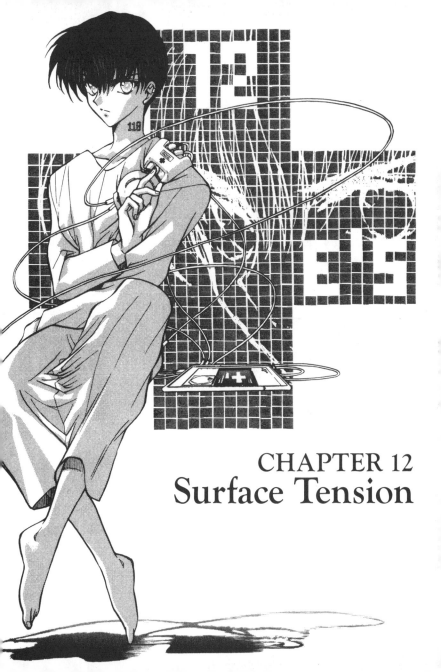

CHAPTER 12
Surface Tension

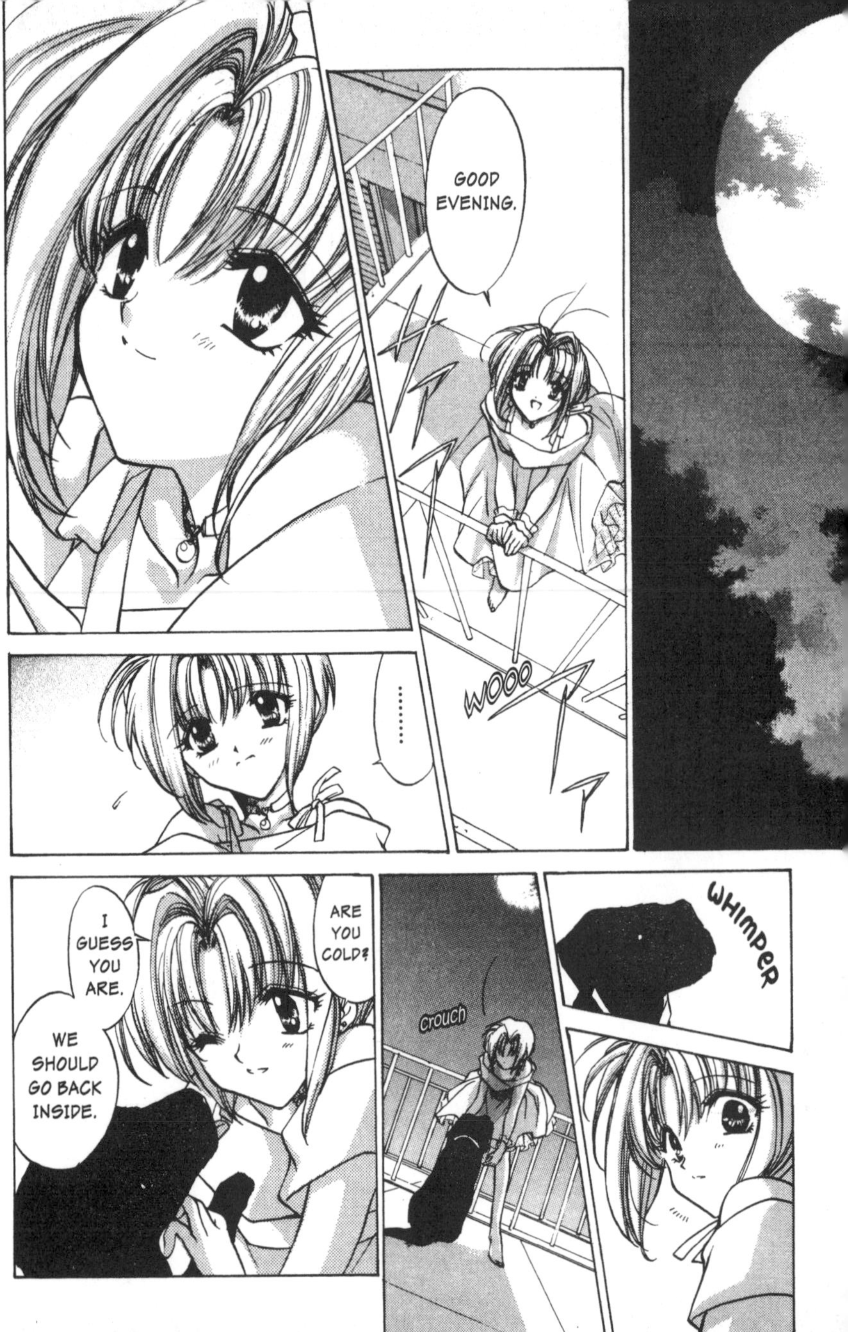
GOOD EVENING.
WOOO
......
WHIMPER
crouch
ARE YOU COLD?
I GUESS YOU ARE.
WE SHOULD GO BACK INSIDE.

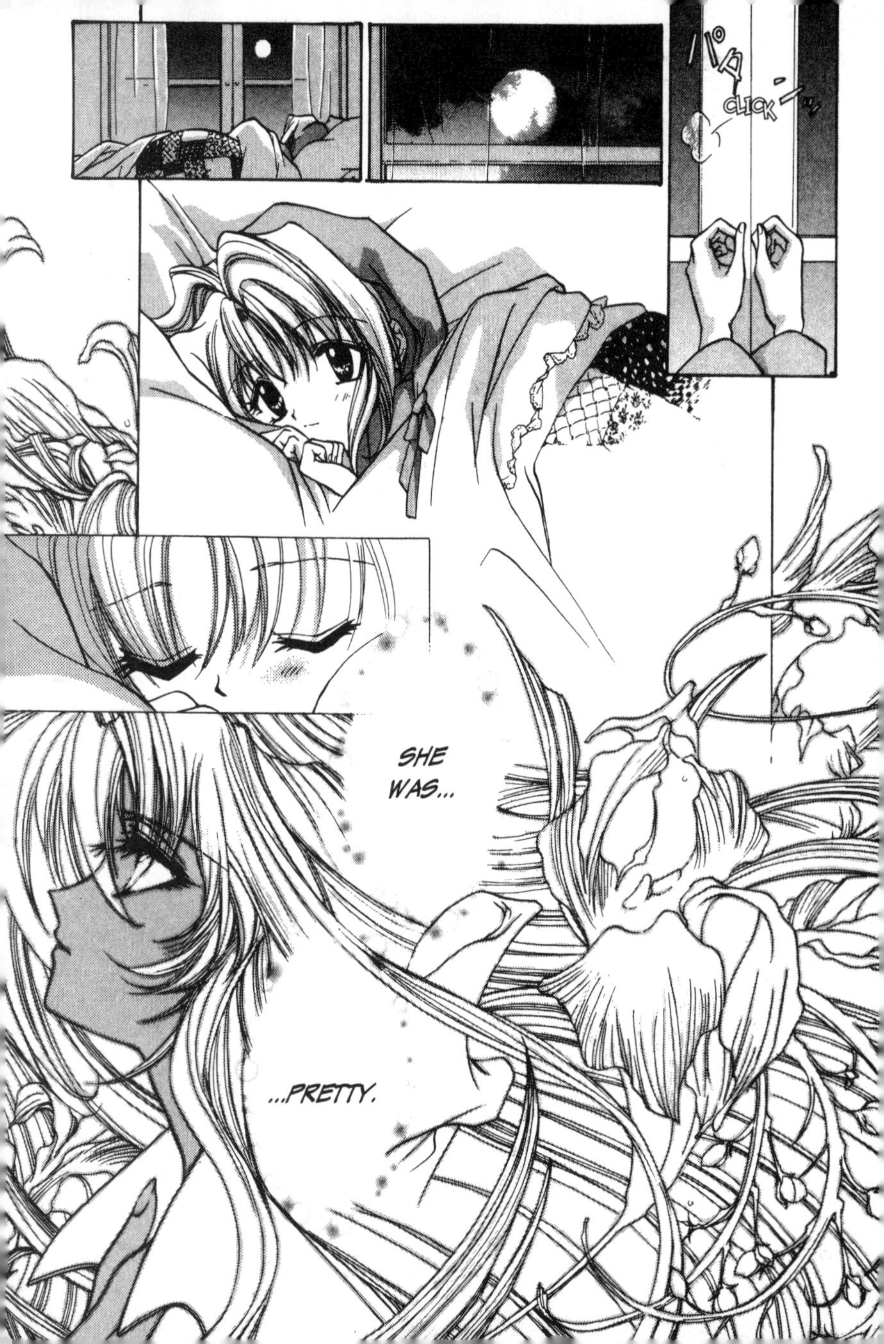
パチ
CLICK
SHE WAS...
...PRETTY.

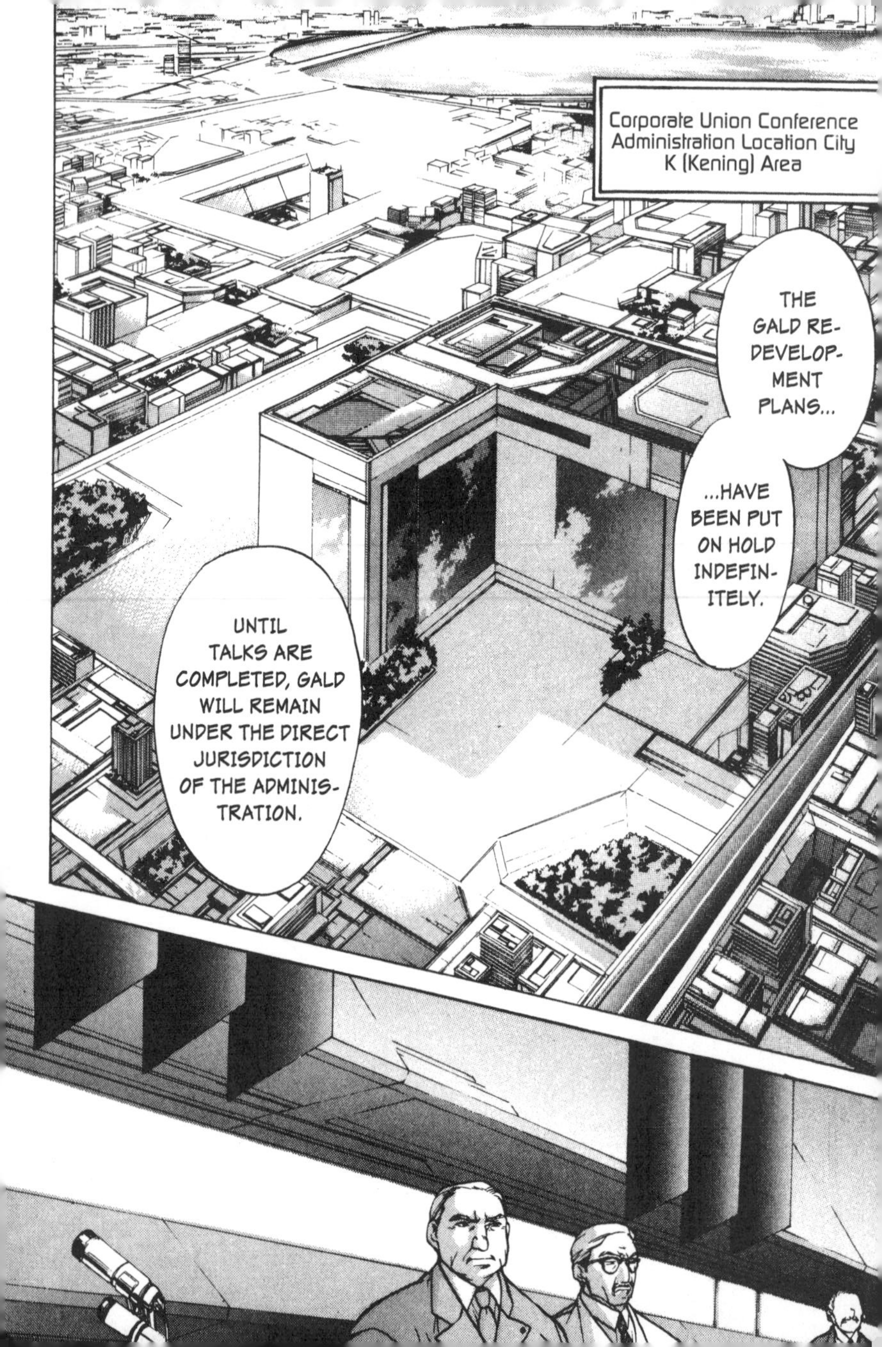
Corporate Union Conference Administration Location City K (Kening) Area
THE GALD RE-DEVELOPMENT PLANS...
...HAVE BEEN PUT ON HOLD INDEFINITELY.
UNTIL TALKS ARE COMPLETED, GALD WILL REMAIN UNDER THE DIRECT JURISDICTION OF THE ADMINISTRATION.

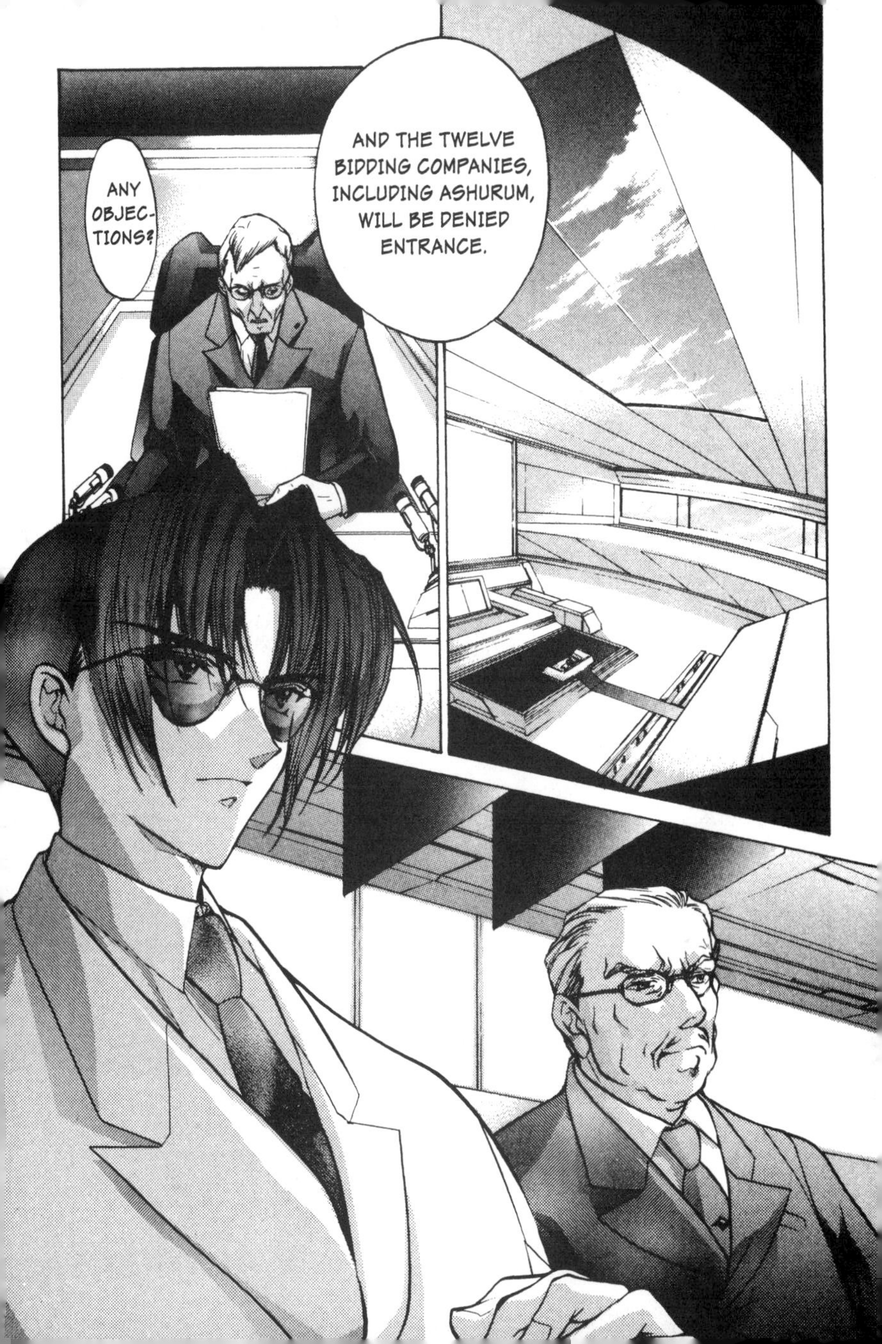
AND THE TWELVE BIDDING COMPANIES, INCLUDING ASHURUM, WILL BE DENIED ENTRANCE.
ANY OBJEC- TIONS?

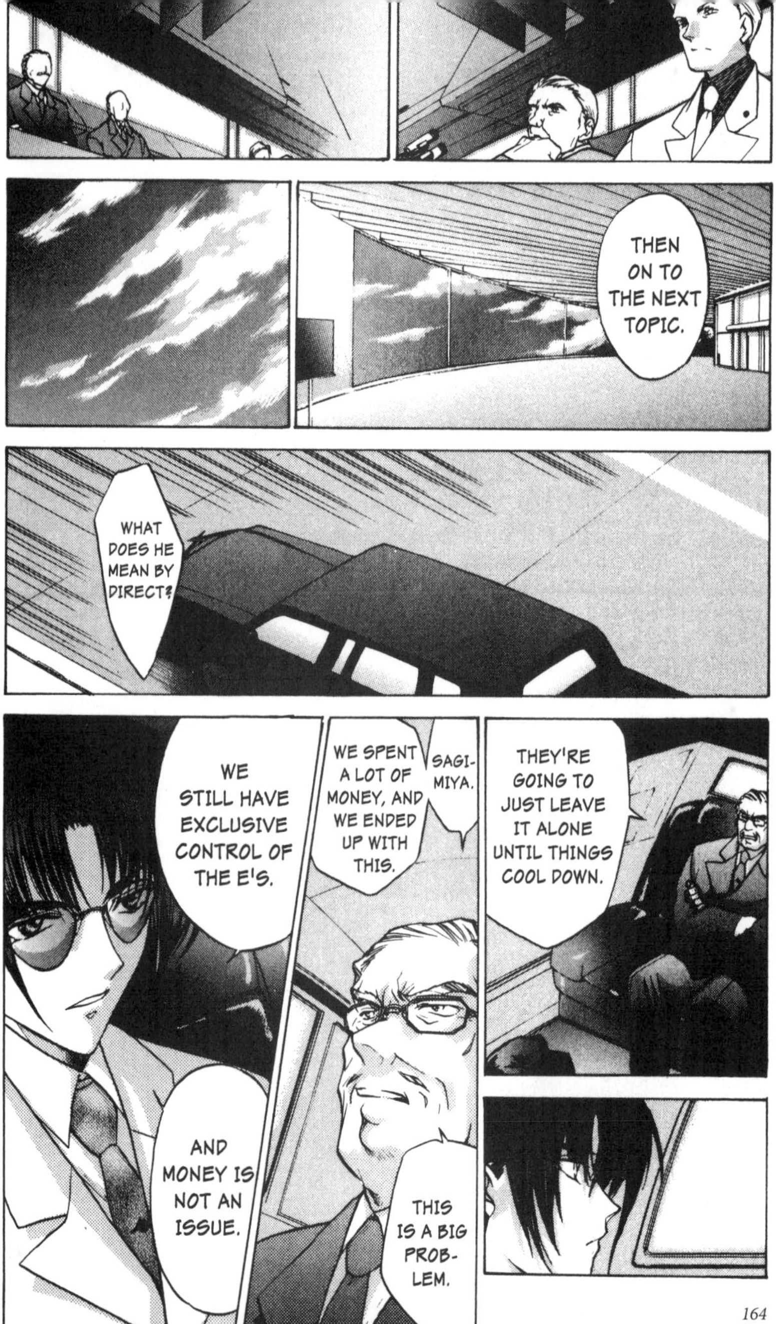
THEN ON TO THE NEXT TOPIC.
WHAT DOES HE MEAN BY DIRECT?
THEY'RE GOING TO JUST LEAVE IT ALONE UNTIL THINGS COOL DOWN.
SAGI-MIYA.
WE SPENT A LOT OF MONEY, AND WE ENDED UP WITH THIS.
THIS IS A BIG PROB-LEM.
WE STILL HAVE EXCLUSIVE CONTROL OF THE E'S.
AND MONEY IS NOT AN ISSUE.

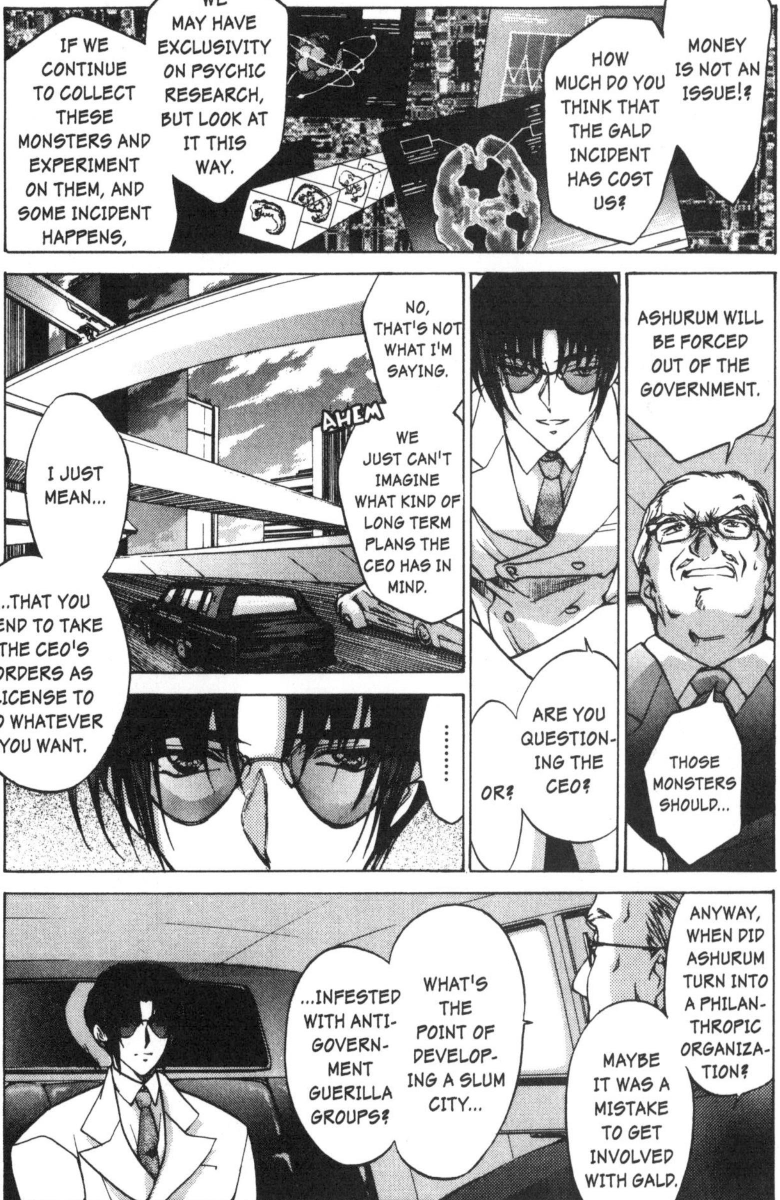
MONEY IS NOT AN ISSUE!?
HOW MUCH DO YOU THINK THAT THE GALD INCIDENT HAS COST US?
WE MAY HAVE EXCLUSIVITY ON PSYCHIC RESEARCH, BUT LOOK AT IT THIS WAY.
IF WE CONTINUE TO COLLECT THESE MONSTERS AND EXPERIMENT ON THEM, AND SOME INCIDENT HAPPENS,
ASHURUM WILL BE FORCED OUT OF THE GOVERNMENT.
THOSE MONSTERS SHOULD...
ARE YOU QUESTIONING THE CEO?
OR?
NO, THAT'S NOT WHAT I'M SAYING.
AHEM
WE JUST CAN'T IMAGINE WHAT KIND OF LONG TERM PLANS THE CEO HAS IN MIND.
I JUST MEAN...
...THAT YOU TEND TO TAKE THE CEO'S ORDERS AS LICENSE TO DO WHATEVER YOU WANT.
......
ANYWAY, WHEN DID ASHURUM TURN INTO A PHILANTHROPIC ORGANIZATION?
MAYBE IT WAS A MISTAKE TO GET INVOLVED WITH GALD.
WHAT'S THE POINT OF DEVELOPING A SLUM CITY...
...INFESTED WITH ANTI-GOVERNMENT GUERILLA GROUPS?

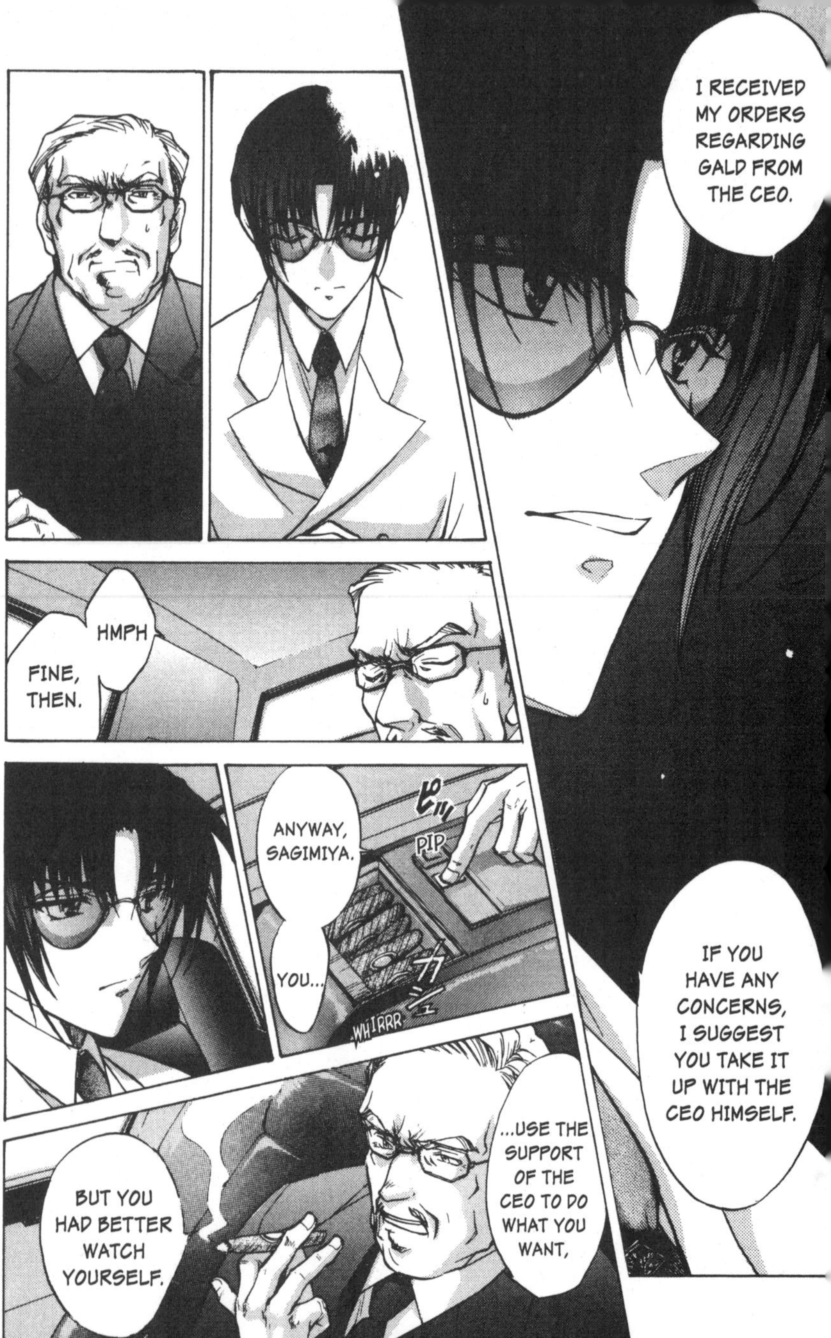
I RECEIVED MY ORDERS REGARDING GALD FROM THE CEO.
IF YOU HAVE ANY CONCERNS, I SUGGEST YOU TAKE IT UP WITH THE CEO HIMSELF.
HMPH
FINE, THEN.
ANYWAY, SAGIMIYA.
PIP
YOU...
WHIRRR
...USE THE SUPPORT OF THE CEO TO DO WHAT YOU WANT,
BUT YOU HAD BETTER WATCH YOURSELF.

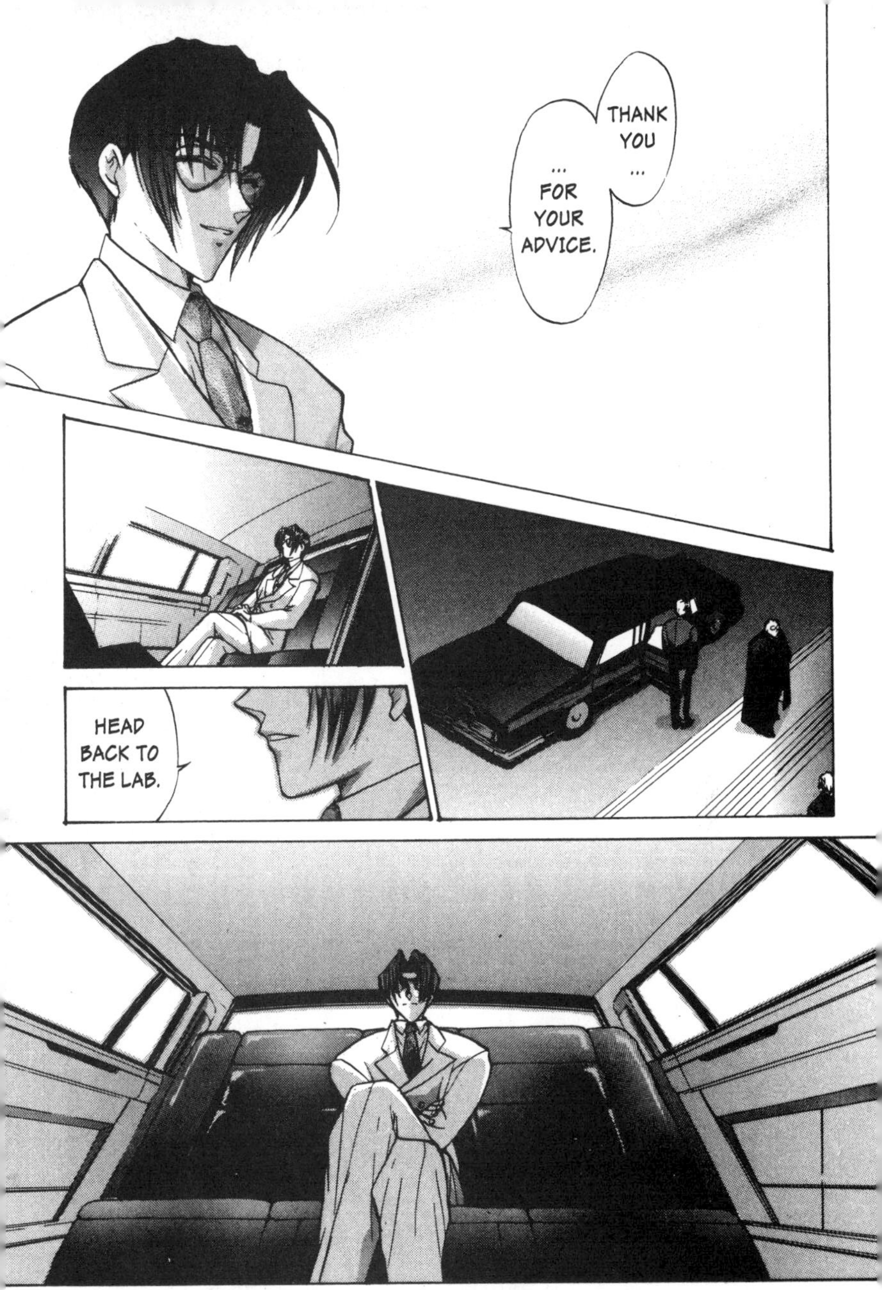
THANK YOU ...
... FOR YOUR ADVICE.
HEAD BACK TO THE LAB.

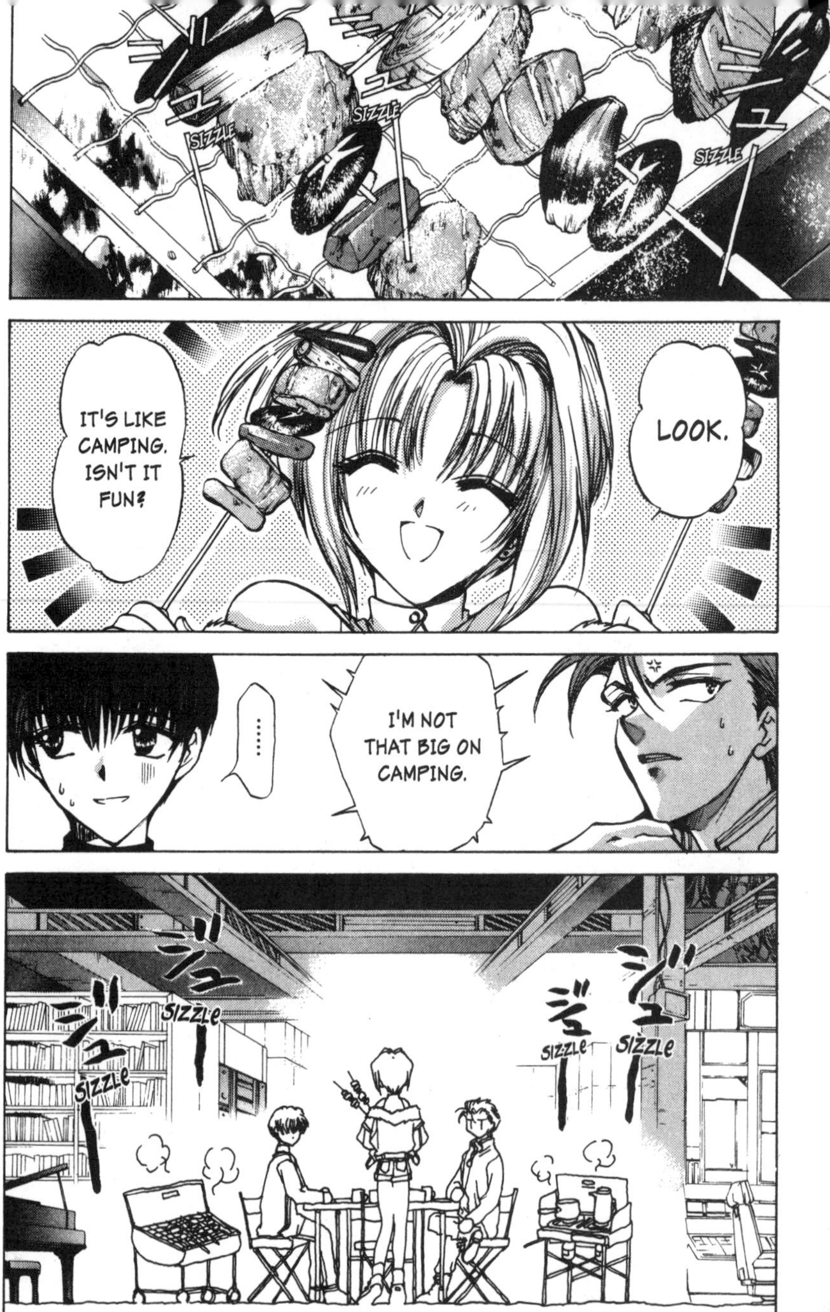
SIZZLE
SIZZLE
SIZZLE
LOOK.
IT'S LIKE CAMPING. ISN'T IT FUN?
I'M NOT THAT BIG ON CAMPING.
......
SIZZLE
SIZZLE
SIZZLE
SIZZLE

Please tell me where I am...... ※

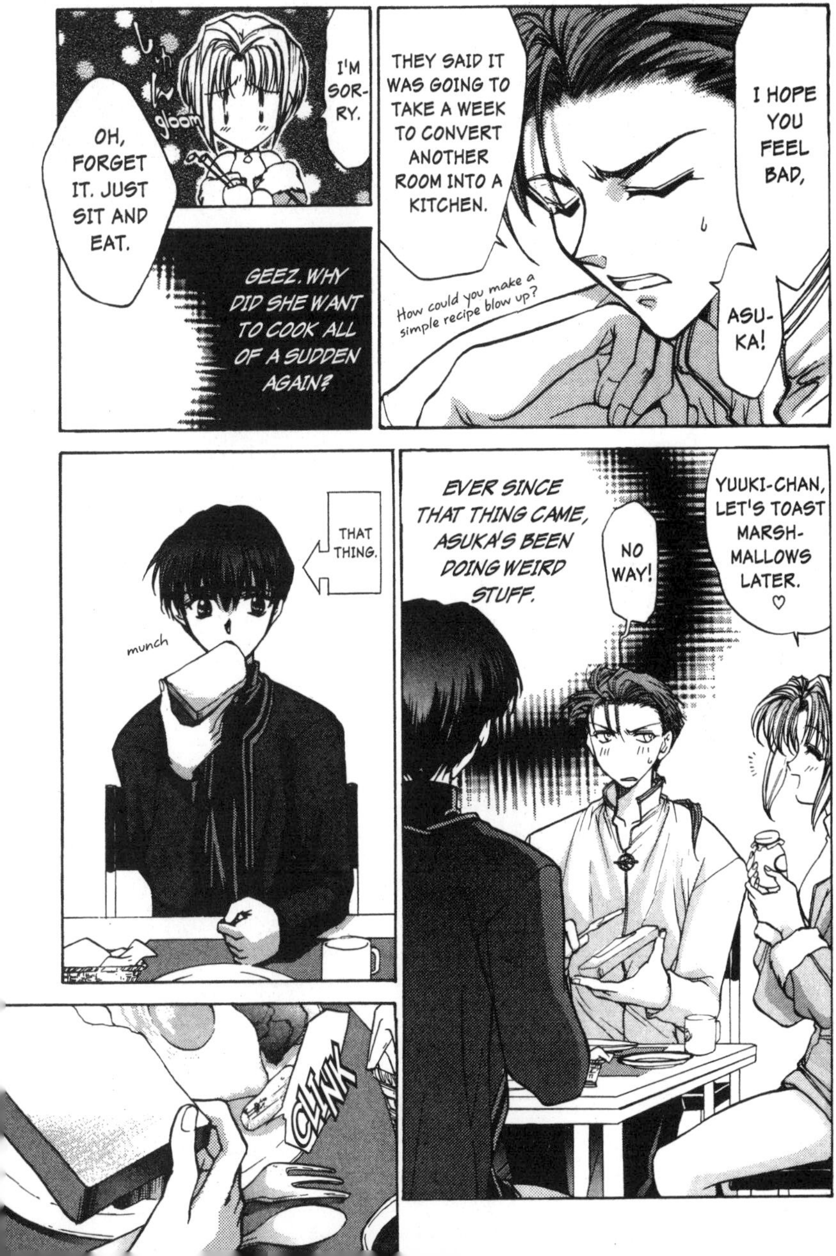
I HOPE YOU FEEL BAD,
ASUKA!
THEY SAID IT WAS GOING TO TAKE A WEEK TO CONVERT ANOTHER ROOM INTO A KITCHEN.
How could you make a simple recipe blow up?
I'M SOR-RY.
gloom
OH, FORGET IT. JUST SIT AND EAT.
GEEZ. WHY DID SHE WANT TO COOK ALL OF A SUDDEN AGAIN?
YUUKI-CHAN, LET'S TOAST MARSH-MALLOWS LATER. ♡
NO WAY!
EVER SINCE THAT THING CAME, ASUKA'S BEEN DOING WEIRD STUFF.
THAT THING.
munch
CLINK

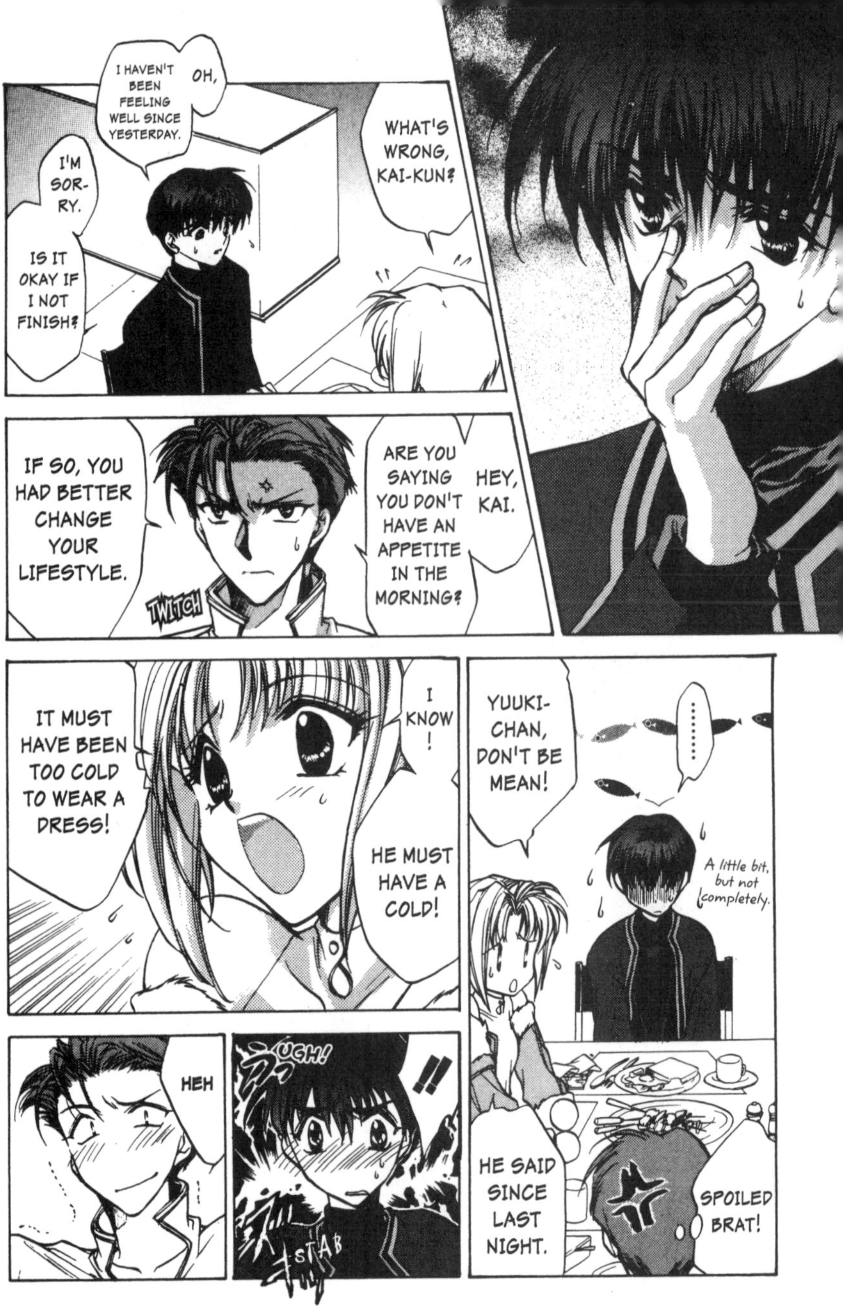

WHAT'S WRONG, KAI-KUN?
OH,
I HAVEN'T BEEN FEELING WELL SINCE YESTERDAY.
I'M SORRY.
IS IT OKAY IF I NOT FINISH?
HEY, KAI.
ARE YOU SAYING YOU DON'T HAVE AN APPETITE IN THE MORNING?
IF SO, YOU HAD BETTER CHANGE YOUR LIFESTYLE.
TWITCH
....
YUUKI-CHAN, DON'T BE MEAN!
A little bit, but not completely.
SPOILED BRAT!
HE SAID SINCE LAST NIGHT.
I KNOW!
HE MUST HAVE A COLD!
IT MUST HAVE BEEN TOO COLD TO WEAR A DRESS!
UGH!
!!
STAB
HEH

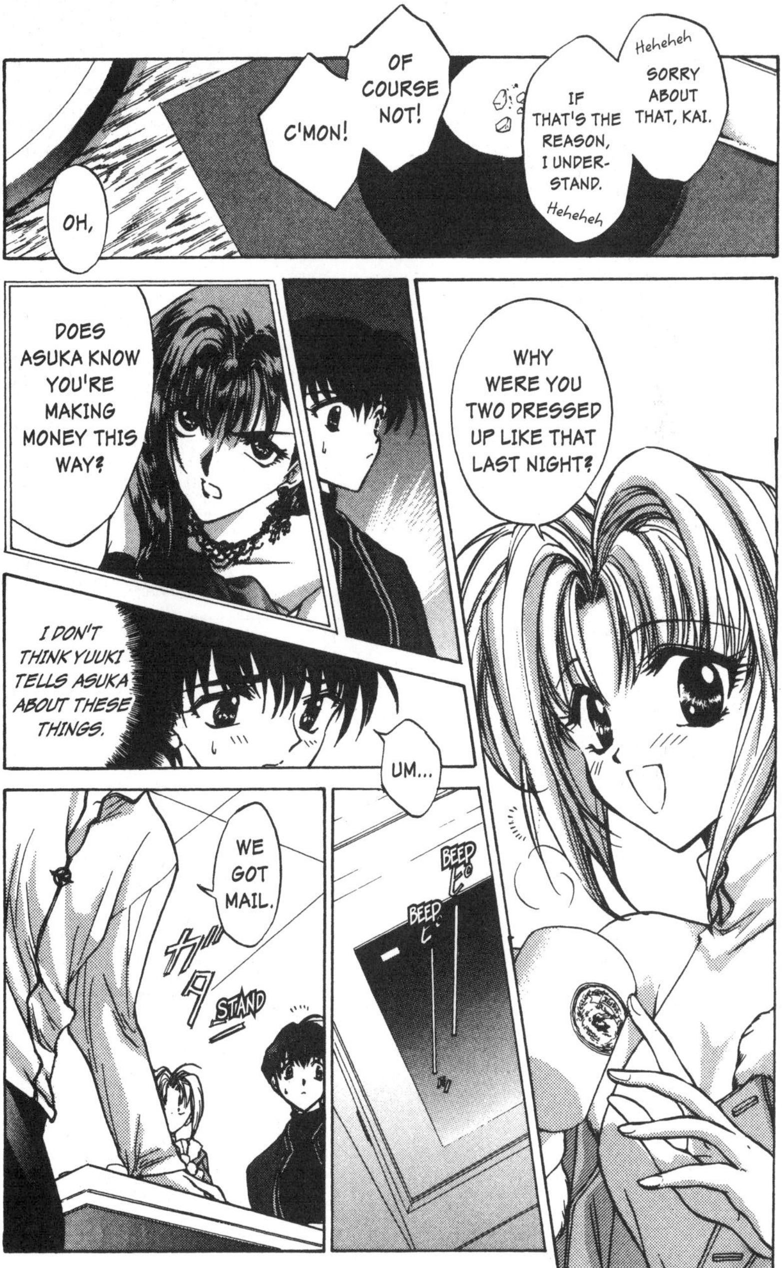
Heheheh
SORRY ABOUT THAT, KAI.
IF THAT'S THE REASON, I UNDERSTAND.
Heheheh
OF COURSE NOT!
C'MON!
OH,
WHY WERE YOU TWO DRESSED UP LIKE THAT LAST NIGHT?
DOES ASUKA KNOW YOU'RE MAKING MONEY THIS WAY?
I DON'T THINK YUUKI TELLS ASUKA ABOUT THESE THINGS.
UM...
BEEP
BEEP
WE GOT MAIL.
STAND

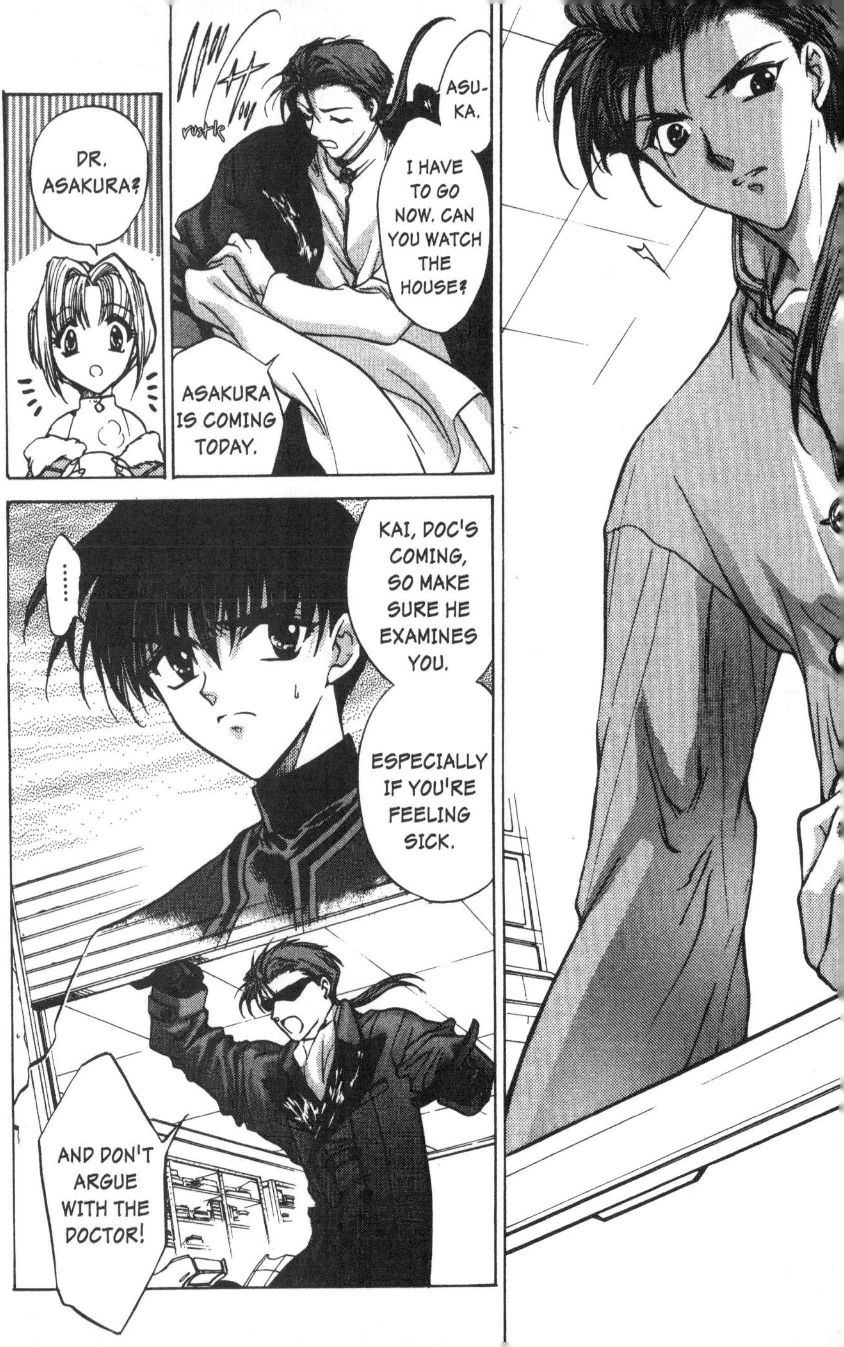
rustle
ASU-KA.
I HAVE TO GO NOW. CAN YOU WATCH THE HOUSE?
ASAKURA IS COMING TODAY.
DR. ASAKURA?
KAI, DOC'S COMING, SO MAKE SURE HE EXAMINES YOU.
ESPECIALLY IF YOU'RE FEELING SICK.
......
AND DON'T ARGUE WITH THE DOCTOR!

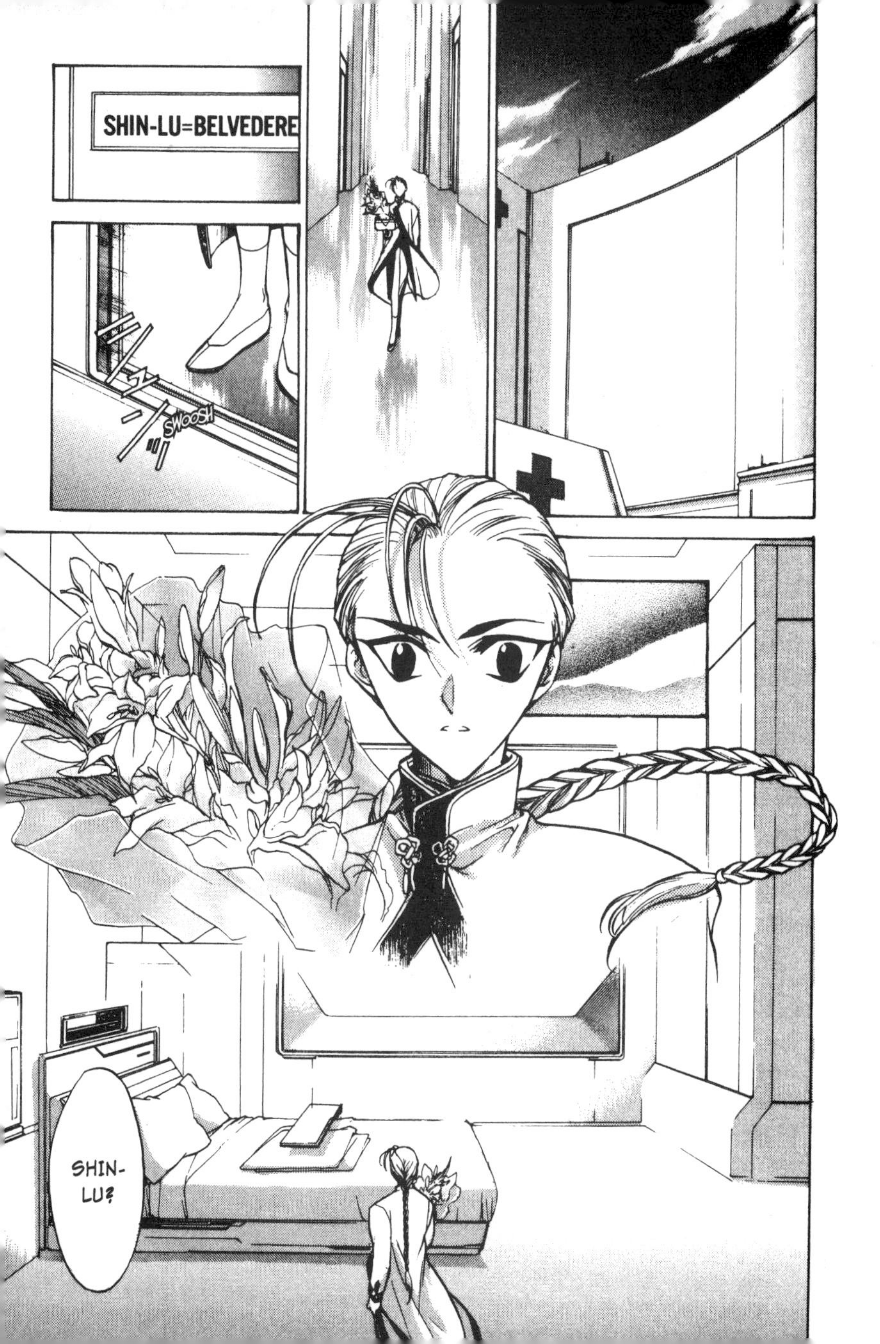
SHIN-LU=BELVEDERE
SWOOSH
SHIN-LU?

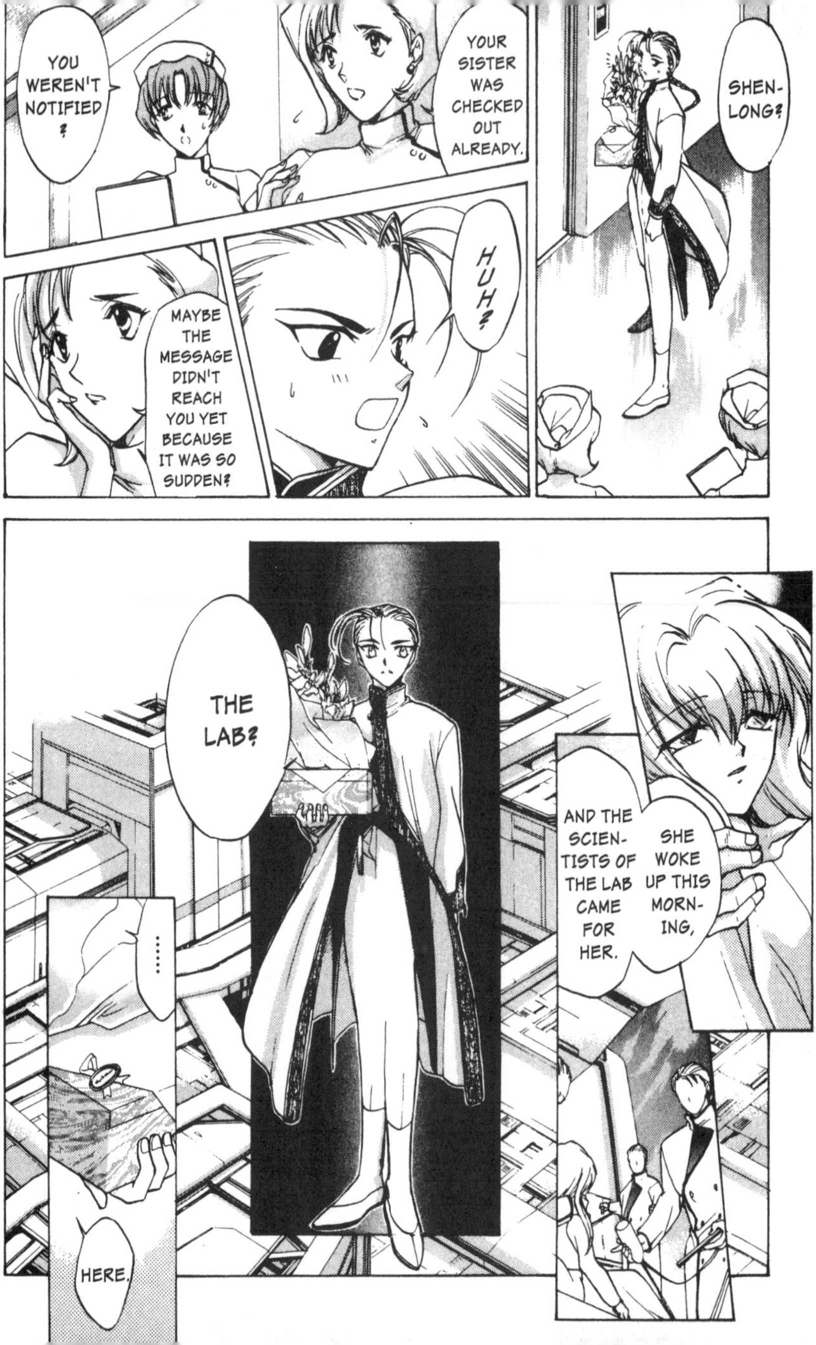
SHEN-LONG?
YOUR SISTER WAS CHECKED OUT ALREADY.
YOU WEREN'T NOTIFIED?
HUH?
MAYBE THE MESSAGE DIDN'T REACH YOU YET BECAUSE IT WAS SO SUDDEN?
SHE WOKE UP THIS MORNING,
AND THE SCIEN-TISTS OF THE LAB CAME FOR HER.
THE LAB?
......
HERE.

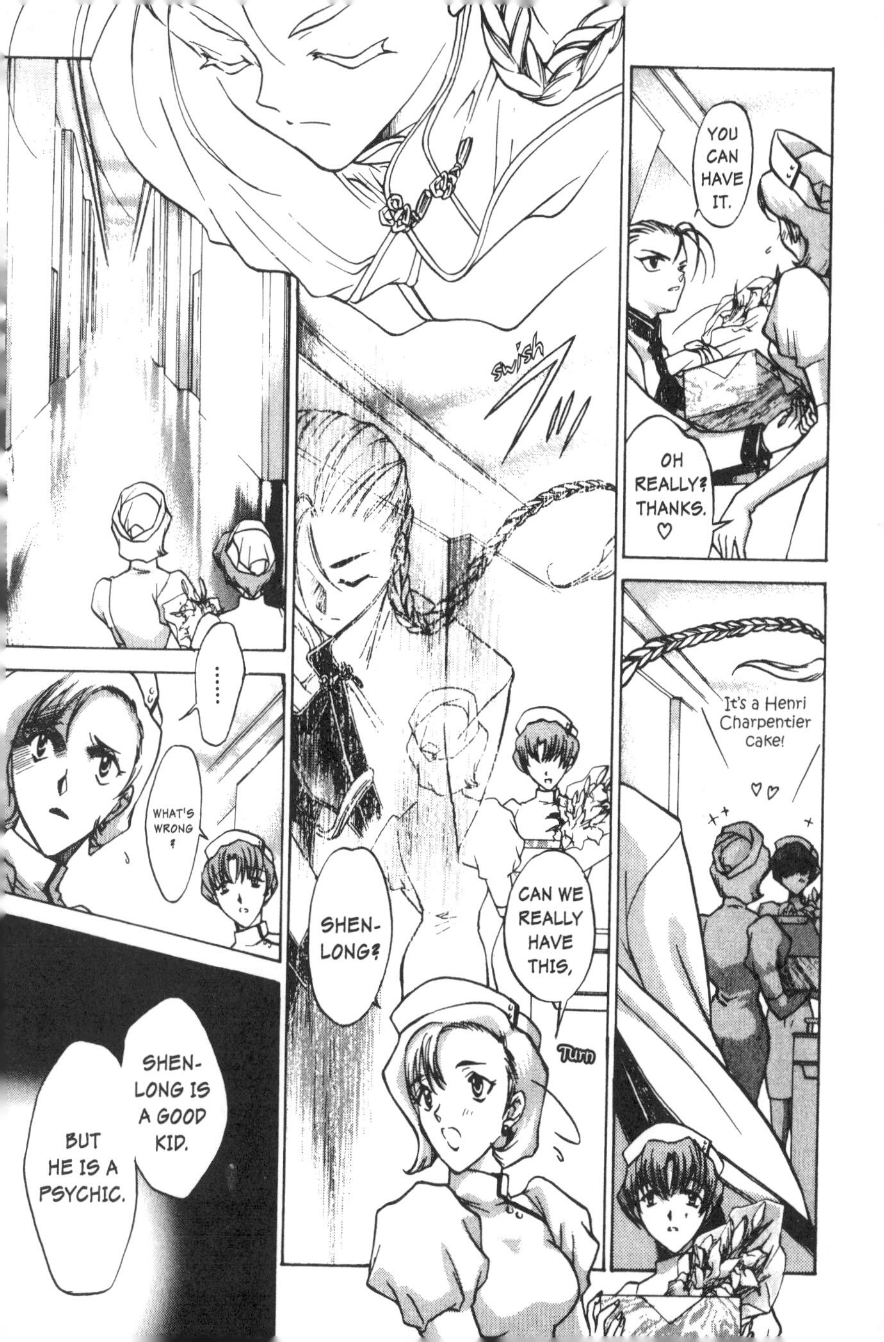
YOU CAN HAVE IT.
OH REALLY? THANKS. ♡
It's a Henri Charpentier cake!
swish
CAN WE REALLY HAVE THIS,
Turn
SHEN-LONG?
......
WHAT'S WRONG?
SHEN-LONG IS A GOOD KID.
BUT HE IS A PSYCHIC.

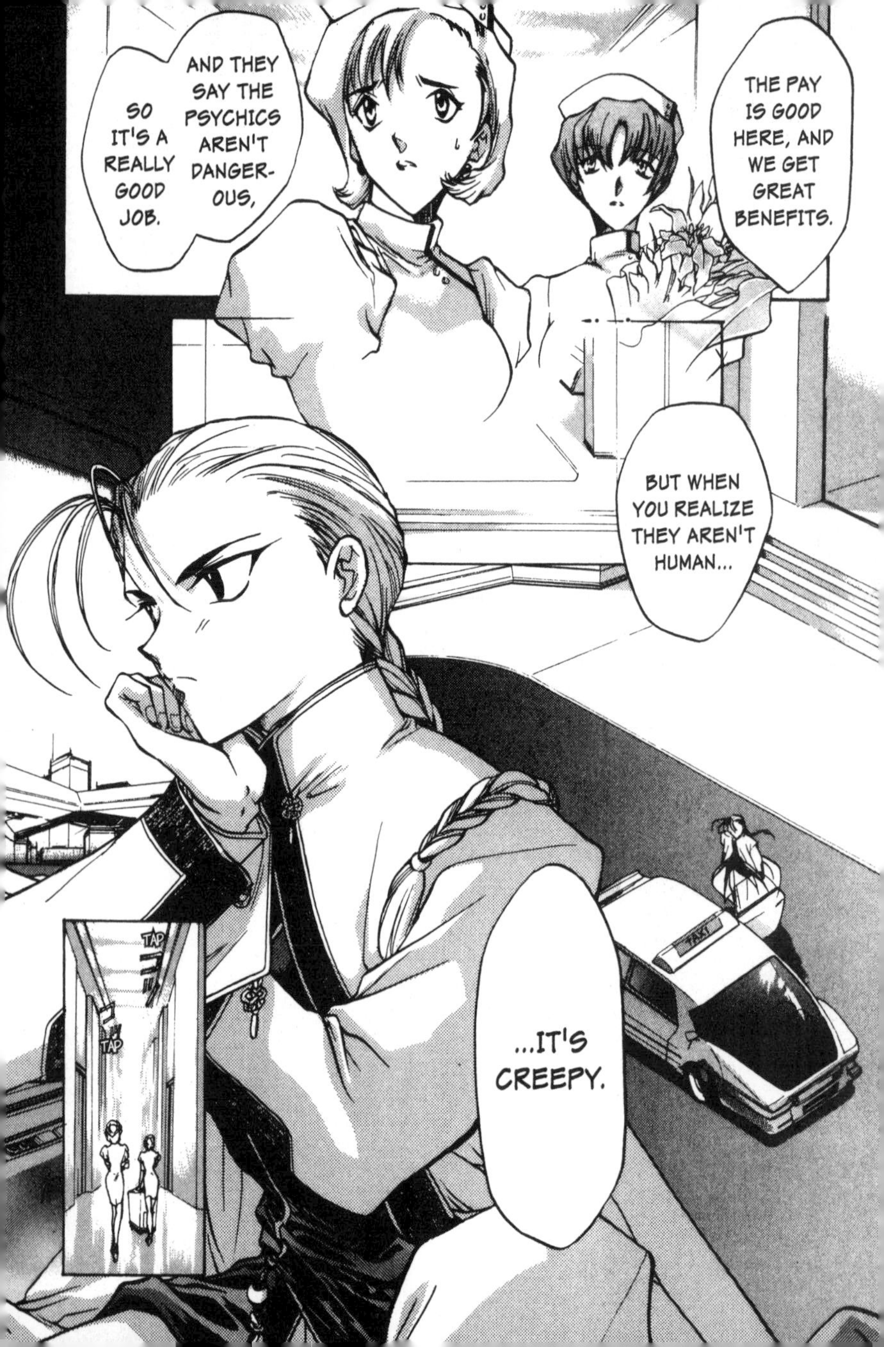
THE PAY IS GOOD HERE, AND WE GET GREAT BENEFITS.
AND THEY SAY THE PSYCHICS AREN'T DANGER-OUS,
SO IT'S A REALLY GOOD JOB.
BUT WHEN YOU REALIZE THEY AREN'T HUMAN...
...IT'S CREEPY.
TAP
TAP

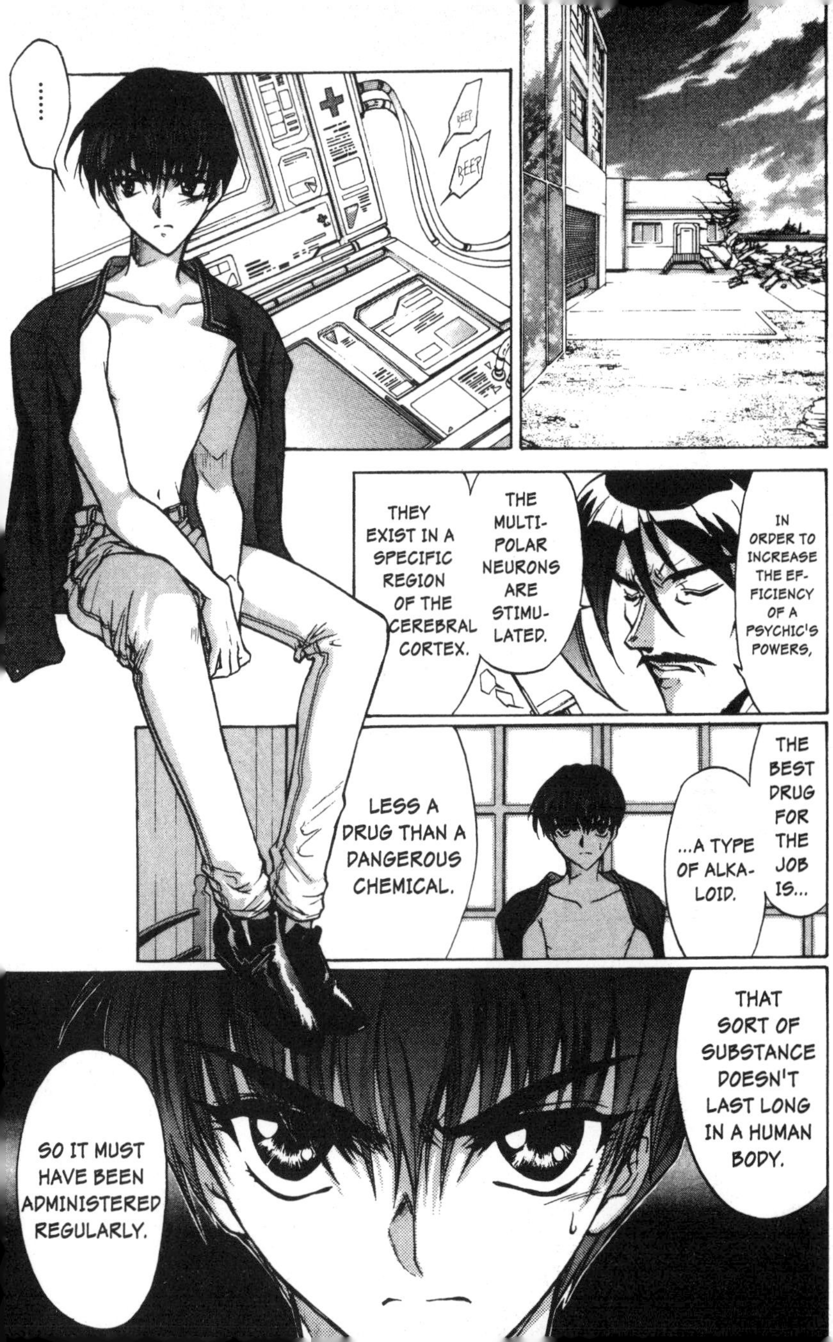
BEEP
BEEP
......
IN ORDER TO INCREASE THE EFFICIENCY OF A PSYCHIC'S POWERS,
THE MULTI-POLAR NEURONS ARE STIMULATED.
THEY EXIST IN A SPECIFIC REGION OF THE CEREBRAL CORTEX.
THE BEST DRUG FOR THE JOB IS...
...A TYPE OF ALKALOID.
LESS A DRUG THAN A DANGEROUS CHEMICAL.
THAT SORT OF SUBSTANCE DOESN'T LAST LONG IN A HUMAN BODY.
SO IT MUST HAVE BEEN ADMINISTERED REGULARLY.

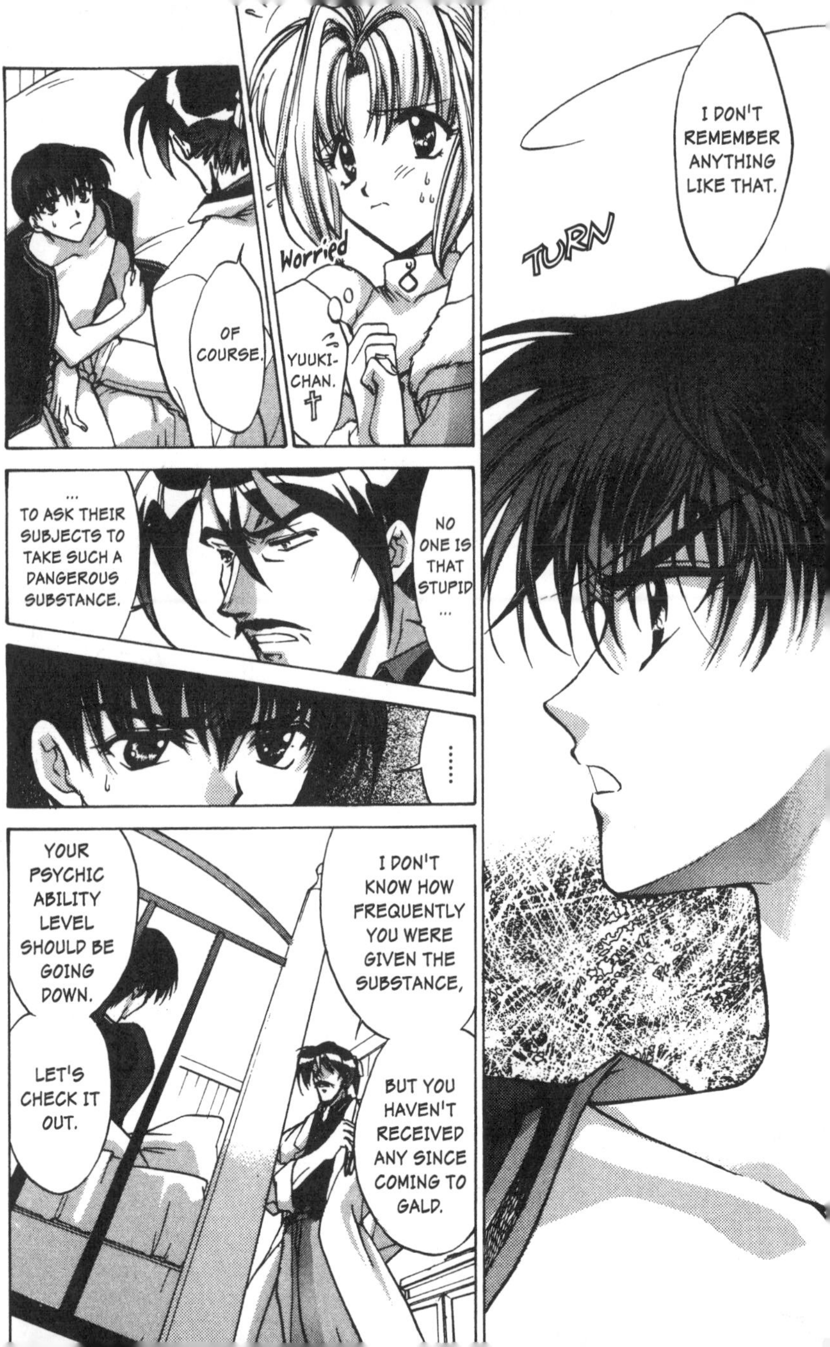
I DON'T REMEMBER ANYTHING LIKE THAT.
TURN
Worried
YUUKI-CHAN.
OF COURSE.
NO ONE IS THAT STUPID ...
... TO ASK THEIR SUBJECTS TO TAKE SUCH A DANGEROUS SUBSTANCE.
......
I DON'T KNOW HOW FREQUENTLY YOU WERE GIVEN THE SUBSTANCE,
BUT YOU HAVEN'T RECEIVED ANY SINCE COMING TO GALD.
YOUR PSYCHIC ABILITY LEVEL SHOULD BE GOING DOWN.
LET'S CHECK IT OUT.

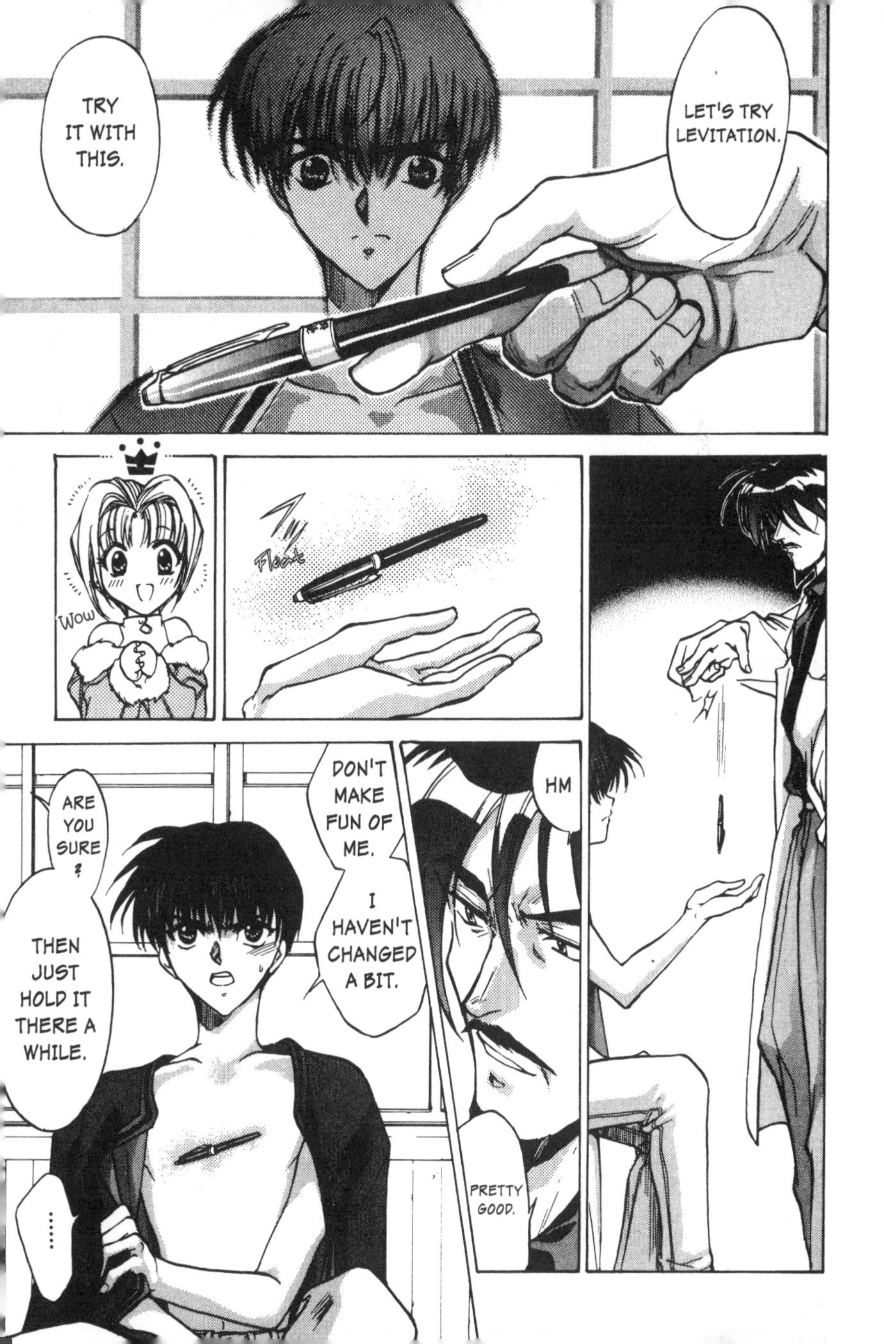
LET'S TRY LEVITATION.
TRY IT WITH THIS.
Float
Wow
HM
PRETTY GOOD.
DON'T MAKE FUN OF ME.
ARE YOU SURE?
I HAVEN'T CHANGED A BIT.
THEN JUST HOLD IT THERE A WHILE.
......

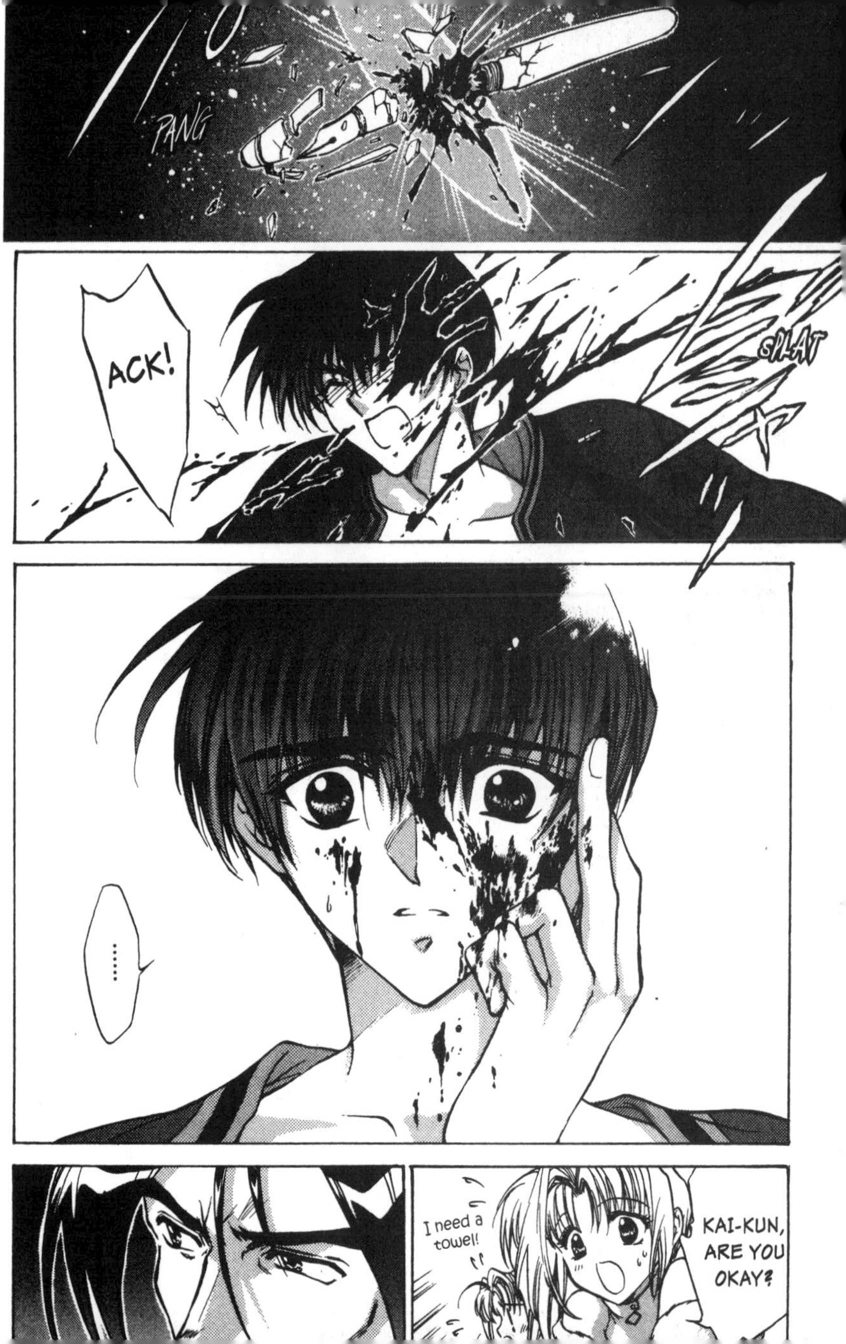
PANG
SPLAT
ACK!
......
KAI-KUN, ARE YOU OKAY?
I need a towel!

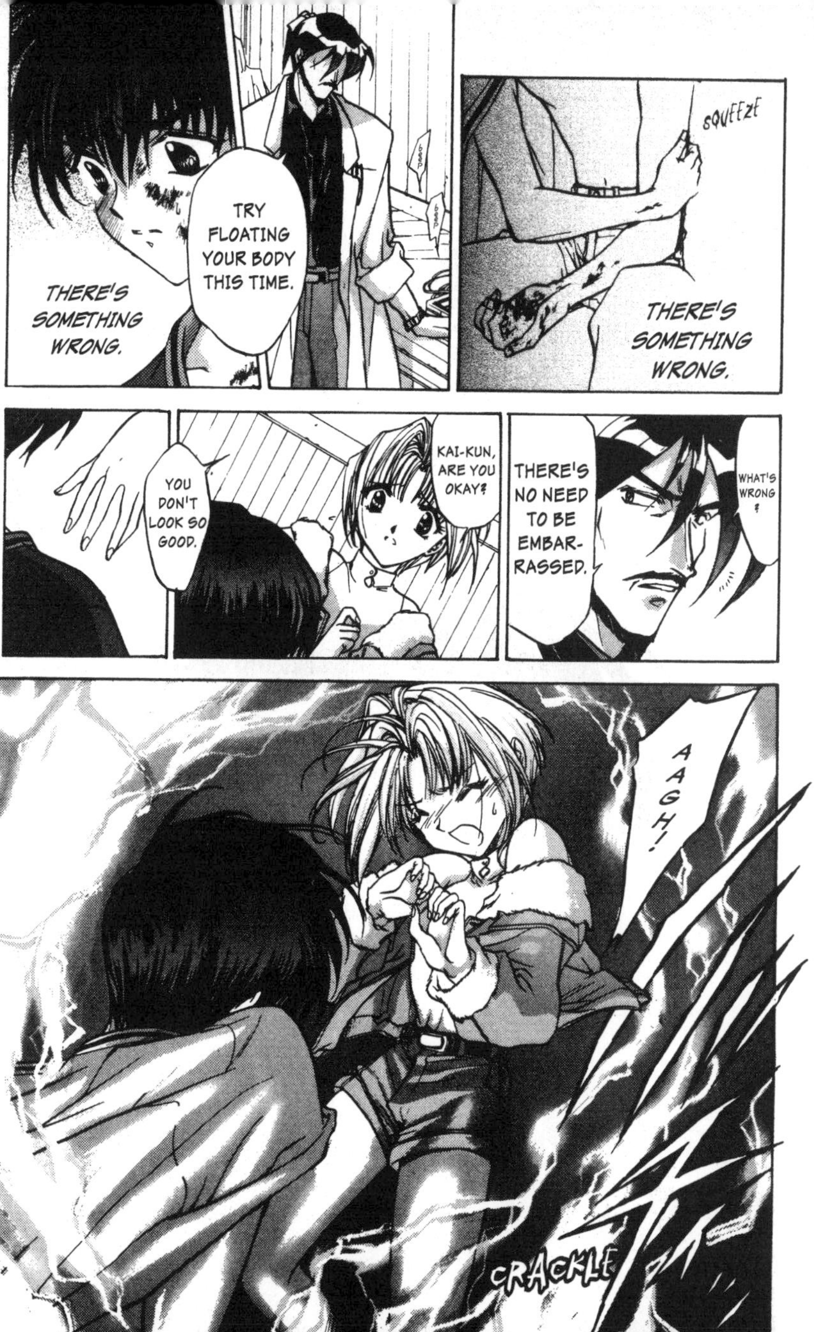
SQUEEZE
THERE'S SOMETHING WRONG.
beep
beep
TRY FLOATING YOUR BODY THIS TIME.
THERE'S SOMETHING WRONG.
WHAT'S WRONG?
THERE'S NO NEED TO BE EMBARRASSED.
KAI-KUN, ARE YOU OKAY?
YOU DON'T LOOK SO GOOD.
AAGH!
CRACKLE

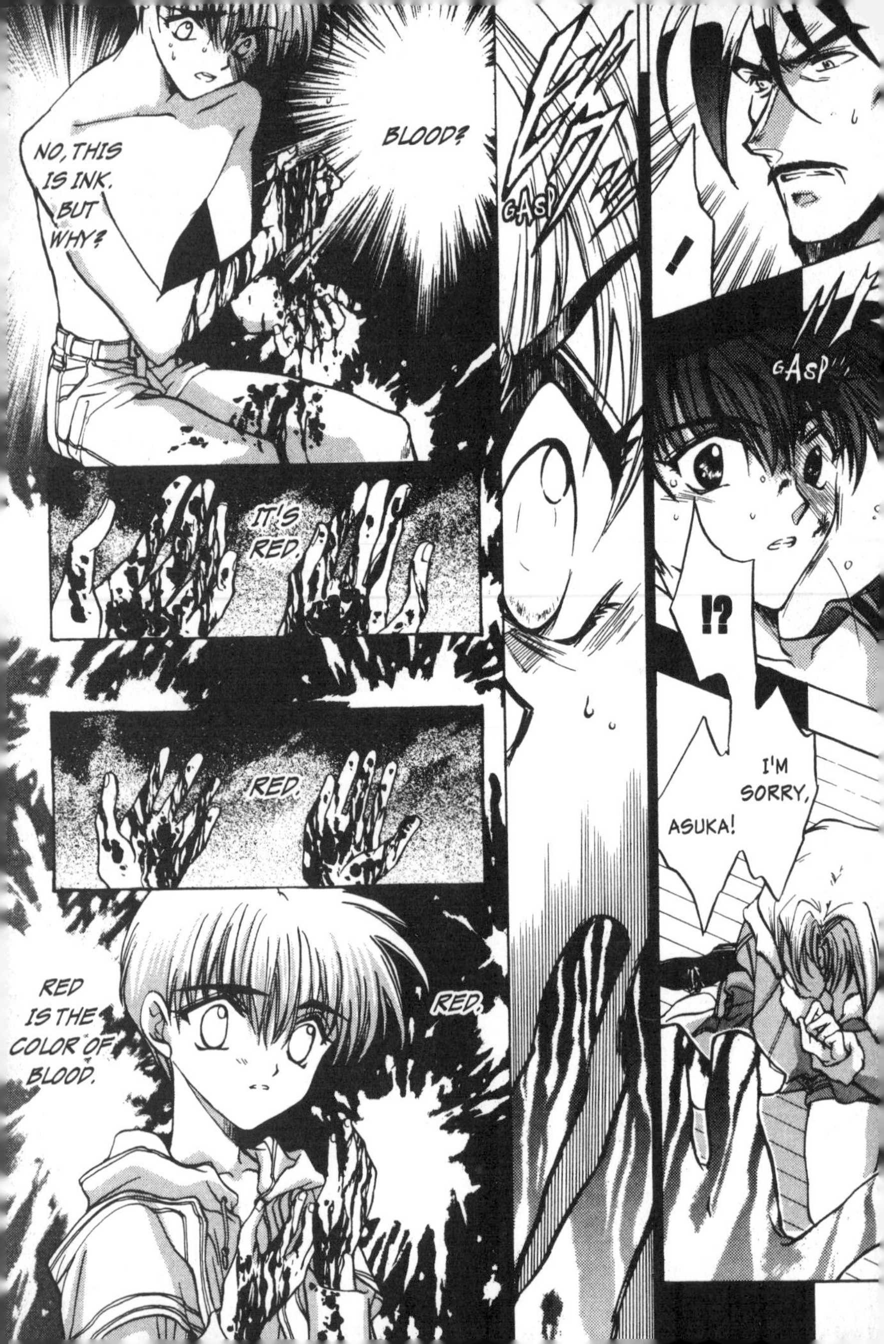
!
GASP
!?
I'M SORRY, ASUKA!
GASP
BLOOD?
NO, THIS IS INK. BUT WHY?
IT'S RED.
RED.
RED.
RED IS THE COLOR OF BLOOD.

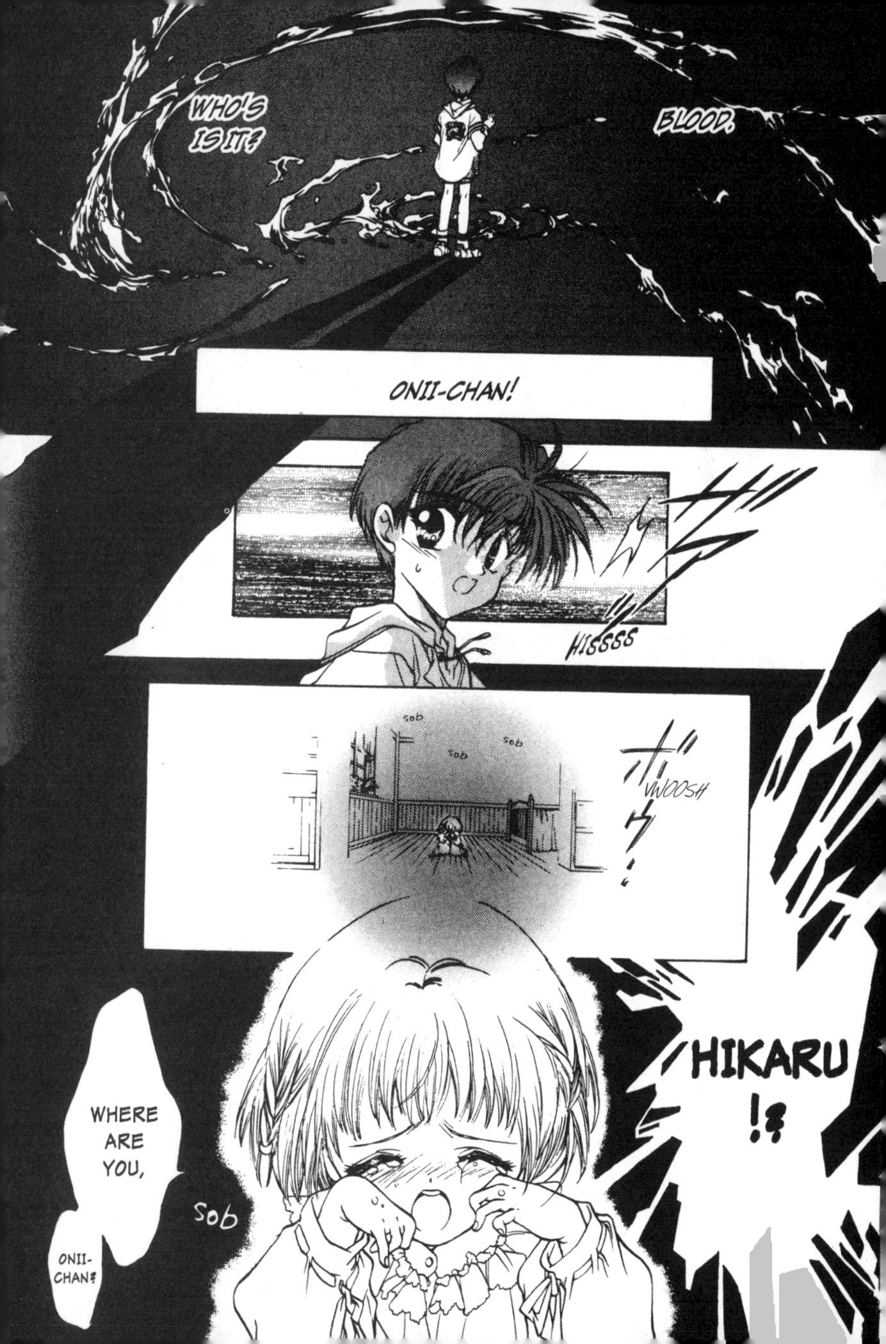

BLOOD.
WHO'S IS IT?
ONII-CHAN!
HISSSS
sob
sob
sob
VWOOSH
HIKARU !?
WHERE ARE YOU,
sob
ONII-CHAN?

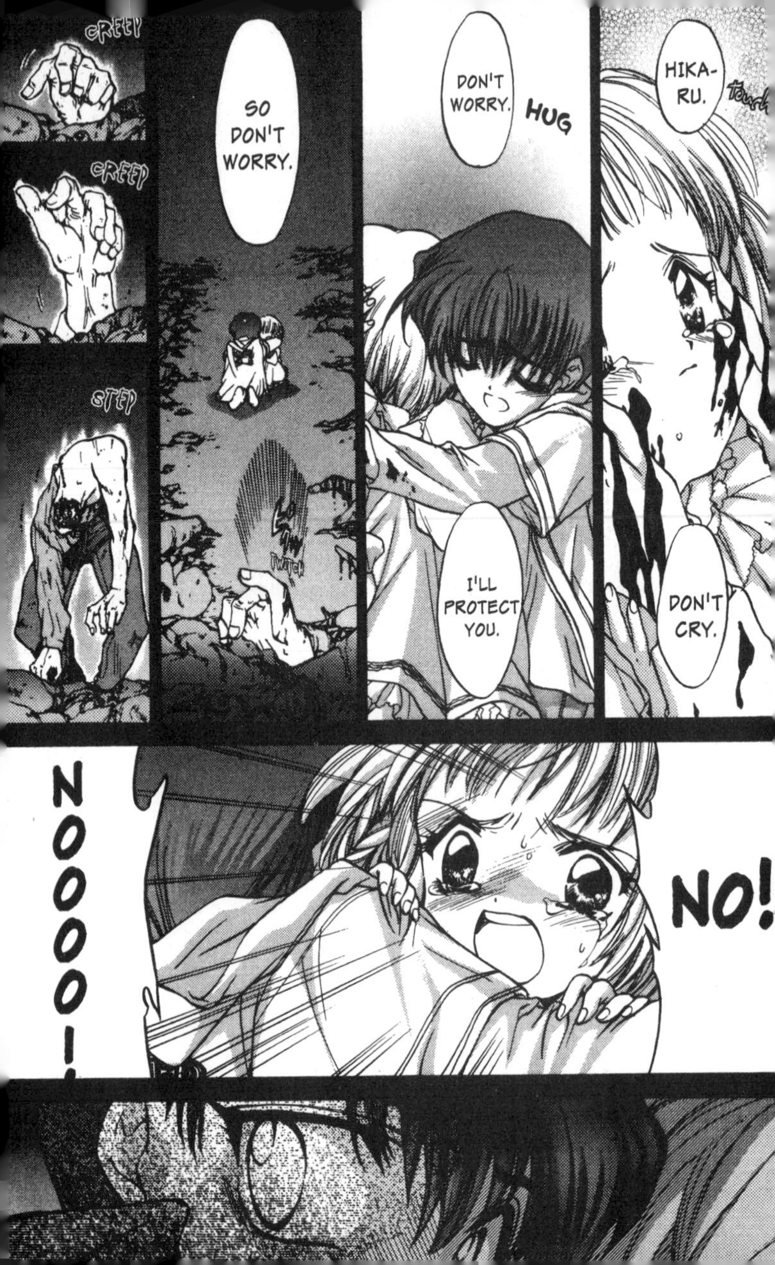
HIKA-RU.
touch
DON'T CRY.
DON'T WORRY.
HUG
I'LL PROTECT YOU.
SO DON'T WORRY.
TWITCH
CREEP
CREEP
STEP
NO!
NOOOOO!

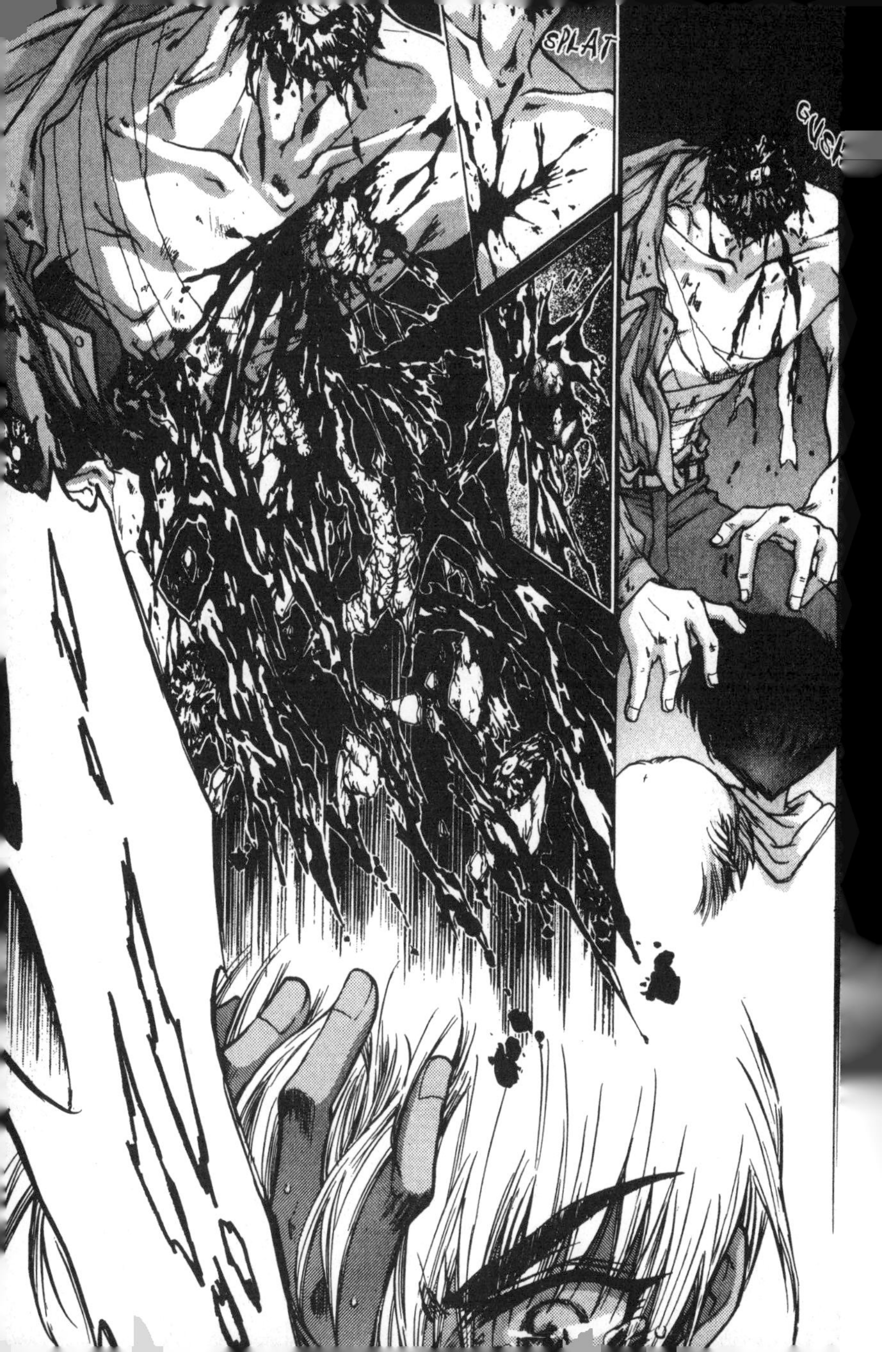
SPLAT

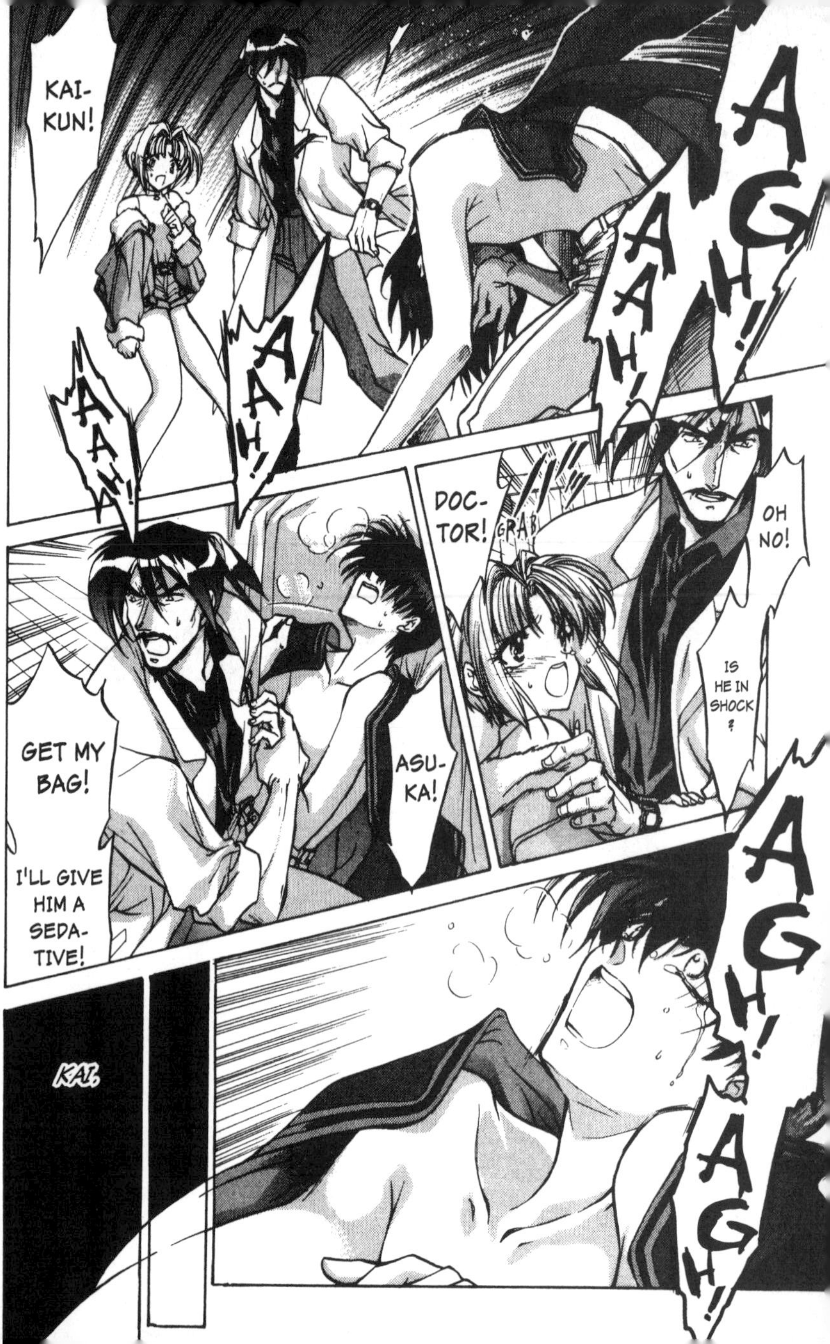
AGH!!
AAH!
KAI-KUN!
AAH!
AAAH!
OH NO!
DOCTOR!
GRAB
IS HE IN SHOCK?
ASUKA!
GET MY BAG!
I'LL GIVE HIM A SEDATIVE!
AGH! AAGH!!
KAI.

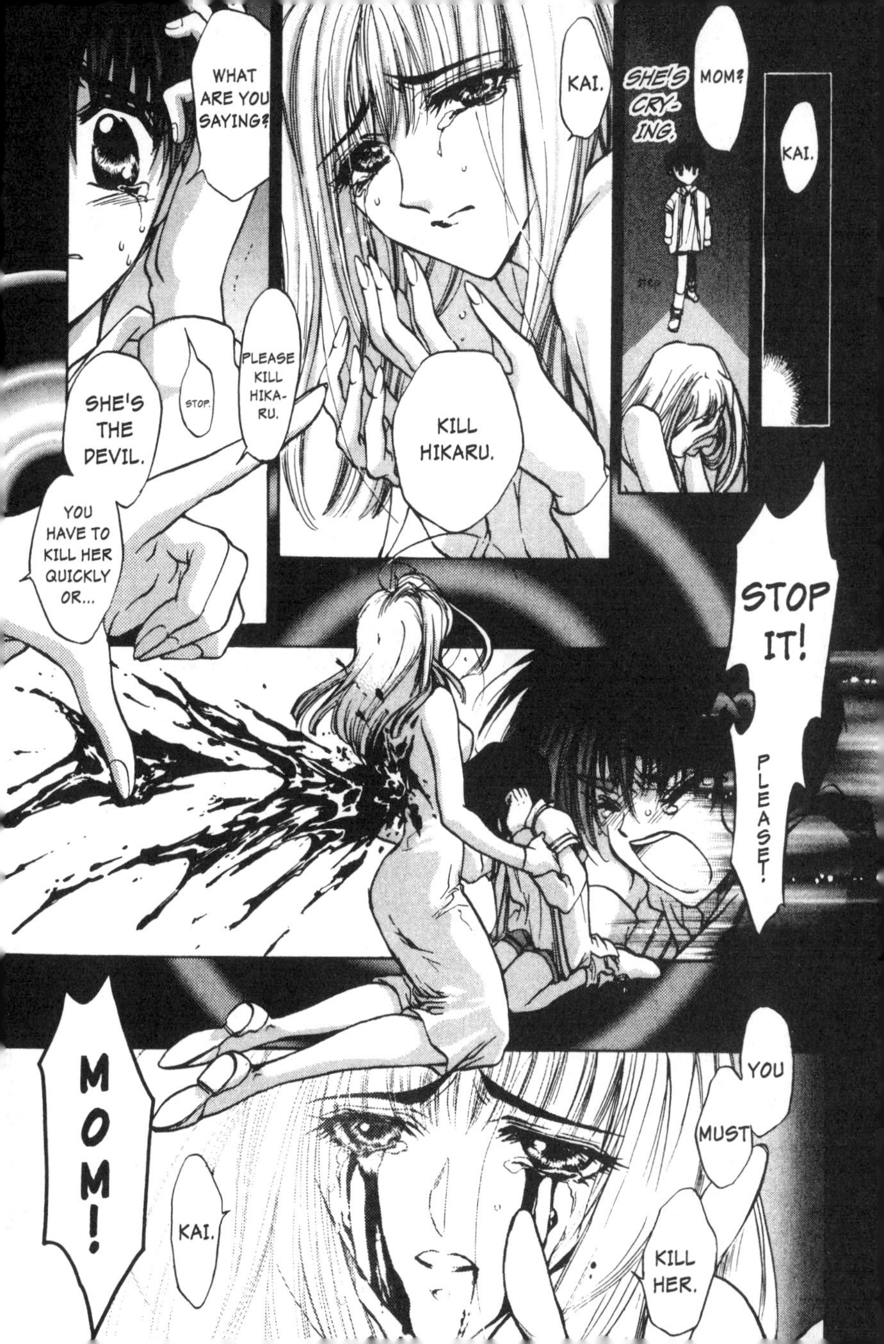
KAI.
MOM?
SHE'S CRY-ING.
KAI.
PLEASE KILL HIKA-RU.
KILL HIKARU.
WHAT ARE YOU SAYING?
STOP.
SHE'S THE DEVIL.
YOU HAVE TO KILL HER QUICKLY OR...
STOP IT!
PLEASE!
YOU MUST
KILL HER.
KAI.
MOM!

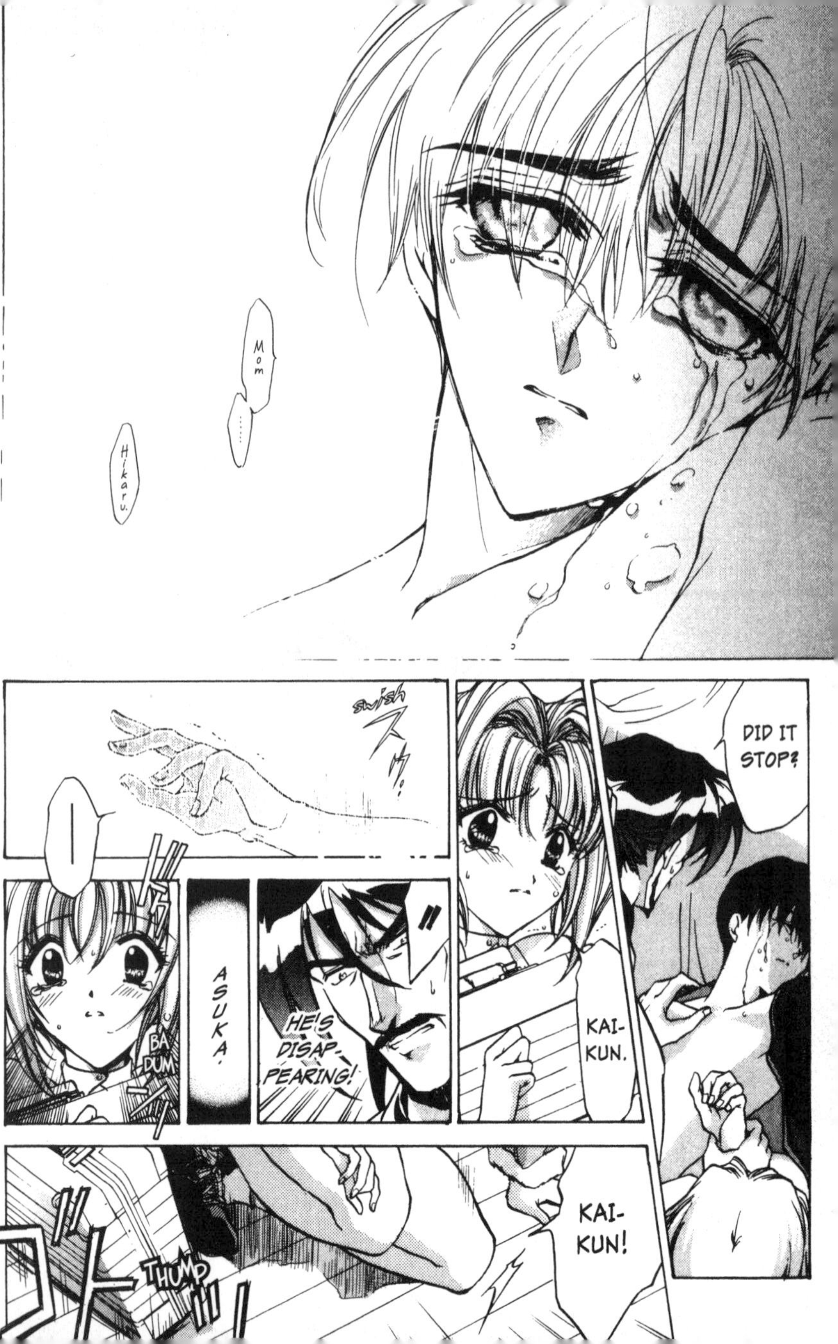
Mom
......
Hikaru.
DID IT STOP?
KAI-KUN.
swish
—
HE'S DISAPPEARING!
ASUKA.
BA DUM
KAI-KUN!
THUMP

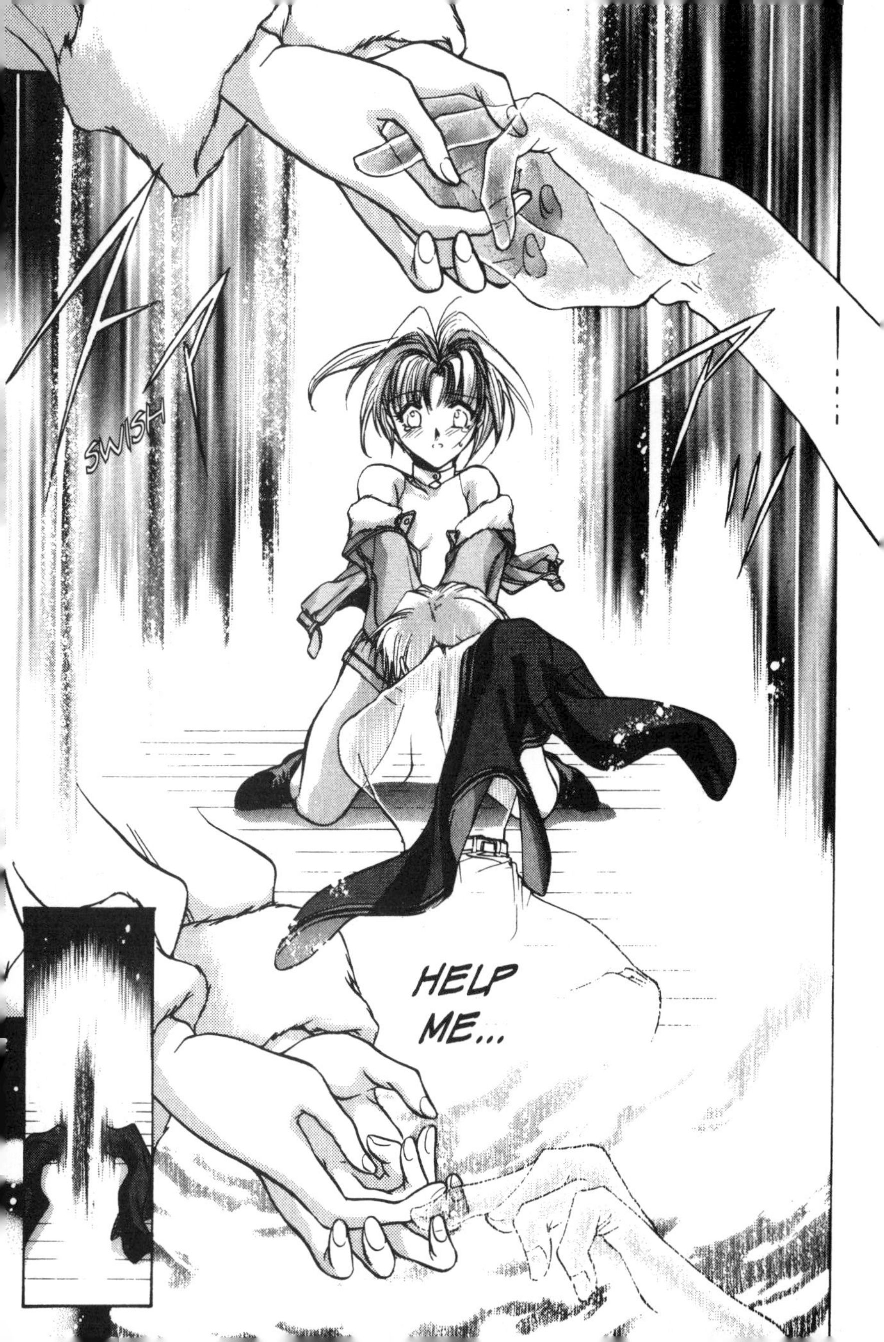

SWISH
...
HELP ME...

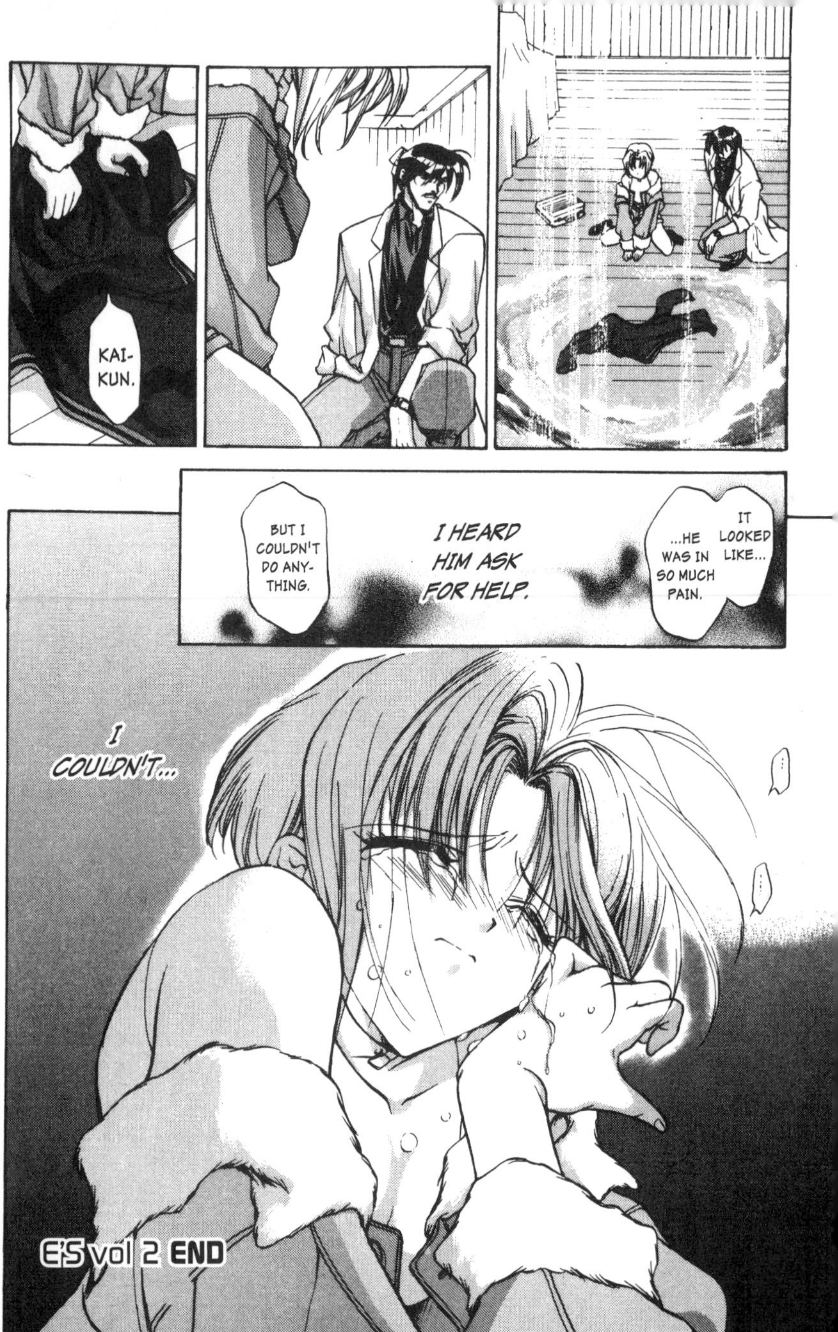
KAI-KUN.
IT LOOKED LIKE... ...HE WAS IN SO MUCH PAIN.
I HEARD HIM ASK FOR HELP.
BUT I COULDN'T DO ANY-THING.
...
...
I COULDN'T...
E'S vol 2 END

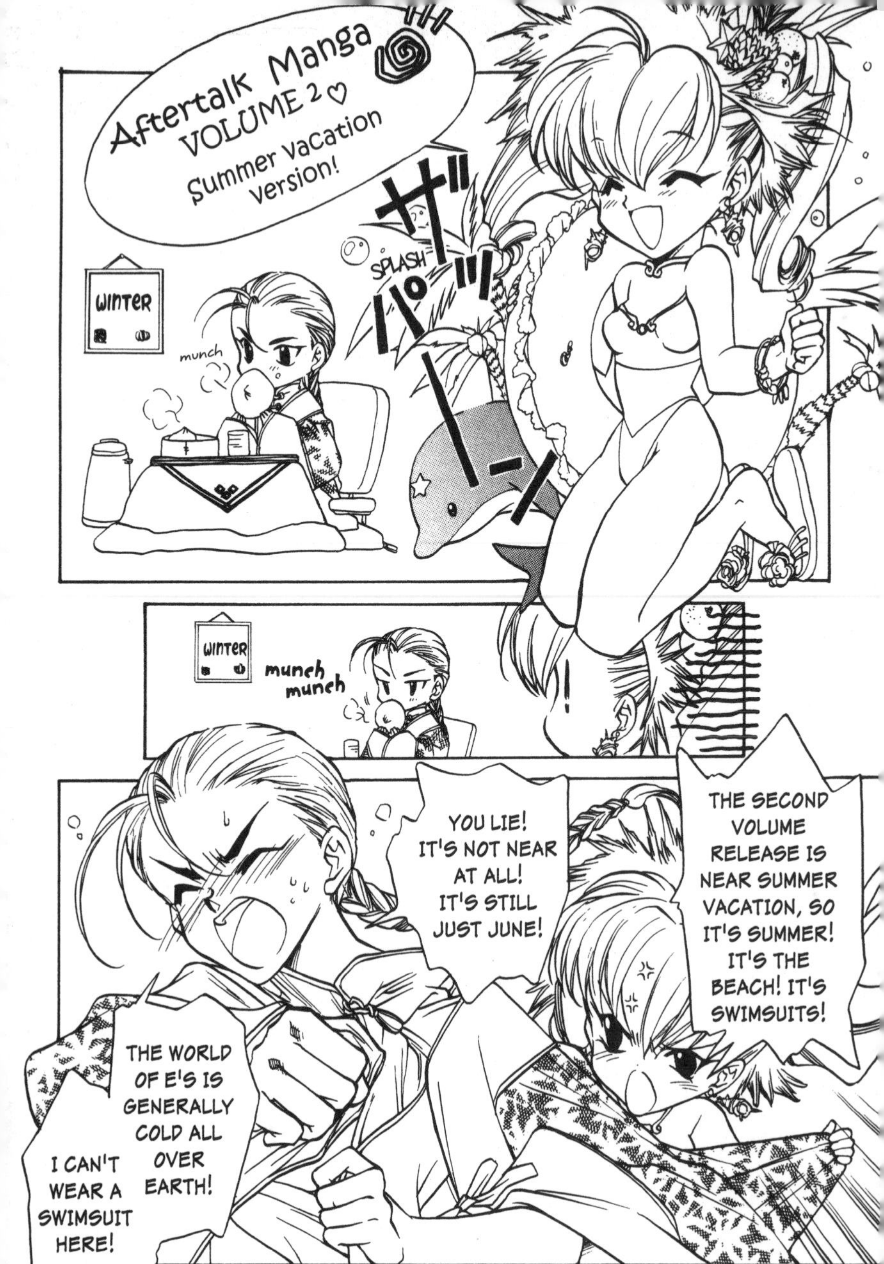
Aftertalk Manga VOLUME 2 ♡ Summer Vacation Version!
SPLASH
WINTER
munch
WINTER
munch munch
THE SECOND VOLUME RELEASE IS NEAR SUMMER VACATION, SO IT'S SUMMER! IT'S THE BEACH! IT'S SWIMSUITS!
YOU LIE! IT'S NOT NEAR AT ALL! IT'S STILL JUST JUNE!
THE WORLD OF E'S IS GENERALLY COLD ALL OVER EARTH!
I CAN'T WEAR A SWIMSUIT HERE!

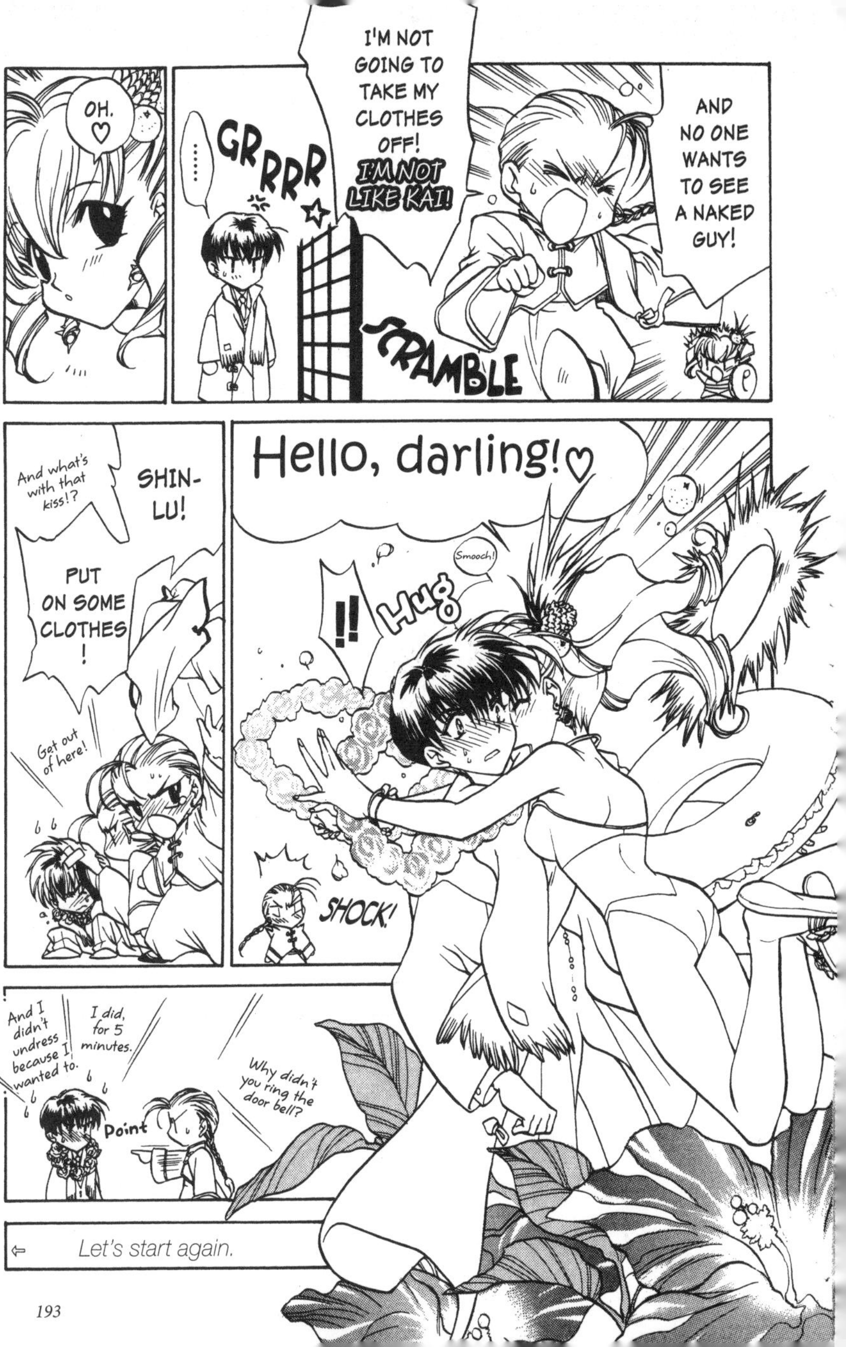

I'M NOT GOING TO TAKE MY CLOTHES OFF! I'M NOT LIKE KAI!
AND NO ONE WANTS TO SEE A NAKED GUY!
SCRAMBLE
GRRRR
......
OH. ♡
Hello, darling!♡
Smooch!
Hug
!!
SHOCK!
SHIN-LU!
And what's with that kiss!?
PUT ON SOME CLOTHES!
Get out of here!
Why didn't you ring the door bell?
Point
I did, for 5 minutes.
And I didn't undress because I wanted to.
⇦ Let's start again.

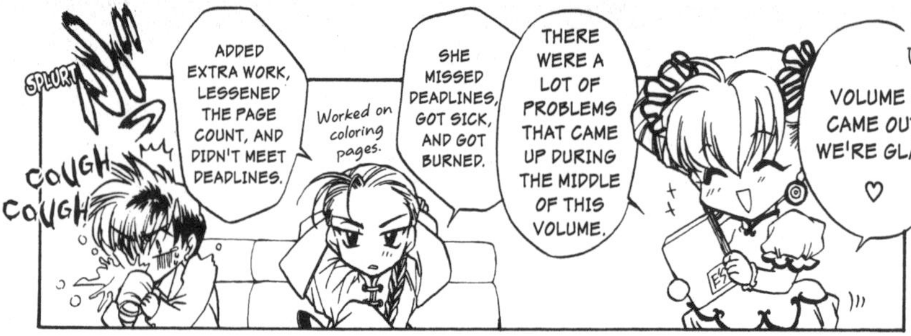
Well, VOLUME 2 CAME OUT. WE'RE GLAD. ♡
THERE WERE A LOT OF PROBLEMS THAT CAME UP DURING THE MIDDLE OF THIS VOLUME.
SHE MISSED DEADLINES, GOT SICK, AND GOT BURNED.
Worked on coloring pages.
ADDED EXTRA WORK, LESSENED THE PAGE COUNT, AND DIDN'T MEET DEADLINES.
SPLURT
COUGH COUGH

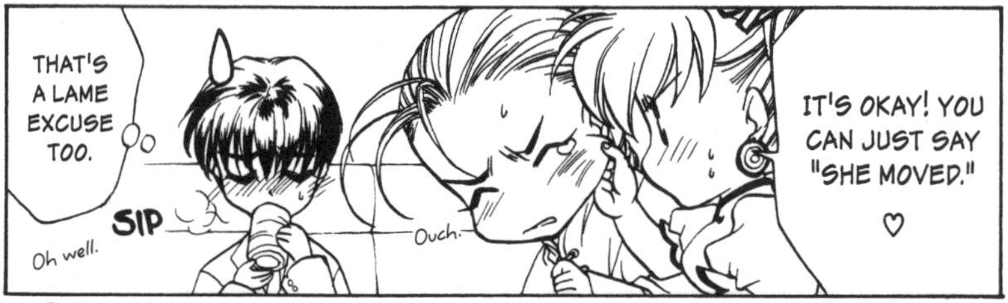
IT'S OKAY! YOU CAN JUST SAY "SHE MOVED." ♡
Ouch.
THAT'S A LAME EXCUSE TOO.
SIP
Oh well.

※ Volume 3 has problems too.

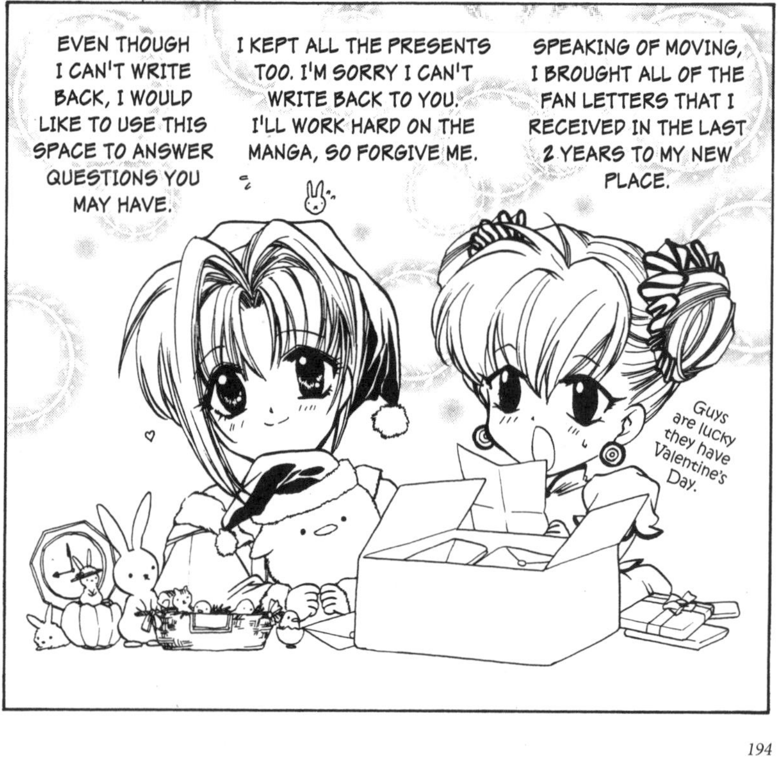
SPEAKING OF MOVING, I BROUGHT ALL OF THE FAN LETTERS THAT I RECEIVED IN THE LAST 2 YEARS TO MY NEW PLACE.
I KEPT ALL THE PRESENTS TOO. I'M SORRY I CAN'T WRITE BACK TO YOU. I'LL WORK HARD ON THE MANGA, SO FORGIVE ME.
EVEN THOUGH I CAN'T WRITE BACK, I WOULD LIKE TO USE THIS SPACE TO ANSWER QUESTIONS YOU MAY HAVE.
Guys are lucky they have Valentine's Day.

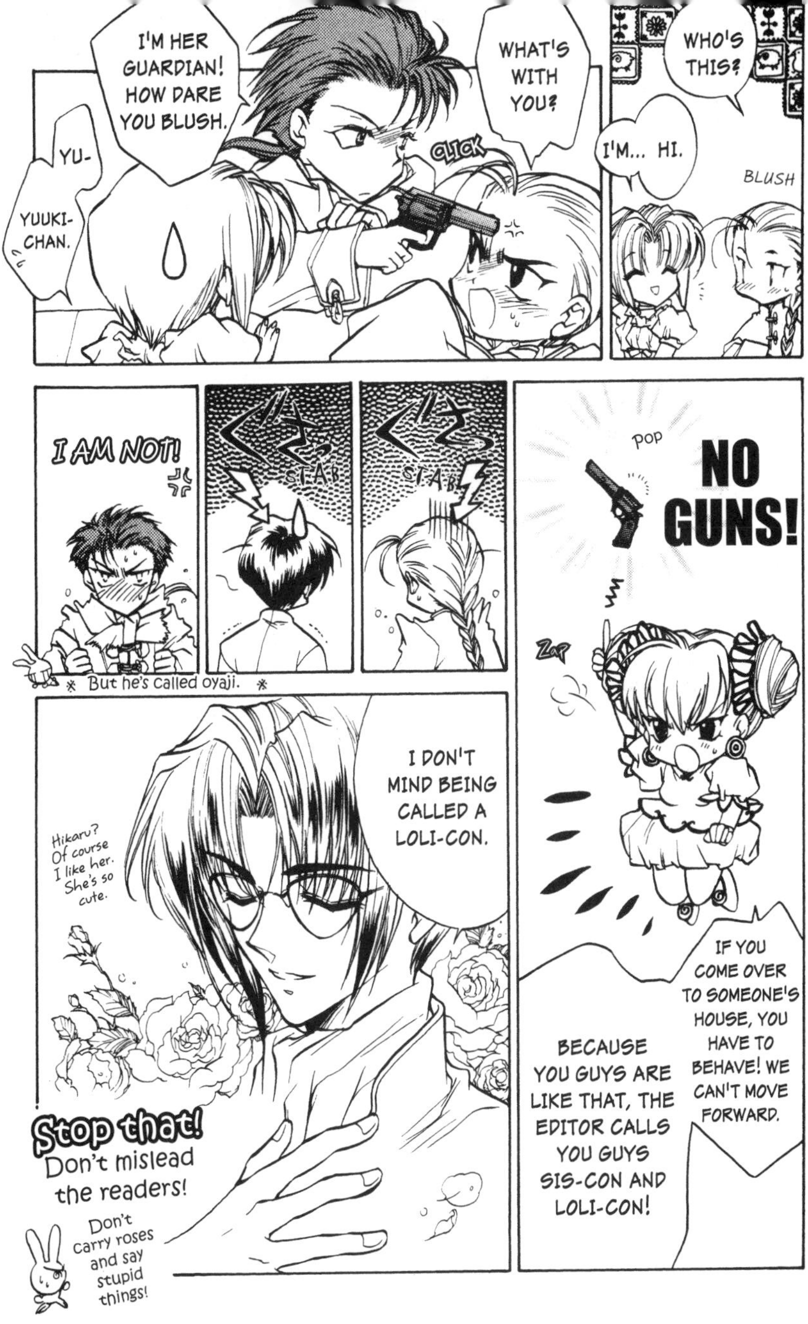
WHO'S THIS?
I'M... HI.
BLUSH
WHAT'S WITH YOU?
CLICK
I'M HER GUARDIAN! HOW DARE YOU BLUSH.
YU-
YUUKI-CHAN.
POP
NO GUNS!
ZAP
IF YOU COME OVER TO SOMEONE'S HOUSE, YOU HAVE TO BEHAVE! WE CAN'T MOVE FORWARD.
BECAUSE YOU GUYS ARE LIKE THAT, THE EDITOR CALLS YOU GUYS SIS-CON AND LOLI-CON!
STAB
STAB
I AM NOT!
※ But he's called oyaji. ※
I DON'T MIND BEING CALLED A LOLI-CON.
Hikaru? Of course I like her. She's so cute.
Stop that! Don't mislead the readers!
Don't carry roses and say stupid things!

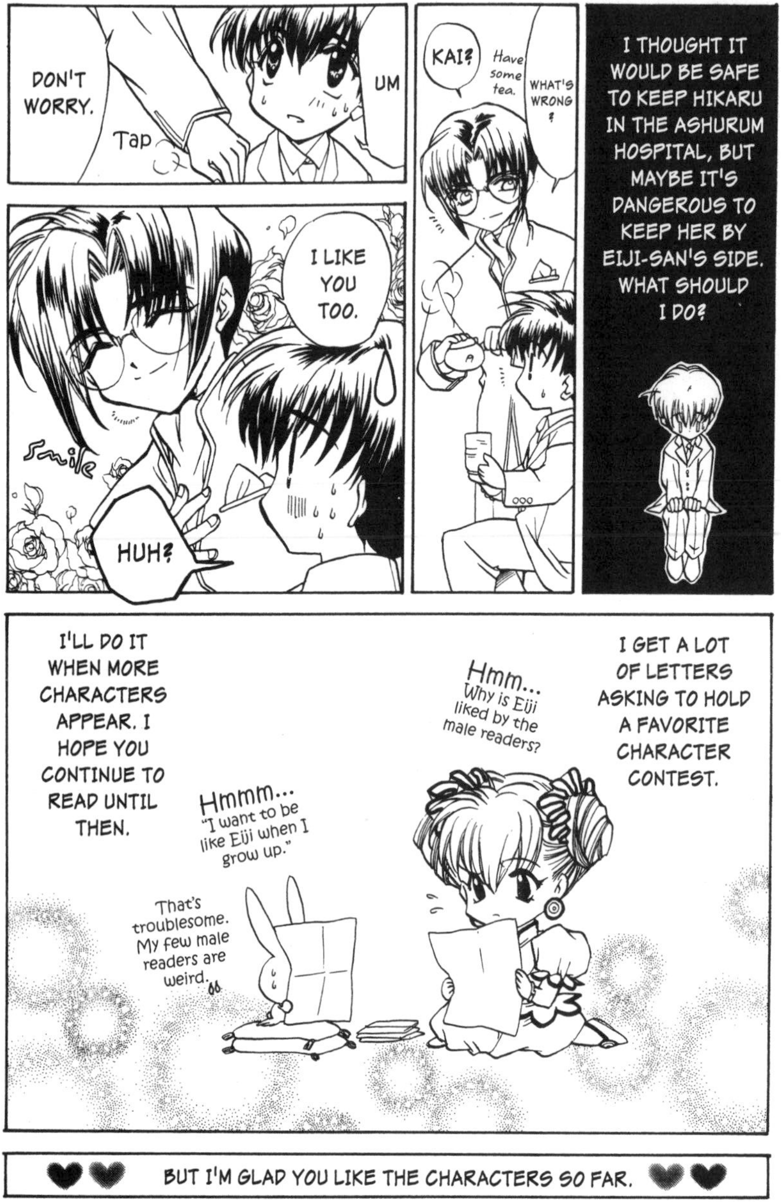
I THOUGHT IT WOULD BE SAFE TO KEEP HIKARU IN THE ASHURUM HOSPITAL, BUT MAYBE IT'S DANGEROUS TO KEEP HER BY EIJI-SAN'S SIDE. WHAT SHOULD I DO?
WHAT'S WRONG?
Have some tea.
KAI?
UM
DON'T WORRY.
Tap
I LIKE YOU TOO.
Smile
HUH?
I GET A LOT OF LETTERS ASKING TO HOLD A FAVORITE CHARACTER CONTEST.
Hmm... Why is Eiji liked by the male readers?
Hmmm... "I want to be like Eiji when I grow up."
That's troublesome. My few male readers are weird.
I'LL DO IT WHEN MORE CHARACTERS APPEAR. I HOPE YOU CONTINUE TO READ UNTIL THEN.
BUT I'M GLAD YOU LIKE THE CHARACTERS SO FAR.

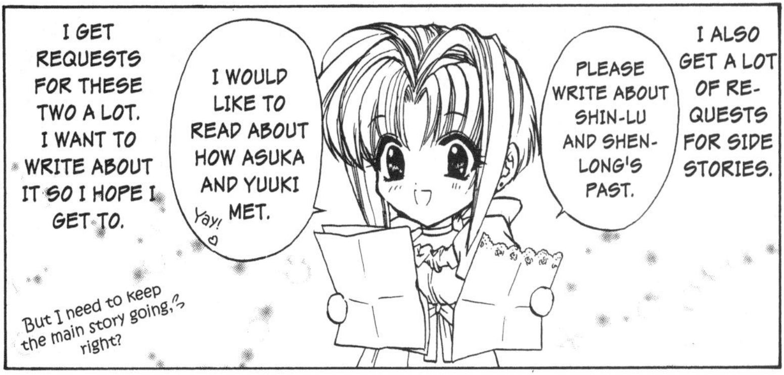
I ALSO GET A LOT OF RE-QUESTS FOR SIDE STORIES.
PLEASE WRITE ABOUT SHIN-LU AND SHEN-LONG'S PAST.
I WOULD LIKE TO READ ABOUT HOW ASUKA AND YUUKI MET.
Yay! ♡
I GET REQUESTS FOR THESE TWO A LOT. I WANT TO WRITE ABOUT IT SO I HOPE I GET TO.
But I need to keep the main story going, right?

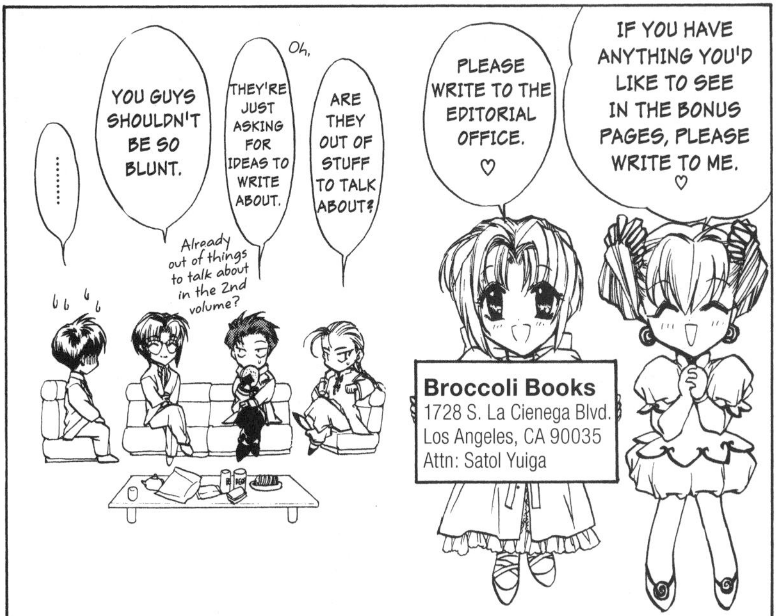
IF YOU HAVE ANYTHING YOU'D LIKE TO SEE IN THE BONUS PAGES, PLEASE WRITE TO ME. ♡
PLEASE WRITE TO THE EDITORIAL OFFICE. ♡
Oh,
ARE THEY OUT OF STUFF TO TALK ABOUT?
THEY'RE JUST ASKING FOR IDEAS TO WRITE ABOUT.
YOU GUYS SHOULDN'T BE SO BLUNT.
....
Already out of things to talk about in the 2nd volume?
Broccoli Books
1728 S. La Cienega Blvd.
Los Angeles, CA 90035
Attn: Satol Yuiga

* Suggestions for Satol Yuiga not accepted, but fan mail is welcome.

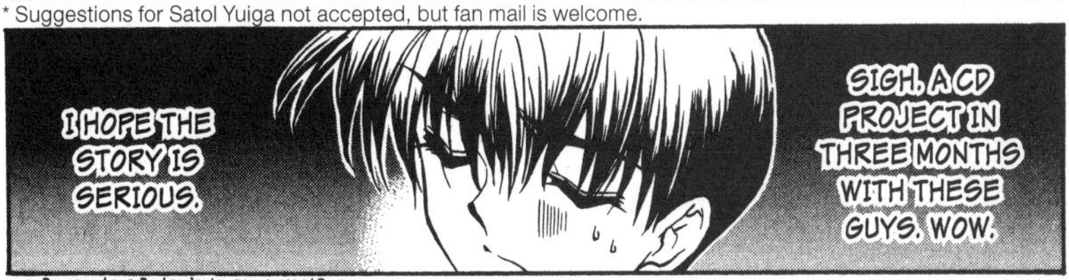
SIGH. A CD PROJECT IN THREE MONTHS WITH THESE GUYS. WOW.
I HOPE THE STORY IS SERIOUS.

※ I wonder? I don't know myself. ※

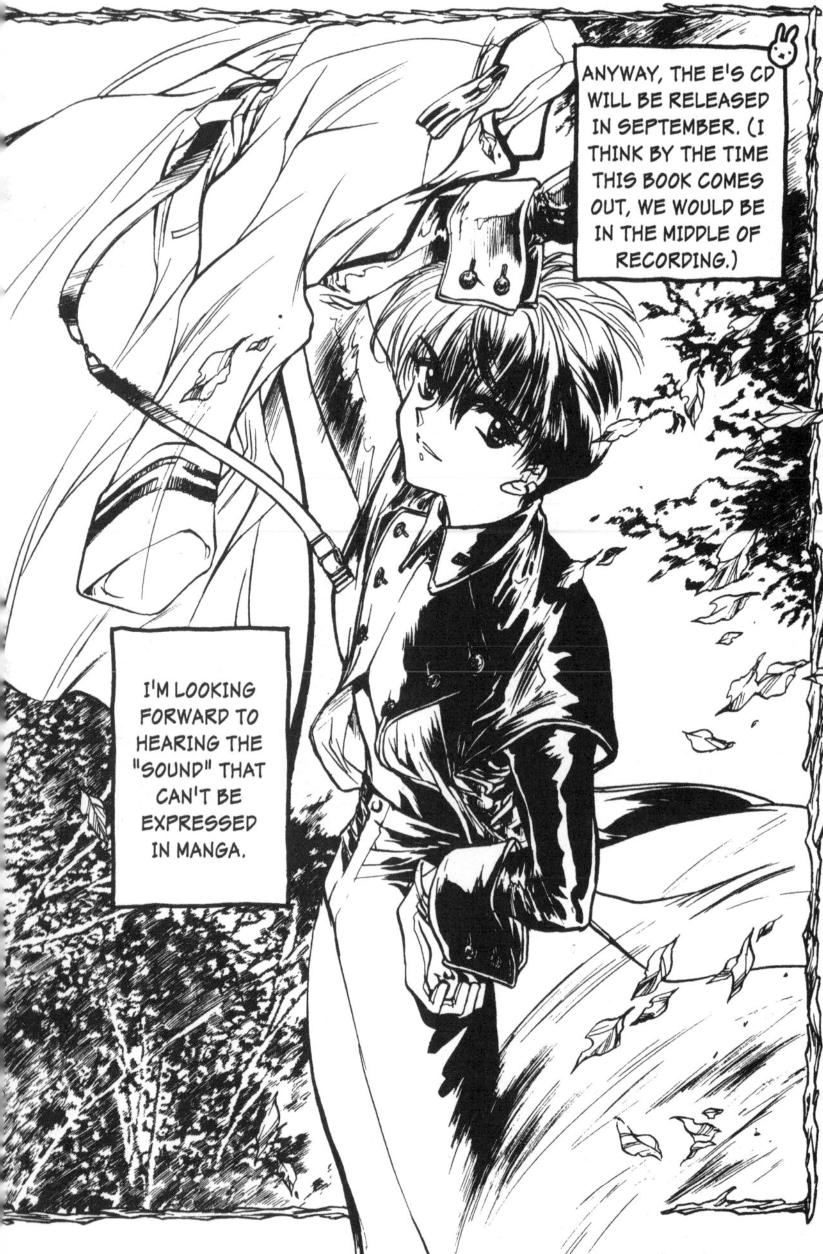
ANYWAY, THE E'S CD WILL BE RELEASED IN SEPTEMBER. (I THINK BY THE TIME THIS BOOK COMES OUT, WE WOULD BE IN THE MIDDLE OF RECORDING.)
I'M LOOKING FORWARD TO HEARING THE "SOUND" THAT CAN'T BE EXPRESSED IN MANGA.

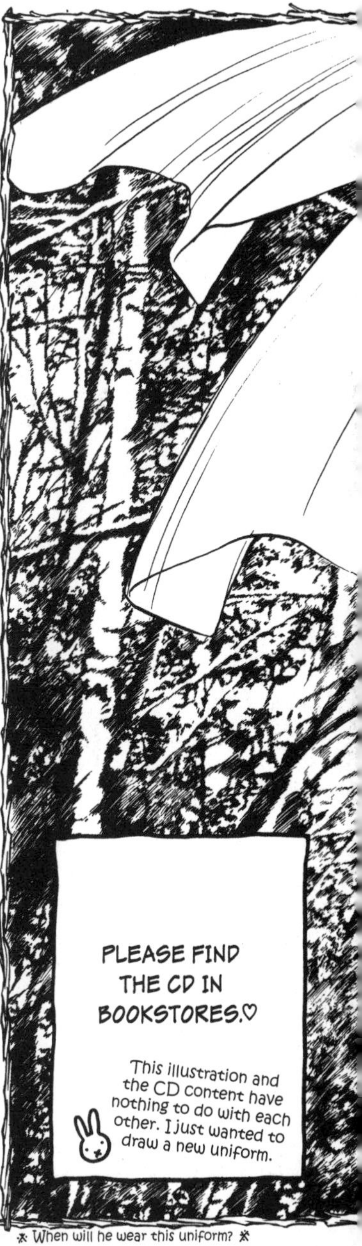
PLEASE FIND THE CD IN BOOKSTORES.♡
This illustration and the CD content have nothing to do with each other. I just wanted to draw a new uniform.
※ When will he wear this uniform? ※

BONUS MANGA, finish with a 4-panel manga

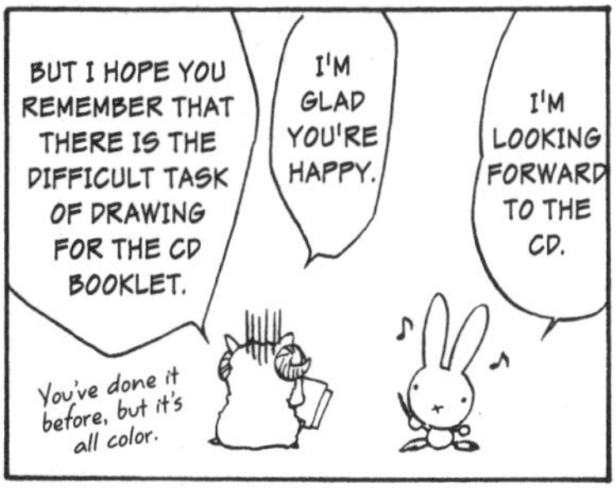
I'M LOOKING FORWARD TO THE CD.
I'M GLAD YOU'RE HAPPY.
BUT I HOPE YOU REMEMBER THAT THERE IS THE DIFFICULT TASK OF DRAWING FOR THE CD BOOKLET.
You've done it before, but it's all color.

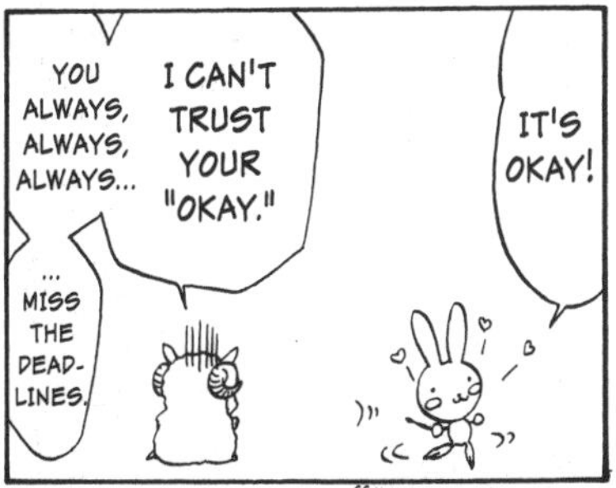
IT'S OKAY!
I CAN'T TRUST YOUR "OKAY."
YOU ALWAYS, ALWAYS, ALWAYS...
...MISS THE DEADLINES.
※ Side scroll effect. ※

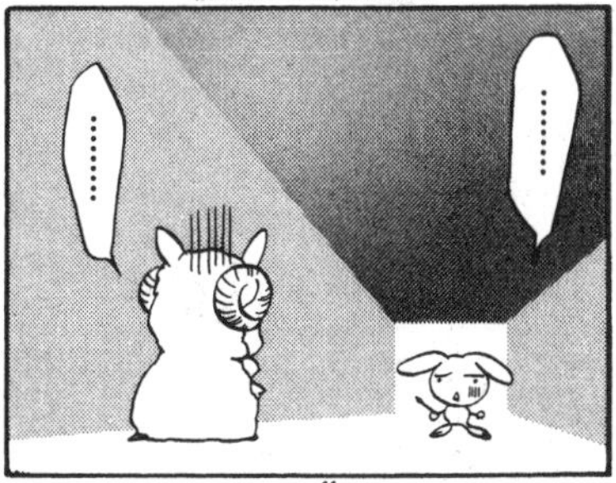
....
....
※ 3D effect. ※

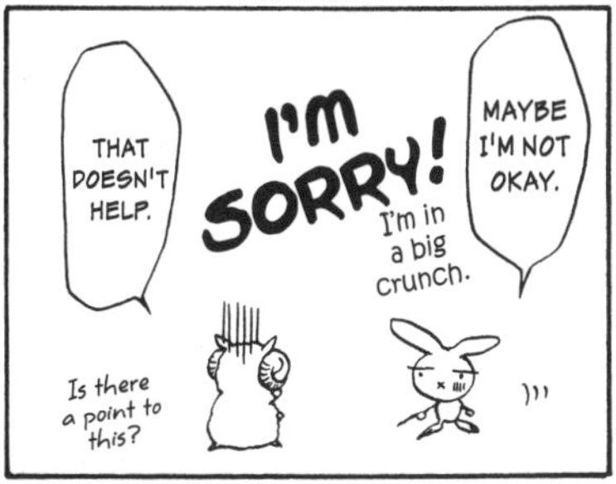
MAYBE I'M NOT OKAY.
I'M SORRY!
I'm in a big crunch.
THAT DOESN'T HELP.
Is there a point to this?

E'S volume 2 bonus manga, end

CHARACTERS CORRELATION CHART

Nice Onii-chan
Killing machine
Not sure anymore
Real Onii-chan
Needs to save
Cares only about money
Money making machine
Wants to help
Brainwashed E'S Psychic

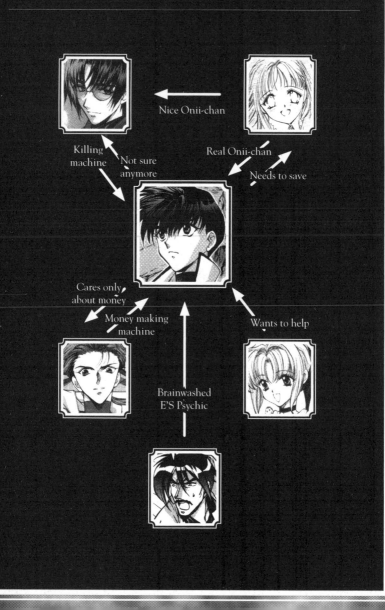

TERMINOLOGY

– A S H U R U M
Ashurum is a government organization that provides shelter to
psychics. Its psychic military branch usually handles criminals
that the regular police and military are unequipped to deal with.
Ashurum is searching for the Sacrament of Calvarias hidden deep
within Gald City.

– C R I D   S T I C K
A stick that acts as both an identification tag and a credit card.

– S A C R A M E N T   O F   C A L V A R I A S
The Sacrament of Calvarias is a mysterious artifact hidden
somewhere in Gald. Ashurum won't let anything stand in its way in
order to obtain it, and Erimiya, head of the guerillas, has charged
Yuuki with finding it first. What is its importance? What power does
it hold?

– G A L D
Gald is a city in ruins and home to a large guerilla organization. The
Sacrament of Calvarias is located within its tattered remains.

– G U E R I L L A S
Guerillas are groups, generally of normal humans, who are violently
opposed to the government. Some guerilla groups incorporate
psychics to carry out some of their tasks.

– P S Y C H I C S
Because of their powers, psychics are viewed as mutants and are
shunned by "normal" society. Ashurum, a government organization,
provides shelter to many psychics, but what is their true purpose
behind this?

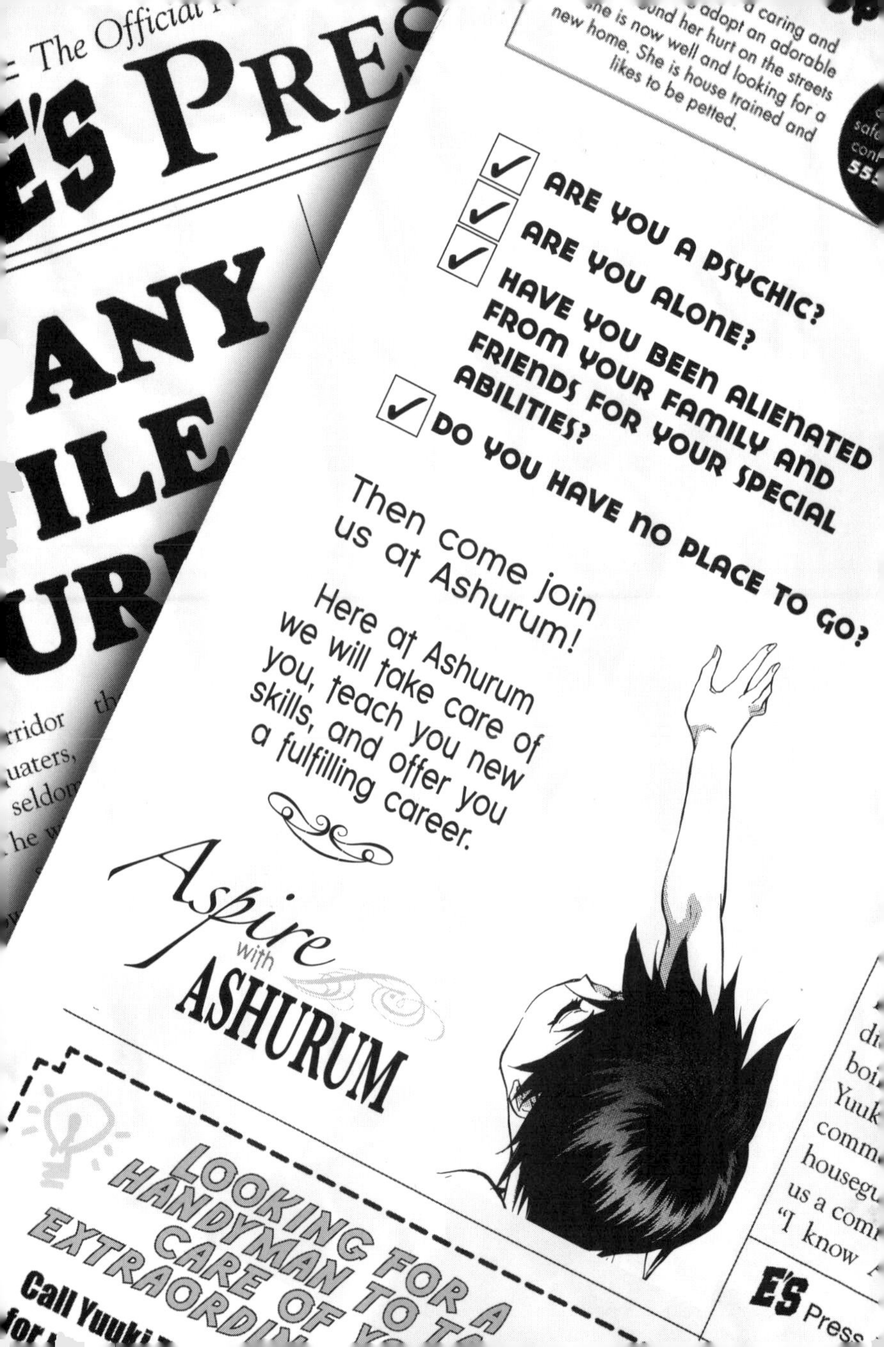

The Official
E'S PRES
ANY
ILE
UR
rridor
uaters,
seldo
he w
und her hurt on the streets
adopt an adorable
she is now well and looking for a
new home. She is house trained and
likes to be petted.
ARE YOU A PSYCHIC?
ARE YOU ALONE?
HAVE YOU BEEN ALIENATED FROM YOUR FAMILY AND FRIENDS FOR YOUR SPECIAL ABILITIES?
DO YOU HAVE NO PLACE TO GO?
Then come join us at Ashurum!
Here at Ashurum we will take care of you, teach you new skills, and offer you a fulfilling career.
Aspire with ASHURUM
LOOKING FOR A
HANDYMAN TO TA
CARE OF YO
EXTRAORDIN
Call Yuuki
dr
boi
Yuuk
comm
housegu
us a com
"I know
E'S Press

Message from the Director

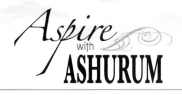

I would like to welcome you to the Ashurum family. We take in psychics of all ages, from young children to adults, who have been discarded by society. We are especially interested in the large number of children abandoned by their parents. When children are revealed to be psychics, many of them are locked up or simply kicked out onto the streets. We welcome these children and teach them to use their powers for the common good.

People think that psychics are a threat to society, but the true danger lies in a society which rejects and excludes psychics. Psychics are just like people, only with a special talent. We here at Ashurum embrace that talent and encourage its development. If you feel rejected from society, please come and join us.

----Director, E. Sagimiya

Individual Rooms

Ashurum provides housing to all employees and their families so that everyone can live in safety and comfort. Our transportation is convenient and makes it easy to get around, especially for those who choose not to teleport.

Research Facility

Ashurum boasts research facilities with the highest technology available. Our psychic research is the best in the world. All psychics undergo routine exams to test and monitor their abilities.

Medical Center

The Ashurum medical center offers up-to-date technology and skilled doctors to keep you healthy. Schedule an examination today. Walk-ins are also welcome.

Individual Laboratories

For our advanced researchers, Ashurum provides personalized laboratories so that you may focus on your research in a comfortable environment.

Academic Campus

Although the campus is not part of Ashurum, We do have close ties with the educational system. Many Ashurum researchers teach in the schools, and many of the top graduates become employees of Ashurum.

Aspire with **ASHURUM**

Aspire with ASHURUM

Shin-lu Belvedere

I had a horrible life until I came to Ashurum. My twin brother and I discovered that we were different from other people when we were quite young. I don't really like to remember my life before I came to Ashurum. When we arrived here, the staff greeted us warmly. We were given food, shelter, medical care and special training that now allows us to help the army and police.

Hikaru Kudou

I've always been here, and everybody is always nice to me. It's my home.

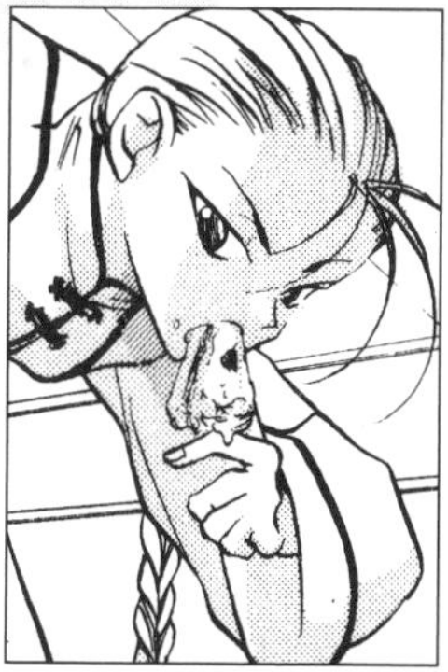

Shen-long Belvedere

I hate humans, so Ashurum is the place for me. I can teleport anytime I want, and don't have to worry about ignorant gawkers. I don't like the fact that weakling psychics like Kai are here, but I get to be with my twin sister, and that's what matters the most.

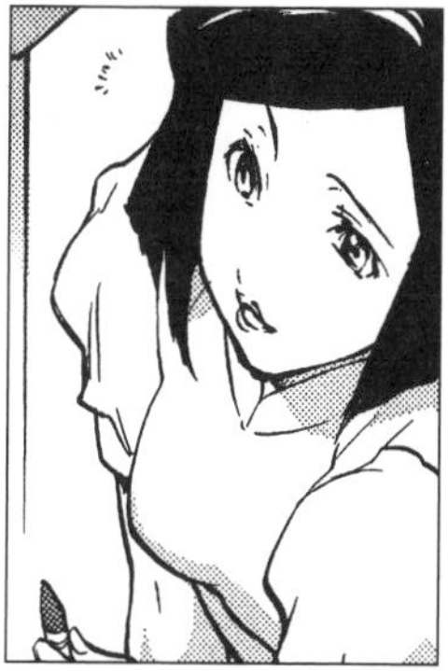

Nurse

Working for Ashurum is great. The salary and benefits are very competitive, and we have great insurance and receive compensation for any accidents.

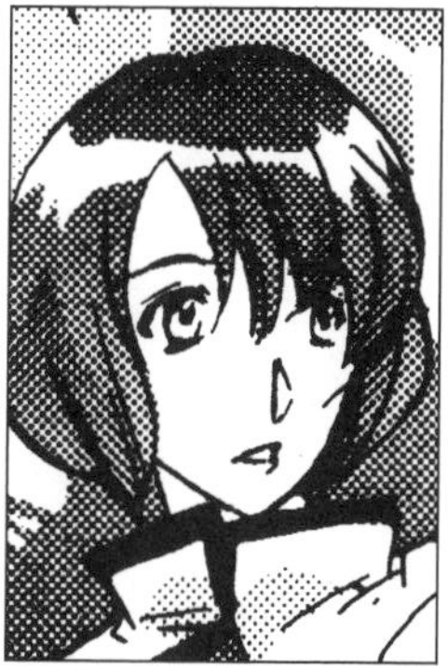

Lab Technician

I never considered psychics to be dangerous or threatening. They are very sweet and kind. If I give them treats they thank me and eat them, if I compliment them on their ability test results they are pleased. My section chief told me to treat them with love and care, like they were human, and that's just what I do.

TRANSLATION NOTES

P 10 M D P L A Y E R – MiniDisc is a data storage medium created by Sony. It can also be used to store music which can be played with an MD player.

T C H A I K O V S K Y S Y M P H O N Y N O . 6 – Symphony No. 6 in B minor, *Pathétique*, Op. 74 is Pyotr Ilyich Tchaikovsky's (1840-1893CE) final symphony. Several days after it premiered he died, possibly from cholera, although there is a theory that it was suicide.

C H A N – A suffix; can be put after any name. It is often used for children, good friends or those younger than oneself.

P 11 K U N – A suffix, usually goes after a boy's name.

P 17 H P A N D M P – In role-playing games, players usually have a set of stats called HP (health points) for life, and MP (magic points) for magic.

P 67 S M G – Stands for submachine gun. Submachine guns are guns generally capable of automatic fire but use pistol cartridges rather than larger and more powerful rifle cartridges.

P 89 S A X S H I O T O X I N T Z – A made up toxin.

P 105 B U R I D A N ' S M U L E – A reference to Buridan's Ass, a paradox wherein a perfectly rational donkey, when placed exactly between two equally desireable bales of hay, will starve since it cannot rationally decide between eating one or the other. It is named after Jean Buridan (1300–1358CE), a French philosopher.

P 175 H E N R I C H A R P E N T I E R C A K E – Henri Charpentier was a famous French chef, who is attributed with creating the dessert crepes Suzette. The cake that Shen-long brings is from a Japanese dessert company of the same name. When the founder of the company decided to dedicate his life to making desserts, he named his shop after the famous chef.

P 183 O N I I - C H A N – An informal Japanese term for "big brother."

P 192 S U M M E R V A C A T I O N V E R S I O N – Satol Yuiga worked on these pages in June of 1998. However the actual release was later in the summer of 1998, which is why Shin-lu is dressed in a bathing suit.

P 195 S I S - C O N – Short for sister-complex; when a person is attracted to their sister.

L O L I - C O N – Short for Lolita-complex; when an older person is attracted to young girls.

O Y A J I – Japanese for "old man."

P 196 S A N – A suffix; can be put after any name indicating respect.

P 198 E ' S C D – This drama CD was released in Japan in 1998.

PREVIEW

– VOLUME 3 –

PRESENTED BY SATOL YUIGA

KAI WAKES UP FROM HIS ORDEAL IN AN UNDERGROUND LABYRINTH, AND IS LED BY A MYSTERIOUS VOICE TO A PLACE WHERE YOUNG PSYCHICS ARE BEING HELD CAPTIVE.

MEANWHILE, YUUKI CONFRONTS MARIA, WHO DEMANDS HE HAND OVER THE PSYCHIC HE IS HARBORING, BUT SHE DOESN'T MEAN KAI! YUUKI SOON LEARNS THAT THERE'S A BOUNTY ON HIS HEAD, AND HE MUST HURRY TO FIND OUT THE DETAILS BEFORE IT'S TOO LATE FOR BOTH HIM AND ASUKA.

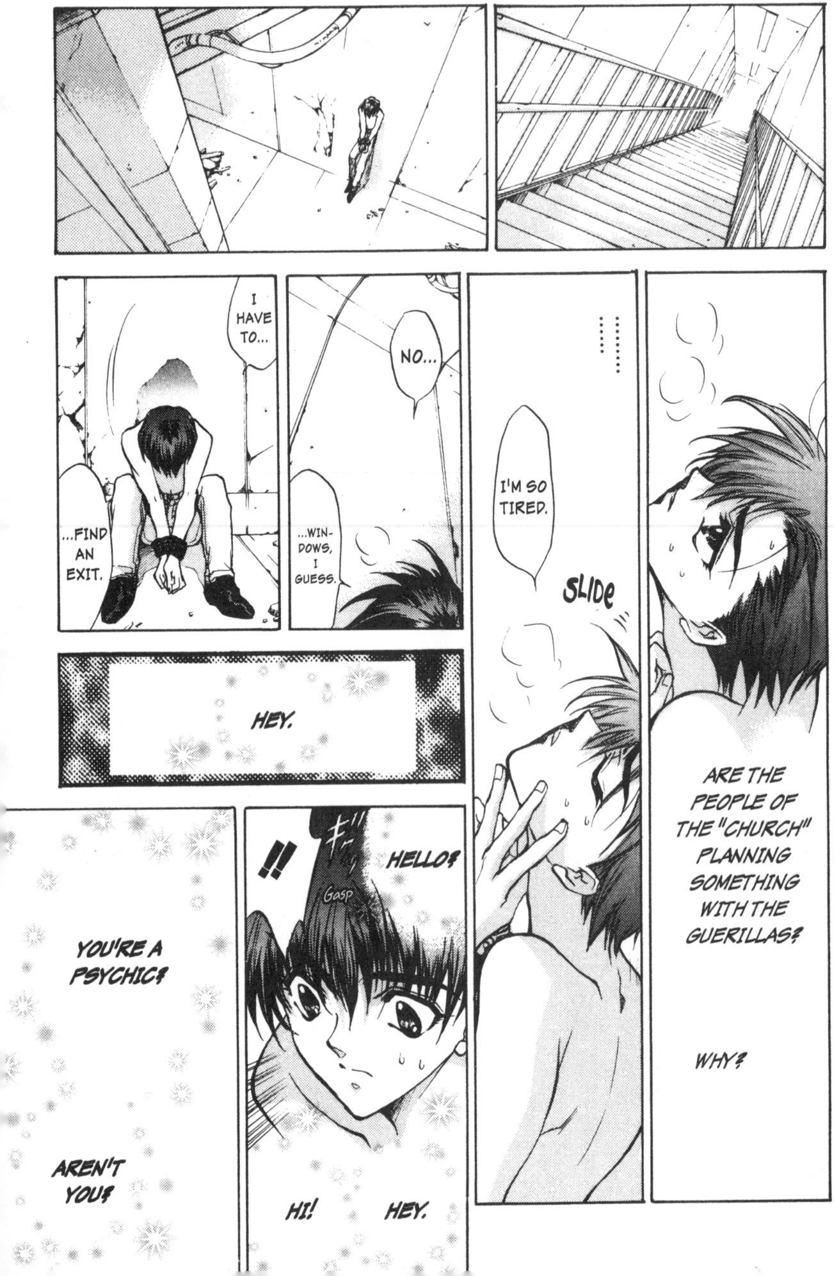
ARE THE PEOPLE OF THE "CHURCH" PLANNING SOMETHING WITH THE GUERILLAS?
WHY?
......
I'M SO TIRED.
SLIDE
NO...
...WINDOWS, I GUESS.
I HAVE TO...
...FIND AN EXIT.
HEY.
HELLO?
!!
Gasp
HI!
HEY.
YOU'RE A PSYCHIC?
AREN'T YOU?

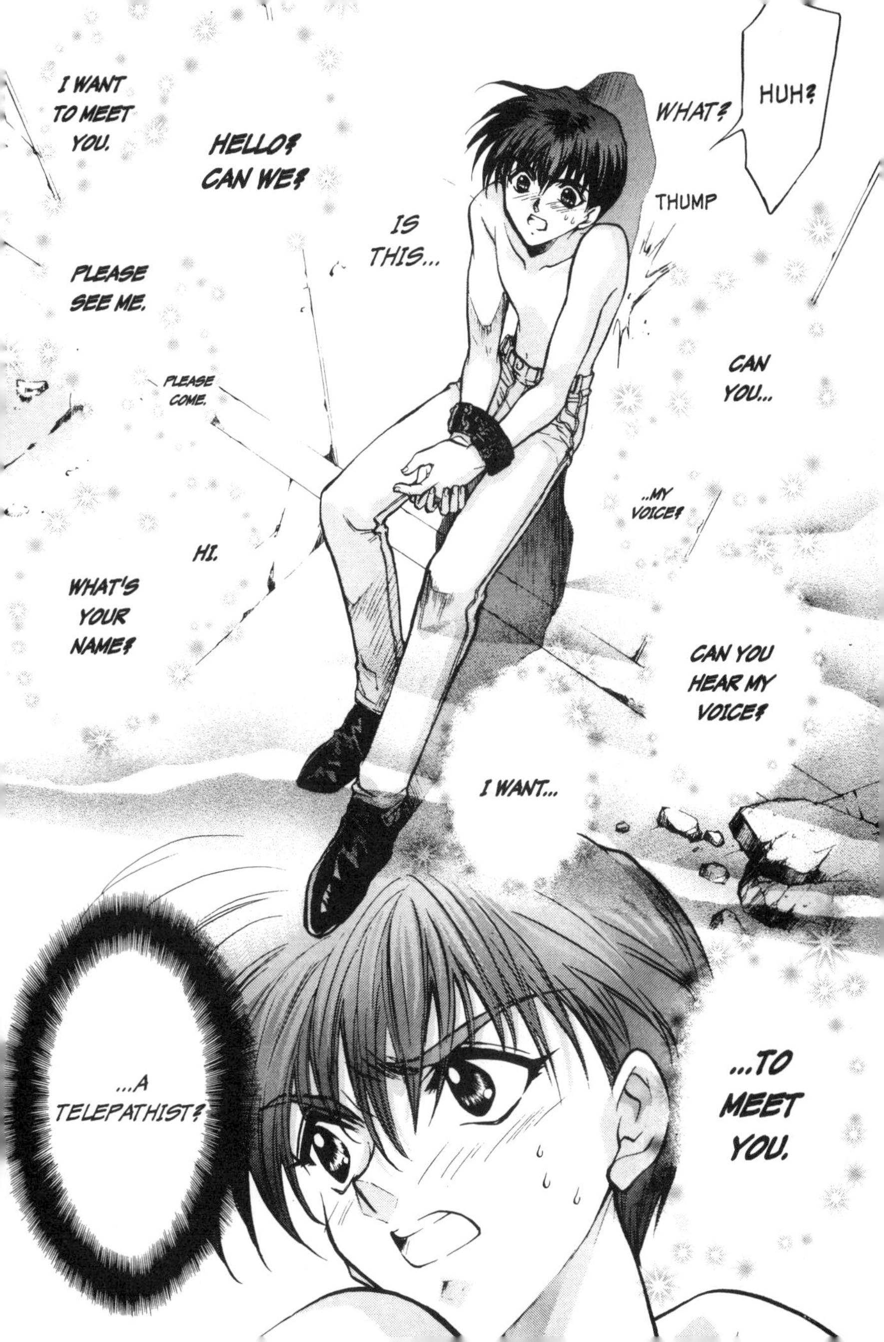
HUH?
WHAT?
THUMP
IS THIS...
HELLO? CAN WE?
I WANT TO MEET YOU.
PLEASE SEE ME.
CAN YOU...
...MY VOICE?
PLEASE COME.
HI.
WHAT'S YOUR NAME?
CAN YOU HEAR MY VOICE?
I WANT...
...TO MEET YOU.
...A TELEPATHIST?

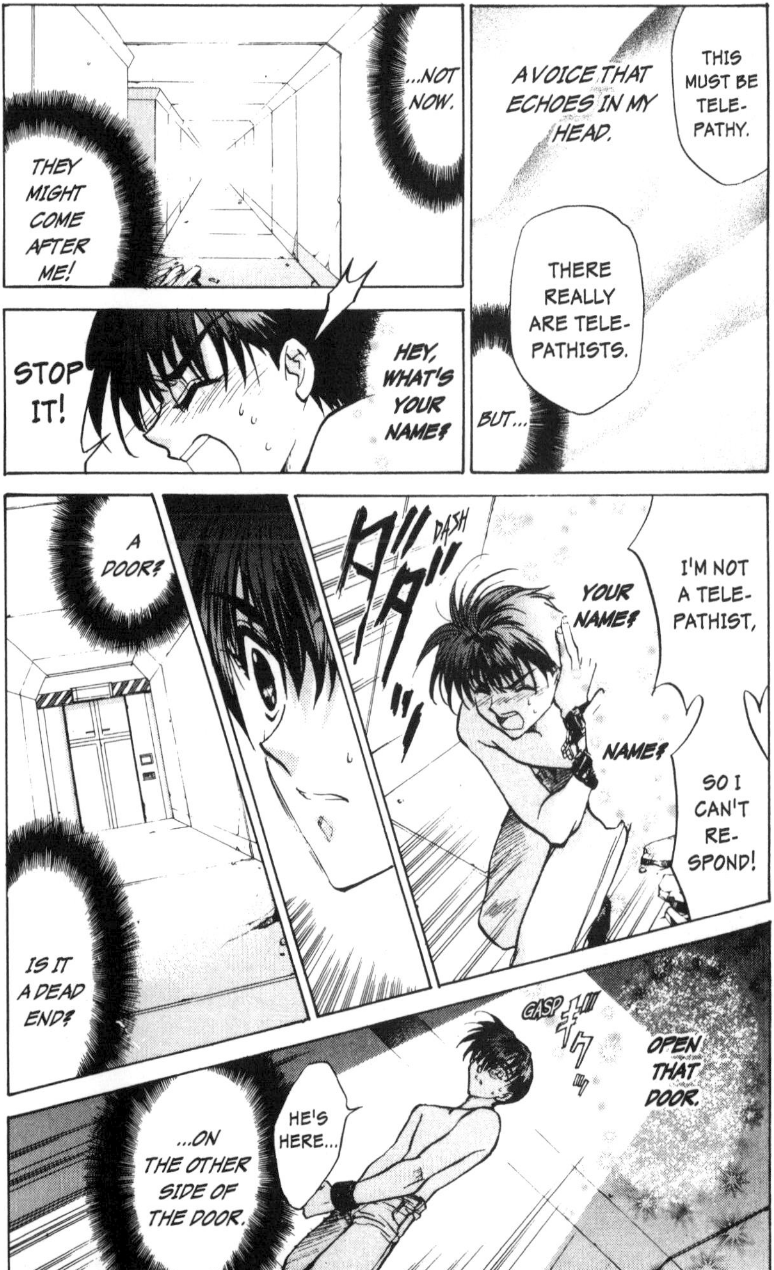
THIS MUST BE TELE-PATHY.
A VOICE THAT ECHOES IN MY HEAD.
THERE REALLY ARE TELE-PATHISTS.
BUT...
...NOT NOW.
THEY MIGHT COME AFTER ME!
HEY, WHAT'S YOUR NAME?
STOP IT!
DASH
I'M NOT A TELE-PATHIST,
YOUR NAME?
NAME?
SO I CAN'T RE-SPOND!
A DOOR?
IS IT A DEAD END?
GASP
OPEN THAT DOOR.
HE'S HERE...
...ON THE OTHER SIDE OF THE DOOR.

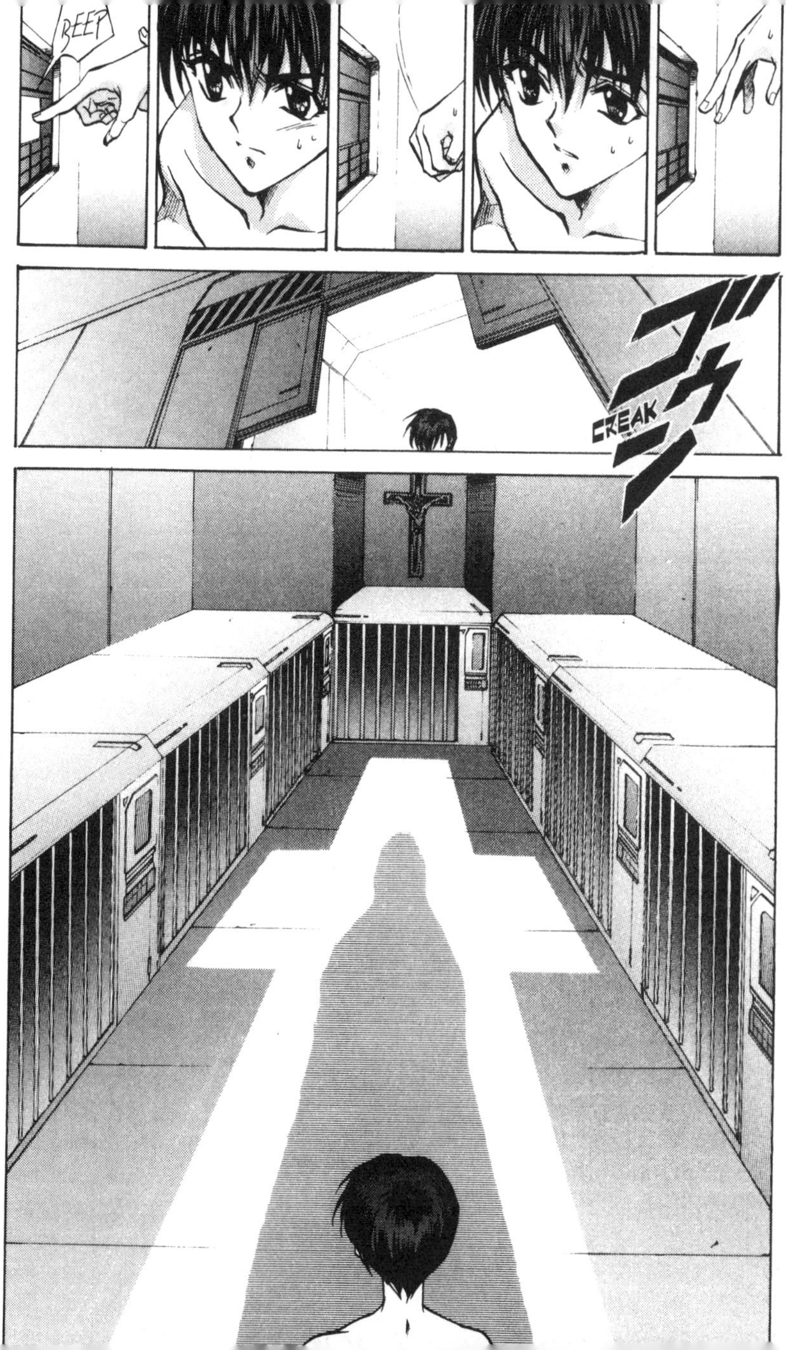
BEEP
ゴウン
CREAK

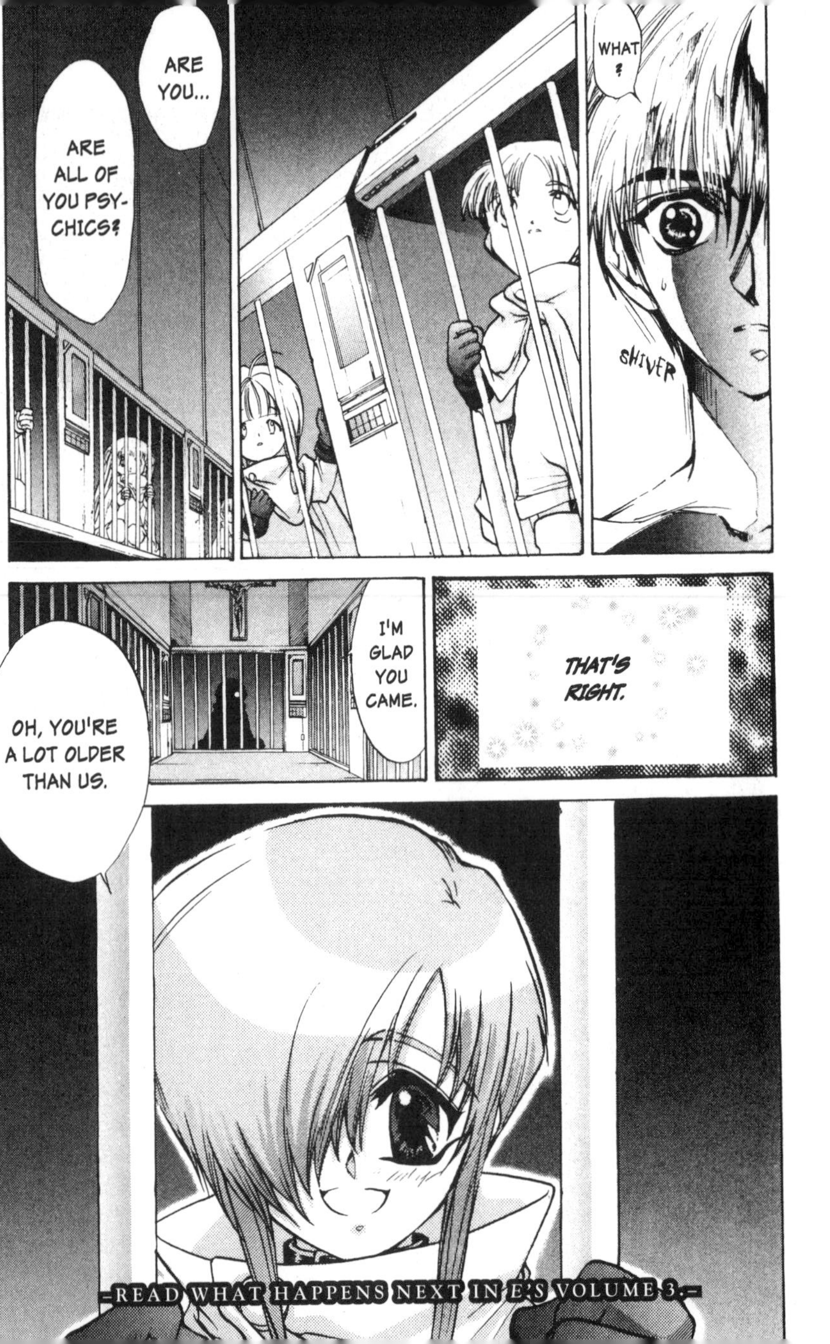
WHAT?
SHIVER
ARE YOU...
ARE ALL OF YOU PSY-CHICS?
THAT'S RIGHT.
I'M GLAD YOU CAME.
OH, YOU'RE A LOT OLDER THAN US.
-READ WHAT HAPPENS NEXT IN E'S VOLUME 3.-

The latest graphic novel from Koge-Donbo, the creator of Di Gi Charat and Pita-ten!

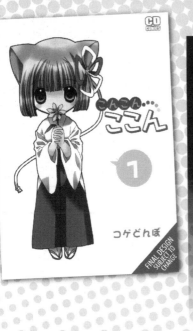

CD COMICS
こんこん……
ここん
1
こげどんぼ
FINAL DESIGN SUBJECT TO CHANGE

Ren just wants to be one of the cool kids, but it doesn't help that secretly he's just a nerdy monster fanatic. That is, until a young girl named Kokon shows up. She claims to be a fox that he had helped years ago and now she wants to return the favor. With the fox girl Kokon by his side, will Ren be able to become the most popular kid in school?

SRP: $9.99

E
Everyone

こんこん……ここん

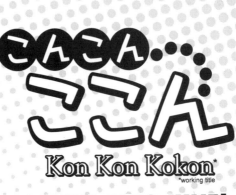

Kon Kon Kokon*

*working title

COMING THIS JUNE!

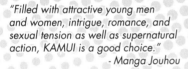

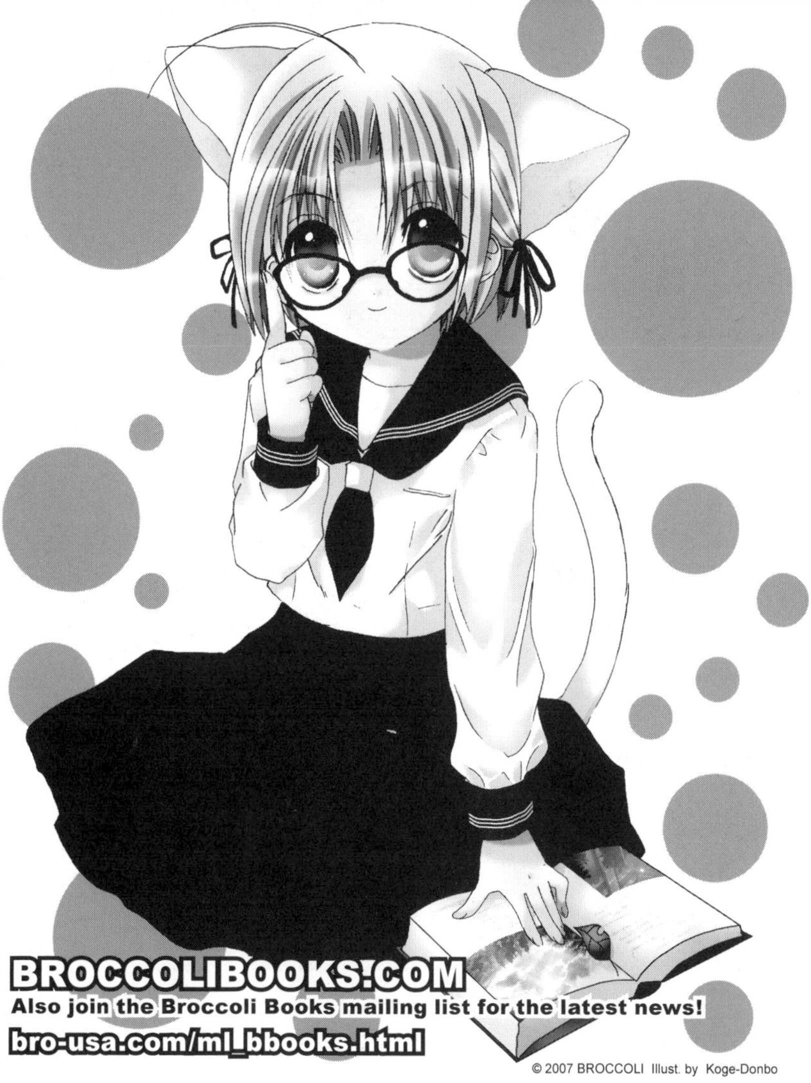

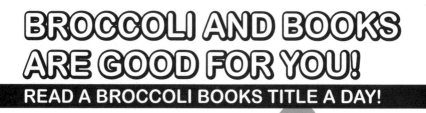

This is the end of the book! In Japan, manga is generally read from right to left. All reading starts on the upper right corner, and ends on the lower left. American comics are generally read from left to right, starting on the upper left of each page. In order to preserve the true nature of the work, we printed this book in a right to left fashion. Those who are unfamiliar with manga may find this confusing at first, but once you start getting into the story, you will wonder how you ever read manga any other way!

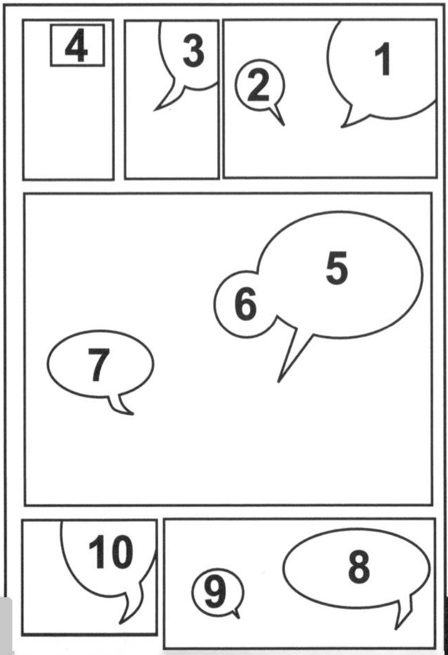
1
2
3
4
5
6
7
8
9
10

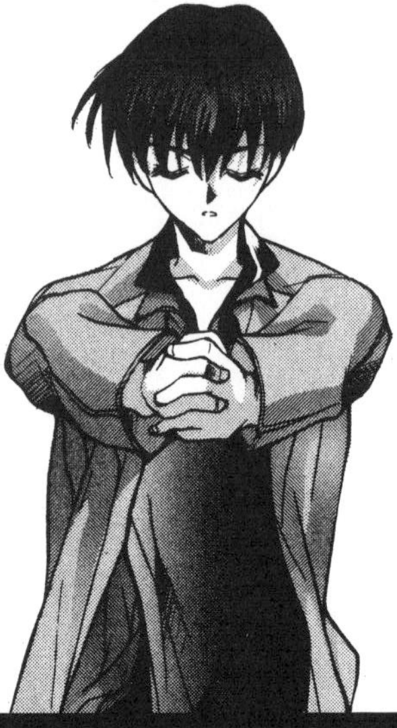

THIS QUESTIONNAIRE IS REDEEMABLE FOR:

E'S Volume 2 Sticker

Broccoli Books Questionnaire

Fill out and return to Broccoli Books to receive your corresponding sticker!*

PLEASE MAIL THE COMPLETE FORM, ALONG WITH UNUSED UNITED STATES POSTAGE
STAMPS WORTH $0.50 ENCLOSED IN THE ENVELOPE TO:**

> Broccoli International
> Attn: Broccoli Books Sticker Committee
> 1728 S. La Cienega Blvd
> Los Angeles, CA 90035

(Please write legibly)

Name: _____

Address: _____

City, State, Zip: _____

E-mail: _____

Gender: ☐ Male ☐ Female **Age:** _____

(If you are under 13 years old, parental consent is required)

Parent/Guardian signature: _____

Where did you hear about this title?

☐ Magazine   ☐ Convention

☐ Internet   ☐ Club

☐ At a Store   ☐ Other

☐ Word of Mouth

Where was this title purchased? (If known)

_____

Why did you buy this title?

_____

_____

_____

_____

02

How would you rate the following features of this manga?

	Excellent	Good	Satisfactory	Poor
Translation	☐	☐	☐	☐
Art quality	☐	☐	☐	☐
Cover	☐	☐	☐	☐
Extra/Bonus Material	☐	☐	☐	☐

What would you like to see improved in Broccoli Books manga?

____

Would you like to join the Broccoli Books Mailing List? ☐ Yes ☐ No

Would you recommend this manga to someone else? ☐ Yes ☐ No

What related products would you be interested in? (Check all that apply)

☐ Apparel ☐ Art Books

☐ Posters ☐ Stationery

☐ Figures ☐ Trinkets

☐ Plushies ☐ Other

Favorite manga style/genre: (Check all that apply)

☐ Shoujo ☐ Anime-based

☐ Shounen ☐ Video game-based

☐ Yaoi

Final comments about this manga:

____

____

____

Thank you!

* While supplies last.
** For residents of Canada, please send an International Reply Coupon (IRC) of $3.00 US made out to "Broccoli International."

All information provided will be used for internal purposes only. We will not sell or otherwise divulge any of the information.

Requests not in compliance with all terms of this form will not be acknowledged or returned. All submissions are subject to verification and become the property of Broccoli International USA. Fraudulent submission, including use of multiple addresses or P.O. boxes to obtain additional Broccoli International USA information or offers may result in prosecution. Broccoli International USA reserves the right to withdraw or modify any terms of this form. Void where prohibited, taxed, or restricted by law. Broccoli International USA will not be liable for lost, misdirected, mutilated, illegible, incomplete, or postage-due mail. Sticker offer is only available to residents of the United States and Canada. For updates to the rules and regulations, please see www.broccolibooks.com.